THE CONLANGER'S LEXIPEDIA

THE CONLANGER'S LEXIPEDIA

by Mark Rosenfelder

YONAGU BOOKS

Yonagu • Chicago • 2013

Contents

Introduction

For those who didn't read the back cover, this book is a guide to understanding and creating **lexicons**.

I've written two books, *The Language Construction Kit* and *Advanced Language Construction*, that focus on **grammar**. If you want to know what sounds can be made, how case works, what you can do with verbs, what's a pidgin, how to create logographs, or how to wrangle morphosyntactic alignment and master polysynthesis, that's where you go. Arguably the sounds and the way the morphology and syntax work are the heart of the language, what makes it itself.

But as every language learner eventually finds out, with some dismay, there's also the 800-pound gorilla of the vocabulary. For the conlanger, this raises new questions— or it should:

- How many words do I need?

- Which ones should I create first?

- Am I just making a complicated cipher of English?

- How are new words created in natural languages?

- What structure does the lexicon have?

- What do I need to know about things to make words for them?

This book answers all these questions, and where that's not enough, it asks its own questions and then answers *those*.

How not to do it

Suppose you need to translate this sentence:

> *The king's court rejected the new queen for her faith.*

You find you don't have any of the content words, so you fire up your word generator and get:

> *dlatla*
> *atlesi*
> *učitlo*
> *iprikoga*
> *speti*
> *briiau*

and match them up to the terms you need:

dlatla	king
atlesi	court
učitlo	reject
iprikoga	new
speti	queen
briiau	faith

With a little grammatical manipulation you have

Učitlo-ño-e atlesi dlatla-ič speti-s iprikoga-s briiau-ke.

reject-impfv-3s court king-gen queen-acc new-acc faith-abl

The king's court rejected the new queen for her faith.

Now, this is not *terrible* conlanging. In fact, for your basic roots, you're just going to have to make them up! But you shouldn't be creating a new *root* every time you need a new *word*.

Let's look at some of the missed opportunities and future problems here.

- 'King' is *dlatla*, 'queen' is *speti*. That matches English, but in many languages the terms would be related (Spanish *rey, reina*, Russian король, королева) or the same (Mandarin *wáng*).

- 'Court' has a historical metaphor built into it. It's borrowed from Old French *cort*, from Latin *cohors*— literally 'cattle-yard'. It was used for 'military attendants, bodyguard'. This must have been jocular at first— picturing the officer's retinue as a herd of cows— but it became quotidian and then formal.

  Does this mean you should re-use a word meaning 'farmyard'? No, but the idea is that political words are a chance to do some conworlding. What did the people surrounding the king look like to your people?

- Do they use the same word for the king's court, the judge's, and the basketball player's?

- 'Reject' is a Latin compound: 'throw back'. It *could* be a basic root, but probably you should build it from something simpler.

- The commonest words tend to be short, so a four-syllable word for 'new' might not be the best choice.

- 'Faith' is used in the sample as a stand-in for 'religion'. *Believing* is a key part of Christianity, but not necessarily other religions. What's the key element of your con-religion?

  As so often in English, we have a triplet— *faith* from Old French, *belief* from Old English, *religion* from Latin. Most languages don't borrow so broadly as English; you should watch out for such multiples and not reproduce them without a good reason.

Beyond this sample sentence, what happens when you need related words, such as these?

> *novel (= story), novelty, newspaper*
>
> *kingdom, regal, royal*
>
> *courtier, courtesan, courtesy*
>
> *faithful, fidelity, believe, religious*

The main point is, please don't reach for the word generator and decide that 'novel' is *etrapi*, 'novelty' is *klado*, 'newspaper' is *peižga*. At the least, try to derive these from your word for 'new'. Better yet, think of different derivations for your words.

That's where this book comes in. It's full of etymological examples, subtle relationships between words, real-world information, and ways languages besides English do things.

Why not a dictionary?

When you need a new word, your first thought may be to use a dictionary— either one for your native language, or for a language you're borrowing from. That's great as far as it goes. But there are two main disadvantages.

- You may just reproduce the etymology you find in the dictionary. Not a bad thing, but it's good to think about alternatives.

- The lexicon has a structure: words are largely defined by *how they relate to other words*. Creating a language, you're really creating a web of words as well as a system of metaphor. Again, if you don't spend any effort on this, you'll just duplicate English.

Every word is a conworlding opportunity. You're deciding what's important to your people and how they see the world. If the word involves technology or culture, you have to think about who first came up with it in your world and how it got to the language you're working on.

Another problem: very often to create a word you need to understand the **real-world referent**. Why is there a class of chemicals called *oxides*? What characteristics of an *elm* would make a good name? At what technological level does *glass* appear? Your general knowledge and even the dictionary may not be enough for such questions.

How does this book help?

This book is arranged **thematically**. Each section concentrates on one semantic field, giving words you might want to create, how multiple languages created them, interesting divergences from English, and just enough encylopedic information to help out.

For instance, the section on color briefly explains the order languages tend to develop color terms, how perceived colors depend on our eyes, and how color might work for other species or planets. It also talks about other color groups you might want to think about: skin and hair color. Finally, it points out relationships that might not be obvious, e.g. to the words *jaundice, rouge, bear*.

The book also presents a specially created frequency list designed for fantasy/sf[1] worlds. This will help answer the perennial question, "Which words are the most useful?"

Many sections would easily expand into a whole chapter! Often that chapter is available in my earlier book, *The Planet Construction Kit*, and I'll point you to it, or to other books.

What else have you got?

The following chapters offer some general help on **wordcrafting**:

- A how-to chapter giving step by step instructions
- When to create alternatives and synonyms
- Building metaphor systems
- Thinking in terms of roots, derivations, and compounding

Following the thematic section is an index of all the words referred to, in case you're not sure which of the thematic sections a word lives in.

Apology to Prof. Levi

My college linguistics professor used to say that "the lexicon is not an encyclopedia." I think this was a corollary of the '70s idea of independence of the language organ, and the desirability of doing syntax with only syntactic facts. I'm afraid I've departed from it, though Prof. Levi's old friend George Lakoff is partly to blame. In cognitive linguistics, the boundaries between language and everything else have grown fuzzier.

---

[1] "Sf" means *science fiction* or *science fantasy* or *speculative fiction*, as you like.

Some of the encyclopedic information may not be to your taste, too. That's fine; this is a reference work, and you can skip what you don't need. The more scientific sections are intended for those with present-day or sf conworlds.

Anyway, I have to satisfy my inner 13-year-old, who would have hated being given (say) a list of the nine most important phyla of Animalia. Gimme 'em all, dammit!

Typographical conventions

If I'm talking about a word, English or foreign, it'll be in *italics,* while a gloss or etymology will be in 'single quotes'. For example, *etymology* derives from Greek 'true-word'.

Following Lakoff's convention, metaphors are named in ALL CAPS.

The word-lists have special typography to indicate **frequency**; see p. 45.

For how to read the **etymological summaries**, see p. 78.

> ‣ A quick reference to another page or book is printed in sans-serif, like this.

Greek and Cyrillic

Aspiring linguists should already know the **Greek** alphabet, at least if they were paying attention in math class. For reference, here's the alphabet with the classical (5th century BC) phonetic values as given by W. Sidney Allen in *Vox Graeca*:

Αα	Ββ	Γγ	Δδ	Εε	Ζζ	Ηη	Θθ	Ιι	Κκ	Λλ	Μμ
a	b	g	d	ε	zd	ε:	tʰ	i	k	l	m

Νν	Ξξ	Οο	Ππ	Ρρ	Σσ	Ττ	Υυ	Φφ	Χχ	Ψψ	Ωω
n	ks	ɔ	p	r	s	t	y	pʰ	kʰ	ps	ɔ:

σ appears as ς at the end of a word.

For the purposes of this book no harm will be done if you pronounce θ φ χ with their post-classical fricative values [θ f x]. But Πλάτων would look at you funny.

And if you know the Greek alphabet, there's little excuse for not reading **Cyrillic**. Here are the basic Russian values:

Аа	Бб	Вв	Гг	Дд	Ее	Жж	Зз	Ии	Йй	Кк
a	b	v	g	d	jɛ	ʒ	z	i	j	k

Лл	Мм	Нн	Оо	Пп	Рр	Сс	Тт	Уу	Фф	Хх
l	m	n	ɔ	p	r	s	t	u	f	x

Цц	Чч	Шш	Щщ	Ъъ	Ыы	Ьь	Ээ	Юю	Яя
ts	tʃ	ʃ	ʃ:		ɨ		ɛ	ju	ja

Russian actually has *two* series of consonants, regular ('hard') and palatalized ('soft'), and these are marked not by modifying the consonants but by changing the normal vowels **а э ы о у** to **я е и ё ю**. That is, да is /da/ and дя is /dʲa/. The second series is also used for the diphthongs j + V, as in союз 'union'.

These rules sometimes aren't enough, and that's where the unlabelled letters come in. The soft sign ь marks the previous consonant as palatalized when there's no following vowel, as in читать 'to read'. The hard sign ъ similarly marks a consonant as unpalatalized; it's rarely necessary except in foreign words, such as Нъю-Йорк 'New York'.

Thanks to palatalization, transliterations of Russian are either inaccurate or ugly; thus my preference for citing forms in Cyrillic.

Date conventions

For brevity I often write 5C for "the 5th century AD", i.e. the 400s, and likewise -13C is "the 13th century BC", i.e. the 1200s BC.

Web resources

URLs have a shorter half-life than books, so I've placed all links on a single site I can make sure will stick around:

http://www.zompist.com/resources/lex.html

What's Almea?

I expect most readers already know about my own conworld, Almea, and its languages, such as Verdurian and Xurnese. If not, be aware that I sometimes use examples from Almea to illustrate approaches you can take.

For all too much information on Almea, see www.zompist.com.

Acknowledgements

Many thanks to the readers who went through the manuscript and offered great feedback: John Cowan, John Baker, Samuel Lereah, Michael Kerns, Phillip Krohn, Sally Burr, Vincent Guerin, Timothy Hawk, and my wife Lida.

Thanks to the following correspondents and ZBB members who suggested words that diverge from English: John Baker, Ugo Lachapelle, clawgrip, Finlay Chalmers, Serafín, Yosi Bellman, Chuma, Qwynegold, Jyri Lehtinen, Eric Aniag, Ars Lande, Yaali Annar, Miłosz Andrzej Mazurkiewicz-Dubieński, Imralu, Anaïs Ahmed, James M. Li, Hans-Werner Hatting, Corundum, Daniel von Brighoff, Ulrike Meinhof, Campbell Nilsen, Aaron Toivo, Soren, John Cowan, Chris de Lisle, Mart van de Wege, Christian Cordeus, Elizabeth Bowen, Pekka Karjalainen, Sacemd Westen.

Thanks to my father, Charles Rosenfelder, for some of the pictures on the cover, and for buying all my books.

A book of this nature offers a myriad opportunities for transcription errors— the web resources page will have an Errata section. (If there are no errors, the preceding statement will be listed as false.)

Mark Rosenfelder

November 2013

How to

If you're the type of person who hates to read instruction manuals, and just grabs the Allen wrench and assembles their Hjärnblödning cabinet the way *you* like, skip to the next chapter.

This one is for people who like to see a detailed plan of attack. It's organized as a series of questions.

How do I create a word?

When I need a word for a conlang, I try to go through this process:

- Could I get by **without it**? Maybe I'm making a distinction just because English does (*like* vs. *love*, *look* vs. *stare*, *come* vs. *go*, *foot* vs. *leg*, and I can just add another gloss to an existing definition.

- Do I already have a **near-synonym**? If I need *rapid* and I already have *fast*, why not use that?

- On the other hand, I may want to **avoid English homophones.** I may have already created a word for *case* in the sense of 'situation', but I may want a different word for the sense of 'lawsuit' or 'declensional category'.

- Can I build it from **existing roots**? The no-brainer is changing parts of speech— if I have *to howl* I should be able to easily form *a howl* or *howling*. Note that for historical reasons English something obscures this: *sight* vs. *see*, *time* vs. *temporal*.

  But you should have other basic derivations: people, place, collection, repetition, causatives, negatives, etc. For instance:

      priest = 'god-man'

      library = 'book-place'

  Locatives greatly extend your vocabulary: e.g.

      climb = 'go up'

      private = 'in house'

  And of course if you have *n* roots, you have n^2 possible two-root compounds!

      disgust = 'hate-vomit'

      city = 'hill-fort'

- Can I use a **metaphor**?

  skull = 'bowl'

  succeed = 'pass through'

- Did I create this word already in **another language**? You should always consider this with technological and cultural terms, but in general people like *cool words* and can borrow almost anything.

- How did **other languages** do it? I often look up the word in a dictionary or two to see how *they* derived the word. You can simply use this book, which contains thousands of natural-language etymologies.

- Consider how your people **feel** about the referent. Is it virtuous or shameful, nice or nasty? Words often express a judgment (as in how we name the *right* hand), and despised things (*swine, ass*) lend their names to other things we dislike.

- Creating a **new root** is always possible— and you'll be doing it a lot— but it should be the last resort.

Does it sound like you need a lot of **extra knowledge** to make all that work? You do, but that's why I've written this book! The introductory chapters tell you what you need to know about derivation, etymology, classes, metaphor. And the bulk of the book gives plenty of examples and helpful explanations in each semantic field.

It could easily be twice as long! But the idea isn't to give you every possibility; it's to show how words work, where they come from, how they change, to spark your own creativity.

Won't re-using roots be boring?

If you follow my advice, you might (say) end up with a whole slew of words based on a simple root like *go*:

enter = 'go in'	*attack* = 'go after'
sail = 'boat-go'	*companion* = 'goes with'
return = 'go back'	*visit* = 'go see'
come = 'go' + benefactive	*road* = 'going place'
suitable = 'go' + reflexive	*lead* = 'make to go'
wander = 'go' + iterative	*remain* = 'un-go'

Couldn't this make the language seem a little wan or repetitive? Esperanto sometimes feels this way, with compounds like *patrino* 'mother' = 'female-father' and *malbona* 'bad' = 'un-good'.

One answer is that the speakers of a language don't really pay attention to even very transparent etymologies. Words like *undergo* or *become* or *today* or *grandmother* are perceived as just normal words. Most of the time we're talking *about* referents *using* our words; it takes a small effort to focus on the words themselves— an effect relied on by cheap comics ("why do we park on the driveway and drive on the parkway?").[2]

Many languages rely on native roots far more than English. German learned words are often very straightforward: 'communicate' is 'share with', 'avoid' is 'move away', 'instant' is 'eye-glance'. Rather than directly borrowing a Romance root, German often calques it: 'chance' is 'to-fall', 'resist' is 'stand against', 'preside' is 'fore-sit', all matching the Latin verbal root.

But there are a few techniques that can reduce the repetition.

First, you can choose **derivational processes** that make the derivation less obvious.

- The simplest is an infix, e.g. Kebreni -*su*-, which means 'made of X':

  siva 'sand' > *sisuva* 'sandy'
  heda 'stone' > *hesuda* 'stony'

- Triliteral root systems can have this effect— Arabic KTB gives *kitāb* 'book', *kutubī* 'bookseller', *maktab* 'office', *miktāb* 'typewriter', *kātib* 'writer', *ʔiktitāb* 'registration', etc.

  ‣ For creating triliteral roots, see p. 100.

- As English trains our eyes to look at the first part of a word, prefixes make a word look more different than suffixes (*standing* is obviously a form of *stand; understand* seems farther off). Swahili, whose morphology is almost all prefixing, is exotic to us. Of course, if your native language is Swahili, it's English that seems strange!

Or you can use the trick used by English and Japanese: hide the derivations by **borrowing** from another language. *Alley, allure, gangplank,*

---

[2] Since we're doing etymology, let's answer the question. Of course, you drive on a *driveway*. A *parkway* was originally a broad boulevard with a grassy (*park*-like) margin. The verb *park* was once to leave a vehicle in a yard (a *park*).

ambient, exit, comity, transit, obituary, acrobat, ion, basis, vademecum, vamoose all directly use 'go', but in another language.

Sound change is also a great obscurer. *Follow* was once a compound *fulgangan* 'full-go'. We can form the future with *going to*, but it's barely recognizable in *gonna* and almost baffling in *I'm'a.*

Old Chinese had a number of productive derivational processes that have been completely obscured by sound change.

(As a reminder, the * means 'unattested' in citations from reconstructed languages like Old Chinese and Proto-Indo-European.)

Nominalizer -n:

ʔwa 'bend' > *ʔwâns* 'wrist'   *yū > jīn*

ŋaʔ 'speak' > *ŋan* 'speech'   *yǔ > yán*

Terminative -ŋ:

wa 'go' > *waŋʔ* 'arrive'   *yú > wǎng*

Iterative s-:

ran 'drip' > *srâ* 'flow'   *lián > shān*

Causative s-:

laŋ 'be sick' > *slaŋ*   *yáng > shāng*

Finally, etymology can be obscured by **semantic change**. E.g. you would hardly guess that *can, learn, wit, ignore,* and *nice* are all based on words for 'know'.

Wait, why can't I just make up roots?

What would happen if you just used a machine-generated root for everything in the lexicon?

The world will continue to rotate, yes, but what you'll have on your hands is likely to have several deficiencies.

- It will be far harder to learn than it ought to be. It'll have too many roots, none of which offer keys to the rest of the vocabulary.

- It will have no personality, no quirks of its own— no distinctive metaphors, no cultural allusions, no amusing or clever etymologies.

- It won't reflect your conworld's history: there won't be subsets of the lexicon pointing to the various cultures that provided your people's technology, or military traditions, or government, or philosophy.

- It will have a lexical structure, but it will be that of English (or your native language, if it's not English). It won't *sound* like English, but it will closely imitate it in ways you're not even aware of.

In short, it won't be a naturalistic language— and it will probably be too difficult and too anglocentric to make a good auxlang or loglang, too.

Which words do I do first?

Creating a respectable vocabulary takes time, so I create words as I need them, and intersperse grammar writing with bouts of word-building.

Geographical terms are always a good place to start, as you'll need them for maps.

▸ See *Nature* and *Water*.

You'll come up with lists of pronouns, auxiliaries, adpositions, and numbers as part of the process of writing the grammar. Writing sample sentences will give you a subset of useful words, too.

▸ See *Grammar* for a list. But use the *LCK* and *ALC* to actually work through the grammar!

There are several word lists in the *LCK* (pp. 260-9); I've sometimes worked through the Swadesh list, repeated for convenience on p. 46.

To get the most out of your wordbuilding time, you should create the commonest words first. To help in this, I've created a 1500-root frequency list based on fantasy and science fiction texts.

▸ See the Fantasy Frequency Wordlist, p. 34.

Another approach is to look at what words are most used in etymologies. If a word is used a lot in derivations, it's probably worth having it in your own language.

▸ See the Etymology Frequency List, p. 89.

But I'd also like to impress upon you that you shouldn't just think in terms of creating *words*. You should think about creating entire *semantic fields*.

Why should I think about semantic fields?

Good question! The bulk of this book is organized by semantic field— things like *Animals* and *Emotions* and *Tools*.

First, as Frédéric Saussure pointed out, words are defined by **how they relate to other words**. A continuum of meaning like *hot, warm, cool, cold* may be divided differently in another language. Words like *break* and *cut* help define each other— prototypically both involve something being divided, but only the latter involves an edged object. If you define words in alphabetical or frequency order, you'll miss these interrelationships— with the result that you'll reproduce the relationships of your native language.

A corollary: what words exist is affected by **culture**. If (say) you just create a word for *aunt* when you run into it, you may never stop to think about how the kinship system for your culture works. Similarly, you might define words for *pink* and *brown* without realizing that many languages don't bother with these words. The semantic field sections of the book will mention things like this.

Second, languages have **classification systems**— e.g. certain animals are grouped together as *birds;* certain social behaviors are categorized as *sins*. Some categories seem pretty natural— though they might differ if your people are not human— but most can vary by culture, which means they're an opportunity for conworlding.

> ‣ See the Classes chapter, p. 46.

And thirdly, there's often **real-world knowledge** that's relevant to coming up with terms in a given area. You can't name chemical substances, for instance, without knowing something about them— what they look like, what they're used for, where they were found and at what tech level. Each of the thematic sections tells you what you need to know to create words in that area.

How do I use the word lists?

Let's look at just one example— words related to fear, from the *Emotions* section.

Fear   **fear, afraid, worry,** terror, dread, anxious, nervous, desperate, alarm, *panic, shy, coward*

The typography gives **frequency** information. So this tells you that you should probably have a word for *fear*, but that you can go a long time without *panic*.

You could of course create an equivalent for each of these words. But that's simply using the English vocabulary at one remove. How can you avoid this?

- Divide up the semantic space differently. There's a gradation from mild *worry* through *anxiety, alarm, fear,* and ending in *panic* and *terror*. You can combine steps, or introduce finer distinctions.

- Think about how these words are differentiated. For instance, besides level of fear, some of these words mix in something else:

  ° *dread* — the particular horror of the unknown or the uncanny

  ° *coward* — the contempt bolder men feel for the fearful

  ° *nervous, shy*— fear of social awkwardness rather than physical harm; *nervous* implies agitation while *shy* is compatible with outward calm

  ° *desperate* — fear combined with rashness

  Ideally, rather than copy English words, you'll think of your own concepts. Perhaps:

  ° fear mixed with disgust

  ° helpless fear, as when one is trapped or outnumbered

  ° fear plus foolishness (being afraid of nonexistent things, or being misled by a demagogue)

  ° fear tempered by the satisfaction of having predicted the situation

How do I use your etymologies?

For most of the high-frequency words, I give etymologies for English and often for half a dozen other languages. For instance:

arrow OE *arwe* 'bow-thing'
• Gk τόξευμα < 'shoot' • Fr *flèche* < 'feather' • Sw *pil* < 'javelin' • OCS *strela* < 'beam of light' • Cz *šip* 'thorn' • Farsi *tīr* 'sharp'

The immediate purpose is to give you a bunch of ideas for when you need to create the word 'arrow'. I've gone through some very large volumes finding these things to make it easier for you (and for me, on my next language). Just grab one!

A little more abstractly, the list should help jump-start your own creativity. How *else* could you express the concept of 'arrow'?

If you get stuck, ask questions like these:

- What are some related words? Maybe they got repurposed ('javelin', 'dart', 'bolt'), maybe the word can express their relationship ('bow-thing', 'skirmisher-weapon').

- If it's a physical object, what does it look like? ('thorn', 'needle')

- What's it made of? ('feather', 'ashwood-thing', 'obsidian')

- What's it used for? ('shoot', 'pierce', 'ranged-killer')

- What striking attributes does it have? ('sharp', 'pointy', 'long', 'whooshing')

- Can you get there by a metaphor? ('beam of light', 'finger')

- Perhaps a broader term narrowed to just this meaning? ('weapon', 'stick')

- Is the thing associated with a particular person or culture? ('nomad-tools', 'of Diana')

Any of these are good choices. There are few wrong answers, but at the least, avoid anachronisms— e.g. an arrow is the archer's equivalent of a 'bullet', but that couldn't be used before the invention of the gun. (But it could work for a futuristic language!)

> ‣ There's a whole chapter on etymologies, p. 78.

What can I do with categories?

See the Categories chapter (p. 46) for an explanation of the concept.

An easy place to start is **supercategories**— that is, words that group together disparate things, like *carnivore, fish, vegetable, sin, crime, planet, art, game, job*. Each of these is really a little conworlding exercise. What do your people include in the concept? Some examples:

- Is robbery a *crime*? A society where you can grab anything at all seems unlikely, but the limits need not be the same as in our culture. The idea of 'robbery' presupposes the idea of 'property', and a culture may find it absurd to claim certain things as property, like 'air'. The powerful often take things that aren't theirs— grazing areas, countries, slaves— and come up with reasons why this isn't 'robbery'.

- Are whales *fish*? You may think that science gives us the answer, but science isn't the boss of language, and even scientists haven't always agreed that genetic descent is the best way to classify life.

- Is lesbianism *perversion*? Not in my conculture Verduria— not out of progressivism, but because it's considered a harmless way to keep girls and women from messing around with men.

- In our culture, defining something as *art* gives it a certain cachet. There may be complicated reasons we do or don't apply the term to dressmaking, industrial design, or storytelling. Similarly, Adam Smith pointed out that few jobs require more variety and depth of knowledge than farming, but because it was so common it was hardly regarded as a *profession*.

- You might have considered *planet* to be out of place on my list, but in fact it's an excellent example! The original definition as a 'wandering' light in the sky would exclude the Earth and include the Sun and comets. The idea of 'a big satellite of the Sun' was challenged by the discovery of Ceres and then by thousands of asteroids. If you're looking at sheer size, the moon Ganymede is larger than Mercury. There's no natural class here; all we can do is pick a definition that suits our needs.

On a more sophisticated level, **all words are categories**. Some may be pretty obvious, like *dog*, but words like *anger, child, hair* all group some things together and exclude others, and you can think about how your people might group things differently.

The discussion in each section of the book will give you more ideas and things to think about.

Classes may also be grammaticalized. One example is gender, discussed in *ALC* pp. 124-134; another is measure words, discussed below, p. 78.

Many older conlangs were based on classification systems; for more on this see p. 73.

How do I create a whole lexicon?

One word at a time. I don't think there's any shortcut to producing a large quality lexicon. Just plug away at it, in between working on the grammar, the sample texts, or other aspects of your conworld.

My rule of thumb is that a language doesn't feel done until I have at least 1500 entries; it starts to feel respectable once there are 2500 or so; and once it has over 6000 it's impressive. To put it another way, if you have 500 words, almost every sample sentence will require inventing a new word; with 2000 you'll need a few per sample text; and with 6000 it'll be fairly rare to stumble over a word you don't have.

For almost all of my languages I keep only a lexicon sorted in romanized form. This keeps related words together and prevents making accidental homophones. Since I work on the computer, it's easy enough to search for a particular English word.

I created a subject dictionary for Verdurian, organized by topic, much like the word lists in this book. This was great for forcing myself to fill out the categories, and to work out how the Verdurians think about things.

Which words can be borrowed?

Almost anything can be borrowed. However, of the first fifty items in the Fantasy Frequency Wordlist, just one was borrowed (*they*); of the first 200, just 20 were borrowed— and English is a copious borrower.

So very common words are the **least likely** to be borrowed. But they're not exempt; note that these borrowings include such everyday words as *get, seem, run, want, face, move, place.*

Words for **technologies** are often borrowed; see the Technology chapter in the *PCK* for a timeline. Think about which of your cultures is expert in different areas, and at what time period. E.g. for English we could list:

Greek	philosophy, art, religion, math, science
Latin	government, linguistics, science
Norse	various everyday words
French	feudalism, heraldry, war, diplomacy, literature, fashion, cuisine
Italian	banking, accounting, architecture, music

Spanish	intermediary for Arabic and Native American terms
German	mining, philosophy
Hebrew	religion
Arabic	math, astronomy, clothing, chemistry

For Japanese, the table would look like this:

Chinese	everything premodern
Portuguese	Christianity, early trade products
Dutch	trading products, shipping terms
German	medicine, science, mountain climbing
English	modern life

If people move to a new area— as when English speakers moved to North America, South Africa, India, and Australia— they'll borrow local terms for animals, plants, cooking, and interesting geological features.

Don't neglect the lure of **coolness**. For centuries the language of culture and sophistication for most of Europe was French; today, for much of the world, it's English. Marginal groups can be the source of cool words as well.

Recall that words **drift** from their original meaning, so don't restrict borrowings to specific domains. Compare the original and present-day meaning of these words:

triumph	rite honoring a Roman general	a great success or victory
shack	a thatched cabin (Nahuatl)	a rough cabin
tycoon	a Japanese feudal lord	big business magnate
yen	an addiction (Chinese)	a yearning or interest
check	threaten the king in chess	test, verify
bungalow	a Bengali house	a small one-story house
swastika	Sanskrit 'well-being'	a symbol of evil
profanity	sacrilege	swear words
cabal	the Jewish Qabbālāh	a conspiracy
cherub	a mighty angel of God	a cute baby

▸ The "Putting it all together" chapter of ALC explains the borrowing strategies I used for Almea.

How do I change meanings?

So you have a proto-language and every word in your main language derives from the parent. Good! Only, in every case it means the same thing. Bad!

The best way to get a feel for meaning change is to look at a bunch of actual etymologies. Browse the wordlists in the book. Check your dictionary, or look up etymological sources online.

Leonard Bloomfield listed eight types of semantic change. (My examples give only the glosses, as we're not focusing on the shape of the words here.)

Narrowing	meet > fight
	young person > girl
	pleasing > joke
	wild animal > deer
	food > meat
Widening	occur by chance > happen
	divide > judge
	nestling > bird
	kill > harm
Metonymy	embrace > kiss
	nape > neck
	chair > hips
	pulpit > the clergy
Synecdoche (part/whole)	board > floor
	enclosure > garden
	bench > bank
	swelling > grave
Hyperbole	evil > fierce
	crippled > boring
	run > walk
	terrorist > dissident
Litotes (understatement)	hit > kill
	kiss > have sex
	right-size > fire people
	neutralize > imprison
	breeze > storm

Degeneration	boy > knave
	farmer > evil person
	blessed > foolish
	matron > slut
Elevation	same clan > well-born
	man > baron
	foolish > fond
	hut > house

I'd add a few more categories. **Metaphors** can be simple (*ball > eye, bowl > skull*) or sophisticated (*fall > happen, look > idea, straighten > govern, debt > sin*).

▸ I could talk about metaphor like a gushing stream— see p. 91.

Another common process I'll call a **resultative**: refer to a process using an early stage of it (*kiss > have sex, prepare > wear*), or a preliminary physical action (*stretch > hold*) or a prerequisite (*be able > help*).

Then there's **reification**, turning an attribute into a thing, which allows it linguistic agency and near-personhood. For instance, we ask *what kind of thing* something is— we just want a description. It's natural to then reify this as a class or category— its *kind*. An author's *style*, the *mood* of the electorate, a culture's *standards of beauty*, a smoker's *addiction* are all complex patterns of behavior that are reified into a single active thing.

▸ See the case study on *nature*, p. 65.

Why do meanings change? Many people feel that words are degraded or destroyed in the process... why would anyone do that?

I don't think linguistics knows for sure, but we can get a hint by looking at why we ourselves use new expressions— that is, why we use slang.

People just like novel, vivid, or exaggerated terms. We don't logically need a new term for 'good', but every generation or region seems to invent one: *bully, nifty, aces, lovely, gone, groovy, bodacious, fantastic, awesome, nice, sweet, wicked.*

Slang dates, of course— dig a Mark Twain character (in *Roughing It*) asking a parson to conduct a funeral in 1860s Nevada:

> *Yes. That's it— that's our little game. We are going to get the thing up regardless, you know. He was always nifty himself, and so you bet you his funeral ain't going to be no slouch— solid silver*

*door-plate on his coffin, six plumes on the hearse, and a nigger on
the box in a biled shirt and a plug hat— how's that for high? And
we'll take care of you, pard. We'll fix you all right. There'll be a
kerridge for you, and whatever you want, you just 'scape out and
we'll tend to it. We've got a shebang fixed up for you to stand behind, in No. 1's house, and don't you be afraid. Just go in and toot
your horn, if you don't sell a clam. Put Buck through as bully as
you can, pard, for anybody that knowed him will tell you that he
was one of the whitest men that was ever in the mines. You can't
draw it too strong.*

Like a maple tree, slang sends out a thousand seeds; most of them die,
but a few take root. Things have been *cool* for almost a century; that one
might be a keeper. Some of Twain's terms could still be used today,
though not always with the same meaning (his *nifty* meant 'smart,
fine'). Men have been *guys* and *dudes* for 150 years. Children have been
kids for three hundred years. If people like the new term enough, it will
become the standard word (Latin *testa* 'pot' > Italian 'head'), perhaps
itself to be replaced later on.

Words don't change immediately; there's a period of overlap where both
meanings can be encountered. For the people involved this causes less
confusion than you might expect— the context or tone or cultural
knowledge serve to indicate the intended meaning. It can be a night-
mare for future historians and critics, though.

The process isn't restricted to slang, of course. Take *literally:* people just
can't be stopped from using it as a mere intensifier: "I literally coined
money." That's a quotation from 1863.

The irony is that the 'correct' meaning is itself a semantic change. It derives from Latin *littera* 'letter'; under Charlemagne there was a reform
to read Latin *literaliter*, according to the letters, as opposed to substituting the greatly changed vernacular pronunciation. The term was extended to literature (a man in 1593 is described as 'literally wise', that is,
learned in literature) and to word-for-word reporting or translation, before reaching its modern meaning of 'truly, non-figuratively'.

The point is, people are constantly 'misapplying' words, for all sorts of
reasons: to be vivid, to come at something from a new angle, to surprise,
to amuse, to express something new or difficult. Your con-people should
be doing this too.

There are words that seem to **resist change**. A sampling of words that
basically meant the same thing in Old English: *arm, bare, begin, body,*

cold, daughter, die, far, gold, grin, head, kiss, knife, land, mean, name, new, red, shadow, small, star, think, time, tree, water, word, yard, young.

Is it that common words don't change as much? Well, here's some words that had a different meaning in Old English: *bad* ('worthless'), *breath* ('odor'), *can* ('know'), *cloud* ('rock'), *dear* ('glorious'), *fast* ('firm'), *fear* ('peril'), *load* ('journey'), *lose* ('perish'), *nice* ('foolish'), *pretty* ('tricky'), *pull* ('pluck'), *soft* ('agreeable'), *walk* ('roll'), *with* ('against').

The bottom line is that you can get away with changing pretty much any word *or* leaving it alone.

How do I make a proto-language?

In my view, an ancestral language is just a language. That's because language, to the best of our knowledge, goes back at least 50,000 years— that is, at least five times the time depth of the longest-attested language families. For all that time, languages must have been pretty much what they are today.

What does change, of course, is technology. Your proto-language should be appropriate to its people's tech level.

- Recall that agriculture, markets, cities, governments, and even high numbers are inventions. If the proto-language is spoken by hunter-gatherers, it shouldn't have words like *harvest, republic, temple, coin, glass, highway.*

Depending on the particulars of your language, you can of course leave out stuff you'd put in a complete grammar. You could work with nothing but a wordlist. However, I'd try to work out at least some of the morphology. You can make satisfying fusional morphologies by applying sound change and analogy to an agglutinative parent; see the *LCK* pp. 163-91.

You can probably leave out most of the syntax section— though the more you work out, the more you can use. (Even if the syntax changed a lot, there may be remnants— as for example we still have SOV in French when the object is a pronoun.)

(Language arguably did get more complex with the invention of writing— not because the grammar got nastier, but because old words as well as dialectal variation can be kept around indefinitely.)

If you're curious what words to include so they make a good basis for the daughter language to build on, see the Etymology Frequency List, p. 89.

Do I need synonyms?

My copy of *Roget's Thesaurus* has quite a few words for *angry*. Let's take a look:

> *angry, angered, indignant, irate, wroth, wrathful, mad, sore, riled, ill-tempered, infuriated, raging, furious, savage, storming, fuming, rabid, vexed, pissed, incensed, provoked, annoyed, irritated, aggravated, peeved, resentful, maddened, inflamed, bristly, cholerous, offended, aggrieved, seething*

Do you need all that? No. In fact, I advise that you **avoid synonyms** most of the time. There are some near-synonyms on the Fantasy Frequency List; feel free to combine them. Life is short, especially if you want to fill a world with half a dozen languages.

Besides, if you concentrate on breadth in the lexicon, you'll find that you've got quite a few synonyms already through the magic of **metaphor**. If you have words for *storms, fire, cooking, insanity, pain, spines*, and *wild beasts*, you've got a good bit of the above list. Technical terms like *bile* (= choler) and *rabies* can be applied here. Of course, you should try to use your own metaphors rather than just re-use all of English's.

You may also find you have alternatives already thanks to a healthy **morphology**. *Angered* is just the participial cousin of *angry*; *wroth/wrathful* are related, as are *furious/infuriated*. If your adjectives can have diminutives, you can double your word count, forming words like *angryish* for *irritated*.

It's a nice touch to supply some **slang** terms; again, the easiest way to form these is to use existing words (like *pissed*).

For your main language, maybe you want to imitate this kind of richness. Recall, though, that English is a weird mixture— a magpie of a language that is not representative of all languages. On the other hand, that gives us a clue: **borrow a lot**. *Wrath* is native; we borrowed *ire* from French, *irate* from Latin, *anger* from Norse. So if you want lots of synonyms, make your people linguistic borrowers (which means creating languages they can borrow from, and a history that inclines them to do it).

Beyond that, of course, many of the words in the list mean something slightly different:

> *furious*   great anger on the edge of being uncontrolled

irritated	a mild anger, often at a small (but persistent) thing
resentful	angry out of a feeling of being treated unfairly
sore	with hurt feelings, seen in a somewhat disparaging way

The take-away point is that the additional terms add nuance, allowing writers to be more expressive.

Languages seem to avoid exact synonyms, but words are distinguished by more than meaning:

- **Region**: e.g. Boston's *T* vs. New York's *subway* vs. Chicago's *el* vs. London's *tube*.

- **Register**: among the anger words, *ire* and *wrath* are now fairly hifalutin, *angry* is neutral, *mad* (for Americans) colloquial, and *pissed off* slangy.

- **Domain**: e.g. the substance known as *sodium chloride* in the lab is *salt* in the kitchen. The kitchen, for that matter, is called the *galley* at sea.

- **Collocations.** Some words are preferred with particular other words— e.g. *place* and *set* are similar in meaning, but you have to *place* a bet and *set* the table. Sometimes an earlier sense can remain indefinitely, protected by such a collocation— e.g. you can still *hold fast* to something, though *fast* in general has changed from 'firm' to 'quick'.

- **Derivations.** Even if two words are interchangeable, like *snake* and *serpent,* their derivations aren't: the musical instrument can only be a *serpent,* while the plumber's tool can only be a *snake*.

- **Attitude**: e.g. the same person may be *bargain-conscious* when we approve of his spending habits, *miserly* when we don't.

I'm not going to provide a list of all the words you might want to create, because a) that would be a big book, and b) you already have that book, it's a dictionary. But remember the lesson of this book: ask yourself *Can I vary this a little (or a lot) from English?* Every language is likely to have a word meaning *angry*, but when it comes to these nuanced terms, there's going to be more variation.

What if it's not perfect?

On my board or in my mail, I run into people who seem to be paralyzed by the choices involved in conlanging. Where do they start? What if they get it wrong?

I think this is one of those problems whose solution seems too simple to accept: *Just make a choice.* Throw a dart at the page; flip a coin. It's art, so there is no wrong answer. It's not even like drawing the human figure, where fidelity to the model can be criticized. It's more like drawing a dragon— who's to say that your idea of a dragon is wrong?

I don't mean that you can't make a poor conlang. I had the advantage of doing my early work off the net, so you can't see it. I suppose my obituary will mention Verdurian, which is the first Almean conlang I made, and definitely not the best. (If you're curious, what bothers me is that I borrowed a lot of French and Russian words too closely. I wish I'd had this book available, so I could look at their etymological sources instead!)

You can always revise the language later. Or just relegate it to a less important nation, or make it a proto-language! Deriving a new language from a parent is liable to produce a much better product, as you can produce irregularities in an organic fashion with sound change, and you have the time depth to play with grammaticalization and etymology.

Since we're talking about lexicons, I'll mention a neat trick for words you've come to dislike: instead of deleting them, repurpose them as synonyms. Languages are such huge things that it's a pity to simply throw out work.

E.g., going back to the initial example in the book: we had *dlatla* for 'king', *speti* for 'queen'. We decide that we shouldn't have a separate root for 'queen'; we make it *dlatlaŋ* instead. But maybe *speti* can be kept as an alternate word, originally meaning 'wife', that was sometimes used for the queen. Or perhaps it can be used for 'prince' or 'consort' or some other term we don't have yet.

I emphasize linguistic knowledge and real-world knowledge a lot, but I also want to underline that you never *have* to use it! Your conlang doesn't have to be artistic, it just has to please you. And please don't think you need a real-world model for every word or etymology.

What should a good lexicon entry look like?

Probably you have a lot of lexicon entries that look like this:

    care - rasfolžer

To be honest, lots of mine look like that too. But a glance at almost any natlang dictionary should show that this 100% interchangeability is very rare.

Here's the current entry for *care* in my English-Verdurian dictionary:

> **care** - *affection* rasfolže; *painstakingness* arastát; *meeting of needs* cumasát; *worry* itësi, orivura
>
> > *care for* cumásuir
> >
> > *take care of* agolec
> >
> > *I don't care* Řo sen troge
> >
> > *He can die, for all I care* Epe šuščan sam sen trogan
> >
> > *I'm beginning to care for these children* Debutai rasfolžer ci-imfáti
> >
> > *Rachel is caring for John* Raheli cumásue Ihanon
> >
> > *Would you please take care of this?* Ut urave agolec eto
> >
> > *Take care crossing the street* Leleno še rekan soa prosiam
> >
> > *Would you care for a cup?* Esce e dy vuleu taš?

The main things to note:

- Different senses are distinguished in the main entry.

- Translations are given for common short phrases— **collocations**. Very often the sense of a word may match between two languages, but the other words you normally use with it don't. For instance, *question* corresponds to French *question*, Spanish *pregunta*. But where we *ask a question*, in French *on pose une question*, and in Spanish *uno hace una pregunta*.

- Full sentences show how the word is used and offer more nuances (e.g. the use of *leleno* 'see' in the imperative *Take care...*)

Here's a simple example from the Verdurian-English side:

> **orto** - toe; protruding part of a baseboard or pedestal; *(slang)* slow student [HORTO]
>
> > *pere orto* big toe
> > *ĝun orto* second toe
> > *co-pav orto* third toe
> > *pav orto* little toe
> > *trogan so el ortam* do the impossible

The organization is the same, but note that I always include the etymology if I have one. (For Verdurian I use the convention, borrowed from Romance philology, that words in the parent language are cited in CAPS.)

The last idiom shows off what I think is a neat little bit of conworlding. Almeans have only four toes, so indeed *trogan so el ortam* 'to touch the middle toe' is to do something impossible!

Fantasy Frequency Wordlist

What words do you need?

You can create words as needed, or work through the lists in the *LCK*. But it can be useful to have a **frequency list**— a list of the most common words.

I've compiled a frequency list based on **fantasy and sf works**. It has two advantages over wordlists you might find online:

- It's oriented toward creating fantasy and sf worlds, so it'll be appropriate for most conlangs.

- The entries are roots, not individual words. E.g. *know* stands not only for *knows, knew, known, knowing* but for *knowledge* and *knower*.

The method

Here's how the list was created.

- I assembled a corpus of over 1.1 million words. This consisted of a bunch of my own writing, plus online-accessible stories by William Morris, Lewis Carroll, Frank Baum, Kenneth Grahame, Edith Nesbit, H.G. Wells, Edgar Rice Burroughs, H.P. Lovecraft, Aldous Huxley, Olaf Stapledon, Fritz Lieber, Cyrus Kornbluth, Andre Norton, R.A. Lafferty, Marion Zimmer Bradley, Suzette Haden Elgin, Mary Gentle, Molly Brown, Neil Gaiman, Connie Willis, Cory Doctorow, and Charles Stross.

- I used a program to find the words, remove affixes, maintain counts, and then sort the words by frequency.

- I removed proper names and interjections, and corrected for words too obviously boosted by the choice of source material. (E.g. *scarecrow* only appeared in the Baum book.)

Grammatical words

I considered removing grammatical words— articles, pronouns, numbers, conjunctions, modals. These are highly dependent on English, and you'll be creating equivalents for them as you work through the morphology and syntax anyway.

However, I decided to leave them in, for several reasons:

- They tell us something about language— it's interesting to see just how much of our texts consists of these words.

- The boundary line isn't that clear. Prepositions seem to add content— except perhaps for words like *of* and *to*. If *must* is removed, what about *need*?

- Once I'd combined lexemes (e.g. *I, me, my, mine, myself* are all counted as *I*), they don't overwhelm the list anyway.

But I urge you to skip over them if you're working through the list. Don't create a word for *the* just because it happens to be the most frequent word in English. Think about whether you want articles at all, and if so whether they work as they do in English. But all that's covered in the *LCK* and *ALC*.

A note on numbers: I left out *thirty, forty, fifty*, because they're almost always no-brainer derivations; for more see *Numbers*. (60/70/80/90 didn't make the list.)

Caveats

The corpus isn't long enough to trust in the tail. E.g. roots like *hazel, oats, pyramid, shallow, torment, wiggle* all appeared 7 times— but they might well have appeared 12 or 0 times in a different corpus. But it doesn't matter, since I've applied a **cutoff** of 64 appearances.

It's a matter of judgment when a derivation has branched off enough to count as a separate root. I separated *gentle* and *gentleman*, for instance, and *love / lovely*, and *apart / apartment*.

In some cases this affects whether a root makes the list. E.g. *signal* and *signify* don't make the cutoff, but they'd easily clear it if they were combined. (But *sign* made it, so I'm not too worried about them.)

For our purposes the English lexicon has two major disadvantages:

- Some annoying **homonyms**. Without a good deal of work I couldn't distinguish pairs like

    bear — animal / tolerate
    lie — untruth / recline
    leaves — pl. of leaf / 3s of leave
    left — not right / past of leave
    found — past of find / establish
    well — interjection / water source / comparative of good

- English makes some distinctions that arguably distort the list— e.g. both *small* and *little* are common words, and probably should just be one word in your conlang.

I haven't used the list slavishly when conlanging, and neither should you. Naturally, if you need a word that's not on the list, create it!

The list

Without further ado, here's the Fantasy Frequency Wordlist.

Here's the **top fifty** words, with their frequencies:

THE	67664	THIS/THESE	5162
BE	38472	FROM	4574
AND	36157	ALL	4251
OF	30282	THERE	4127
I	28158	ONE	3952
A	28063	BY	3834
HE	27395	WHAT	3767
TO	26694	SO	3637
YOU	16424	SOME	3587
IT	15814	OUT	3534
IN	15723	GO	3464
THEY	14366	OR	3430
NOT	14121	WILL	3387
HAVE	13869	KNOW	3357
THAT/THOSE	13095	SEE	3303
SHE	12742	NO	3301
WITH	8107	UP	3228
WE	7884	COME	3203
AS	7820	IF	3123
FOR	7814	THEN	2967
DO	7752	INTO	2882
BUT	7446	LIKE	2808
SAY	7036	WOULD	2785
ON	6922	COULD	2773
AT	6069	WHICH	2762

These fifty words total 553,087 instances, or just over 50% of the corpus.

And here's the **next 150** words, each of which occurs at least 620 times. They make up a further 12.5% of the corpus.

This and the remaining tables are to be read line by line. That is, it's *look, think, when...* not *look, now, time...*

LOOK	THINK	WHEN	WHO	CAN
NOW	MAKE	ANY	MAN	GET
TIME	MORE	ABOUT	DOWN	TAKE
OTHER	BACK	WEAR	GOOD	ONLY
HAND	OVER	LONG	THAN	TELL
VERY	WAY	LITTLE	BEFORE	WELL
LIFE	EYE	JUST	HERE	HOW
THING	THROUGH	TWO	EVEN	FIND
GIVE	ASK	FEEL	WHERE	AFTER
FIRST	FACE	HEAD	AGAIN	EVERY
SEEM	OWN	GREAT	TURN	STILL
DAY	OFF	WANT	AWAY	UPON
TOO	DOOR	OLD	MOVE	MUCH
MUST	PEOPLE	THOU	NEVER	THOUGH
RIGHT	NEW	STAND	LIGHT	SPEAK
YEAR	DEAD/ DEATH	HEAR	TRY	REAL
CITY	LAST	OPEN	BEGIN	MIGHT
SIDE	WHY	AGAINST	ANOTHER	LET
HOUSE	WORK	SHOULD	WHILE	ROOM
THREE	RUN	ONCE	PLACE	WOMAN
BECAUSE	WORLD	END	MIND	MOST
UNTIL	NOTHING	WORD	ARM	NIGHT
VOICE	LEFT	AROUND	WAR	HOLD
DARK	MEAN	KEEP	CLOSE	WITHOUT
CALL	FAR	MOMENT	YET	SMALL
EACH	MANY	FOOT	SUCH	TOWARD
COURSE	POINT	SIT	TALK	FALL
ENOUGH	WALL	HIGH	BEHIND	UNDER
FRIEND	MAY	NEED	STAR	LAND
ALMOST	WATER	BODY	NEAR	BRING

(*Life* includes *live*; *give* includes *gift*; *move* includes *motion*; and *though* includes *although*.)

Here's the **next 300** roots, each of which occurs at least 248 times:

follow	child	build	put	half
human	walk	watch	kind	few
(a)sleep	god	same	sure	sudden
strange	along	grow	air	lead
ever	young	stop	across	hard
between	round	also	love	lay
reach	late(r)	become	leave	white
pass	quite	wait	home	return
serve	true	power	set	always
name	red	shall	break	under-stand
answer	laugh	black	wonder	meet
heart	slow	strong	green	hour
large	horse	king	ring	use
help	ship	smile	part	fear
among	sound	happen	show	lord
believe	fight	four	deep	next
kill	silent	cry	boy	fire
together	send	lose	perhaps	bad
full	present	care	soon	remember
floor	start	die	second	clear
both	draw	animal	lady	step
low	rest	simple	learn	wish
stone	rather	father	appear	girl
certain	sun	possible	office	ground
since	change	play	order	big
least	explain	hundred	minute	breath
eat	hair	shake	above	short
cold	else	catch	question	son
space	shoulder	wood	free	less
party	whole	blood	indeed	tip
sea	direct	alone	guard	lie
(un)able	inside	story	sword	line
matter	color	travel	read	bright
gold	beauty	carry	final	force

morning	past	prince	quick	enter
system	already	cover	please	five
tree	suppose	peace	earth	ride
dream	machine	planet	control	continue
touch	colony	river	sort	finger
either	within	leg	mouth	easy
listen	pull	differ	expect	magic
table	spirit	hope	reply	bed
save	wise	reason	window	entire
fly	however	decide	interest	ear
nature	blue	act	distant	ready
stay	add	surprise	cut	burn
nor	gray	sense	thousand	person
realize	rise	soft	form	forward
idea	alien	drop	army	horror
remain	wide	front	hang	hide
mountain	moon	outside	beside	safe
sing	bear	escape	bit	creature
ten	weapon	metal	shadow	enemy
master	maybe	drive	fair	street
quiet	six	center	chief	forget
throw	soldier	top	pain	several
clothes	discover	raise	rule	suggest
edge	hot	road	rock	skin
fact	figure	complete	glad	sight
heavy	write	state	rose	except

The first 500 roots, above, make up 74% of the corpus.

Here's the **next 400 roots**, each of which occurs at least 122 times:

strike	dance	shut	trouble	happy
sign	case	danger	south	week
crowd	pick	sky	instant	whisper
hall	roof	twenty	fast	anger
teach	train	attack	notice	number
ago	pay	(a)wake	fool	silver

country	fill	blow	book	dear
instead	palace	poor	duke	council
dress	none	commit	secret	whatever
wild	field	lean	spend	(in)visible
beyond	choose/ choice	society	mother	wave
group	command	doubt	early	mere
difficult	art	consider	battle	below
general	thick	attention	glance	huge
destroy	offer	(e)special	fine	food
maid	age	create	whether	wrong
brother	chance	cross	express	hunt
language	plan	prison	repeat	wind
climb	direction	faint	level	memory
straight	stretch	eight	hill	perfect
push	chair	lift	month	rich
thank	settle	box	gate	noise
roll	shape	defend	judge	lip
lot	self	town	advance	glass
visit	dry	during	family	grass
plain	allow	business	sharp	shout
warm	nod	shoot	brain	marry
north	support	empty	intend	thus
alive	mad	study	tire	agree
hate	miss	paper	process	approach
evident	race	receive	fellow	further
imagine	queen	bow	exact	loud
neck	warn	actual	afraid	giant
tear	curious	hole	shit	swing
circle	dust	search	deal	lock
narrow	thin	history	knife	often
seven	succeed	stream	captain	charge
empire	hop	immediate	size	bare
monster	pretty	bend	knee	tin
garden	sick	chamber	comfort	pale
piece	yellow	manage	problem	cosmos
damn	flash	pause	tall	respect

important	inform	tale	clean	probable
smell	weak	west	arrive	attempt
check	gun	accept	message	report
fit	remake	sweet	usual	evil
hurry	pocket	proud	speed	tea
trade	drink	third	view	boss
cause	guess	hurt	odd	press
slight	spring	agent	beast	corner
position	slip	spear	brown	mark
scream	bank	boat	fail	member
vision	worry	east	recognize	stick
conquer	dog	loose	produce	promise
valley	radiate	spread	blind	finish
intelligent	island	music	particular	cat
cloud	condition	path	serious	tight
tooth	fish	law	nose	century
gaze	picture	respond	terrible	ugly
cave(rn)	exist	money	throat	track
village	experience	haste	jump	quarter
rush	somewhat	demand	middle	paint
seat	temple	threat	beneath	gentle
object	swift	wife	arrow	base
cheek	effect	forest	game	sorry
surface	therefore	ahead	bug	forth
revolt	beat	bone	cheer	flesh
passage	castle	couple	desert	dim
mar	mile	bird	fuck	gather
join	sigh	tone	trust	belong
companion	frighten	journey	smoke	station
suspect	cast	luck	mighty	shine
blink	protect	scene	tiny	win
bind	hunger	joy	kiss	oppose
pleasant	born	calm	flat	single
steel	store	community	govern	ought
shock	worth	dine	dozen	familiar
flower	heat	local	marble	march
prepare	hit	refuse	resist	tower

bottom	glow	plant	stuff	main

We're now up to 900 roots making up 81% of the corpus.

And here's another **600 roots**, each of which occurs at least 62 times:

subject	desire	effort	purpose	record
require	steal	ancient	bottle	court
evening	excite	rag	satisfy	stair
today	cool	dare	manner	observe
pleasure	afternoon	car	company	nice
stage	trick	active	snake	terror
confuse	hesitate	remind	concern	science
admit	busy	explore	honor	iron
onto	prove	situation	struggle	anxious
disappear	egg	firm	folk	include
necessary	physical	police	spot	steady
wander	wash	weigh	contact	converse
drift	future	helium	occupy	welcome
boot	civilize	duty	fresh	fur
mass	sand	adventure	assure	drag
occasion	twist	unless	vast	account
corridor	creep	elder	extreme	naked
seek	slide	statue	trail	beg
block	daughter	describe	neither	nobody
wing	belt	claim	eager	maintain
sir	survive	arrange	band	content
grip	individual	mistake	mount	range
square	treat	violent	weary	increase
public	trap	worship	awful	bar
breast	devil	grin	hell	job
note	practice	priest	raid	reflect
slave	surround	tongue	common	defeat
develop	meat	murder	murmur	normal
pursue	wine	burst	coat	examine
kick	neighbor	provide	snow	suffer
thrust	buy	camp	detail	lone
nine	relate	remove	school	screen
smooth	bomb	deem	leap	match

cease	craft	insist	invite	letter
obvious	relief	rough	scout	tar
vanish	absolute	communicate	crawl	explode
ill	muscle	test	tunnel	wrist
argue	assist	capture	enormous	exclaim
freeze	sad	wound	accord	conscious
count	cup	emerald	fat	flame
gesture	mouse	pack	protest	utter
baby	bread	character	chest	fashion
grab	pink	proper	rare	reveal
signal	suit	twice	universe	ally
bother	delight	display	farm	ghost
heal	lack	military	skill	stupid
complain	divide	gentleman	medical	noble
post	proceed	shift	shrug	victory
ancestor	aunt	bag	guide	majesty
map	million	rabbit	row	brief
claw	double	jewel	nation	silk
trip	unite	yard	audience	complex
convince	grace	hat	ruin	supply
sweat	twelve	uncle	ceiling	cell
chapter	descend	glory	grave	image
organize	pilot	rain	snap	swim
hotel	nervous	result	sex	soul
throne	chain	dirt	emotion	extend
mechanical	permit	sister	contain	crack
dawn	educate	gain	limb	nought
occur	pray	scar	startle	various
advise	bush	caution	fortune	limit
politics	religion	sail	shudder	trace
baron	broad	brush	enjoy	favor
generate	glare	impatient	pity	scarce
tonight	avoid	desk	female	hero
kitchen	knock	meal	opposite	peer
possess	solid	squad	sweep	admire
bore	desperate	dull	fade	fling

key	mirror	opportunity	pair	passion
patient	sink	swallow	venture	authority
brave	curse	declare	due	flitter
grasp	kid	operate	ray	separate
spy	strip	absent	beam	bolt
culture	determine	energy	engine	gleam
grandmother	meter	obey	page	peasant
perceive	pile	represent	stiff	tomorrow
wet	address	barbarian	comment	demon
event	fog	insect	load	major
mental	mutter	plate	rapid	responsible
roar	robe	term	tube	clever
confident	feature	galaxy	invade	lake
link	lunch	mission	mystery	nasty
origin	polite	pool	share	stride
tremble	upper	accompany	apart	astonish
depart	globe	heap	summer	task
triumph	aim	arch	aware	blade
board	harm	male	pace	patch
perform	stable	structure	whistle	class
dread	faction	fist	ignore	inch
material	measure	merchant	program	reside
scale	sell	spider	stare	stir
stomach	tail	amid	bridge	collect
fix	float	handle	interrupt	labor
prefer	rate	remote	witch	amuse
attract	cloth	cook	fancy	fate
fruit	intense	mix	overhead	progress
switch	abrupt	assume	balance	constant
expand	fierce	flow	gasp	greet
impress	practical	pure	royal	scrap
shiver	waste	combat	design	dwell
echo	equip	fleet	forever	instruct
misery	parent	preside	rank	risk
treasure	value	wrap	cruel	duck
hook	idiot	indicate	kilometer	locate
recover	taste	accomplish	adult	aside

bitter	compare	custom	discuss	engage
frown	gravity	joke	meanwhile	motor
populate	powder	twin	announce	area
cloak	correct	current	forehead	lamp
native	panel	puzzle	queer	sob
yell	behave	breakfast	concentrate	mention
mess	pattern	propose	storm	winter
annoy	blast	hail	hiss	hollow
ice	orbit	significant	silly	total
whip	alarm	amaze	bath	brilliant
delicate	fold	husband	purple	rope
string	swear	wheel	bless	bury
curtain	false	gap	relax	shame
wizard	frame	launch	loyal	pour

That makes **1500** roots; if you created all those words, you'd have a very respectable lexicon and a good chance of handling quite a lot of fantasy- and sf-related material.

These 1500 roots make up 87% of the corpus.

There is an **electronic version** of this list on the web resources page (p. 12).

Word priorities

To make word priorities clear, I've used this **typographical scheme** for all the wordlists in the book:

- The first 200 roots are in **BOLDFACE CAPS**.

- The next 300 are in **bigger type**.

- The next 400 are in **boldface**.

- The remaining 600 roots are in normal type.

- Finally, nice-to-have words (those not on the above lists) are in *italics*. There are over a thousand of these. The index itself makes a handy word-list for the most ambitious conlangers.

Again, if you need a word, don't be held back by these categories, just create it!

The Swadesh list

For convenience, I've listed the 200-item list created by Morris Swadesh, also found in the *LCK*. Words *not* in the Fantasy Frequency List are *italicized.*

Words in Swadesh's earlier 100-item list are in **bold**.

Adjectives

Numbers	**one, two**, three, four, five
Colors	**black white red green yellow**

Oppositions

good, bad	**long**, short
new, old	wide, narrow
warm, cold	thick, thin
dry, wet	**fat**, heavy
sharp, dull	left, right
near, far	**many**, few
big, small	**all**, some

Miscellaneous	**round, full**, dirty, right (correct), rotten, smooth, straight, other

Nouns

Substances	**earth, water, stone, fire, sand, smoke,** *ashes,* dust, ice, salt
Time	**night**, day, year
Weather	**rain, cloud**, snow, fog, wind
The sky	**sun, moon, star**, sky
Geographical	**mountain, road**, woods, lake, river, sea
Body parts	**head, neck, hand, foot, skin, knee, breast,** *belly,* back, leg, *fingernail*
The head	**ear, eye, hair, mouth, nose, tongue**, tooth
Internal	**blood, bone, heart, meat,** *liver,* guts
Animals	**bird, dog, fish,** *louse,* snake, animal, *worm*
	tail, egg, claw, *feather, horn,* wing
Plants	**tree, leaf,** *bark,* **seed,** *root,* flower, fruit, grass, stick
People	**person, man** (male), **woman**, child
Family	father, mother, wife, husband
Miscellaneous	**name**, fear, rope

Verbs

Life and death	**die**, **kill**, **sleep**, live
Movement	**come**, **walk**, **fly**, **swim**, float, turn
Body position	**stand**, **sit**, **lie** (down), fall
Mouth actions	**eat**, **drink**, **bite**, blow, breathe, *suck*, *spit*, *vomit*
Perception	**see**, **hear**, smell
Cognition	**know**, think
Speech acts	**say**, sing, laugh, count,
Daily life	play, hunt, throw, wash, *sew*, *wipe*
Conflict	fight, hit
Tool usage	cut, tie, dig, *stab*
Manipulation	**give**, hold, push, pull, *rub*, *scratch*, *squeeze*
Physical states	**burn**, flow, freeze, *split*, *swell*

Grammatical words

Conjunctions	**not**, and, because, if
Prepositions	at, in, with
Personal pronouns	**I**, **thou**, **we**, he, you (pl.), they
Demonstratives	**this**, **that**
Locatives	here, there
Question words	**what**, **who**, how, when, where

All about classes

A lot of this book is about creating **classes** or categories. Words *are* classes— to create a word *bird* is to define a class which some things in the universe belong to and some don't. And words are arranged in class hierarchies— e.g. a *robin* is a *bird*, and a *bird* is an *animal*.

As Steve Martin observed, people who speak another language have a *different word* for *everything*. At a deeper level, they also have a *different classification system* for everything. One of the purposes of this book is to help you think about how to create such a thing.

Classification is the subject of George Lakoff's *Women, Fire, and Dangerous Things*. That's the best place to go for more information, though you may or may not be interested in his detailed demolition of traditional logic-based theories of categorization.

Six types of class

We often tie ourselves into knots when thinking about meaning, and one reason, I think, is that we insist on treating all words the same way. Let's look at some of the ways we can look at defining words, and some of the problems.

Algorithm

The easiest type of words to think about are those defined by a formula or algorithm. These are widely used in science and technology:

radius	the distance from the center of a circle to its circumference
compiler	a program which transforms human-readable code into applications directly executable by a computer
iamb	a metrical unit composed of an unstressed syllable followed by a stressed one
velar	having a point of articulation at the velum
momentum	the product of mass times velocity
hydrogen	an atom whose nucleus contains just one proton
sucrose	a molecule $C_{12}H_{22}O_{11}$
planet	a body which orbits a star, is large enough to be nearly round in shape, and is the dominant gravitational object in its orbit

In terms of the dots-for-referents diagrams I used in the LCK (p. 100), these might be pictured like this:

• MOMENTUM

With a word defined algorithmically,

- There is no internal variation. Either the word fits or it doesn't.

- Referents without the formula are of no help in learning the word.

- The word is learned by explicitly passing on the formula, and if you don't know the formula you don't know the word.

- The linguistic signals of prototypes (below) don't work. It doesn't make much sense to say "Strictly speaking line A is a radius" or "Technically, this molecule is sucrose."

- However, *roughly* can be used as a signal that the formula doesn't quite match: *The island is roughly triangular.*

So far so good, but the trouble is that people of a pedantic mindset, like logicians and lexicographers, prefer formulas and try to apply them to everything. Most everyday words do not have clear thick boundaries.

Family resemblance

Logicians once hoped that any word could be defined by a set of shared features. Ludwig Wittgenstein explains why this doesn't work, focusing on the word *game*:

> Consider for example the proceedings that we call "games". I mean board-games, card-games, ball-games, Olympic games, and so on. What is common to them all? — Don't say: "There must be something common, or they would not be called 'games'"–but look and see whether there is anything common to all. — For if you look at them you will not see something that is common to all, but similarities, relationships, and a whole series of them at that. To repeat: don't think, but look! —

> Look for example at board-games, with their multifarious relationships.

Now pass to card-games; here you find many correspondences with the first group, but many common features drop out, and others appear.

When we pass next to ball-games, much that is common is retained, but much is lost.— Are they all 'amusing'? Compare chess with noughts and crosses. Or is there always winning and losing, or competition between players? Think of patience. In ball games there is winning and losing; but when a child throws his ball at the wall and catches it again, this feature has disappeared. Look at the parts played by skill and luck; and at the difference between skill in chess and skill in tennis.

Think now of games like ring-a-ring-a-roses; here is the element of amusement, but how many other characteristic features have disappeared! sometimes similarities of detail.

And we can go through the many, many other groups of games in the same way; can see how similarities crop up and disappear.

And the result of this examination is: we see a complicated network of similarities overlapping and criss-crossing: sometimes overall similarities.

I can think of no better expression to characterize these similarities than "**family resemblances**"; for the various resemblances between members of a family: build, features, colour of eyes, gait, temperament, etc. etc. overlap and criss-cross in the same way. – And I shall say: 'games' form a family.

(*Philosophical Investigations*, §66-67)

Was Wittgenstein right? Do the lexicographers actually fail at this? The *American Heritage Dictionary (AHD)* defines *game* as "A way of amusing oneself; a diversion." That does fail to capture important points (such as rules and competition) and also fails to exclude other amusements (such as opera, cocktails, web browsing, and masturbation).

A better attempt is made by the philosopher Bernard Suits in *The Grasshopper*: "playing a game is the voluntary attempt to overcome unnecessary obstacles." That's not bad, though what's the obstacle in playing the lottery, or dodgeball? Suits's definition also fits conlanging or stamp collecting or dancing, none of which are exactly games.

Maybe you can come up with something cleverer. But that misses the point, which is that we don't learn the word *game* from definitions, no matter how clever. We learn it by playing a bunch of games and being told that they are 'games'.

You can evade the whole issue by just defining a word in your conlang that glosses as 'game'. That's not a bad thing, but is every cultural practice in your conworld a copy of English? Is there any other word that has the complexity of *game* or *judge*?

Once you start noticing words like *game*, you'll see them all over. What's a *woman*, for instance? None of these attempted definitions quite work:

- Has breasts or a womb. (These might have been removed.)

- Can bear a child. (Many women are infertile, too young, or too old.)

- Has XX chromosomes. (People with androgen insensitivity live as females but are XY, and there are other variations. Plus, other species have other chromosome types.)

- Has a vagina. (Certain intersex conditions are not clear-cut; plus, transgender women may not yet have had surgery.)

- Prefers men. (Duh, lesbians.)

- Acts like a woman. (You can be as butch as you like and still be female.)

- Identifies as a woman. (Works for transgender people, but many people just don't worry what sex they identify as.)

This is very distressing for some people, who want their boundary lines thick and clear— but you can only have that when you have consensus on a useful formula.

Often a word is formulaic in science, but not in ordinary language. Biologists find it useful to define *female*, and their criterion is that the female is the sex that creates larger gametes. That's fine for biological work, but it doesn't mean that biology has the last word when it comes to culture, law, or religion! It just means that biology has found that definition useful as a technical term.

Our culture reveres dictionaries— though the ordinary type has only existed for a few centuries. Many books and articles begin with a definition— elaborate, gerrymandered, and mostly forgotten in Chapter Two. If an author has to create a definition, they're not working from the social consensus; they're just following an eccentric procedure for saying what they want to talk about!

Prototype

Many common words— biological kinds, emotions, personality types, simple actions and attributes, tools, colors, and more— show **prototype** effects. Characteristics of these words:

- There is significant internal variation.

- Some referents are better examples than others. Linguistic signals include *That's a real bird; he's a **man's** man; that's a proper risotto.*

- There is often a best example or model member. E.g., the prototype *bird*, for Americans, is probably something like a robin or a sparrow.

- There are valid edge cases. Linguistic signals include *Technically a tick is an arachnid. Strictly speaking that's legal.*

- There are close but invalid edge cases: *Technically rabbits are not rodents.*

- The word can be learned by generalizing from multiple examples.

Clumpy space

The semantic space— the sea of possible referents— can be visualized as diffuse but clumpy. Some clumps are obvious enough that most cultures will have them as concepts, with similar boundaries, but others are messier.

E.g. dogs are a pretty obvious clump, and most languages have a word for them. (To my knowledge, no language with access to both cats and dogs fails to distinguish them.)

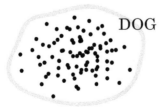

On the other hand, the distinction between *love* and *like* is much fuzzier. English happens to distinguish them, French doesn't:

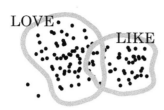 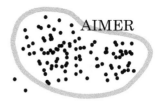

We learn many of these words as children, not from definitions but from examples. If there's a dog in the family, the child quickly learns that it's *doggie*— but she hasn't learned the word yet, only one referent.

She soon encounters dogs in the neighborhood, stuffed dogs, dogs in pictures. At first she may extend the concept incorrectly— e.g. she uses *doggie* for a stuffed lion, or she fails to recognize that the chihuahua next door is a *doggie* like her family's own beagle.

Eventually, of course, she uses the words as everyone else does. (Though perhaps her prototype is still the family dog. When my niece Lisa was a toddler, she drew pictures of cats without tails. Quite reasonably, since her family cat was a Manx!)

Prototype effects

Prototype effects have been extensively studied since the work of Eleanor Rosch. They include:

- *Gradability*: Respondents can provide judgments on how good an example of a class a particular member is.

- *Reaction time*: Respondents are given statements like *A chicken is a bird* and asked if it's true or false. Response times are shorter for prototypical members.

- *Example production*: Respondents are more likely to name the prototype when asked to list members of the class.

  (I might add that if you ask a cartoonist to draw it, they'll probably draw the prototype. From this we can learn that the prototypical hunk of cheese is Swiss, with really big holes.)

- *Asymmetry in reasoning*: New information about a prototypical member is more likely to be generalized to marginal members than the reverse. E.g. Lance Rips found that subjects assumed that a disease would readily spread from robins to ducks, but not the reverse.

Prototype effects should not be confused with graded categories. The idea is not that robins are 100% birds, chickens 50%, and penguins just 20%. They're all birds, but some are better examples than others.

Cloud relations

The boundaries between prototype-words live in tension with all the other nearby words. And the boundaries can shift.

For instance, over the history of English, *dog* moved from being just one breed to refer to the whole species:

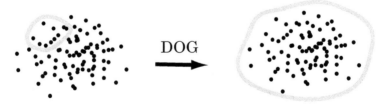

Similarly, *girl* once referred to any child, male or female, and came to be applied only to females:

Often a narrower word grabs some set of referents from another. E.g. a *chair* is anything you can sit on, minus *stools* which are backless and *benches / couches* which are multi-person and hard or soft respectively.

Map division

For some semantic spaces, a prototype plus the pressure of nearby words might be all you need. Continua, for instance: the *heat* continuum can have two nodes (*hot / cold*) or four (*hot / warm / cool / cold*) or some other number. You don't need a formula for the boundary, just a general rule to use the term closest to the prototype.[3]

A two-dimensional example is color, as colors are defined not only by hue but by saturation. E.g. *orange* and *brown* pick out the same hue, but *orange* is more saturated.

It's not uncommon for a term to be used only within one domain. E.g. *blond* can be used of hair or wood and not much else. *Lukewarm* is fine for drinks but not the weather. *Scrambled* is mostly applied to eggs. Almost anything can be *beautiful* but only a few things (people, clothes, landscapes, pictures) can be *pretty*.

Prototypes and formulas

Many words seem to have prototypes *and* formulas. Birds, for instance, aren't just an assemblage of things-like-robins. They have a conceptual unity: feathers, a body plan with wings in place of arms, beaks, no teeth, egg-laying, and flight. (This is really a Wittgensteinian family resemblance: some birds lack feathers or can't fly, and very early birds did have teeth.) As a bonus, they form a valid cladistic class— they have a common ancestor.

Similarly, though *chair* has prototype effects, chairs can also be defined as things made to sit on. A few things you can sit on are not chairs be-

---

[3] The continuum may vary in different domains, however. A *cool star*, for instance, is far hotter than a *hot car engine*.

cause they're named by other words (e.g. *sofa, car seat*), but if you can't sit on it at all, it's pretty much disqualified from chairhood.

Some words are learned as prototypes and are redefined as formulas. *Father* is first learned, no doubt, as a name. The logical next step is that the child applies the word to the adult male in other households; but they don't yet understand the relation to parenthood— as Barbara Partee noticed when she was asked by young children if she had a 'father'— she eventually realized that they were asking if she had a husband. The adult usage is defined with a formula, but retains prototype effects— we might call one man *more fatherly* than another, or say *he's a real father*.

Function

Some things don't even make sense except in terms of another object. A *glove*, for instance, would be a baffling construction if we had never seen a hand.

These are just a special case of formulas, but I point them out because they're not the prototypical example of nouns. An alien could probably work out an idea of *horse* given enough examples of horses, but no number of *keys* would explain that word, till he'd been shown a *lock*.

Script

Some actions are best thought of as scripts. (Lakoff calls them ICMs, for *idealized cognitive models*, though in more recent work he uses the catchier *frames*) A fairly complicated procedure has to apply for them to make sense. Consider what it means to *judge*.

- Person J presides over a formal meeting whose purpose is to settle a dispute between two parties A and B.

- J has specific cultural authority to make such decisions, involving much training and experience.

- Party A, who brought the suit, must explicitly accept J's authority. (A may be the state rather than a private party.)

- B need not accept J's authority, but J has the cultural power to compel B to follow her dictates anyway.

- J must be engaged in the formal meeting, rather than (say) discussing the case at home in bed with her husband.

- The parts of the procedure which involve investigation and argumentation are over.

- The *judgment* is a formal statement which requires certain performative or ritual elements. (E.g., it must be delivered in court, must be audible, must be recorded, must not be followed by the words "... Ha, I'm just horseshitting you.")

- J's decision will have practical effects on A and B which can be practically enforced. (There may or may not be a way to formally challenge it.)

This too is a formula, but a particularly elaborate and culturally determined one. An alien trying to record the meaning of *judge* would not really have succeeded unless he got it all down.

Scripts can vary by time or place, or require subjective judgment calls, or cultural rules. This is troublesome for the necessary-and-sufficient-condition crowd, but ordinary speakers have no problem with such words... at least, under close to prototypical situations!

Many words have a nice clear formula, but it sounds pedantic or odd to insist on it in all cases. A *bachelor*, for instance, is an unmarried adult male. But it doesn't sound right to say that a widower, or a monk, or a man with a long-term girlfriend, is a bachelor. Part of the script for bachelorhood is that the man is *in the market* for marriage. Someone who for whatever reason is not marriageable is not felicitously described as a bachelor.

Lakoff captures this with the *idealized* in ICM. A model doesn't have to match reality precisely. In fact, we can refer to multiple, conflicting ICMs, discussing which is appropriate— his term is *framing* the situation. A simple example:

> *Peter isn't stingy, he's thrifty.*

Thrifty has a frame which includes the tenet *Saving money is good*; *stingy* has one that says *Saving money is bad*. The sentence is an implicit comment on which ICM better applies to Peter. This is hard to handle in traditional theories of meaning, which have no place for human subjectivity, much less direct evaluation of competing frames.

Polytypes

Why is it that many people don't believe in male superiority, and yet make a point of saying they aren't *feminists*? Pretty obviously they are not applying a formula or an ideological checklist. I'd say that they are contemplating the entire perceived history of feminism— Gloria Steinem and Bella Abzug and Susan Brownmiller and Hillary Clinton, lesbians in birkenstocks, Women's Studies programs, some blog post that's in the news— and comparing themselves to *that*.

This isn't simply a prototype, as it's composed of multiple people, behaviors, symbols, and quotations. It's close to the traditional idea of *stereotype*, but it's not always negative, so instead I'll call it a *polytype*.

Words for political movements are usually polytypes— e.g. *fascist* and *socialist* are used for little more than 'political things I hate'. Cultural movements (*Romantic, Impressionist, pop, punk, geek, otaku*) are polytypes. Attempts at definitions are always gerrymandered and quickly forgotten; they are usually introduced by enumerating examples.

Many terms of value are polytypes— *cool, hip, elegant, weird, kitsch, tacky, lame, compelling, exciting*. With some of these, there's the added complication that a statement seemingly about the world is really about our own experiences— after all, nothing is a *cliché* when you hear it the first time.

It's often said that **race** is a social construct. I hope you linguists and conlangers understand that *all* words are social constructs. But my point is that *race* is far from a 'natural kind'; it's a polytype.

- Much of the reason we think it's clear is because we're really thinking about prototypes— e.g. George W. Bush vs. Clarence Thomas. Plenty of real-world people aren't easy to classify, and many people have passed for black or white depending on where they lived and who they associated with.

- The determination varies by region. The same person might be called *black* in the UK and *Asian* or *Middle Eastern* or *Hispanic* in the US.

- It varies over time. To most Americans today, Italians and Jews are *white*; in 1880 people felt vehemently that they were not.

- Americans are hypersensitive, in a strange princess-and-the-pea way, to any hint of black descent. I'm half-German and half-Norwegian in descent, but no one would insist that I'm therefore 100% German. But someone half-black and half-white... or far less black than that... registers to many people as *black*.

If you point all this out, many people will insist that no, it's perfectly clear to *them*. This can be explained as a prototype effect: they have an idea of a prototypical white or black man, and as the *prototypes* seem easily distinguished, they think the *classes* are, too. They also may not have much experience with edge cases that wouldn't fit their prototypes as well.

Saying that a word doesn't fit a formula, or is a social construct, doesn't mean it's useless. Race words still communicate information. But they don't handle edge cases well, and generalizations based on them are notoriously bad— which is why we talk about stereotypes.

Connotations and frames

With stereotypes and value words, we get into the territory of the speaker's emotions and attitudes. Very often the speaker is less interested in conveying a fact than in reporting his feelings about it . And this is lexicalized in a wide swath of words: *good, evil, sin, crime, horrible, pleasant, adorable, lazy, greedy, bitch, brat, asshole, jerk, moocher, chauvinist pig, wetback, unprofessional.*

When you're creating a word, you might ask yourself, what do they call it when they're angry?

Bertrand Russell jocularly spoke about "irregular verbs", such as:

> *I am firm, you are obstinate, he is a pig-headed fool.*

> *I am righteously indignant, you are annoyed, he is making a fuss over nothing.*

> *I have reconsidered the matter, you have changed your mind, he has gone back on his word.*

Or, from the BBC show *Yes, Minister:*

> *I give confidential press briefings, you leak, he's been charged under Section 2A of the Official Secrets Act.*

Lexicographers rarely acknowledge the issue— e.g. the AHD defines *frivolous* as "unworthy of serious attention, trivial", which misses the point that it's a word for slapping down *other people's* behavior. If we approve of the pastime, it's a *hobby* or *relaxation* or *art.*

Words that simply communicate an attitude are simple enough; more complex are words that— without our quite knowing it— help put across an entire perspective— a **frame**. Lakoff talks about this in *Don't Think of an Elephant* and *Moral Politics.*

Lakoff uses the example of *tax relief.* The word *relief* implies a metaphor: TAXATION IS A DISEASE. *Relief* is always positive; opposing *relief* makes you a bad guy. The phrase helps put across the idea that taxation is always bad; it's a brilliant piece of conservative political framing. Liberals even adopted the term, helping to spread the frame.

A liberal example would be *civil rights*. It's hard to be against *rights*! Rights are things you're supposed to have; the word itself declares how right that is. This was a more successful framing than talking about *integration* (which was easily opposed— many people just didn't like mixing races) or *racism* (1950s opponents of civil rights were explicitly white-supremacist, so the term was simply descriptive, and didn't offer a competing frame).

Or there's *piracy* to describe downloading music for free. This is framing because there's no social consensus that doing so is bad, much less a crime. The intent is to equate downloading with looting and murder on the high seas. This may not be as successful a frame, partly because pirates are viewed as romantic rogues more than as criminals— old villains inspire more affection than hatred.

As partisans have already internalized their frames, their terms don't always appeal to the undecided. The communists were famous for prose overheated to the point of ridiculousness (*imperialist running dog, democratic people's republic, paper tiger, petty bourgeois lackey*), and modern rightwingers' invocation of *treason* or *socialism* is just as foolish— fun for the converts, silly to anyone else.

The French have a useful term for the fervid, stereotyped drivel of the politician: *langue de bois,* literally 'wooden tongue'.

For the conlanger, the lesson is to think about your conpeople's beliefs, fears, and obsessions. What frames and metaphors do their belief systems use? What do they fight about so intensely that even the terms they use are loaded?

If you're inventing controversies and the terms to go with them, recall that the terms with bite imply a split in the community. People invent terms for abuse for minorities, but when 90% of the people agree with you there's no real fight. E.g. Mounia and Joausi face an invasion by the Ombutese. It's likely that there would be invective for the Ombutese, but almost no one supports the enemy, so there's no need for clever propaganda against the Ombuto-lovers. Much more controversial is the idea that the two nations must unite to fight the enemy; the arguments between pro- and anti-union movements would produce interesting terms.

Time drains invective of its force. *Tory* was once a term for Irish bandits, *Whig* for a band of Scottish insurgents. They were applied jocularly and then proudly to the major British political parties.

Basic categories

Not all categories are created equal. Some are **basic-level**, a concept explored by Roger Brown in *Social Psychology*.

There's an animal living next door, and you want to refer to it. Do you call it a *thing*, an *animal*, a *mammal*, a *carnivore*, a *canine*, a *dog*, a *terrier*, or a *fox terrier?*

For most purposes you'd say it's a *dog*; that's the basic-level category. Other examples include *cat, oak, gold, water, chair, car, red, happy, sit.* Words at this level have some common traits:

- The words tend to be shortest and most frequent.

- If you ask for names of things (e.g. you take your informant around the village and point to things), they're the easiest to elicit.

- They're learned first: a child learns *dog* before she learns super-categories like *carnivore* or subcategories like *terrier.*

- They're perceived holistically, as a gestalt. To perceive lower categories you have to look at picky distinctive details; higher categories often can't be perceived directly at all, but are abstracted. (You can't really *see* that something is a 'piece of furniture'; you see that it's a *chair* or a *bookcase* or whatever, and deduce it.)

- We have distinctive actions or functions for basic-level words— e.g. a *chair* is to sit on, a *bookcase* is to store books on, a *dresser* is for keeping clothes.

- The things themselves have distinctive behaviors. E.g. *dogs* bark and wag their tails; *cats* meow and barf in your shoes.

As an illustration of the first point, compare the words for 'dog' and 'animal' in various languages:

English	*dog*	*animal*
French	*chien*	*animal*
Russian	собака	животное
Greek	σκυλί	ζῶον
Hindi	*kuttā*	*jānvar*
Arabic	*kalb*	*hayawan*
Swahili	*mbwa*	*mnyama*
Turkish	*köpek*	*hayvan*

Indonesian	*andjing*	*binatang*
Finnish	*koira*	*eläin*
Japanese	*inu*	*dōbutsu*
Mandarin	*gǒu*	*dòngwù*

Non-basic terms are more likely to be borrowed— e.g. *animal, hayvan, dōbutsu* are all borrowings (from Latin, Arabic, Chinese respectively).

For the conlanger, basic-level words are the most useful to create; not only are they common, but they're the building blocks for other levels of categorization.

Brent Berlin calls these *natural kinds*. This is an unfortunate term, as it's fairly evident that these categories are 'natural' *for human beings*. If we were dolphins we wouldn't need a word for *chair* at all, and we'd distinguish between all sorts of marine rather than land animals.

Berlin has observed that different languages tend to agree on creating basic terms at the level of the genus— examples include *oak, maple, pine, rose, dog, cat, raccoon, human*. This isn't an accident; Carl Linnaeus based his system on the most easily perceived and understood level, the genus, and worked upwards and downwards from that.

On the other hand, are *Heptathela, Liphistius,* and *Ryuthela* 'natural kinds'? Undoubtedly not— not to us humans. They're three of the 3700 genera of spiders; here the basic-level term is *spider* (biologically a 'class').

Basic-level categories arguably vary by culture, as well. For the modern urban-dweller, as Berlin points out, it may well be that *tree* and *flower* are the basic-level categories.

Defining a system

The bulk of this book presents various categories and ways to classify them— emotions, animals, materials, artworks, etc.

What makes a good classification? Let's start with a purposely bad one:

> *Esas ambigüedades, redundancias y deficiencias recuerdan las que el doctor Franz Kuhn atribuye a cierta enciclopedia china que se titula* Emporio celestial de conocimientos benévolos. *En sus remotas páginas está escrito que los animales se dividen en (a) pertenecientes al Emperador, (b) embalsamados, (c) amaestrados, (d) lechones, (e) sirenas, (f) fabulosos, (g) perros sueltos, (h) incluidos en esta clasificación, (i) que se agitan como locos, (j) innumerables, (k) dibujados con un pincel finísimo de pelo de camello, (l) etcétera,*

(m) que acaban de romper el jarrón, (n) que de lejos parecen mos-
cas.

These ambiguities, redundancies, and deficiencies recall those which Dr. Franz Kuhn attributes to a certain Chinese encyclopedia which is titled *The Celestial Emporium of Benevolent Knowledge.* In its remote pages it is written that animals are divided into (a) those belonging to the Emperor; (b) embalmed ones; (c) tame ones; (d) suckling pigs; (e) sirens; (f) fantastic ones; (g) wild dogs; (h) those included in this category; (i) those which shake as if mad; (j) innumerable ones; (k) those drawn with a very fine camel-hair brush; (l) others; (m) those which just broke the vase; (n) those which look like flies from far away.

—Jorge Luis Borges, "El idioma analítico de John Wilkins"[4]

Borges was critiquing a conlang, by the way, that of John Wilkins, an example of the sort of universal classification that was popular in the 17th century. (For more on Wilkins see p. 73). These are fun to work out, but pretty useless at the highest levels.

The 'Chinese' encyclopedia is invented, but he also mentions the catalog of the Institut International de Bibliographie in Brussels, whose 1000 categories include the following:

262. The Pope

268. Dominican schools

282. The Roman Catholic Church

283. The Sabbath

294. Hinduism, Buddhism, Shinto, and Taoism

298. Mormonism

How could we do better?

- The subdivisions should 'make sense'— they either form a useful clump, or can be defined with a formula.

  Ideally, the category supplies what Wittgenstein couldn't find for 'game'— a common element or organizing principle. This

---

[4] I've included the original partly to point out how much smoother it is. The cumbersome repetitions of 'ones' and 'those' are not needed in Spanish.

might depend on our scientific knowledge. Compare the successive definitions of *acid*:

- ° having a sour taste (ultimately from Latin *acer* 'sharp')

- ° able to corrode metals (especially important with the medieval discovery of the mineral acids)

- ° turning litmus paper red (known to Robert Boyle, late 1600s)

- ° containing oxygen (Lavoisier's idea— incorrect, but the source of the word *oxygen*)

- ° delivering H+ ions (Arrhenius, 1884)

- ° donates a proton (Brønsted & Lowry 1923)

- ° accepts a pair of electrons (Lewis 1923)

- They divide up the semantic space fairly equally. A good subset of emotions might positive vs. negative, or they could be associated with the four flavors sweet, sour, sharp, bitter. A pretty bad subset would be "righteous indignation" vs. "everything else".

As we'll see under *Animals* and *Plants*, modern biological classifications based on genetic descent are very often of the latter type, which is fine for talking about genes but isn't very useful for ordinary people!

People's interests change over time, of course— in 1895, when the Brussels institute was founded, multiple pedantic distinctions within Christianity vs. a single classification for South and East Asian religions might well have fit the books on hand.

- The same item shouldn't fall into multiple categories. E.g. what would the *Celestial Emporium* do with a tame suckling pig which just broke a vase?

- Definitions should use the same sort of criteria. E.g. a classification of plants shouldn't be partly based on form and partly on how humans use them. A classification of languages shouldn't be partly based on cognacy and partly on region— as early ones often were.

But note that you can have several classifications of the same semantic field! For plants, in fact, we have a genetic taxonomy **and** terms based on use, such as *weed* or *herb*. For languages we have family groupings and *also* typological categories.

Classifications also suggest **cultural values**. Here are some examples, in the form of questions:

- What's the prototypical art form? Is it restricted to the elite (painting, opera) or something anyone can enjoy (epic poetry, dance)?

- Which emotions are the good ones? Does your culture value compassion, honor, piety, or valor the most?

- Which of these are *animate*: plants, bacteria, rivers, fire, planets, books?

- If your language grammaticalizes *humans*, what happens with gods, babies, corpses, dolls, talking animals in fables, robots, or newly discovered aliens?

- Which sexual practices are immoral?

- Which social classes are the best? (*Noble* and *aristocrat* originate as compliments; *villain, churl* went from class designators to insults.)

- Are bankers, merchants, and lawyers viewed as respectable professionals or as despicable parasites?

A case study: Nature

Lakoff talks about *radial categories*— words whose senses radiate out like a tree. The concept is best explained with an example; let's look at the lexeme *nature* (with its derivations, especially *natural*).

We get the word from French *nature*, which gets it from Latin *nātūra*. If we look at various senses of the word— the leaves of the tree, so to speak— they seem inexplicably various, even contradictory:

- Particularly talented: *He's a natural.*

- Particularly idiotic: *Love is like a great natural...*

- Relating to the landscape: *I like nature more than cities.*

- Given citizenship by the state: *naturalized.*

We could throw up our hands and just list these separate senses, but if we think of the senses as a tree, they all relate.

1. The root sense is the **character or quality** of something— what it's like. At one point in Gaul, Caesar sent to know *quālis esset nātūra montis*, what was the character of the mountain. What he wanted was a description.

1.1. An individual hill has its particular character; the **class** of hills can also be said to have a character.

> *John Daus, 1560: "Aristotel, Plinie, and suche other like, haue wrytten of the nature of Plantes, Herbes, Beastes, Metalles and Precious stones."*

1.2. An individual man has a particular character, what he's like— this sense is close to **temperament**:

> *Harriet Martineau, 1833: "My brother has it not in his nature to feel jealousy."*

1.2.1. The *nature* of certain individuals happens to be similar— they have a certain temperament in common. We can reify that **collective quality**, and then compare it to the temperaments of others.

> *Temple, 1668: "There are some Natures in the World who never can proceed sincerely in Business."*

1.3. In Old and Middle English, the obvious translation of *nature/natura* was *cynd/kind*. This had a back-effect when Englishmen applied other senses of *kind* to *nature*. *Kind* could mean 'offspring' (it's related to *kin*), and one meaning of *kindly* was 'by birth'. This was applied to *natural*:

> *Shakespeare, 1591: "Whom should he follow but his natural king?"*
>
> *KJV, Paul to Peter: "We, who are Jews by nature, and not sinners of the Gentiles..."*

1.3.1. One's *natural* children were those **begotten** rather than adopted.

1.3.2. What you get at birth is your **genetic inheritance**, as opposed to your culture or upbringing— often expressed as the opposition of *nature vs. nurture*.

1.3.3. Presumably related to the birth process is the old sense of *nature* as the female **genitals**:

> *R. Androse, 1569: "Take the nature of a female Hare made into pouder."*[5]

1.3.4. Privileges the state gives at birth may be granted by law instead. We still speak of *naturalization* as the process of **granting citizenship**.

---

[5] When thou visitest R. Androse's house, taste not his alchymical concoctions.

1.4. A behavior which follows from a person's character is *natural*— it's what is **to be expected**. This is a very common meaning with the adverb, *naturally*. Compare French *naturellement* which often has the meaning 'of course'.

> *Temple Bar, 1890: "It comes quite natural to a poor woman to sit up the night with a sick neighbour."*

1.4.1. English 'kind' shares the idea of 'type, character'. A frequent meaning shift is from class X to only the better examples of X— a 'man of character' means a man of *good* character, and similarly 'kind' came to mean 'proper, fitting', and then to a particular kind of proper behavior— **affection** or family feeling. This too was applied to the word *nature*.

> *Hartshore, 1841: "There's often more nature in people of that sort, than in their betters."*

Hamlet's father describes his own murder as "strange and *unnatural*", which includes both of these senses: it was abnormal and unexpected, and also defied family affection, as it was a fratricide. Similarly Lady Macbeth prepares for a murder by banning "compunctious visitings of nature".

1.4.2. Another disapproved departure from the norm is perversion. The natural is thus reduced to **sexual propriety**, though this sense is largely used in the negative:

> *KJV, Paul: "And likewise also the men, leaving the natural use of the woman, burned in their lust one toward another..."*

1.5. *Nātūra* was the usual translation of Greek φύσις, which also meant 'kind, character'. But the Greek philosophers had also used φύσις with a rather surprising sense, to refer to **everything**. Parmenides wrote a poem on φύσις, normally translated as *On Nature*; we could also render this *About Everything*.

Now, as C.S. Lewis remarks, "'Everything' is a subject on which there is not much to be said." Almost as soon as the concept was invented, it was demoted, by contrasting it with something else— God, the heavens, Grace, chaos, the human world. Logically all these things are part of Everything, but all these demotions are more interesting to talk about than the original sense.

1.5.1. Aristotle defines φύσις as that which is subject to change— that is, Everything minus the unchangeable, which meant either the eternal truths of mathematics, or the unmoved Mover, God. (This was not the same as the gods, who were part of φύσις.) Thus *nature* comes to mean the **created world** in general— in modern terms, everything made of matter and energy.

1.5.1.1. One powerful derivational process is what Lewis calls the *methodological idiom*. Aristotle had to define φύσις, but once he'd written a book on it, the things-of-φύσις — the φυσικά — are now a discipline. *Physics*—or Latinized, *natural philosophy*— thus comprises the things in Aristotle's book: the elements, motion, causation, optics, chance. This term has now mostly been taken over by **science**, though we can still occasionally speak of *naturalists* in the sense of 'scientists', and one of the leading journals of science is called *Nature*.

1.5.1.1.1. Over the centuries chemistry and biology have been subtracted from **physics**, giving the modern meaning.

1.5.1.1.2. Most of natural philosophy, for centuries, went way over most people's heads. But they had an interest in one practical application— medicine. Thus a *physician* became a term for a **healer**.

1.5.1.1.3. An almost comic usage of the methodological idiom is to contrast physics with what came after it in Aristotle's œuvre— which happened to be discussions of God, unity, being, cause, and potentiality. These were τὰ μετὰ τὰ φυσικά, the things after *Physics*— in short *metaphysics*. Today this can mean anything from ontology to various versions of the supernatural.

1.5.1.2. The senses of **the material and the ordinary** can be combined, contrasting with the *supernatural*— miracles, angels, ghosts.

1.5.2. Aristotle's φύσις included the heavenly bodies, but they seemed far above the realm of 'mutability', close to God. In the medieval period nature was therefore restricted to the **sublunary world**:

> *Chaucer, ~1400: "Eche thing in [Nature's] cure is under the Mone that mai waxe and wane."*

Pliny the Elder's *Historia Naturalis* covers more or less everything in this category, including art, geography, and engineering. Later the term *natural history* tended to exclude the works of humanity— though ethnology, the study of people not like us, still got in.

1.5.2.1. Rather than being just a collection of things, *nature* could be reified into a sort of spirit or force immanent in the created world, or in a particular object. The sense of **vital power or strength** was retained for a long time:

> *John Dryden, 1672: "Reason's a staff for age when nature's gone."*

Nature [journal], 1890: "The fungus.. as it goes destroys the 'nature' of the wood."

1.5.2.2. This vital spirit soon developed into a **personified Mother Nature**, a potent female allegorical figure still invoked today.

1.5.2.2.1. The domain of medieval Nature was the whole earth, but often the boring bits— the rocks and the air— were left out; Nature was **life**.

1.5.2.2.1.1. When we speak of "Nature, red in tooth and claw" (Tennyson, 1850) we're restricting the idea further to **animal life**. We talk about "when nature calls" when a particularly low animal urge asserts itself.

1.5.3. In Christianity, God is the creator of Nature; but Nature has become estranged from God. Thus *Nature* comes to mean the **fallen world**, contrasted with *Grace*.

KJV, 1 Cor: "But the natural man receiveth not the things of the Spirit of God..."

KJV, 1 Cor: "It is sown a natural body, it is raised a spiritual body."

The original Greek is not φυσικός but ψῡχικός, belonging to ψῡχή, the animal spirit, the non-rational part of the soul.

1.5.3.1. This sense may combine with the expectable (1.4) to refer to **excusable frailty**. "It's only natural", we say to paper over some sin.

1.5.4. An ancient idea is that the world was created not *ex nihilo* but out of something basic and simple— disorder or chaos. Nature is thus **what is not chaos**; Milton describes the Abyss as "the womb of Nature and perhaps her grave". The idea that the world had to be organized or set out is also the metaphor behind the Greek κόσμος (related to *cosmetics*).

1.5.5. Partly from the sense of 'the sublunary world', but also influenced by 1.3 (birth) and 1.4 (the expected), we get the natural as what is **not interfered with**, mostly by man. Thus a *natural* cotton is undyed; the *natural* behavior of a dog is to poop on the rug; Aristotle advises studying biological specimens in their '*natural* condition' (κατα φυσιν), i.e. good undamaged examples. The interference may be framed as negative (in which case the natural is unspoiled, pure) or as positive (in which case it's primitive, raw, or unrefined).

1.5.5.1. Our technological civilization has a love/hate relationship with its own artifice. One of our luxuries is to value things with **minimal**

technological processing— e.g. *natural foods. Natural childbirth* does its best to avoid doctors and hospitals.

1.5.5.2. The processing can also be abstract or procedural, so that natural means **simple**, without complications. In mathematics the nonnegative integers are *natural numbers*. In music a *natural* is a note that's neither sharp nor flat.

1.5.5.2.1. Base *e* logarithms are called *natural*. They're **easier** to calculate with and **less arbitrary** than base 10, which we use simply because we have ten fingers.

1.5.5.2.2. A recent science article asked "Is nature natural?" It was referring to a modern debate over whether the fundamental constants of physics are **readily derived from basic theory**— as electromagnetism flows neatly from Maxwell's equations. (The 'unnatural' alternative is that there exists an infinite froth of universes each with its own set of constants, most of which wouldn't allow stars to form; in this view we just happen to live in the tiny percentage of habitable universes.)

1.5.5.3. A death **without violence or accident** is said to come from *natural causes*. Of course violence (and accidents) are part of ordinary biological life, but evidently we classify them as 'interference'.

1.5.5.4. One salient form of interference is training or education. So a *natural talent* is one who is **untrained yet capable**. Being talentless is just as *natural* in this sense, but as in 1.4.1 (natural affection), the word is being used to refer only to positive examples.

1.5.5.5. If we frame interference or artificiality as *unnatural*, the greatest artificiality is urban life. Thus *nature* is identified with **the countryside**. Farmland is highly organized by centuries of human activity, but to the city dweller it's the epitome of getting back to *nature*. In the quote below, the poet equates Nature with British landscapes rather than, say, sand deserts or lava flows:

> *James Thomson, 1730: "At large, to wander o'er the vernant earth / In various hues, but chiefly thee, gay Green! Thou smiling Nature's universal robe!"*

1.5.5.6. A slightly different opposition is within human society, between our primordial *nature* (whether our character as human beings, or our biological inheritance) and what governments and institutions give us. We might call this the **pre-organized**. It has two branches, depending on whether the writer approves or disapproves of the interference.

1.5.5.6.1. If we worry that law and governments are inherently corrupt, then nature is a sort of **primitive human state of grace**. The OED defines *natural law* as "doctrines based on the theory that there are certain unchanging laws which pertain to man's nature, which can be discovered by reason, and to which man-made laws should conform; freq. contrasted with positive laws."

1.5.5.6.2. Or if we consider that humans need a good deal of civilizing, then a *state of nature* is **barbarity**— "nasty, brutish, and short" (Hobbes). Samuel Johnson suggested that a man whose father's killer gets off on a technicality may conclude "I am among barbarians who refuse to do justice. I am therefore in a state of nature and consequently... I will stab the murderer." (The barbarians he was speaking of were the Scots.)

1.5.5.6.3. One salient indicator of the primitive is that he doesn't wear clothes. Thus a *naturist* is a **nudist**.

1.5.5.7. Rather than the complications of urban civilization in general, we may concentrate on the vices of sophistication. Here the *natural* is what is **simple and without affectation**. E.g. Milton has Adam and Eve in Paradise eating frugally: they didn't "burden nature". The French *au naturel* may be used for things cooked simply or not at all, or left unadorned or unclothed.

1.5.5.8. In older thought what is most human, what most distinguishes us from the animals, is reason. This may be the source of the old sense of *a natural* as an **idiot**:

> Shakespeare: *"Love is like a great natural that runs lolling up and down to hide his bauble in a hole."*

1.6. Especially in the Renaissance, realism became a value in art. **Realism** can be thought of as depicting things as they are— that is, their *nature*. 19th century critics spoke of *naturalism* in approval of more realistic painting or literature.

1.6.1. A painting may capture a realistic but instantaneous image of the world— thus the French term (occasionally borrowed into English), *nature morte*, literally 'dead nature'— a **still life**.

What do I do with that?

If you liked this extended discussion, I recommend C.S. Lewis's *Studies in Words*, which expands on the story and covers a dozen or so other words in similar detail. You can also browse any word in the *Oxford English Dictionary*, which teases out all the senses of a word and their historical relationships, in far more detail than your desk dictionary.

But perhaps *nature* is a special case, and most words are nowhere near this complicated? Nah, this is pretty common. Look at the meanings of *nice* or *mean* or *tree* or *run* in your dictionary, or Lakoff's fifty-page analysis of the word *over* in *Women, Fire, and Dangerous Things*.

It can be fun to imitate this process directly. E.g. in my conlang Xurnese, the word *ende* '**path**' is fraught with meaning.

- The root meaning is 'path, way, trail'; in the parent language, Axunašin, it's a nominalization of *en* 'to, toward'.

- It's a root metaphor in the Endajué religion— the way to live, the way things go. The name of the religion itself derives from *ende dzu ez* 'the path between all'.

- To be off the Path is a serious thing, the closest thing in Endajué to damnation. Thus *tegendi* 'pathless' is one of the harshest insults (much harsher than sexual references), and *end' eš* 'against the path' is the strongest of curses.

- *Ende* is commonly used for 'morality, correct behavior.' The metaphor is used in other ways— to lose the path, *ende pope*, is to 'go astray, go wrong'; *misustri* 'muddy' is used for 'morally difficult'.

- *Endevaus*, 'point the way', is to advise or mentor.

- To wish someone well, or say goodbye, you can tell them *Oyes ende yu šu*— "May your path be pleasant."

- It can also be used for methods or skills, as in the *Jueši endi*, the Ways of War.

- The physical disciplines of Endajué were also called *endi*.

- The traditions or ways of a group are its *éndex* (a collective of *ende*). Sub-meanings are 'culture' and 'precedent'.

- The 'way things go' is also applied to the whole universe, and thus *ende* can be used in many of the senses of *nature*. (But not all, as the ideas of 'type' and 'by birth' are not present.)

- A path implies direction and movement, so *ende* can be used for 'purpose, progress'.

Now, as ever, you can just imitate English and sweep the whole mess under the carpet. You translate *nature* as (say) *kest* and you're done. But this isn't very naturalistic. (Quick, which sense is that?) E.g. my Russian dictionary gives these possibilities for 'nature': природа, натура, нрав, характер, свойство, качество.

At the very least, try to distinguish some of the different senses of the English word and give different equivalents for each. Ideally, think about what the core senses are, and follow a few of the branches.

This is one reason that for my most developed language, Verdurian, I maintain an English-Verdurian lexicon: it makes it easier to keep track of the different translations of an English word.

Puzzling over etymologies, or foreign dictionaries, can help. This book is designed to help you learn to analyze senses, contrast words, create metaphors, think about how a word can work in a way unlike English. But ultimately it's a way of seeing— you learn to be conscious of how meanings radiate and change.

Classifications of everything

It can be fun to classify *everything*. Indeed, to learn the categories of things is to learn about the things, which is another reason that *natural philosophy* was an early term for *science*. How your people classify the world is a glimpse into their cosmology and philosophy.

As modern science developed, not a few savants believed that we'd be well ahead if we could just *classify everything correctly*. As John Wilkins (a bishop and one of the founders of the Royal Society) plainly put it:

> Yet this I shall assert with greater confidence, That the reducing of all things and notions, to such kind of Tables, as are here proposed (were it as compleatly done as it might be) would prove the shortest and plainest way for the attainment of real Knowledge, that hath been yet offered to the World.
>
> —*An Essay Towards a Real Character and a Philosophical Language* (1668)

Here's his overall classification, encompassing 40 Genera:

General
    Transcendental things
        I General **Bα**
        II Mixed Relation **Ba**
        III Relation of Action **Be**
    Words
        IV Discourse **Bi**
Special
    V Creator **Dα**
    Creature (i.e. things created)
        Collectively:
            V World **Da**

Distributively
  Substances
    Inanimate:
      VII Element **De**
    Animate
      By species:
        Imperfect vegetative
          VIII Stone **Di**
          IX Metal **Do**
        Perfect vegetative (Plant)
          Herb:
            X Leaf **Gα**
            XI Flower **Ga**
            XII Seed-vessel **Ge**
          XIII Shrub **Gi**
          XIV Tree **Go**
        Sensitive
          XV Exanguious **Zα**
        Sanguineous:
          XVI Fish **Za**
          XVII Bird **Ze**
          XVIII Beast **Zi**
      By parts:
        XIX Peculiar **Pα**
        XX General **Pa**
  Accidents (i.e. attributes)
    Quantity
      XXI Magnitude **Pe**
      XXII Space **Pi**
      XXIII Measure **Po**
    Quality
      XXIV Natural Power **Tα**
      XXV Habit **Ta**
      XXVI Manners **Te**
      XXVII Sensible Quality **Ti**
      XXVIII Sickness **To**
    Action
      XXIX Spiritual **Cα**
      XXX Corporeal **Ca**
      XXXI Motion **Ce**
      XXXII Operation **Ci**
    Relation
      Private
        XXXIII Oeconomical **Co**
        XXXIV Possessions **Cy**
        XXXV Provisions **Sα**

Publick
XXXVI Civil **Sa**
XXXVII Judiciary **Se**
XXXVIII Military **Si**
XXXIX Naval **So**
XL Ecclesiastical **Sy**

The bulk of Wilkins's book is an expansion of each of these categories, plus general discussion. (So, yes, it was the 17th century equivalent of this book.) Under *Animals* he takes the time to calculate the number of animals that would fit into Noah's Ark, not neglecting the provisions for both animals and crew. To our relief, he concludes that the dimensions of the Ark were sufficient for its purpose.

Borges notes that Wilkins divides metals into imperfect (*cinnabar, mercury*), artificial (*bronze, brass*), dross (*filings, rust*), or natural (*gold, tin*). It was such earnest naïvetés that led him to postulate the *Celestial Emporium* (p. 62).

Wilkins then creates a symbolic code for representing each category; the top level looks like this:

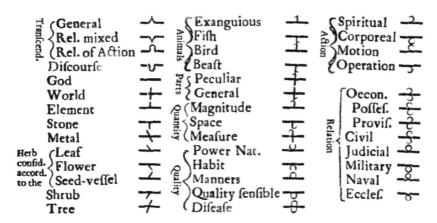

The bishop must have been a trial to his typesetter.

Finally he outlines a phonetic equivalent. The first two letters specify the Genus, as given above. (Personally I find it inelegant that the first letter doesn't correspond to his higher-level categories. E.g. D ends up referring to God, the world, elements, stones and metals.)

Subclassifications add more letters:

De	Element
Deb	Fire

Debα	Flame
Ti	Sensible Quality
Tid	Colour
Tida	Redness
Go	Trees
Gob	Pomiferous Trees
Gobα	Deciduous; Visible Blossoms; Esculent when ripe; More round: Apple

The most successful work along these lines was the taxonomy of Carl Linnaeus, published over the period 1735-58. His system, much adapted, is still used today. One reason his system caught on was perhaps that the names it provided didn't depend on the higher-order classification. Wilkins's system would have been completely upended if science turned out not to support the category of *Pomiferous Trees.*

The classifying impulse can be said to have given us modern chemistry as well— Lavoisier emphasized finding irreducible elements, while Mendeleev's periodic table suggested the ultimate structure of atoms.

Peter Roget's *Thesaurus* (1852) included a classification, whose top-level categories (in a modern edition) are these:

Abstract Relations
Existence
Relation
Quantity
Order
Number
Time
Change
Eventuality
Causation
Power
Space
Space in General
Dimensions
Structure, Form
Motion
Physics
Physics
Heat
Light
Electricity and Electronics
Mechanics

Physical Properties
Color
Matter
Matter in General
Inorganic Matter
Organic Matter
Sensation
Sensation in General
Touch
Taste
Smell
Sight
Hearing
Intellect
Intellectual Faculties and Processes
States of Mind
Communication of Ideas
Volition
Volition in General
Conditions
Voluntary Actions
Authority; Control
Support and Opposition
Possessive Relations
Affections
Personal Affections
Sympathetic Affections
Morality
Religion

The Dewey Decimal Classification, used in many libraries, has this overall shape:

000	General works
100	Philosophy and psychology
200	Religion
300	Social sciences
400	Language
500	Science
600	Technology
700	Arts and recreation
800	Literature
900	History and geography

Fun fact: A really pedantic library could store all its fiction under the appropriate number: 813.

The problem with such classifications is ultimately that there's no consensus on what the top levels are. Classifying physical things is barely doable, but there's little consensus on the supercategories for *shape, number, rotate,* and *speech.*

Plus, even if you create a system that works to your satisfaction, no one will want to hear about it. That's why the thematic sections of this book are listed alphabetically!

Chinese classifications

Chinese comes with no less than three built-in categorization systems.

Radicals and phonetics

The vast majority of *hànzì* (Chinese characters) are formed by combining two graphemes, the **radical** and the **phonetic** (*ALC* p. 56).

The 214 traditional radicals form a comprehensive but maddeningly inconsistent classification of almost all words. Often the system works— e.g. here's some of the *hànzì* that use the 水 'water' radical:

水	*shuǐ*	water	池	*chí*	pool	沤	*òu*	soak
汁	*zhī*	juice	讯	*xùn*	flood	泛	*fàn*	flood
汗	*hàn*	sweat	汐	*xī*	tide	没	*mò*	sink
江	*jiāng*	river	汤	*tāng*	hot water	泳	*yǒng*	swim

The phonetics, of course, suggest the sound of the word. E.g. 汐 has the phonetic 夕 *xī* 'evening'. Something that sounds like *xī* but has a meaning associated with water— if you know Chinese, that points you nicely to 'tide'.

Well, it also points you to 溪 *xī* 'brook', whose phonetic is 奚 *xī* 'what'. It's just bad luck that there are two 'water' terms pronounced *xī* — though fairly common bad luck as Mandarin has ferociously merged syllables. In Middle Chinese these pairs were distinct: 汐/夕 were pronounced *zjäk*; 溪/奚 were *kʰiei* and *ɣiei*. The latter pair illustrates that phonetics don't have to be identical; they often just rhyme— e.g. the phonetic for 汗 *hàn* is 干 *gàn* 'trunk, work'.

Even more precisely, they rhymed, and the initial was at the same place of articulation, 2000 years ago when the system was devised. Sometimes they've diverged spectacularly, as in this set:

		Mandarin	Old Chinese	
也	*yě*	*la?*	also
池	*chí*	*d-lai*	pool
地	*dì*	*lâih*	earth
他	*tuō*	*lhâi*	other
施	*shī*	*lhai?*	spread

But this is rare, and we can say that the system more or less works... till we look at some of the other words that have the water radical:

汇	*huì*	gather	沦	*lún*	fall	法	*fǎ*	follow
汉	*Hàn*	Chinese	沃	*wò*	fertile	沽	*gū*	trade
汲	*jí*	extreme	沟	*gōu*	groove	沮	*jǔ*	stop
沧	*cāng*	dark blue	注	*zhù*	stay	治	*zhì*	control

There's a story behind many of these, of course— e.g. *Hàn* was originally the name of a river; *cāng* is the color of water (etymologically the same as 苍 *cāng* the color of the sky). But of course etymology is hidden to the speakers; the lesson is that a classification system embedded in the language is going to be ruined by sound and meaning change.

Measure words

The other classification system is part of the spoken language— the **measure words**, used in expressions like *sān tiáo máojīn* 'three towels'. The measure word 条 *tiáo* simply means 'strip', and we use it as a measure word in English too: *a strip of cloth, a strip of paper*. Textbooks will tell you that *tiáo* is used for "long and narrow things"— which is more or less true, but consider this list of words that use *tiáo* as their measure word:

bèizi	quilt	*jiāng*	river	*tǎnzi*	blanket
chuán	ship	*jiē*	street	*wéijīn*	scarf
chuángdān	sheet	*kùzi*	trousers	*wéiqún*	apron
diànxiàn	wire	*lù*	road	*xiāoxi*	news
gǒu	dog	*qúnzi*	skirt	*yìjiàn*	idea
hé	river	*shéngzi*	cord	*yú*	fish

huángguā   cucumber   *shǒujīn*   towel

Like many linguistic categories, this is a radial category (p. 65). E.g. there's a subcategory of flat square things (*quilt, sheet, blanket, towel, apron*), presumably because some of these can be long and narrow. Once *trousers* are in (either because they're strip-like or sheet-like), that invites in the related *skirt*. *Dog* and *idea* are mysteries!

Using etymologies

I've provided etymologies for all the words on the Fantasy Frequency List. The idea is to give ideas on how words are constructed as well as how their meanings change over the centuries.

To save space and keep the book readable, I've boiled what is often a complex and contested story down to a line or two. First, let's talk about how to decode it. Here's an example:

second   Lt *secundus* 'following' > '2nd' > '2nd division by 60'
              • Fr *deuxième* 'two'

That is, *second* derives from Latin *secundus*, which is a participle derived from *sequī* 'follow'. The sense 'second' is a narrowing of meaning from 'following'. You can divide an hour or a degree of arc by 60, then do it again; the *second* such division gave its name to the measurement.

The • symbol separates **different roots**. Here the idea is that the French word for 'second' is not related to *second*, but derives straightforwardly from the word for 'two'.

(French, Latin, and Greek words are often relevant to other English roots. E.g. *cloth* cites Latin *textum* and French *étoffe*, which underlie *textile* and *stuff*.)

My major sources are Carl Darling Buck's 1500-page *Dictionary of Selected Synonyms in the Principal Indo-European Languages* and the *Oxford English Dictionary*, 2nd edition, both good places to go for more information. For French I've used the Larousse *Dictionnaire étymologique*, for Latin the Routledge dictionary, and for Chinese Axel Schuessler's *Etymological Dictionary of Old Chinese*.

Languages

The **source language** may use these abbreviations:

IE	Indo-European
Gk	(Classical) Greek
ModGk	Modern Greek
Lt	Latin
Fr	French
It	Italian
Sp	Spanish
Rum	Rumanian
Rom	Romance
OE	Old English

ME	Middle English
ModE	Modern English
Ger	(Modern High) German
Sw	Swedish
Norse	Old Norse
OCS	Old Church Slavonic
Cz	Czech
Pol	Polish
Rus	Russian
Lith	Lithuanian
Ir	Irish
Skt	Sanskrit
Qu	Quechua
Ch	Chinese (citations are Mandarin)

Romance means that the word is shared among the Romance languages but isn't classical Latin (at least, not in a way obvious to etymologists).

I've tried to give the language where the given derivation was transparent. E.g. *auctor* 'author' was a simple person nominalization in Latin, from *augēre* 'grow, increase'; it wasn't in French, where the verb had been lost.

It's generally a safe bet that the immediate source for a Latin or Greek word was French. Often the initial borrowing was more French (*autour, dette*), which was later corrected to look more Latin (*author, debt*).

I usually cite French words in their modern spelling— which is a pretty good phonemic system for 12th century French anyway. But of course the source for many English words was Norman French, and this is occasionally worth pointing out— e.g. to explain *carry* from *carier* rather than modern *charrier*.

I use ME or ModE where the earliest citation in the OED is from those periods. Sometimes a word may be older and just not show up in the literature; e.g. *spot* has cognates in other Germanic languages (so it must date back to OE) but isn't attested till 1200 (so it's marked ME).

Germanic refers to pre-OE developments in the Germanic family; it doesn't mean German. I occasionally refer to *Low German* which may refer to any of the coastal Germanic languages, including Dutch.

If an entry is marked **uncertain**, it means that the further etymology is unknown or disputed. You don't need an etymology or a semantic change for *every word* in your conlang— just most of them!

Glosses

If a word has no **gloss**, the primary meaning can be assumed to be pretty close to the English— e.g. *sound* derives from Latin *sonus*, which means 'sound'.

It's something of an art to write glosses; the goal here is to summarize the word's meaning as briefly as possible *in a way that illuminates the etymology*. Don't mistake the gloss for a full dictionary entry!

For instance, *nervous* is taken back to Latin *nervōsus* 'sinewy', an adjectivization of *nervus* 'sinew'. The full definition of *nervus* from Routledge's Latin dictionary is 'sinew; nerve; bowstring; string (of a lute etc.); fetter; prison; strength, vigor.' 'Sinew' is the root meaning; bowstrings were often made of sinews, and the other meanings are obvious metaphors. Anatomically, nerves look a lot like sinews, and the word *nervus* had been in use for centuries before Galen demonstrated their connection to the brain.

Or, *require* points to Latin *requīrere* 'seek again'; the aim is to illustrate how the word was formed from *re-* 'again, back' + *quærere* 'seek, ask'. But of course *requīrere* already had other, lexicalized senses: 'search for, require, question, miss.'

Abbreviations used:

nomn.	nominalization
adjn.	adjectivization
verbn.	verbalization
dim.	diminutive
abbr.	abbreviation
<	derives from
>	develops into
=	interpreted as
‖	parallel to
poss.	possibly
prob.	probably

' '

If a gloss uses an English derived form, it's intended to suggest a similar derivation in the source language. E.g. *ancestor* is traced to Latin *antecēssor* 'foregoer', indicating that this is a person nominalization from *antecēdere* 'precede'.

> \> This indicates a semantic change.

A chain of derivations may have occurred in the source languages, the intermediaries, or English. E.g.

quite Lt *quiētus* 'quiet' > 'free, clear' > 'clean, complete'

Latin *quiētus* meant 'quiet, calm, peaceful'; in medieval Latin *quitus* had taken the meaning 'undisturbed, free, clear'; in English it became 'clean, complete', and finally *quite* was used for the modern sense of 'entirely'.

> \< Read this as 'ultimately derives from'— it's a remote connection that would not at all be obvious to speakers.

> \= I use = mostly for restatements of the gloss that make the transition to the modern meaning clearer. E.g.

explode Lt *explaudere* 'clap out' = 'drive off the stage' > 'expel with force'

Here 'clap out' is how the word was *formed*, from *ex* 'out' + *plaudere* 'clap'; the *usage* was to drive someone off the stage by clapping. This led to the sense 'reject scornfully', which gave the scientists of the 1600s the physical metaphor 'expel violently', which became the modern sense.

‖ I use ‖ where words are related, but the original meaning is unclear or just complicated. E.g. Ch *tăn* 'dark' poss. ‖ 'ripe, black' indicates that the Chinese word (Old Chinese *tʰəmʔ*) may be cognate to words meaning 'ripe, red' (e.g. Bahnaric *dum*) and 'black' (e.g. Saek *ram*), but we don't know which sense is primary. I've left them in because these connections could be just as inspiring to a conlanger as firm attestations.

OE

I've used the standard (first-cited) OED form for OE words (be aware that there was both dialectal and scribal variation). This includes two quirks of that august but old-fashioned source:

- It uses acute accents for long vowels— i.e. á = [aː]. As a corollary, when Tolkien uses acutes he means long vowels too.
- Actual OE used the glyph ȝ for sounds pronounced [g, dʒ, ɣ, j]. The OED uses g for [g dʒ] and ȝ for [ɣ j]— the distinction is actually Middle English.

OE [æ, y, ð] are pronounced with their IPA values; þ is of course [θ].

Different roots

Most entries cite the derivation of the word in languages besides Modern English. Different languages are separated by the • symbol.

The etymological information here is even briefer; the intention is always to summarize the etymology in order to give you ideas as a conlanger. E.g. for *woman,* one of the entries is

> It *donna* 'lady'

This should be taken as short for "The main Italian word for *woman* is *donna* whose etymology is (summarized as) 'lady'."

My aim is to highlight different ways of constructing the word, so I don't include multiple examples of the same derivation. E.g. *approach* comes from French '(come) near to'; no need to add Breton *tostaat,* Ger *nahen,* OCS *približiti,* Lith *artintis* which are also derivations of 'near'.

If the connection is really remote, I'll throw in a < sign. E.g. for *wave* there's the entry

> Lt *unda* < 'water'

Latin *unda* derives from a variant of IE **wed-,* the root of *water* and *wet.* You can read < as 'ultimately from'. Latin speakers were likely not aware of this, especially as the Latin word for 'water' is different (*aqua*).

I've generally left out words where the derivation is unknown or speculative. E.g. Buck thinks OCS *zvězda* for 'star' *might* be synaesthetic (e.g. an imitative squeal applied to flickering lights). But it seems to be just a guess, so I skipped it.

I've used **Latin and Greek** a lot as examples, because the words are so useful in understanding English, especially our scientific vocabulary. *Nota bene:*

- Latin nouns are given in the nominative singular— e.g. *flōs* 'flower'. When the oblique root differs, I give it too— in this case it's *flōr-.* The oblique root generally underlies the inherited Romance term (e.g. French *fleur*) and is used in derivations (*floral*).

  But to save space, I'll mention only here that the oblique root for words in *-tio* is *-tiōn-,* as in *nātio* 'birth, race, nation', accusative *nātiōnem.* And participles in *-ans, -ens* have oblique roots in *-ant, -ent-.*

- Latin verbs are given in the infinitive, but Greek verbs in the present first person singular. E.g. κάμπτω is really 'I bend', not 'to bend'.

- I cite Latin words with j and u, following my dictionary. The Romans didn't use these letters, but then they didn't have macrons or lower case either.

IE

Take IE glosses with a healthy sprinkling of salt. A word like *nas- can be confidently given as 'nose', since it exists with that meaning in almost every IE language. On the other hand, Gk θάνατος 'death' is related to Sanskrit *dhvan-* 'be extinguished'... which was the IE meaning? Either could be the origin of the other sense, or both could derive from something else.

Or take OE *wrecan* 'drive, avenge' (source of *wreak*), Lt *urgēre* 'press, impel', Skt *vraj-* 'stride, go', Lith *vargas* 'misery'. Pokorny suggests an IE meaning 'push, drive, pursue', but this seems to be seeking a linguistic lowest common denominator. Any IE gloss is just a good guess.

As an example of what might go wrong, consider these Romance words:

Fr *quitter*	leave, give up (source of English *quit*)
Sp *quitar*	remove, take away; *quitarse* leave
Port. *quitar*	cancel, release
It *quitanza*	receipt

If we didn't know Latin, we would probably guess at a root meaning 'remove', with developments 'remove oneself' = 'leave', 'remove (a debt)' > 'cancel' > 'receipt (for a cancelled debt)'. Neat and tidy, except that these words derive from Latin *quiētus* 'calm, quiet'!

I've generally omitted such problematic cases, though sometimes I'll list cognates and you can make of the semantic relationship what you will.

The *American Heritage Dictionary of Indo-European Roots,* by Calvert Watkins, is an excellent resource if you want to look further.

Chinese etymologies

You may recall hearing Chinese 東 *dōng* 'east' refers to the sun rising through the trees. And that's true of the **character**— the (traditional) *hànzì* is a combination of 日 *rì* 'sun' and 木 *mù* 'tree'. But that's not the origin of *dōng*, which Axel Schuessler traces to Old Chinese *tloŋ and relates to Chepang *tʰoŋ* 'lighten, be bright', and possibly to Tibetan *tʰon* 'come out'. The Chinese (Ch) etymologies given in the word list, like those of all the other languages, relate to the spoken language.

Due to the writing system, and a 2000-year tradition of defining education as mastery of the ancient classics, Chinese is like hoarders' apartments, where nothing is ever thrown away.

As an example, looking for *admit* in the sense of 'have to recognize', my *Times* dictionary suggests 承认 *chéngrèn*. If you look up 承 you'll get definitions like

1. bear, hold, carry
2. undertake, contract, take charge
3. be indebted
4. continue, carry on, succeed
5. for, owing to, due to

And if you look up 认 you'll find

1. understand, recognize, know, realize, make out
2. acknowledge, confess, admit, own (up to)
3. adopt, apprentice

Obviously these are Lakoffian radial categories (p. 65), but which sense is primary? This is where Schuessler's dictionary is invaluable: he indicates the earliest meanings (in this case 'lift, hold up' and 'know', respectively), and possible Sino-Tibetan cognates or other sources. So the etymology is 'lift-know'?

Not exactly, because this is just one of many, many instances where Mandarin has constructed a compound out of two synonyms, in order to avoid the ambiguity that plagues the single-character lexicon. As we saw, 认 already means 'admit', but it means a bunch of other things too. 承 somewhat arbitrarily narrows down the meaning to 'recognize, acknowledge, admit'.

All this gets summarized as

• Ch *rèn* < 'know'

Again, this is exactly how I treat the other languages (e.g. Fr *avouer* < 'vow'), but Chinese is unusual in the wide semantic range of its morphemes, and I want to emphasize that there's very often a story like this behind every word.

Another example: *bare* (as in 'bare feet') is 赤裸 *chìluǒ*. If you look up these characters, they both mean 'bare, naked'. It makes no sense to say that the etymology of *bare* in Chinese is 'bare-bare'; it's another two-synonym compound. But the earliest meaning of 赤 is 'red', so that's what's in the word list.

Sometimes the Mandarin compound is transparent— e.g. *alien* is 外来 *wàilái* 'outside-come'. As usual, the absence of < indicates that the derivation is understandable.

Finally, if you know Mandarin or you're studying it, you'll find that my glosses often don't match your dictionary. Again, that's because I'm giving etymologies. Often the gloss goes back to Old Chinese or even to Sino-Tibetan.

Touristic highlights

Some of my favorite English etymologies are the ones where the meaning has changed quickly and many times:

fast	OE 'firm, fixed' > 'determinedly' > 'quickly'
fog	'grassy, mossy' > 'fleshy' > 'murky' > 'misty'
nice	Lt 'not knowing' > 'foolish' > 'fine' > 'kind'
pretty	OE 'tricky' > 'clever' > 'admirable' > 'pleasing'

Then there's words that only date back to Middle English, when I'd have expected something older: *ago, bad, boy, cut, grab, rabbit, smell, talk, whip, wrap.*[6]

I mentioned how homonyms complicate wordlists; what surprised me in researching was how many turn out to be the same etymon after all:

trip	'stumble / travel'
lot	'chance token / a bunch'
mess	'serving / disorder'
might	'power / possible'
fair	'pretty / just'

In some cases the original sense wasn't what I would have guessed: *dull* was 'obtuse' not 'blunt', *leave* was 'let remain' not 'go', *worship* was

---

[6] There's a reason for the rabbits: they were introduced to England by the Normans.

'value' not 'praise'; the root meaning of *interest* was 'a share', not 'curiosity, concern'.

Etymology Frequency List

Since I have over 3000 etymologies at hand, I thought it'd be fun to see what words come up most often in the glosses. So I ran them through the frequency program.

Here's all the words that appear more than ten times:

of	to	be	out
in	make	go	with
stand	no, not	one	up
place	from	put	on
by	for	know	together
turn	at	come	back
down	man	bend	cover
do	hand	under	thing
carry	good	stretch	cut
head	look	move	off
run	away	have	light
strong	take	against	all
bright	form	see	seize
sit	before	high	hold
lead	work	as	fall
part	set	strike	care
late	like	long	measure
point	same	seek	side
small	spread	two	face
flat	order	prepare	shine
walk	arm	circle	clear
mark	mind	open	right
sharp	show	straight	water
well	what	wind	again
bear	break	end	firm
fit	give	heart	hide
hit	live	people	swell
throw	time	toward	after
big	build	cause	child

day	divide	draw	dwell
earth	flow	forward	full
hollow	into	low	press
speak	step	think	way

The standout here is 'stand', which underlies English *assist, constant, distant, exist, insist, instant, resist, rest, stable, stage, stanza, state, station, statue, stay, steady, understand*, as well as non-English words meaning *admit, always, be, big, brave, build, can, cease, finger, form, happen, help, hour, immediate, last, old, place, rise, room, ship, soldier, tail, thick.*

Metaphors

A few decades ago, metaphor was one of those things that linguists promised that they'd take care of eventually, sometime after finishing the legendary complete grammar of a language.

For non-linguists, metaphor is largely something that happens in poetry (*my love is like a red red rose*) or those amusing snippets from *The New Yorker* titled "Block That Metaphor!":

> And if history is any guide, the claiming of a scalp this large will only add fuel to a pyre that is already licking at the heels of several even better-known CEOs.

Largely through the work of George Lakoff, however, metaphor has proved to be close to the heart of language— how we understand the world, how the grammar itself works, and above all how words are created.

Lakoff and Mark Johnson cover the subject in *Metaphors We Live By*, but the best introduction I've read is the Metaphors chapter in Guy Deutscher's *The Unfolding of Language*.

The ubiquity of metaphor

If you think of metaphor as a marginal thing, it may be useful to look at a sample of ordinary prose, which I've purposely taken from a very dry non-poetic source:

> The long period of struggle between "nativists" who benefited from a weak <u>throne</u>, and their opponents who <u>pressed</u> for political changes on the Chinese model and sought to <u>strengthen</u> the imperial institution, was <u>drawing</u> to a close. <u>Under</u> Chongzong the adoption of Chinese cultural norms <u>reached</u> new <u>heights</u>. Latent opposition to that policy, however, was not wholly eradicated.
>
> —F.W. Mote, *Imperial China 900-1800*

I've underlined the obvious, open metaphors. The nativists were not worried about the ruler's actual chair, much less whether it was solidly constructed. Their opponents were not physically pushing on anything; the "imperial institution" was not strengthened like Schwarzenegger; no one was literally underneath Chongzong.

The metaphor for *draw* here is not 'sketch' but the earlier meaning of 'drag'. But once we open the etymological dictionary, the list of metaphors grows until it encompasses almost every word in the passage:

long	space metaphor applied to time
period	Gk 'going in a circle' > 'cycle' > 'stretch of time'
between	the rivals are seen as if playing on a football field
opponent	one who pushes against
change	Lt 'exchange, barter', i.e. transfer physical objects
model	an architect's plan
sought	a physical search extended to a conceptual one
institution	something made to stand up
close	Lt 'shut (like a door)'
cultural	Lt 'cultivate (the ground)'
norm	a carpenter's square
latent	Lt 'hidden'
opposition	placement against
eradicated	pulled up by the roots

Note that every one of the metaphors I've pointed out is from the concrete to the abstract. The physical meanings come first, semantically and temporally. You can't understand the idea of groping for a political end (strengthening the imperial institution) before you understand searching for a physical object.

Ways to build words

In the literary sense, these are all dead metaphors. No one pictures a carpenter's square anymore when using the words *norm, normal, normality, abnormal, paranormal.* You won't get a poetry prize for comparing your love to a flower. But as you can turn dead plants into thatch, dead metaphors turn into language.

The inventors of words in natural languages faced the same problem as conlangers. You might think they had a wide range of methods:

1   Metaphor

2   Borrowing

3   Derivation (e.g. *polis* 'state' > *political, policy*)

4   Phonetic symbolism (perhaps the origin of *struggle*)

5   Make it up from scratch

Borrowing and derivation are extensively used, but they only hide the problem— as we've seen, borrowed words are themselves built from concrete metaphors.

Many words originate in phonetic imitation (*sob, hiss, jump, fart, laugh, murmur, roar, babble*), and by a sort of synaesthesia these can be applied to things that aren't sounds. E.g. *flash* was originally onomatopoeia— it was applied to the sound of rushing water, and then to flames, lightning, and gunfire. *Hurry* was originally an attempt to convey the sound of rapid whirring or whizzing, and was then applied to the sort of rapid motion that produces these sounds— thus the sense 'commotion', preserved in *hurly-burly*. But these are not really alternatives to metaphor but sister processes for moving from the concrete to the abstract.

That leaves creation from scratch. This is the mainstay of the conlanger, but outside slang it's rather rare in natural languages, even in modern times. One clear example is Murray Gell-Mann's *quark*. But as any conlanger knows, creation *ex nihilo* is tiring— it's easier to use an obscure model, as in fact Gell-Mann did, borrowing the word from James Joyce.

In any case, the lesson is that just throwing sounds together is just not what natural languages do. That leaves a general method:

- Create a stock of simple physical words.

- Extend them to abstract senses using metaphor.

- Hide the whole process by making most of it occur in a parent or neighboring language.

If you want to fake it— you need a word for *art* right now, dammit, and haven't made any other languages to borrow from and don't feel like taking the time to create a derivation— well, go ahead. I've sure done it many times. But I feel bad about it and hope to go back sometime and fill in that missing etymology.

Metaphor in grammar

Perhaps you're thinking that metaphor may pervade the messy world of lexemes, but the grammar itself is nice and abstract.

Not a chance; metaphor pervades the grammar too.

- Locatives (including adpositions) are often derived from parts of the body— e.g. *(in) back* from the back, *front* from the forehead, Hebrew *le-yad* 'to the hand' = 'next to'; Mursi *tutuo* 'of the mouth' = 'in front of'; Nahuatl *i-yōllò-co* 'in its heart' = 'inside'.

- With the TIME IS SPACE metaphor, locative expressions become temporal ones: we're *in* summer like we're *in* a room; an hour is *longer* than a minute; dawn comes *before* noon.

- Mandarin grammatical markers often originated as verbs of motion or transfer: accusative *bǎ* < 'grasp'; dative *gěi* < 'give'; comitative *gēn* < 'follow'; terminative *dào* < 'arrive'.

- Demonstratives are spatial: *this* points to something near me, *that* to something farther away. Very often this spatial meaning is extended to form third-person pronouns or articles. Often they form first and second-person pronouns as well— e.g. Japanese *anata* 'you', etymologically 'over there'.

- A common way to express the future is with movement verbs: e.g. English *I'm going to read it,* French *Je vais le lire,* Zulu *baya-kufika* 'they're arriving', lit. 'they go to arrive'.

- Similarly, French *je viens de le lire,* literally 'I come from reading it', expresses the near past: "I just read it." Irish expresses the same idea with a spatial locative: "I'm after reading."

- Many languages express the imperfective using a locative— e.g. Icelandic *Ég er að lesa* 'I am in reading' = 'I'm reading'. This is another example of TIME IS SPACE.

- Spanish has two verbs 'to be', one referring to a temporary state (*Estoy borracho* 'I'm drunk'), the other a permanent condition (*Soy borracho* 'I'm a drunk'). The verb *estar* derives from Latin *stāre* 'stand', using the common metaphor STANDING IS REMAINING, also preserved in such words as *state, station, statue, constant, stay, steady.*

- English *do* is used to form negatives and questions (*You don't know, do you?*) and historically the regular past tense suffix *-ed* is a form of 'do'. But *do* is a worn-down ordinary verb; its Indo-European meaning was 'put, set, lay down'.

- French *faire,* from Latin *facere* 'make, do, fashion', is used to form the causative: *Il m'a fait rire* 'He made me laugh'. The idea of making a physical thing is used for the more difficult idea of causing someone to do something.

- In Spanish *hacer,* from the same source, is used in expressions of time and weather: *hace trece años* 'it was thirteen years ago'; *hace frío* 'it's cold'. The semantic shift may be the same as in expressions like "That makes six carloads", i.e. it amounts to that.

Or consider how languages express the concept of possession— it's conveyed in terms of simple location, or direction, or holding, or seizing (see *Possession,* p. 308).

But English *have* doesn't mean anything, does it? In fact it falls in the last category; it derives from an Indo-European root **kap* meaning 'seize', more faithfully preserved in Latin *capture*.[7]

Even possession is a fairly concrete idea, readily grasped by toddlers. It's applied in turn to much more abstract ideas:

- In the Germanic and Romance languages, 'have' is used to form the perfect— as in English *I've read the book.* The metaphor here could be stated COMPLETION IS POSSESSION.

- In early Romance, *habere* expressed obligation: *parabolāre habeō* 'I must speak'. (The same metaphor of OBLIGATION IS POSSESSION has been re-expressed in modern Spanish: *Tengo que hablar.*) *Habere* used in this way simplified, and the meaning weakened to simple futurity— *parabolāre habeō* became simply *parlerai* (French), *hablaré* (Spanish), etc.

---

[7] Compare colloquial *He got it*. Children often mistake this as *He gots it*, 'correcting' what now looks like a strange use of the past tense.

Derivation

I've often emphasized (*LCK* p. 21, 83; *ALC*, p. 243) creating a robust derivational morphology. When you create a root (say *marry* or *read*), you should make it a habit to create the obvious variants. Here's a handy list of useful derivations:

nominalization	*marriage*
verbalization	*lecture*
adjectivization	*marital*
participle	*married, marrying*
person	*reader, mari* [Fr 'husband']
feminine/masculine	*esposo/esposa* [Sp 'spouse' m/f]
place	*reading room*
thing, tool	*lectern*
process, study	*the art of reading*
instance	*a reading*
negative	*unmarried*
causative	*cause to read*
diminutive	*little reader; read a little*
augmentative	*big reader*
ability	*marriageable*
liking, prone to	*bibliophile*
must be done	*prolegomena*
+ locative	*endogamy*
partisan	*polygamist*
collection	*readables*
badness	*misreading*

Derivation should also be your go-to method when you need a new word. Creating a new root is the easy thing to do, and your first thought should be to avoid it, and instead build the new words out of roots you've already got.

As an exercise, suppose you just have these fifty words:

back	*big*	*birth*	*body*	*breath*
day	*end*	*face*	*fall*	*field*
fold	*flat*	*foot*	*give*	*go*
good	*hand*	*hang*	*hear*	*here*
high	*hold*	*house*	*in*	*long*
make	*man*	*night*	*not*	*old*
one	*out*	*point*	*push*	*see*
side	*sit*	*small*	*spear*	*stand*
sun	*talk*	*there*	*throw*	*turn*
two	*wall*	*want*	*water*	*way*

With two-word combinations alone, you could define 2500 more words. For instance:

throw-water	= *sprinkle*
small-man	= *dwarf*
two-birth	= *reborn*
push-fall	= *knock down*
small-talk	= *chat*
old-old	= *ancient*

How could you express the following words using the above list? These go from easy to hard. There is no right answer, but if you're stumped, see p. 103.

come	first	woman	swim	king
forward	clothes	prefer	exterior	ocean
temple	palace	kill	meaning	desire
friend	support	noon	mountain	send
earth	reject	kick	sigh	build
soul	child	nation	city	climb
excite	emotion	seek	god	possess
remain	nobody	event	return	simple
slave	skin	stable	handsome	story
wash	east	dusk	defeat	foreigner
warrior	assist	floor	fence	exalted
half	morality	collapse	inject	judge
wait	convert	mercy	digression	hermit

Such compounds may strike you as a little *too* transparent— though I think it's only the newfangledness that causes this reaction; there's nothing odd about existing compounds from these words, like *Sunday, backhand, waterway*. But you can easily hide the transparency by sound change (*wife-man > woman*) or by borrowing the compound from another language (*small-man = homunculus, in-hanging = impending*).

English may keep the words of a compound apart (*fruit stand*), join them with a hyphen (*stand-in*), or fuse them (*understand*). This is just a typographic choice; German prefers fusion (*Hoheitsgewässe* 'territorial waters', *Fahrkartenkontrolle* 'ticket inspection'); French avoids it (*machine à écrire* 'typewriter', *salle de bains* 'bathroom'). It's entirely moot in Chinese, which doesn't put spaces between words. To a linguist, compounds are lexical entries (*lexemes*) like any other word.

What's the root?

The wordlists in this book give the simplest form of the root, which in English often means no suffix at all. This may be a noun (*hate > hatred, hateful*), a verb (*decide > decision, decisive*), an adjective (*wide > widen, width*), or several of these at once (*love* = V + N, *cool* = A + V, *fat* = A + N).

Don't always make the root form the same as in English! Compare these derivations in English and French:

health > healthy	N > A	*sain > santé*	A > N
beauty > beautiful	N > A	*beau > beauté*	A > N
draw > drawing	V > N	*dessin > dessiner*	N > V
fly > flight	V > N	*vol > voler*	N > V
born > be born	A > V	*naître > né*	V > A

While we're at it, don't always use the same **valence** (*ALC* p. 140) as in English. Again, using English and French:

he obeys her	transitive	*il obéit à elle*	intransitive
I looked at him	intransitive	*je l'ai regardé*	transitive

In English *like* is something we do to the thing liked; in Spanish it's something the thing does to us:

> **Me gusta la morfología.**
>
> 1s.dat like-3s.pres the morphology
>
> *I like morphology.*

It's common for a root to survive **only in derivations**— e.g. the underlined roots in *hinterland, cobweb, lukewarm, kith and kin, mulberry*. These are sometimes called *cranberry* morphemes, though that's not quite accurate— that *cran* is just *crane*, the bird. A Latin example is the root in *consīderāre, dēsīderāre* 'consider, desire'.

These are particularly common with negatives: *ruthless, insipid, unkempt, distraught, nonchalant*.

Vaguely related

What if you'd like to base one word on another, but none of your processes quite works?

You could have a 'generally related' morpheme, like Esperanto *-um-*: *okulo* 'eye' > *okulumi* 'ogle'. Or use reduplication, which lends itself naturally to intensifiers but can be used for almost anything— Spanish *chiquitito* is especially small/endearing; Mandarin *gège rén*, reduplicating the measure word, becomes a quantifier, 'every man'.

Or, just boldly re-use a derivation irrespective of its meaning. Gender woks well for this, as in Spanish *naranja* 'orange' > *naranjo* 'orange tree', French *fil* 'thread' > *file* 'line'.

Another process that's easy to miss is **sound symbolism**, which creates patterns like English *gleam, glitter, glint, glass, glow, gloss* or *hop, bump, leap, stamp, thump, tamp, trample*, German *knacken, knarren, knarschen, knuuren, knattern* (all words for sounds; recall that both *k* and *n* are pronounced), Cuzco Quechua *ch'uqchay, ch'unqay, suq'uy, suqsuy, wilq'uy, winq'uy* (all verbs of sucking or gulping, making heavy use of aspirates and uvular *q*).

Words that suggest a sound can be extended to other senses— e.g. *flash* was first used of liquids, then extended to flames. *Hurry* was first used of a whirring sound, then for any sort of busy activity, even soundless.

Automatic derivation

Once you have a word— say, *basket*— it's automatically available for a number of uses. You could think of these as applying nonce null-morpheme derivations.

- We can use it for anything that looks like the object. *Why are you wearing that basket?*

- It can be used for a toy, a model, or a picture of the object. Magritte could paint a basket and write *Ceci n'est pas une corbeille*, but he's just being paradoxical; we have no problem saying that the thing on the canvas is a basket.

- It can be stretched to cover something it doesn't quite mean, perhaps if we don't know the proper word: *I put the arrows in my... oh what is it. My arrow basket.*

- It can be applied to the mental domain— e.g. mental *baskets* could refer to temporary or permanent memories, or to the notion of categories.

- We can use it as shorthand for people or activities associated with the item. E.g. at arts & crafts hour, we might say *The baskets finished first*, referring to the people who chose to make baskets.

- Pretty much anything can be used as an insult—*basket case* is already lexicalized.

- For verbs, causatives extend the base meaning (to *walk a dog* is to make him walk) and its metaphors (*walk the batter*). *Drench* was once the causative of *drink*, but has taken its own path, generalizing the meaning to 'applying (too much) water'.

We normally don't think about this, but I think it's worth pointing out for conlangers, as this sort of nonce extension is surely the first step in lexicalization. Mull over a word and see what you can apply it to.

I also point these automatic derivations out because some lexicographers don't seem to realize that they are general rules! The *AHD*, for instance, gives one sense of *basket* as "Something resembling a basket in shape or function."

How to create a triliteral system

Hey, let's create a conlang— I'll call it Dučian. It's totally not a triliteral system like Hebrew, Arabic, or Old Skourene (*ALC* p. 240), just a normal language with fixed roots.

Primitive Dučian

The basic verbal template is

   person-modifier-stem-tense

The person prefix is simply the personal pronoun, e.g. *ana* 'I'.

Examples of stems include *ktum* 'cover', *ptil* 'twist', *cih* 'laugh', *pil* 'be low'. They are fixed stems, as in any respectable language, certainly not triliteral roots, because this is not a triliteral system.

For now we'll just worry about two tenses. The past tense is -*u*; the future is the zero morph ø.

So we can build words such as these:

ana-ktum-u	I covered	*ana-ktum-ø*	I will cover
ana-ptil-u	I twisted	*ana-ptil-ø*	I will twist
ana-cih-u	I laughed	*ana-čih-ø*	I will laugh

The modifier slot is used for various prefixes that modify the meaning. For instance, there's a causative *n-*, and also the stem can be repeated for an intensive meaning:

   ana-n-čih-u   I made someone laugh

> *ana-čih-čih-u*   I laughed a lot, I laughed like crazy

There's also an adjectivization *ša-*, so we can form *ša-pil* 'low'. This normally takes a case ending— e.g. *ša-pil-um* 'low (accusative)'. The modified root can also be used as a new verb 'make low'— e.g. *ana-ša-pil-u* 'I made (something) low'.

The laryngeal mutation

Now that we have a verbal system, let's mess it up. First we'll borrow an idea from Ferdinand de Saussure. In the 19th century, Proto-Indo-European had been reconstructed, but its vowels were something of a mess. Saussure posited that the vowel in all verbs was a simple **e*, but that this could be followed by a consonant which colored the vowel, and often ended up changing it. For instance, the *ew* in the root **bhewg* 'flee' changed to *u* in Latin— thus *fugio* 'I flee' (cf. *fugitive*).

Explaining roots with *a* was more of a trick; Saussure simply suggested an unknown *a*-coloring consonant X, as in **peXs* 'protect', seen in Latin *pāstor* 'shepherd'. Hermann Möller suggested that X could be a laryngeal, such as the *ḥ* in Arabic *Baḥrain*. But X had not survived in any known Indo-European language.

Saussure was vindicated with the discovery of Hittite in the 1920s, which had retained laryngeals in precisely the spots he had predicted— e.g. *paḥs* 'protect'.

Let's apply this idea to Dučian. *H* is laryngeal; let's say that final *-h* turns the previous vowel into *a*, but intervocalic *-h-* does nothing. That affects the root *čih*:

> *ana-čih-u*   I laughed   *ana-čah-ø*   I will laugh

More destruction

A few more sound changes:

- When used as a prefix, the pronoun *ana* is reduced to *a*. (As an independent, emphatic pronoun, it remains *ana*.)
- Final vowels are lost.

The verb forms above thus become:

a-ktum	I covered	*a-ktum*	I will cover
a-ptil	I twisted	*a-ptil*	I will twist
a-čih	I laughed	*a-čah*	I will laugh

Oops, losing the final -*u* merged past and present. But thanks to the laryngeal mutation, 'laugh' isn't affected. The Dučians may decide that the future of 'laugh' was formed by changing the stem vowel to *a,* and then generalize this pattern to all verbs:

a-ktum	I covered	*a-ktam*	I will cover
a-ptil	I twisted	*a-ptal*	I will twist
a-čih	I laughed	*a-čah*	I will laugh

While we're at it, let's say that reduplicated forms are simplified— the final consonant of the first syllable is lost. So the intensive of 'I laughed' is now *a-či-čih.*

Syncope

In *ALC* (p.174) I mentioned the devastation wrought upon Nishnaabemwin by syncope. The rule there is that every other short vowel is eliminated (except the last):

makizin > mkizin		'shoe'
makizinan > mkiznan		'shoes'
ni-makizin > nmakzin		'my shoe'

Let's apply a syncope rule to Dučian: the middle syllable of a three-syllable word is deleted. Note the pre- and post-syncope forms:

ša-pil-um	*šaplum*	low (acc.)
a-ša-pil	*ašpil*	I lowered
a-či-čih	*aččih*	I laughed (int.)

The form *ašpil* 'I lowered' looks a lot like the other verbs above, like *aktum* 'I covered'. It would be only natural to apply analogy and create adjectives for these parallel to *šaplum:*

šaplum	low (acc.)
katmum	covered (acc.)
patlum	twisted (acc.)

The intensive *aččih* is also easily generalized to other roots— e.g. *apittil* 'I twisted a lot'.

The end result

What did we end up with? Let's look at some of the forms for a single root:

aptil	I twisted
aptal	I will twist
patlum	twisted (acc.)
apittil	I twisted a lot
anpatil	I was twisted

We started with an invariable root *ptil*, but thanks to the vowel mutation and syncope, the only common elements are the three consonants *p-t-l*. Various grammatical operations are performed by adding various vowels within this frame (as well as using prefixes and suffixes).

In fact Dučian is now a triliteral system like those of the Semitic languages.

This is a simplified view of how Semitic is thought to have developed; it's based on Guy Deutsch's analysis in *The Unfolding of Language*. (Dučian is named for him, with a Saussurian *eu* > *u* change.) The actual forms are based mostly on Akkadian. Note that once you have the basic system— triliteral roots plus templates— it's easy to create new templates, expanding and complicating the morphology.

If you want to create a triliteral system you certainly don't have to imitate the details above, but I find it a fascinating example of a few relatively simple changes combining to produce a completely new system.

Some possible derivations

Some possibilities for deriving words... if you came up with something different, great!

come	here-go
first	one-way
woman	birth-man
swim	water-go
king	big-spear
forward	face-way
clothes	body-hang
prefer	want-want
exterior	out-side
ocean	big-water
temple	god-house
palace	big-house
kill	end-breath

meaning	point-talk
desire	want-see
friend	side-man
support	stand-back
noon	sun-high
mountain	big-high
send	give-there
earth	water-field
reject	throw-out
kick	foot-push
sigh	long-breath
build	make-house
soul	breath
child	small-body
nation	big-field, birthishness
city	in-walls
climb	high-go
excite	go-go
emotion	push-out, in-talk
seek	see-see, want-hold
god	high-one
possess	hold, in-hand
remain	long-stand, sit-there
nobody	not-body, not-one
event	fall-out
return	back-go
simple	one-fold
slave	house-hand, foot-man
skin	body-wall
stable	standing, long-there
handsome	good-see
story	talk-long
wash	water-push
east	sun-birth
dusk	day-end, sun-sit
defeat	sit-face, make-fall
foreigner	there-man, out-man

warrior	spear-man
assist	give-hand
floor	house-foot, house-flat
fence	field-wall
exalted	held-high
half	one-out-two, small-two
morality	good-way
collapse	fold-small, fall-in
inject	push-in
judge	hear-two-sides
wait	hang-there, long-sit
convert	talk-turn, make-fold
mercy	hold-hand
digression	side-talk
hermit	want-no-man

Word size

As a rule of thumb, you might figure that the length of a word correlates with its importance to your culture's speakers... or more precisely, to their ancestors.

As a quick test of this idea, here are the major body part terms for French sorted by number of phonemes:

2   *œil cou nez dent joue sein hanche main rein peau*
    (eye neck nose tooth cheek breast hip hand kidney skin)

3   *tête bouche langue front cil taille bras doigt poing pouce paume coude pied cœur foie chair*
    (head mouth tongue forehead eyelash waist arm finger fist thumb palm elbow food heart liver flesh)

4   *oreille lèvre gorge menton cheveux poil barbe épaule jambe génou cuisse mollet talon plante vagin anus poumon*
    (ear lip throat chin hair whisker beard shoulder leg knee thigh ankle heel sole vagina anus lung)

5   *visage poignet orteil pénis cerveau*
    (face wrist toe penis brain)

6   *mâchoire moustache intestin bout de sein*
    (jaw moustache intestines nipple)

7 *nombril abdomen estomac utérus*
   (navel abdomen stomach uterus)

Seems like a fair heuristic, so long as you don't take it too literally.

Some of these words have synonyms; note that the more colloquial or vulgar term is usually shorter:

abdomen	*ventre*
visage	*gueule*
vagin	*chatte, con*
pénis	*verge*

Learned terms are often derivations or compound terms, and thus longer. Japanese is an exception, since the native vocabulary has a much more longwinded phonotactics than the many Chinese borrowings.

If a word becomes more common, it tends to be shortened:

omnibus > bus
taxicab > cab
nuclear bomb > nuke
clitoris > clit
personal computer > PC
communist > commie

Chinese requires some caveats. It follows the heuristic, in that long expressions are often abbreviated to two or four characters. However, sound changes have caused so many mergers of syllable types that to ensure comprehension, words sometimes have to get *longer*— rather as the *pin-pen* merger in Southern American English has resulted in the disambiguating expression *ink pen.*

Malleability

It's hard to spend a lot of time looking at etymology, or the history of the senses of a word, or foreign dictionaries, without concluding that meanings are arbitrary and highly malleable.

To put it another way, our **folk theory** of meaning tells us that definitions are fixed, natural, and black-and-white. Thus people get bent out of shape when they notice a word being used in a new way.

Politics is full of examples: it disturbs some conservatives when *mother* is applied to a mother's lesbian partner, or when *rape* is applied within a marriage, or when they're told that *race* isn't a simple biological fact. Liberals may be bothered when conservatives refer to a *fetus* as a *child,* or to the lack of regulation as *freedom,* or when children use *gay* to mean *stupid.* Both sides may be nonplussed when asked to call a transgender person with a penis a *woman.*

Sometimes we defer to the experts, even when there's no need to. In the US, there's a widespread belief that *summer* 'officially' begins at the solstice, though this is merely the astronomical definition, and not appropriate for meteorology, nor is it universal in English-speaking countries. Likewise, we accept the taxonomist's assertion that *whales* are not *fish.*

On the other hand, people aren't likely to accept the modern biologist's view that *fish* are not a class, and the physicists' usage of *work, force,* and *power* is viewed as an idiosyncrasy, irrelevant to ordinary language.

What's wrong with the folk theory?

- As for the **fixed** part, well, there's recorded history. Meanings change broadly and constantly, as if speakers were engaging in a conspiracy to make the dictionary obsolete. Speakers not only adapt words to new situations, but insist on changing basic vocabulary— e.g. bringing in new words for *head* or *dog* or *mountain* or *noon* apparently at whim.

- The **natural** part of the folk theory is also disproved by change, but also by comparison to other languages, which divide up semantic space in different ways.

- Most human languages have no written form and no dictionaries; they aren't learned through **definitions**. And the core words of our language are still learned not from books but from other people, by a process of internal generalization from examples. Logicians and lexicographers like formal definitions because they're easy to work with, but they distort our understanding of how language works.

- The **clear boundaries** part is also disproved by experience— people are constantly using words to refer to something outside the dictionary definition— by metaphor, as humorous exaggeration, by interference from another speech variety, or for simple lack of a better term.

- The traditional view doesn't have a place for prototypes, family-resemblance words, basic-level categories, radiating meanings, or speaker's meanings.

Speaker's meanings

The last term deserves a closer look. C.S. Lewis in *Studies in Words* talked about **word's meanings** and **speaker's meanings**. E.g., for the sense of *furniture* as 'moveable articles in a house', the OED cites one Lichefield, in 1582, referring to "All the furniture for his Chamber and Kitchin". But the common sense of *furniture* at that time was 'furnishing'— either the act of equipping, or any sort of provisions or equipment. Lichefield might well have been using the general sense of 'equipment', which here happens to match 'furniture' in the modern sense.

The thing is, if enough people use a word in a narrowed or expanded way, that generates a new sense, or even takes over the word's meaning. We can no longer speak, as one Knowles did in 1603, of soldiers "differing... in language, countenance, and manner of furniture". We'd have to say *equipment.*

Another example is the contemporary use of *girl* for older women; it would be completely unsurprising if the word ends up as a synonym for *female.* Similarly *guy* is a colloquial term for 'men'— but women use it among themselves, especially as a vocative ("Hey, guys, should I dump this asshole?"), and it may well turn into a term for 'people' or 'friends'. Lewis gives the example of *immorality*, which comes to mean *lechery* because the only type of immorality most people want to talk about is sexual.

This process is baffling if we think of words in terms of their definitions— if *girl* **means** 'young woman', how could anyone ever use it for an older woman? That's why I use the named-clump-of-referents idea. Each actual reference is a sort of vote on the 'meaning' of the word, and if enough people use the word in a new way, then the boundary shifts.

Let's take another example. Suppose your friend says *It'd be a sin to miss this preacher.* What's going on?

- The speaker means that it would violate God's law to skip the sermon.

- The speaker recognizes that that's the meaning of *sin* but is exaggerating as a way of reinforcing the value he puts on going to the talk.

- The speaker is using a subsidiary sense of *sin*, namely 'a pity, a shame' (which itself originated from such exaggerations).

We don't always know. What's more, the speaker may not be able to tell you. Sometimes people are making a proposition clear enough to please a logician. But often they're no more clear than they have to be. The speaker is communicating that it'd be bad if you didn't hear this preacher; he doesn't need to qualify the exact nature of the badness.

(Of course, he might be departing even more from a literal reading— e.g. maybe you both disdain this preacher and it's pure irony. Perhaps the preacher is named Zinn and he's making a pun. Perhaps he's even advising you to aim carefully when you throw the pie.)

Semantic space

My dot diagrams use the metaphor of *semantic space*. Still, what is that space? It can be quantified when it comes to colors or linear scales, but in domains like *furniture* it's just a way of indicating that referents vary in all sorts of ways.

In the '60s and '70s, some linguists felt that if we could reduce language to predicate logic, we'd be done. Consider the following sentences:

> *Sadly, they never saw each other again.*

> *Unfortunately, they never saw each other again.*

> *Regretfully, they never saw each other again.*

The three adverbs mean three different things, and yet the overall effect is about the same. We can imagine a speaker using any of the three to express her thought. (And because of such situations, we can imagine a word for 'poor fortune' becoming a word for 'downcast'— this is in fact the story of *unhappy*.)

But the predicate logic version wouldn't capture the closeness of these words. If you need a dissertation topic, perhaps you could work on a consistent way to quantify this idea of semantic closeness.

It's not just emotions that are malleable; we can also describe bare facts in entirely different ways:

> *They never saw each other again.*

> *That was their last meeting.*

> *The two of them spent the rest of their lives apart.*

> *Would their paths cross once more? It was not to be.*

Another way of looking at this is to ask what it would take for a robot to understand that these four sentences describe the same situation. It requires more than understanding perception, and meetings, and trajectories; it requires making connections between them— e.g., knowing that it's normal (but not absolutely necessary) for participants in a *meeting* to *see* one another. It requires extensive, well-integrated real-world knowledge. So much for treating language as arbitrary symbols, apart from the world!

Summary

The linguistic point of view strikes some people as anarchic— inviting or celebrating degradation and barbarity. But to observe how language works is not to take a moral stand on it, any more than a naturalist studying lions is an advocate of chasing down animals and eating them raw. There's nothing wrong with speaking the standard language and appreciating the meanings and fine distinctions it gives us.

On the other hand, once you've understood how malleable meaning is, you can't really unlearn that and go back to the folk theory of fixed, god-given definitions.

To sum up,

- People are constantly using words outside the dictionary definition. This may be a nonce usage, but if it's widely adopted it will shift or extend the word's meaning.

- Outside technical terms, definitions aren't that important anyway: most words learned by generalization with little formal guidance.

- Words are fluid, changing according to the whim of the speech community.

- There's generally nothing in nature which determines the definition of a word. Another language, or the same language in a hundred years, might see things differently.

- This fluidity is really not worth getting upset over, any more than we're upset that water doesn't hold its shape.

Or to boil it down even more, all languages are conlangs— they're just erratic collective ones.

Thematic section

Some reminders:

- Sections are alphabetical. Hopefully you'll soon be familiar with my categories and flip to them quickly; if not, use the index.

- The typography of words gives frequency information; see p. 45.

- Non-English words are followed by their etymology, not a gloss. See p. 81 for how to read the etymologies.

ANIMALS

animal
Lt < *anima* 'soul, breath'
• Gk ζῷον 'living' • Ch *dòngwù* 'move-thing'

beast
Lt *bestia*
• OE *déor* < 'breath' • Ch *shòu* 'wild animal' poss. < 'hunted'

bird
OE *brid* 'young bird'
• Gk ὄρνις < 'rising' • Sp *pájaro* 'sparrow' • Ir *éan* < 'fly' • Lith *paukštis* < 'young' • Skt *pakṣin-* 'winged'

bug
ModE uncertain

cat
Lt *cattus*, uncertain
• Gk αἴλουρος 'quick-tail' • Lt *fēlēs* poss. 'marten' • Rum *pisică* < a call for cats • Ch *māo* imitative

dog
OE *docga*, originally just one breed
• generic OE *hund*, Lt *canis*, Gk κύων < IE **ḱuon-* • ModGr σκυλί 'puppy'

duck
OE *duce* 'diving'
• Lt *anas anat-*, Ger *Ente* < IE • Sp *pata* imitative

fish
OE *fisc*, cognate to Lt *piscis*
• ModGk ψάρι < 'dainty'

horse
OE *hors* < 'run'
• Lt *equus*, Gk ἵππος < IE **eḱwo-* • Lt *caballus* 'work-horse' • Lith *arklys* 'plower' • Rus лошадь < Turkish *alaša* 'pack horse' • ModGk ἄλογος 'unreasoning'

insect
Lt *insecta* 'cut up' = 'segmented', calque on Gk ἔντομα
• Cz *hmyz* < 'crawl' • Pol *owad* < 'annoyer' • Ch *kunchóng* 'many' + 'insect, worm'

monster
Lt *monstrum* '(divine) warning, portent'
• Ger *Ungeheuer* 'unfamiliar' • Ch *guàiwù* 'strange thing'

mouse
OE *mús*
* It *topo* < 'mole' • Sp *ratón* 'big rat' • Lith *pelė* 'gray'

rabbit
ME, possibly from Flemish

snake
OE *snaca* < 'crawl'
• Lt *serpens -ent-* 'creeper' • OE *wyrm* 'worm' • Lith *gyvatė* 'animal' • OCS *zmija* 'earth' • Cz *had* < 'harmful, loathsome' • Ch *shé* poss. 'winding thing'

spider
OE *spíþra* 'spinner'

+
dragon, troll, orc, werewolf, gnome, elf, vampire, zombie

nest, lair, hive; pollinate, swarm, graze

herd, tame, hunt, stalk

Animal names not in the Frequency List will be found in the tables below.

Taxonomy

Whether you want to create your own creatures, or just make sure you've covered everything, it may be useful to look at **taxonomy**.

Karl Linnaeus organized all life, and the minerals for good measure, in his *Systema Naturae* (1735). He used the ranks *class, order, genus, species,* and *variety.* He proceeded based on anatomical similarity; with Darwin, of course, the idea became to represent lines of descent.

The ranks now used, using the dog and the dogwood as examples:

domain	eukaryotes (multi-celled organisms)	eukaryotes
kingdom	animals	plants
phylum (animals) *division* (plants)	chordates	angiosperms (flowering plants)
class	mammals	eudicots (two-leafed embryos, three-bulbed pollen)
order	carnivores	*cornales* (incl. hydrangeas)
family	canids (incl. foxes)	*cornaceae* (incl. tupelos)
genus	*Canis* (incl. wolves, coyotes, jackals)	*Cornus* (dogwoods)
species	*lupus* (gray wolf, dog, dingo)	*florida*, flowering dogwood— eastern US

Intermediate levels can be created in bewildering detail.

The primary need of researchers is not so much classification as identification; for this the last two ranks are used, in Greco-Latin form: *Canis lupus, Homo sapiens, Cornus florida, Escherichia coli.*

In the last few decades genetic analysis has been available, and the result is an ongoing revolution and a confusing stew of new and contested names. The best course is to procure a time machine, then acquire the 2050 edition of this book. For a conworlder, however, the important levels are class, order, and genus.

Most ordinary language words correspond pretty closely to the **genus** level, as with *dogwood* above. Only for very familiar genera (like *Canis*) do we have distinct words for separate species.

The **order**, for mammals at least, is likely to be a familiar and useful classification— e.g. carnivores, primates, rodents.

When we're devising classifications, the most useful classes are those with roughly equal numbers. E.g. a useful classification of nations would be by continent, or socioeconomic level; a not-useful classification would be 'Australia' vs. 'All the rest'. Biological classifications, unfortunately, are very often like the latter— e.g. *Archaea* (below) are tiny relative to the other two domains; placental mammals make up the vast majority of mammals; of these 40% belong to just one class, rodents.

Non-scientific language tidies up biology by ruthlessly combining classes based on how interesting they are to humans. Thus a fairly complicated set of clades are all grouped together as *fish*, and a large number of phyla are tossed into the *worm* bucket.

Domains

The top of the biological tree is quite simple:

Bacteria   Single cell, no cell nucleus. The name is from Greek 'staff', after the shape of the first ones observed.

Archaea   Single cell, no cell nucleus. The first exemplars were extremophiles, and many archaea use unusual energy sources such as ammonia or hydrogen gas. But not all are exotic; they include the methanogens in your digestive system. They're distinguished from bacteria by genetics— many of their cell mechanisms are closer to eukaryotes.

Eukarya   Cells with nuclei (hence the name, Greek 'true kernel'[1]); includes all multicellular life.

Your first question, no doubt, is "what about **viruses**?" Viruses have genetic material— indeed, they're just a bit of DNA or RNA plus a capsule to hold it— and thus can evolve and reproduce. But, crucially, they can't reproduce by themselves— they have to hijack a living cell.

It's not known whether viruses are decayed versions of full cells, or bits of DNA/RNA that evolved the ability to move between cells, or something that predated other forms of life. Or a bit of all three.

---

[1] Greek εὐ- is normally 'good', as in *euphony,* but in taxonomic names should be taken as 'true'.

Obviously, the ancient Romans knew nothing about them; *vīrus* meant 'slime, poison'. They were discovered by Dmitri Ivanovsky (1892).

Kingdoms

The bacteria and archaea are not usually divided into kingdoms.

The kingdoms of eukaryotes, according to a widely accepted classification by Robert Whitaker (1969):

Protista	protists— unicellular or at least not differentiated into tissues
Plantae	plants— usually multicellular; cell walls contain cellulose; most turn sunlight into energy (photosynthesis)
Fungi	mushrooms, yeast, molds— cell walls contain chitin
Animalia	animals— generally multicellular and moving

As an example of the current flux in taxonomy, here's a rather different set of kingdoms according to the International Society of Protistologists (2005):

Excavata	flagellate protozoa
Amoebozoa	lobose amoeboids, slime molds
Opisthokonta	animals, fungi, various flagellates
Rhizaria	foramins, radiolarians, and other amoeboids
Chromalveolata	some algae types, kelp, diatoms
Archaeplastida	land plants, green algae, red algae, glaucophytes (another type of algae)

Phylums of *Animalia*

As you look over the list, you're going to think, "That's an awful lot of worms." But most are trivial. The nine major phyla, accounting for 96% of described species, are boldfaced.

1 Parazoa	'alongside animals'	multicellular but no tissues/organs; no symmetry
Porifera	'pore bearers'	sponge— sessile as adults, rely on ambient water flow

Placozoa	'broad animals'	a single species: a flat undifferentiated mass; moves using cilia
2 Eumetazoa	'true over-animals'	animals with symmetric bodies
2.1 Radiata	'radiating'	radial symmetry
Ctenophora	'comb carriers'	comb jelly
Cnidaria	'nettles'	coral, sea anemone, jellyfish, various parasites
2.2 Bilateria	'two-sided'	bilateral symmetry
Orthonectida	'straight-swimmers'	tiny, very simple parasite
Rhombozoa	'rhombus animals'	tiny wormlike parasite of cephalopods
Acoelomorpha	'no-coelom shape'	small gutless worm
Chaetognatha	'long-hair jaw'	arrow worm— marine, predatory on plankton
2.2.1 Deuterostomia	'second mouth'	dent in embryo develops into anus
Chordata	'corded'	chordates, with a nerve cord, including all the **vertebrates**; the others are tunicates and lancelets (both marine)
Hemichordata	'half-corded'	acorn worm, sessile pterobranch
Echinodermata	'porcupine skin'	five-fold and marine: starfish, sea urchins, sand dollar, sea cucumber
Xenoturbellida	'strange turbulence'	simple gutless marine worm
2.2.2. Protostomia	'first mouth'	dent in embryo develops into mouth
2.2.2.1 Ecdysozoa	'stripping animal'	Periodically molts outer layer of body
Kinorhynca	'moving snout'	tiny segmented animals in mud or sand, no circulatory system
Loricifera	'lorica bearers'	tiny sediment-dwellers with a little protective case (*lorica*), discovered only in the 1970s
Priapulida	Greek god Priapus	marine predatory worm

Nematoda   'thread-form'   roundworm, with full tubular gut

Nematomorpha   'thread shaped'   horsehair worm— larvae parasitic, adults free-living in water

Onychophora   'claw bearers'   velvet worm— soft-bodied predator with stubby legs; bears live young

Tardigrada   'slow walker''   water bears— tiny segmented animals found in moss or lichen; can tolerate extreme pressure, temperature, or radiation

Arthropoda   'joint-feet'   exoskeleton, segmented body, jointed appendages: trilobites, insects, spiders, horseshoe crabs, crustaceans, centipedes, millipedes

2.2.2.2 Platyzoa   'flat animals'   no coelom (fluid-filled cavity alongside gut) or a pseudocoel

Platyhelminthes   'flat worms'   flatworms— unsegmented, no body cavity, no circulatory system; includes tapeworm, fluke

Gastrotricha   'stomach hair'   hairybacks— microscopic, covered with cilia, and hermaphroditic

Rotifera   'wheel-bearer'   rotifers— microscopic, mostly freshwater; named for their wheel-like cilia which sweep food into the mouth

Acanthocephala   'thorn head'   thorny-headed worms— parasitic worms with a spiny proboscis for attaching to the host

Gnathostomulida   'jaw-mouth'   jaw worms— tiny animals in wet sand and mud; no body cavity; one-way gut; hermaphrodites

Micrognathozoa   'small jaw animal'   Just one species— a tiny thing with a complicated jaw structure, restricted to some springs in Greenland

Cycliophora	'circle-bearers'	Tiny creatures living as symbionts on the mouthparts of lobsters; discovered in 1995
2.2.2.3 Lophotrochozoa	'crest-wheel animals'	first four: a crest of cilia on the larva; remaining phyla: a lophophore, a crest of ciliated tentacles
Sipuncula	'small tube'	peanut worms— unsegmented marine worms
Nemertea	after the nymph Nemertes	ribbon worms— mostly marine; known for a proboscis which everts to capture prey
Mollusca	'soft things'	Mollusks— mostly marine, very diverse: snail, slug, squid, octopus, nautilus, clam, oyster, scallop, mussel, chiton, and various worms
Annelida	'ringed'	segmented worms, of many types, including the earthworm and leech
Phoronida	from a name of the goddess Isis	horseshoe worms—anchored in chitinous tubes underwater, with a crown of soft tentacles covered with cilia, which draw food into the mouth; has a simple set of blood vessels
Bryozoa	'moss animals'	Tiny, sessile marine animals, with a crown of tentacles on a goblet-shaped body, itself on a long stalk
Entoprocta	'internal anus'	Similar to bryozoa but the anus is inside the crown of tentacles, and they have no coelom
Brachiopoda	'arm-feet'	Marine filtering animals with hard shells
Echiura	'viper-tailed'	spoon worms— marine worms, unsegmented, with a proboscis poking from the head used to feed

Vertebrates

The original definition of vertebrates was 'animals with a backbone', which however produces a problem with hagfish, which have a skull but no spine.

The traditional five classes are of course fish, amphibians, reptiles, birds, and mammals. But the birds are derived from reptiles (and thus taxonomically *are* reptiles), which along with the mammals derived from amphibians, and everything came from fish.

Plus it turns out **fish** is not a defensible category. Fish form three or four classes (the hagfish and lampreys are sometimes split):

> **Agnatha** 'jawless'— jawless fish.
>
> > *Hagfish, lamprey*
>
> **Chondrichthyes** 'cartilage-fish'— cartilaginous fish
>
> > *Shark, ray, chimaera*
>
> **Osteichthyes** 'bone-fish'— fish with true bones, divided into:
>
> > **Sarcopterygii** 'flesh-wings'— lobe-finned fish, with very thick fins, directly ancestral to the legs of all other classes of vertebrates
> >
> > > *Coelacanth, lungfish*
> >
> > **Actinopterygii** 'ray-wings'— ray-finned fishes, with thin fins made of skin supported by spines
> >
> > > *All other fish*

Amphibians ('both-life', i.e. living both on land and in the water) are divided into three orders:

Anura	'no tail'	frog, toad (90% of all amphibians)
Caudata	'tailed'	salamander, newt, siren
Gymnophiona	'naked-serpent'	like snakes, but without scales

An extinct group called *labyrinthodonts* ('maze-teeth', from their elaborately folded dental structure) gave rise to the reptiles.

Reptiles ('crawlers') lay eggs with an amniotic sac (which allows them to be laid on land), are cold-blooded, and have scales. They are divided into four extant orders:

Testudines	'tortoise-ish'	turtle
Sphenodontia	'wedge-tooth'	tuatara

Squamata	'scaly'	lizard, snake (largest group)
Crocodilia	'pebble-worm'	crocodile, alligator, caiman

Reptiles, like Ozymandias, have fallen far from their former glory. The overall tree relating the modern amniotes with the ancient monsters looks something like this:

1 Synapsida

    1.1 Mammals

2 Sauropsida

    2.1 *Anapsidea*— survived by turtles

    2.2 *Diapsidea*

        2.2.1 *Ichthyosauria*

        2.2.2 *Lepidosauromorpha*— including plesiosaurs and placodonts; survived by tuatara, snakes

        2.2.3 *Archosauromorpha*

            2.2.3.1 *Crurotarsi*— survived by crocodiles

            2.2.3.2 *Avemetatarsalia*— includes the dinosaurs proper; survived by birds

Mammals

'Mammal' is a very late word, created by Linnaeus from Lt *mamma* 'breast, teat'; as bulging mammaries are only characteristic of humans and bovines, the Finnish *nisäkäs* 'things with nipples' is more accurate... except that monotremes lack nipples. Russian млеко-питающее 'milk-feeding' covers everything.

There are three divisions of (living) mammals:

Monotremes 'one-hole', which lay eggs and have just one opening (*cloaca*) at the lower end; have 10 rather than 2 sex chromosomes; confined to Australia/New Guinea.

platypus, echidna

Marsupials (< 'pouch'), whose young are born undeveloped and are carried in a pouch; extinct in Eurasia.

Americas: opossum

Australia: kangaroo, koala, wombat, Tasmanian devil

Placental mammals, which are nurtured during a long period through the mother's placenta.

The orders of placental mammals are:

Euarchontoglires	'true ancestors' + 'dormice'	
Rodentia	'gnawing'	Largest order by number of species
		springhare, beaver, gopher, mole rat, guinea pig, capybara, porcupine, hamster, mouse, rat, squirrel, chipmunk
Lagomorpha	'rabbit-shaped'	*rabbit, hare, pika*
Scandentia	'climbers'	*tree shrew*
Dermoptera	'skin-wings'	*colugo* (small gliding animal)
Primates	'principal'	*monkey, ape, you and me*
Laurasiatheria		
Eulipotyphla	'true fat blind'	insectivores: *hedgehog, mole, shrew*
Chiroptera	'hand-wings'	*bat*
Perissodactyla	'uneven toes'	*horse, donkey/ass, zebra, tapir, rhinoceros*
Cetacea	'whales'	*whale, dolphin, porpoise*
Artiodactyla	'even toes'	*camel, pig, giraffe, deer, moose, antelope, cattle, sheep, goat, hippopotamus*
Pholidota	'scaly'	*pangolin (scaly anteater)*
Carnivora	'meat-eater'	*dog, wolf, fox, cat, lion, tiger, bear, seal*
Xenarthra	'strange joints'	restricted to Americas; slow metabolism
Cingulata	'banded'	*armadillo*
Pilosa	'hairy'	*sloth, anteater*
Afrotheria	'African beasts'	
Macroscelidea	'big hips'	*elephant shrew*
Afrosoricida	'African shrews'	*tenrec, golden mole*
Tubulidentata	'pipe-teeth'	*aardvark*
Hyracoidea	'hyrax-like'	*hyrax*
Proboscidea	'trunked'	*elephant*
Sirenia	mythological sea-nymph	*dugong, manatee*

Birds

The orders of birds have imposing names, but almost all are just Greek or Latin for "shaped like <prototypical member>".

Struthioniformes	*ostrich, emu, kiwi*
Tinamiformes	*tinamou*
Anseriformes	*duck, goose, swan*
Galliformes	*chicken, turkey, grouse, quail, partridge, pheasant*
Charadriiformes	*gull, button-quail, plover*
Gaviiformes	*loon*
Podicipediformes	*grebe*
Procellariiformes	*albatross, petrel*
Sphenisciformes	*penguin*
Pelecaniformes	*pelican, heron, egret, ibis*
Phaethontiformes	*tropicbird*
Ciconiiformes	*stork*
Cathartiformes	*vulture*
Phoenicopteriformes	*flamingo*
Falconiformes	*hawk, falcon, eagle*
Gruiformes	*crane*
Pteroclidiformes	*sandgrouse*
Columbiformes	*dove, pigeon*
Psittaciformes	*parrot, cockatoo*
Cuculiformes	*cuckoo, turaco*
Opisthocomiformes	*hoatzin*
Strigiformes	*owl*
Caprimulgiformes	*nightjar*
Apodiformes	*swift, hummingbird*
Coraciiformes	*kingfisher, hoopoe, hornbill*
Piciformes	*woodpecker, toucan*
Trogoniformes	*trogon*
Coliiformes	*mousebird*
Passeriformes (songbirds)	*oriole, crow, raven, lark, swallow, martin, warbler, thrush, starling, wren, sparrow, cardinal, tit, robin*

On the farm

A farming community won't be satisfied with just one word referring to
Bos taurus. Let's look at some of the terms relating to **cattle**:

cattle	generic term (plural)
cow	female adult
bull	male adult
calf	young (under a year)
yearling	young (over a year)
ox	castrated adult male
steer	a young ox [in British usage]
beef	meat from cattle
veal	meat from calves
muck	cattle dung

A similar array could be made for horses, pigs, sheep, goats, dogs, and
even deer. This is typical for European languages, but you can also take
a more analytical approach— Chinese makes do with various compounds of *niú*.

There's also a wide variety of terms for referring to animal anatomy,
inside and out, though probably the only parts you need to provide
names for are things your people eat.

Horses

In a premodern society, you weren't a farmer unless you had your own
cow, but you were rabble till you had your own horse. A man with a
horse was a noble in Latin (*eques*) as well as French (*chevalier*). Having a
horse made you part of the *cavalry*, the elite of the army, and imposed a
higher standard of behavior (*chivalry*). The military rank *marshal* is
etymologically 'horse-servant'.

Naturally, there was a rich terminology relating to horses— equipment
(*saddle, bit, harness, stirrup, reins*), movement (*walk, trot, canter, gallop*),
ages and purpose, anatomy. A sampling:

attaint	a wound on a horse's leg
barding	ornamental covering for a horse
bayard	a bay-colored horse
bishop	to file a horse's teeth to hide its age
boggle	to startle at an imagined specter (a bogey)

bronco	a wild or untamed horse
caparison	an ornamental cloth spread over the saddle
cob	a short-legged, stout horse, suitable for heavy riders
colt	a young male horse (older than a *foal*)
curvet	a leap in which the fore-legs are raised together, followed closely by a spring of the hind-legs
dressage	training of a horse
farrier	one who shoes or treats horses
founder	an inflamed foot, from overwork
gee	a command to a horse to turn right (left is *haw*)
hackney	a horse of middling quality
hobby	a small or middling horse; then a toy horse or horse costume; then a trivial avocation (a metaphor on riding a toy horse)
jade	an inferior or worn-out horse
kelpie	a Scottish water-demon in the shape of a horse
lunge	a long rope used in training horses
pastern	the part of the horse's foot between fetlock and hoof
stud	a collection of horses, originally one used for breeding

Types of dung

Muck (above) isn't alone; the OED offers the following specific types of dung:

button	sheep
crottels	hare
fewmets	deer (and dragons, according to T.H. White)
fiants	badger, fox
frass	insect larvae
grattishing	deer
guano	sea-birds or bats
lesses	boar, bear, wolf
metessing	hawk
purl	horse, cow, or sheep
scumber	dog or fox

spraints	otter
tath	farm animals
treddle	sheep or goats
waging	fox

If you don't use them in your conlang, they also make good, inscrutable responses in Internet arguments.

Quechua, which lent us *guano*, also has *taha,* the dung of llamas, rabbits, or sheep; *uccha-khawa,* horse's or ass's dung; *chhuchu,* dried burro dung, and *warkha,* balls of dung on a sheep's coat.

Kind of gross, to city dwellers; but recall that dung is valuable as a source of fuel or as fertilizer. It can be used directly as a building material, or as a component of adobe or daub (the plaster-like substance used in wattle-and-daub construction). Hunters use it for tracking. Guano can be mined for phosphorus, and was once a key source of saltpeter, used for gunpowder. Sal ammoniac could be produced from camel dung. Tanners used dung to soften hides, though this could also be done with brains.

Dung and urine have been used in medicines. Urea, used in many cosmetics, was isolated from urine, though now it's produced inorganically. The estrogens in Premarin are still collected the old-fashioned way, from horse urine. Have you heard of honeydew honey? The bees collect sap which has been, um, run through an aphid first. I'll stop now.

Speciesism

As humans, we're interested in seeing where we fit in the big picture, so we see increasing detail (more names, more related terms) the closer the animals affect us.

If your conpeople happen not to be mammals, you should be careful not to copy a mammalian worldview! If they're birds, they should have far more words for other birds than for their remoter relatives the mammals. If they're invertebrates, they might well group most of the vertebrates together under broad terms as loosely as we talk about 'worms' or 'bugs'.

On your world elves and dragons may well be real; but are there also mythical monsters? That is, in a fantasy world, what do people make up as *their* fantasy?

art	Lt *ars art-* 'skill' < 'fit together' ‖ *artus* 'joint'
	Ger *Kunst* < 'knowledge' • Lith *dailė* < 'beautiful' • Rus искусство < 'trial' • Ch *yì* < 'accomplished' < 'cultivate'; cognate to Japanese *geisha*
audience	Fr nomn. of 'heard'
	• Ger *Publikum* • Ch *tingzhòng* 'hear-crowd'
culture	Lt *cultūra* 'cultivation, tending'
	• Ch *wénhuà* 'literature-change'
dance	Fr *danser* < Frankish **dintjan* 'move to and fro'
	• Gk χορεύω < 'courtyard' • Sp *bailar* < Gk βαλλίζω < 'throw' • Lith *šokti* 'jump'
+	*academy, exhibit, gallery*

Genres

What genres are recognized as fine art? The **Greeks** recognized nine Muses; it may be telling that the generic μοῦσα gave her name to one particular art, *music*. A shrine to the Muses, μουσεῖον, became our *museum*.

epic poetry	**Calliope**
history	**Clio**
love poetry	**Erato**
song, elegy	**Euterpe**
tragedy	**Melpomene**
sacred poetry	**Polyhymnia**
dance	**Terpsichore**
comedy	**Thalia**
astronomy	**Urania**

The focus is on metrical poetry, with obvious extensions to music, dance, and theater. History slips in as the main 'none of the above'. Astronomy is an odd choice, not really explained by the fact that Thales wrote a book on astronomy in metrical form.

Calliope has a different meaning now— a deafening steam-powered musical instrument associated with the circus... an example of the gradual demotion of imaginative figures. The muse would be bemused.

Xurno, an Almean country actually ruled by artists, divides art into these categories, which also make up the major ministries of the government:

busumudo	poetry, including epics, oratory, philosophy
dzuzovugudo	drama
aujikalu	music
šukecudo	painting, drawing and enamelling
jadzudo	sculpture, including architecture
rimixau	weaving, including tapestry and clothes-making
cauč	dance
xeracudo	gymnastics

A major shakeup in Xurnese society was the agitation for a Salon of Prose (*gejupudo*). As an art form this includes what we would call the novel, but the real issue was whether art included scholarship, or science. (How many civil wars are conducted over issues of classification? Quite a few, actually, if you consider divisions based on religions and belief systems.)

Language arts

book OE *bóc* < 'beech'

• Gr βύβλος 'papyrus' < city exporting it • Lt *liber* < 'inner bark' • Latvian *grāmata* < 'writing' • Skt *grantha-* 'bundle'

brush Fr *brosse* '(broom made of) small twigs'

• Lt *pēniculus* dim. 'tail' • Sp *cepillo* dim. 'bough' • Rum *perie* < 'feathers'• Rus щётка 'bristle'

chapter Fr *chapitre* < Lt dim. 'head'

• Ch *zhāng* 'distinguished, display'

history Gk ἱστορία 'inquiry'

letter Lt *littera* 'grapheme', in plural 'message'

Grapheme: • Gk γράμμα < 'write' • Sw *bokstaf* 'book-staff' • Latvian *burts* 'magic symbol' • Ch *wén* 'grapheme' < 'soot'

Message: • Gk ἐπιστολή 'message' < 'sent to' • Sp *carta* < 'paper' • Sw *bref* < 'short' • Lith *laiškas* 'leaf' • Rus письмо 'writing' • Ch *xìn* 'something entrusted'

mystery Gk μυστήριον 'secret rite' < 'close (the eyes)'

• Ger *Geheimnis* 'secret, private' < 'house' • Ch *shén* 'spiritual'

page Lt *pāgina* < 'fixed'

• Gk σελίς 'deck, block' • Dutch *bladzijde* 'leaf-side'

perform Old Fr *perfourmer* < 'per' + either 'form' or 'furnish'

• Fr *exécuter* 'execute (a task)', *jouer* 'play (a role)'

play OE *pleʒan* 'move energetically'

read	OE *rǽdan* 'consider, make out, interpret' • ModGk διαβάζω 'carry across' • Lt *legere* 'pick up, gather' • OCS *čitati* 'read, count' • Ch *dú* < 'say aloud', *kàn* 'look'
record	Lt *recordārī* 'back to heart' • Fr *rapporter, noter* • Ch *lù* < 'carve'
scene	Gk σκηνή 'tent, stage'
stage	Old Fr *estage* 'standing place'
story	Gk ἱστορία 'inquiry' • Sp *cuento* < 'reckon' • Ch *gùshì* 'event-matter'
tale	OE *talu* ‖ 'speak', 'number'
write	OE *wrítan* 'score, write' • Gk γράφω 'scratch' • Lt *scrībere* < 'cut, carve' • Gothic *mēljan* 'mark' • OCS *pĭsati* < 'color, paint, adorn' • Ch *xiě* 'depict'
+	*poem, rhyme, alliteration, rhythm, chant, ballad, refrain, chorus, metaphor*
	proverb, maxim, oratory
	theater, comedy, tragedy, fantasy, romance, epic, myth
	pen, pencil, typewriter, ink, script
	essay, edit, translate, fiction, manifesto, newspaper, maga- zine

The oldest of art forms is surely **storytelling**, which requires only language and an audience capable of wondering what happens next. Adding meter gives you poetry and takes you close to music; divide out the roles and you have drama.

Words for **writing** reflect the physical technology, and tend to stick around even if the tech changes. E.g. in Germanic 'writing a book' meant carving on tablets of beechwood; in Sanskrit you were scratching on palm leaves; in Akkadia it meant pressing a stylus into wet clay. A *page* was originally a column within a scroll. In Latin you distinguished a *volūmen* (< 'roll') for a scroll, from a *cōdex* (< 'block of wood') for a set of attached pages— originally a joined set of wooden tablets. In French you still write with a feather (*plume*) on papyrus (*papier*) even if it's really a Bic on wood-pulp paper.

For **Verduria**, I divided literature into these genres:

pomäe	chronicle, myth, legend
racont	tale, story, account
šant	song

cevai	chant
ralinë	drama
kallogi	speech, oratory
onemu	treatise, essay, account, manual
curayora	argument, proof, discourse, manifesto

▸ For different approaches to poetry, see the *LCK*, p. 160.

In early work on Verdurian, I tried to create words for various **aesthetic** effects; I defined them using prototypes and associated words, such as:

gažë	Henrik Ibsen	*engagé*, involved, angry, reforming
paléty	Dorothy Parker	pathos, sadness, empathy
cümorge	Nietzsche	defiant, ridiculing, power-obsessed
ɖumäg	Jonathan Swift	*Weltschmerz*, misanthropic

I don't think the experiment was successful: it was hard to explain why these particular attitudes needed names, and providing etymologies was a headache. The better approach is through conworlding:

- We do have a word for satire like Swift's: *Swiftian*. So, invent some cultural figures who gave their names to a style, mannerism, or attitude.

- Artistic movements do have codewords, such as *engagé* above, a word describing the existentialist's choice to be involved in the world with other human beings. To create such terms you need to name some movements and consider their views, as well as what they're reacting against.

To put it another way, the magic in these words is not in their derivation (which tends to be simple— *Weltschmerz* = 'world-ache'), it's in the art and ideology behind them. And those in turn often respond to the historical context— e.g. an unsuccessful revolution may lead to feelings of alienation and disenchantment, or to a new radicalism.

Visual arts

draw	OE *draʒan* 'drag' > 'attract' > 'sketch'
	• Fr *dessiner* 'design' • Ch *huà* 'paint, figure'
picture	Lt *pictūra* 'painting'
	• Fr *tableau* 'panel' • Sp *cuadro* 'square' • Ger *Bild* poss. < 'fitting'
paint	Lt *pingere*, cognate to words meaning 'speckled, write, adorn'
	• Breton *liva* 'dye' • Ger *malen* < 'mark, spot' • Rus писать 'write' • Skt *likh-* 'scratch'

statue Lt *statua* < 'stand'

• Gk ἄμαλγα 'ornament' • Ir *dealbh* 'form' • Breton *skeudenn* 'shadow' • OE *manlīca* 'man-like' • Ger *Bildsäule* 'picture-pillar' • Rus изваяние 'carving' • Skt *pratimā-* 'measure against' • Ch *diāoxiàng* 'carve-likeness'

map Lt *mappa* 'tablecloth'

• Fr *carte* < 'paper' • Ger *Plan* • Ch *dìtú* 'earth-picture'

+ *chart, cartoon, film*

Japanese uses the same word (*kaku*) for 'write' and 'draw', while Mandarin *huà* (also the final syllable in Japanese *manga*) suffices for both 'draw' and 'paint'.

Painting can be classified by **medium**, for instance:

- Early paintings made heavy use of minerals, e.g. blue from copper oxides, black from soot, red from iron oxide. Greens and yellows were from plant products and faded, which is one reason some ancient art looks like it only uses earth tones.

- *Tempera*, which is egg yolk plus an acid such as vinegar or even beer. It's vivid and permanent, but dark colors and variations of shading are difficult.

- *Enamel*, which uses melted powdered glass— very expensive; dates back to ancient Egypt.

- *Fresco*, dating back to -15C Crete— painting on fresh plaster. The pigment bonds with the plaster and thus is very lasting.

- *Oils*, popularized in the 15C. The pigment is mixed directly with the oil, which allows a luminous transparency of color, a great range of hues, and fine shading.

- *Watercolor*, with water as the main medium, plus pigments and substances that add body.

- Modern substances such as *acrylic*.

It can be fun to work out a set of schools or **styles**, parallel to terrestrial terms such as *Pre-Raphaelite, Renaissance, baroque, rococo, Romantic, Impressionist, Cubist, Abstract Expressionist*. Some of this may just be fashion (e.g. a cycle of elaboration and minimalism), but consider also new technology (perspective; the invention of oil painting; the camera which changed artists' attitude toward realism) and contact with new cultures (as Western art was influenced in the 19C by Japanese styles, and in the early 20C by African).

Music

beat	OE *béatan*, uncertain
measure	Fr *mesure* < Lt *mētīrī* < IE, cognate to Gk μετρέω, OE *mæd*
meter	Gk μέτρον 'measure'
music	Gk μουσική 'of the Muse'
	• Ch *yuè* poss. ‖ 'joy'
note	Lt *nota* 'mark'
sing	OE *singan*
	• Gk ἀείδω ‖ 'sound' • ModG τραγουδῶ 'chant tragedy' • Lt *canere* < IE
+	*melody, lyrics, chord, harmony*

Instruments

Ethnomusicologists may use the Hornbostel-Sachs system, which classifies instruments by what is vibrating:

- *Idiophones*: the whole instrument

- *Membranophones*: a stretched membrane

- *Chordophones*: a string

- *Aerophones*: a column of air

The Western orchestra is traditionally divided into

woodwind	*flute, oboe, clarinet, bassoon, saxophone*
brass	*horn, trumpet, cornet, tuba*
percussion	*drum, timpani, bells, cymbals, tambourine*
strings	*violin, viola, cello, bass*
keyboard	*piano, organ, harpsichord*

You might also want words for the vocal ranges of singers, e.g. *soprano, alto, tenor, bass* in Western music. The male and female vocal ranges actually overlap somewhat, and of course how many divisions you make for each sex is arbitrary.

Performance spaces

David Byrne in *How Music Works* points out how the choice of performance space influences music. E.g. the Gregorian chant was performed in huge stone cathedrals, where notes linger and thus even the mildest dissonance sounds terrible. Polyphony and more adventurous intervals appeared when the performance space shifted to salons and concert halls. African music is traditionally performed outdoors, which acoustically favors percussion.

Scales and intervals

Music varies by culture, but the basics are provided by acoustics. If a note has frequency f, a note with frequency $2f$ is particularly harmonious—in fact we perceive it as the 'same note' an *octave* higher. E.g. if f is 220 Hz, the A below middle C, $2f$ = 440 Hz, the A above middle C.

The note $^3/_2 f$ goes well with both. In the A scale that gives us 330 Hz = E; the A-E *interval* is a *fifth*. The ratio $^4/_3$ is almost as consonant, giving us 293.3 Hz or D— a *fourth*. Medieval harmony relied heavily on octaves, fifths, and fourths.

The interval between E and D is $^3/_2 \div ^4/_3 = ^9/_8$ — a *tone*. The even closer $^{16}/_{15}$ is a *semitone*. We can now build the A major scale with the sequence *tone, tone, semitone, tone, tone, tone, semitone*:

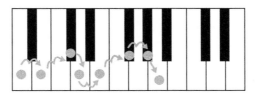

The keys on the keyboard are one semitone apart. If you apply the same pattern starting at C you'll find that you hit only the white keys.

The natural A minor scale is formed with *tone, semitone, tone, tone, semitone, tone, tone*— which also hits only white keys, but sounds much different:

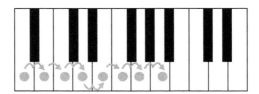

If you actually tune to these ratios, you're using *just temperament,* and you'll find that you have to retune your instrument when you change keys. This is awfully inconvenient for keyboardists, so it's perhaps not surprising that when the clavier became popular, there was a switch to *equal temperament,* where the semitone is defined as $\sqrt[12]{2}$ (about 1.05946) rather than $^{16}/_{15}$ (about 1.06667). Now D becomes 293.665 Hz. The ear is fooled and the keyboardist can play in any key.

Western scales are *heptatonic*— e.g. C major has 7 notes, C D E F G A B. To play all the keys you need to divide all the tones into semitones, thus the 12 keys on the keyboard, the basic of *dodecaphonic* or *12-tone* music.

English names the keys with letters, but French uses *ut ré mi fa sol la si*, from the first syllable of each line of a medieval hymn. German uses the letters as in English, except that *B* is our B-flat, and *H* is our B-natural.

There are lots of other ways to form scales. *Pentatonic* (five-note) scales are used worldwide, for instance. Some music uses smaller intervals than the semitone.

All this just touches the surface of music theory, of course, but it's a good start for conlanging.

ASTRONOMY

STAR	OE *steorra*, cognate to Lt *stēlla*, Gk ἀστήρ
	• Ir *réalta* 'bright thing' • Ch *xīng* poss. ‖ 'clear'
sun	OE *sunne*
	• Ir *grian* < 'heat' • Skt *ravi-* 'reddish' • Ch *tàiyáng* 'great-(sun)shine'
earth	OE *eorþe*
	• Lt *terra* < 'dried' • Rum *pamînt* 'floor' • Ir *talamh* < 'surface' • Skt *pṛthivī-* 'wide'
planet	Gk πλανήτης 'wanderer'
	• Ch *xíngxīng* 'walk-star'
moon	OE *móna* < IE 'measure'
	• Gk σελήνη 'brightness' • Lt *lūna* < 'light' • Pol *księżyc* dim. 'prince' • Skt *çaçin-* 'hare' (from its markings) • Ch *yuè* poss. ‖ 'white', 'clean'
cosmos	Gk κόσμος 'order, ornament', i.e. 'well-arranged place'
	• Ch *yuzhòu* 'space-eternity'
universe	Lt *ūniversum* 'whole world' < 'turned as one'
galaxy	Gk γαλαξίας 'milky'
	• Ch *yínhé* 'silver-river'
orbit	Lt *orbita* 'wheel track' < 'wheel, circle'
+	*constellation, nebula, comet, meteor*
	horizon, zenith, nadir
	equinox, solstice, eclipse, nova, opposition, conjunction

▸ For creating your solar system, see the PCK, p. 38.

For fantasy you don't need much more than *sun, moon, star, earth*. Most of the other terms above were created after the invention of the telescope, and are thus multisyllabic and Latinate. *Zenith* and *nadir* however are reminders of the advancement of the medieval Arabs.

If your culture has been trekking the spaceways for centuries, astronomy and astronavigation are everyday realities, and we can expect shorter and more informal words to develop— as with transport, where we say *car, bus, taxi, plane* in place of the earlier *automobile, omnibus, taximeter cabriolet, aeroplane.*

How do you name your **planets**? Once people actually live on them, they're not going to call them *Alpha Centauri A IV*. Westerners named the planets after gods, but the Chinese named them after elements (p. 183). If they were named when they were just points of light, relevant factors may be inner vs. outer planet, color, and brightness. If they're named by spacefarers, other facts may come into play: ring systems, size, composition, tidal locking, terrain types. If they have inhabitants, we can ask them for their name, but they're likely to have several!

Similarly, future societies need not define astronomical terms by how they look in the sky— e.g. like clouds (*nebulae*) or spilled milk (*galaxy*).

Naming the key locations in an **orbit** should be straightforward, except that we've created specialized terms for when the earth is one of the bodies involved— e.g. *apogee* for the farthest point in a satellite's orbit, and *perihelion* for when the earth is closest to the sun. Astronomers started making terms based on each celestial body— I think my favorite is *apomelasma* for an orbit round a black hole— but there's really no need for more than one root. The consensus seems to be to use *apoapsis* for the farthest point and *periapsis* for the nearest. (The other body, if massive enough, lies at one of the *foci* of the ellipse. More equal-massed bodies will have elliptical orbits round a common *barycenter*.)

The same pedantry threatens to give us *selenology, areology,* etc., but it's more accepted to call them all *geology.*

This comes from Greek γῆ, 'earth', but we should be clear about what was being referred to. Greek and Latin had four terms that were translated *world* in the KJV:

- γῆ, Lt *terra*, the earth (as opposed to the heavens). The goddess *Gaia* represents another form of this root.

- οἰκυμένη, the inhabited earth, Lt *orbis*, represented in the ecclesiastical term *ecumenical* (= *universal*).

- αἰών, a generation or era, Lt *saeculum*. As Christianity posited a new age, the present one became disreputable— thus the term *worldly.*

- κόσμος, the universe; Lt *mundus*.

All of these are frequently used in a demoted sense— John writes that all the κόσμος had gone after Jesus (7:19), when the meaning was only that quite a few had; when Jane Austen mentions "a truth universally acknowledged" she is not venturing even as far as the Moon.

Premodern people are of course not aware of being on a planet at all. Once they are, they have to name it. *Earth, Terra,* Russian земля, and Mandarin 地 *dì* refer to land or soil. *World* (like French *monde*) can refer to the Earth, but retains a more general sense, so that we can speak of *other worlds.* To a marine species the name of the planet might be *Ocean.*

In ancient societies, studying the stars helps you with your calendar as well as with navigation. Rain was all-important, so looking at the sky for clues to its intentions was natural; and when planets were given heavy symbolism their approaches could seem fraught with significance— leading to **astrology**. Planets were linked to temperaments (p. 274)— which gave people new descriptive terms for personality types, and for other things: a *constellation* was originally the configuration of the planets at one's birth; a *disaster* was an ominous astronomical event— a 'bad star'; *being in the ascendant* referred to which planet or sign of the zodiac was currently rising above the horizon.

The conjunction of weather and astronomy is neatly illustrated by the words *meteor* and *meteorology*. Both derive from Greek μετέωρον 'celestial phenomenon', itself from μετέωρος 'lifted up, lofty'.

The names for astronomical events are straightforward: *equinox* 'equal night' (i.e. equal to the day), *solstice* 'sun stands still' (as it's slowest then), *nova* 'new (star)', *eclipse* 'fail to appear'. For *eclipse* Mandarin has *shí*, originally 'eat'— the celestial body was being eaten by a monster.

THE BODY

ARM
OE *arm* < IE 'arm, joint'
- Gk βραχίων 'shorter' • Norse *handleggr* 'hand-bone' • Skt *bhuja-* 'bend' • Ch *gē* < 'armpit'

BACK
OE *bæc*
- ModGk ράχη < 'spine' • Lt *dorsum* poss. < 'turned down' • Sp *espalda* < 'shoulder' • Lith *nugara* 'mountain ridge' • Skt *pṛṣṭha-* 'stands out' • Ch *bèi* < 'carry on back'

BODY
OE *bodiȝ* prob. < 'tub'
- Gk σῶμα < 'swelling' • Dutch *lichaam* 'body-husk' • OCS *tělo* 'surface' • Skt *çarīra-* 'covering' • Ch *shēn* poss. < 'stretch out'

breast
OE *bréost* < 'swelling'
- Lt *mamma* < babytalk • Fr *sein* < 'fold' • Sp *teta* 'nipple' • OCS *sŭsĭcĭ* < 'suck' • Rus грудь < 'big, swell' • Ch *rŭ* < 'suckle' poss. < 'drink'

chest
Gk κίστη 'box, chest'
- Khmer *truuŋ* < 'shield'

finger
OE *finger* poss. < 'five'
- Lt *digitus* 'pointer' • Cz *prst* < 'stand forth' • Rus палец 'thumb' • Skt *aṅguli-* 'crooked'

fist
OE *fýst*
- Lt *pugnus* ‖ 'fight' • Ch *quàn* 'curled'

flesh
OE *flǽsc* poss. < 'split'
- Gk σάρξ < 'cut' • Lt *caro carn-* 'share' • OCS *plŭtĭ* 'covering, crust' • Ch *ròu* prob. < 'soft'

FOOT
OE *fót* < IE **ped-*, cognate to Lt *pēs ped-*, Gk πώς
- OCS *noga* < 'claw' • Skt *caraṅa-* '< 'move'

HAND
OE *hand* prob. < 'seize'
- Ir *lámh* 'palm' • Breton *dourn* 'fist' • OCS *rǫka* 'collect' • Ch *shŏu* poss. < 'taker'

knee
OE *cnéow*, cognate to Lat *genū*
- Sp *rodilla* dim. 'wheel' • Lith *kelys* 'leg' • Ch *xī* < 'joint'

leg
Norse *leggr* 'bone (of leg or arm)'
- Gk σκέλος 'bent' • It *gamba* 'hoof' • Sp *pierna* < 'ham' • Ger *Bein* 'bone' • Skt *jaṅghā-* < 'step' • Ch *tuĭ* 'thigh'

limb
OE *lim*

shoulder
OE *sculdur* < 'scapula'
- Fr *épaule* < dim. 'sword' • Ger *Achsel* 'shoulder joint' • Lith *petys* < 'flat' • Ch *jiān* ‖ 'arm'

skin
Norse *skinn*
- Gk δέρμα < 'tear' • Lt *pellis* < 'cover' • OCS *koža* 'goatskin'

wrist	OE *wrist*
	• Fr *poignet* < 'fist' • Sp *muñeca* < 'protuberance' • Ch *wàn* 'thing which bends'
+	*nipple, navel, waist, hip, abdomen*
	thumb, knuckle, palm, elbow
	thigh, calf, heel, sole, toe
	vulva, vagina, clitoris, penis, testicles, anus

Languages don't always agree on body part names.

- Quechua doesn't distinguish arm/hand (*maki*). Curiously it does distinguish leg/foot, while other languages don't— e.g. Russian нога is both.

- Spanish uses the same word (*dedo*) for fingers, thumbs, and toes. Russian палец covers both 'finger' and 'thumb'.

- We have names for the upper and lower leg (*thigh, calf*) and the lower arm (*forearm*), but not the upper arm.

- In French, a hair on your head is a *cheveu* (usually seen in the plural, *cheveux*); a hair elsewhere is a *poil*.

- Latin divides *breast* into *pectus* 'front of chest' and *mamma* 'mammary'.

- Japanese has separate words for the upper back (*senaka*) and the lower (*koshi*).

English terms for the **genitals** are all highly marked for register. The anatomical terms are simple descriptors in the original Latin: *vulva* 'wrapper', *vāgīna* 'sheath', *pēnis* 'tail', *labia* 'lips'. Slang terms are generally humorously disdainful (*rod, dick, snatch*), though there's also slightly ridiculous euphemisms (*member, manhood, pearl*).

Word for the genitals don't *have* to be derived— so far as I can see Quechua *raka* 'vagina' and *lani* 'penis' are basic roots just like *simi* 'mouth' or *sinqa* 'nose'.

The head

cheek	OE *céace* 'jaw, cheek'
	• Lt *bucca* < 'blow' • Ir *pluc* 'lump' • Ger *Wange* < 'curve' • Cz *líce* 'face'
ear	OE *éare* < IE **aus-*, cognate to Lt *auris*, Gk οὖς
	• Farsi *goš* < 'hear'

EYE OE *éaʒe* < IE *okw-, cognate to Lt *oculus*
- Ir *súil* 'sun' • Rus. глаз < 'ball' • Avestan *dōiθra-* < 'see' • Ch *yăn* < 'knob, bulge'

FACE Fr < Lt *facies* 'appearance, form'
- Fr *visage* 'seeing' • OCS *lice* 'cheek' • Rum *obraz* < 'form'

forehead OE *forhéafod* 'fore head'
- Gk μέτωπον 'between' • Danish *pande* 'pan' • Ger *Stirn* < 'spread out' • OCS *čelo* 'rise, hill' • Ch *é* < 'face, confront'

hair OE *hǽr*
- Ch *tóufa* 'head-growth'

HEAD OE *héafod*
- Lt *caput*, Gk κεφαλή < 'head, bowl' • Fr *tête* < 'pot' • OCS *glava* 'bald' • Ch *tóu* poss. < 'skull'

lip OE *lippa*
- Breton *muzell* 'muzzle' • Lith *lūpa* 'hanging flesh' • OCS *ustĭna* dim. 'mouth' • Rus губа < 'swelling' • Ch *chún* < 'rim'

mouth OE *múþ* prob. < 'chin'
- Gk στόμα 'muzzle' • It *bocca* < 'cheek' • Lith *burna* < 'opening' • Rus рот < 'projection' • Skt *vadana-* < 'speak' • Ch *kŏu* poss. < 'hollow'

neck OE *hnecca* 'nape'
- Lt *collum* < 'round' • Rum *gît* 'throat' • OE *swíra* < 'column' • Farsi *gardan* 'turn'

nose OE *nosu* < IE *nas-, cognate to Lt *nāsus*
- * ModGk μύτη < 'cuttlefish snout' • Skt *ghrāṇa-* < 'smell'

throat OE *þrote* < 'swelling'
- Lt *gula* < 'swallow' • Gk σφαγή 'narrow' • Sp *garganta* imitative • Ch *hóu* poss. ‖ 'neck'

tongue OE *tunge* < IE *dṇghwā-, cognate to Lt *lingua*
- Gk γλῶσσα poss. 'pointy' • Ch *shé* ‖ 'lick'

tooth OE *tóþ* < IE *dont-, cognate to Lt *dens dent-*, Gk ὀδών
- OCS *zǫbŭ* 'tooth, bolt, tusk'

+ *chin, jaw, beard, moustache, eyelash; bald, shave*

Japanese *ago* encompasses both the chin and jaw, and *hige* is both beard and moustache.

In English the region between the nose and mouth can be called the *upper lip*; this sounds strange to the Japanese, who call it *hana no shita*, the area 'under the nose'.

Yidiɲ has *yaniŋ* for the side of the face, between the eye and ear.

Body part words seem inordinately prone to metonymy. I don't think Romance speakers actually confused the cheek and mouth; *bocca* must have been jocular, though the joke kind of eludes me.

There are complexities in the use of body part words that are so common we hardly notice them. The *eye* is the eyeball, right? But if your eyes are *blue*, that refer to the iris only; if your eyes are *slanted* it refers the shape of the eyelids; and someone with a *good eye* is being complimented on their vision. A *large mouth* means something different to a painter and to a dentist.

We all have the same eyes, but what we *notice* depends on culture. Takao Suzuki points out (in *Words in Context*) that Turkish writers describing pretty girls concentrate on the features that would not be hidden by a veil— even when they are describing modern women who don't wear one. E.g., from Ömer Seyyfetin:

> She is the most beautiful girl in Istanbul! Large shiny dark eyes...
> Rich, soft black hair... And incredible fair skin with pure, dream-
> like whiteness.

Suzuki goes on to note that Japanese writers describing a face unfailingly mention the nose, while Europeans often omit it. Europeans also deduce character from the shape of the chin or jaw— weak, determined, aggressive— while the Japanese simply describe the shape.

Animals

claw	OE *clawu*
	• Fr *griffe* < 'scratch' • Ch *zhuā* < 'grasp'
egg	OE *ǽʒ* < IE *ōwo, poss. ‖ 'bird' (cf. Lt *ōvum, avis*)
	• Latvian *uola* 'pebble' • Lith *kiaušis* dim. 'skull'
fur	Fr *fourrure* 'lining (of a garment)' > source of the lining
	• It *pelliccia* 'of skins' • Dutch *bont* < 'multicolored' • Rus мех < 'leather sack' • Cz *kožešina* 'hide' • Norse *loð-* 'hairy' • Ch *máo* 'hair'
hide	OE *hýd*, cognate to Lt *cutis*
scale	Norse *skál* 'bowl'
tail	OE *tægl* < 'fringe, hair'
	• Gk οὐρά < 'stand out' • Sp *rabo* 'turnip' • Welsh *cynffon* 'hind-staff' • Danish *hale* 'shaft' • Ger *Schwanz* 'swing'
wing	Norse *vængr* < 'blow, flutter'
	• Gk πτέρυξ < 'feather' • Lt *āla* 'arm joint' • Ger *Flügel* < 'fly' • OCS *krilo* 'go in a circle'

+   *beak, bill, feather, fin, hoof, horn, mane, tusk*

In Indonesian, *bulu* means both feathers and fur. Latin *penna* serves for both 'feather' or 'wing' (but is commonly pluralized for the latter).

Czech *kůže* is 'skin, hide, leather', but doesn't cover the skin of fruit (*slupka*).

The same body part may have a different name for **animals**:

- A Spanish speaker's leg is a *pierna*; her dog's leg is a *pata*. French makes the same distinction— *jambe / patte*— except that horses have *jambes* too! *Pata/patte* also cover 'paw'...though in Spanish predators known for their claws, like lions, have *zarpas*.

- In French, the mouth is *bouche*, but for animals *gueule*.

- The *udder* is usually distinct from the *breast,* though Greek μαστός could be used for both. English *teat* is now restricted to animals.

Body part names can be applied to other species by analogy, but often, for whatever reason, names are changed— e.g. apparently the trunk of an elephant seems too different from a *nose* to be called that. We call the closing parts of an insect's mouth *mandibles,* perhaps to underline the oddness of their closing horizontally rather than vertically.

If your conlang's speakers are **non-human**, obviously the basic body part names should be based on their anatomy rather than ours. Note that the 'back' of a quadrupedal creature is really the top surface!

Organs and substances

blood   OE *blód* poss. < 'burst out'
                    • OCS *krŭvĭ* < 'raw' • Ir *fuil* 'wound' • Skt *rakta-* 'red'

bone   OE *bán* uncertain
                    • Ger *Knochen* 'knuckle' • Lith *kaulas* 'long hollow thing'

fat   OE *fǽtt* < Germanic 'fattened'
                    • Fr *graisse* < 'thick'

heart   OE *heorte* < IE *ǩerd-*
                    • Rum. *inimă* < 'soul' • Ch *xīn* ‖ 'life', 'mind'

muscle   Lt *músculus* dim. 'mouse'

shit   OE (unattested, but supported by cognates)
                    • Lt *cacāre* < babytalk, *merda* prob. < 'stink' • ModGk σκατά < 'separate' • Welsh *tom* < 'mound' • Danish *møg* 'soft' • Rus кал 'mud' • Sw *dynga* < 'cover' > 'fertilize'

stomach	Gk στόμαχος 'throat' < 'mouth'
	Gk κοιλία 'hollow' • Ger *Magen* < 'bag-like object' • Latvian *pazirds* 'under-heart'
sweat	OE *swætan* < IE, cognate to Lt *sūdor*
	• Rum. *nqduşi* 'swelter' < 'no breath' • OCS *potŭ* < 'hot'
tear	OE *téar* < IE, cognate to Lt *lacrima*, Gk δάκρυ
	• Ch *lèi* < 'flowing thing'
+	*liver, lungs, womb, kidney, brain, intestines*
	skeleton, skull, rib, spine, pelvis
	spit, snot, urine, semen, fart, menstruation

Many languages use the same word for 'belly' and 'womb', e.g. OE *innoþ*, OCS *črĕvo*, Skt *jaṭhara-*.

Bones and organs are often named for nearby parts (*femur* 'upper thigh', *humerus* 'shoulder') or for their shape (*clāvicula* 'little key', *pelvis* 'basin', *mūsculus* 'little mouse'). An ancient or prestige language, if you have one, is good for learned or euphemistic terms.

Primitive humans were presumably familiar with internal organs more from animals than from their own bodies. In any case, organs and body parts also serve as names for cuts of **meat**— e.g. *sirloin* = 'above the loins'. OE *hamm* 'back of the knee' developed into *ham* 'salted dried pig thigh'.

Extensions

The basic **directions** or **surfaces** may be named from body parts— *side, back, bottom*. *Front* derives from the Latin for 'forehead'.

Names of body parts make good starting points for **clothing** or armor— e.g. *leggings, breastplate, bracers* and *brassiere* (from French *bras* 'arm'), *collar* (< Fr 'neck'), German *Handschuh* 'hand-shoe' for 'glove'.

The word for *tongue* can be used for *language*; Quechua uses 'mouth' (*simi*) instead.

These terms are also liberally applied to other objects, sometimes rather loosely: chairs have *legs* though old-style bathtubs only have *feet;* pliers have *teeth;* bottles, lakes, and guitars have *necks*. The OED lists no less than fourteen mechanical or architectural uses of *throat*.

In Xurnese, I used body parts for the ranks of the **army**; see *Military Ranks*, p. 386. **Numbers** are often based on body parts; see p. 287.

Bodily actions

FEEL	OE *félan* 'handle, touch' > 'perceive', prob cognate to Lt *palpāre*
	• Gk ψηλαφάω < 'pluck' • Sw *känna* < 'know, perceive'
gesture	Late Lt *gestūra* 'carrying'
	• Ger *Gebärde* < 'conduct' • Ch *shŏushì* 'hand-power'
hang	OE *hón*
kick	ME *kike* uncertain
lay	OE *lecgan*
lean	OE *hleonian*
	• Fr *pencher* < 'hang' • Sp *inclinarse* < 'bend down'
POINT	Lt *pūnctum* 'pricking, dot, point'
	• Fr *montrer* 'show' • Sp *señalar* 'signal'
reach	OE *rǽcan*
	• Fr *atteindre* 'stretch to'
rest	OE *ræstan*
	• Fr *se reposer* < 'put back' • Sp *descansar* 'de-tire' • Ch *xiū* poss. < 'shade'
shrug	ME uncertain
	• Sp *encogerse de hombros* 'shrink shoulders' • Ger *Schulterzucken* 'shoulder-jerk' • Ch *sŏngjiān* 'high shoulder'
SIT	OE *sittan* < IE *sed-*, cognate to Lt *sidēre*, OCS *sěděti*
STAND	OE *standan* < IE *stā-*, cognate to Lt *stāre*, OCS *stojati*
touch	Fr *toucher* < 'knock', imitative
	• ModGk αγγίζω 'approach' • Welsh *cyffwrdd* 'push with' • Dutch *aanraken* 'hit' • Ger *berühren* 'move' • Rus трогать prob. < 'snatch' • Ch *chù* 'knock against'
+	*slap, scratch, caress, hug*

▸ See also *Movement,* p. 276 and *Possession,* p. 308.

The prototype for actions, and thus for verbs, are the things the body can do.

Humans are unusual among placental mammals in being particularly helpless at birth— infants have to learn how their body works and how it interacts with the world.

Like the body part names, these words are extremely fruitful for metaphors. The positional words can be used as locatives for just about anything; the limb actions can be used for anything that moves.

We use *feel* for both the sense of touch and for emotions, but these are different in French (*tâter* vs. *éprouver*).

See p. 91 for why *stand* is almost the only word you need.

English uses *sit, stand, lie* directly for both a change in state and a position, though it can use the progressive for the latter *(be sitting)*; French prefers different verbs:

sit	*s'asseoir*	*être assis*
stand	*se lever*	*être debout*
lie	*se coucher*	*gésir, être allongé*

Mouth/breath/eyes

blink	ME uncertain
	• Fr *cligner* poss. < 'close'
blow	OE *bláwan* < IE imitative, cognate to Lt *flāre* > Fr *souffler*
	• Gk πνέω 'breathe'
breath	OE *bráp* 'odor, smell'
	• Lt *spīrāre* imitative • Fr *souffle* < 'blow' • Latvian *elpe* < 'weak, faint' • Ch *hūxī* 'exhale-inhale'
faint	Fr *feint* 'feigned' > 'sluggish, spiritless' > 'weak'
	• Ger *schwach* 'powerless' < 'swaying' • Ch *hūn* 'dark'
frown	Old Fr *froignier* uncertain
	• Ch *zhòuméi* 'wrinkled-brow'
gasp	Norse *geispa* 'yawn'
glare	Middle Dutch *glaren* < 'gray'
grin	OE *grin*
hiss	ME imitative
kiss	OE *cyssan*, imitative
	• ModGk φιλῶ < 'love' • Lt *osculārī* 'little mouth' • Fr *embrasser* 'embrace' • Irish *pōgaim* < 'peace' • OCS *lobŭzati* < 'lick' • Rus целовать < 'greet' • Ch *wěn* '(close) lips'
laugh	OE *hlehhan* < Germanic **klak-*, imitative
	• Lith *juoktis* < 'joke' • Pol *śmiać się* < IE 'laugh, smile' • Ch *xiào* poss. < 'belittle'
nod	ME uncertain
sigh	past tense of OE *sícan*
	• Fr *soupirer* 'under-breathe'

smile	ME *smīlen* < apparently Low German < IE, cognate to Skt *smi-*
	• Fr *sourire* < 'under-laugh' • Rum *zîmbi* < '(show) teeth' • Breton *mousc'hoarzin* 'mask a laugh'
swallow	OE *swelӡan*
+	*yawn, bite, chew, sneeze, drool, choke, vomit, swallow, cough, suck, spit, whistle, snore*

▸ See also *Speech*, p. 338.

Strangely for English speakers, languages often use the same word, or close variants, for *laugh/smile*.

As the least perceptible material associated with life, *breath* is the natural metaphor for the soul— *spirit, psyche,* and Hebrew *ruakh* are all formed this way. Chinese 气 *qì* is also associated with breath, but in metaphorical form it's a kind of life force that courses through the body (p. 244).

Mouth actions can be recycled for machinery, pipes, or any sort of opening or consumption. E.g. the wind *blows,* acid *eats away* substances; a *soufflé* is 'blown up'.

Neat fact: your lips are red because they're an extension of the lining of your mouth.

Drives

(a)wake	OE *wacian* < IE 'lively, vigorous'
	• Pol *czuwać* 'feel, notice' • Welsh *dihuno* 'un-sleep' • OCS *buditi* < 'perceive, be conscious' • Ch *xǐng* < 'sober, clean'
hunger	OE *hungor* ‖ Lith *kanka* 'pain'
	• Gk λῑμός < 'waste away' • Ir *gorta* < 'burn' • OCS *gladŭ* < 'desire' • Qu *mikuymanta* '(away) from food' • Ch *è* ‖ 'fast'
sex	Lt *sexus* poss < 'cut' = 'a division'
	• Gk γένος 'kin, race' • OCS *polŭ* 'half' • Pol *płeć* 'flesh' • Ch *xìng* 'nature, property'
(a)sleep	OE *slápan* < 'weak, loose'
	• Ir *codail* 'be still' • Ch *shuì* prob. < 'droop'
tire	OE *tíorian* 'fail, weaken, weary'
	• Gk κάμνω 'toil' • Lt *fatīgāre* < 'enough' • Sp *cansar* < 'turn aside' • Cz *mdlý* < 'slow' • Rus уставать < 'cease' • Ch *lèi* ‖ 'weak, faded'
+	*thirst, sated*

▸ See also *Sex*, p. 327.

Hunger and thirst, especially, are used for any kind of desire. Conversely, *lust* once just meant 'desire' but has specialized to one type of it.

Cajun French distinguishes *échiné* 'tired from lack of sleep' from *lasse* 'tired from exertion'.

BUILDINGS

Like clothing, architecture immediately gives away location in time and space. Although you presumably wouldn't put a strip mall into a medieval kingdom, it's easy to create other anachronisms, like dividing a keep into modern living and dining rooms, or decorating the tables with knife, fork, and spoon.

The city

arch
Fr *arche* < Lt 'curve'
• Ger *Bogen* 'bow' • Ch *gǒng* < 'join the hands'

block
Fr *bloc* < Germanic

bridge
OE *brycg* < 'beam'
• Gk γέφῡρα 'dam, dyke' • Lt *pons pont-* < 'path' • Lith *tiltas* < 'ground' • Ch *qiáo* < 'cross-bar'

CITY
Fr *cité* < Lt *cīvitas cīvitāt-* 'body of citizens'
• Gk ἄστυ < 'dwelling' • Lt *urbs* poss. 'enclosure' • Fr *ville* < 'villa' • OE *burg* 'fortress' • Sw *stad* 'place' • OCS *gradu* < 'yard' • Ch *chéngshì* 'wall-market'

gate
OE ʒeat 'opening'
• Lt *porta* < 'passage' • OCS *vrata* 'shut' • Cz *brána* 'defense' • Ch *dàmén* 'big door'

road
OE *rád* 'act of riding' > 'course'
• Gk ὁδός < 'walk' • Lt *via* poss. < 'seek' • Fr *route* < 'broken' • Rus дорога < 'drawn out' • Skt *mārga-* 'animal (path)'

square
Old Fr *esquare* < 'make square' < Lt *quattuor* 'four
• Gk τετράγωνον 'four-cornered' • Ir *cearnóg* < 'corner' • Sw *fyrkant* 'four-edge' • Ch *fāng* 'side, region'

street
Lt (*γia*) *strāta* 'paved way' < 'laid down'
• Gk ἄγυια 'leading' • Fr *rue* < 'wrinkle' • Sp *calle* < 'path' • Rus улица < 'opening' • Skt *rathyā-* 'chariot (way)' • Ch *xiàng* poss. < 'village'

town
OE *tún* 'enclosure'
• Danish *by* < 'dwell' • Ch *yì* prob. < 'shelter'

tunnel
Old Fr *tonel* 'cask' > 'type of net' > 'tube, passage'

village
Lt *villāticum* 'of a villa'
• Lt *vīcus* 'dwelling' • Sp *pueblo* 'people' • Rum *sat* < 'moat' • Ger *Dorf* < 'field' • Skt *grāma-* 'community' • Ch *lǐ* < 'fence'

+
port, neighborhood, alley, sewer, forum, plaza, courtyard, cemetary, park

For basics on cities, see the *PCK* p. 114. Recall that for most of history, a place with 10,000 inhabitants was a very respectable city.

Our neat size distinction *city/town/village* is largely accidental; French does just fine with *ville* for both *city* and *town*. *Ville* derives from Latin *villa* 'country house'; a *village* is just a collection of villas. That the French word for 'city' derives from a small rural settlement suggests how far post-Roman Europe declined from urbanization.

We misread Greek history, making it seem much more urban than it was, by taking πόλις as 'city'; it was really a small state— the dense settlement that was its capital was an ἄστυ. Latin *cīvitas* was the citizenry, the community of *cīvēs* 'citizens', thus parallel to πόλις; it only later came to be 'city'. Mandarin *chéngshì* 'wall-market' neatly captures two of the major purposes of a city, trade and protection; the latter is also at the root of *town*.

Ancient Greek colonists referred to the *metropolis* the 'mother country'; the word came to mean 'capital or chief city' and in modern times 'very large city'.

Largely by borrowing, we've accumulated a wide variety of names for types of **streets**. *Boulevard* has an interesting history; it meant 'rampart' (in Germanic form *bulwark*), and was applied to the promenades created when Paris's walls were torn down, and then to similar large streets. In Manhattan *avenues* are north/south and *streets* are east/west; in St. Petersburg, Florida, it's the reverse; Chicago is a mess.

A *road* is generally a route outside the city (though particular roads may retain the term after being engulfed by city sprawl). Compare German *Straße* which can be used for any paved road or street.

Types of buildings

bath	OE *bæð*
home	OE *hám;* cognates often refer to people, e.g. Latvian *saime* 'household'
hotel	Fr *hôtel* < 'hospital' < Lt 'of guests'
HOUSE	OE *hús* poss. < IE 'cover'
	• Lt *domus* < 'build' • Gk οἶκος < 'settlement' • Sp *casa* < 'hut' • Fr *maison* < 'staying' • Ir *teach* < 'cover' • Bulgarian *kŭšta* < 'tent' • Ch *fáng* 'room'
office	Lt *officium* 'doing before' = 'service, duty'
	• Fr *bureau* 'desk' • Ru контора 'counting house' • Ch *bàngōngshì* 'manage-public-room'
palace	Lt *Palātium* 'Palatine hill' > Augustus's mansion there

prison Fr *prison* < 'seizing'
  • Gk εἰκτή 'shutting in' • Fr *geôle* < dim. 'cage' • Latvian *cietums* < 'hard' • OCS *temĭnica* 'darkness' • Rus тюрма < 'tower' • Ch *yŭ* ‖ 'control'

station Lt *statio* 'standing'

tower Lt *turris*
  • OE *stépel* < 'lofty' • Pol *wieża* < 'tent(-shaped)'

+ *tent, hut, shed, cabin, apartment, shelter*

What **buildings** exist depends on the type of society.

• Where civic life is a priority, as in ancient Rome, you'll get stadiums, agoras, theaters, baths.

• You'll only get shops, inns, and workshops when there's a market economy. In medieval Europe most craftsmen worked in their home; they rarely had enough goods for a showroom, but sold items from their front windows, or from a stall out front.

• A city could get by without walls only in a very secure realm, such as early Imperial Rome or Persia.

• It wasn't till the 1800s that factories dominated the cityscape; huge stores appeared in the later half of the century.

If you're looking to fill out a map, consider:

• Government: *palace, castle, office, prison, ministry, customs house, archives, constablery*

• Cultural: *scriptorium, forum, library, school, academy, university, monument, theater, museum, concert hall*

• Religious: *church, temple, monastery, shrine, cemetary*

• Recreational: *bath, pool, tavern, inn, hotel, restaurant, brothel, arena, stadium, race track, park, garden, gambling den, opium den*

• Infrastructure: *port, warehouse, stable, railroad station, airport, spaceport, aqueduct, reservoir, fountain, sewer, hospital*

• Commercial: *market, shop, bank, brokerage, factory, brewery, mill, department store, tannery*

The house

corridor It *corridore* 'place to run (between buildings)'

ceiling	ME < Lt 'make a canopy', either from 'chisel' or 'sky'
	• Fr *plafond* 'flat base' • Sp *techo* 'roof' < 'covered' • Ch *tiānhuābiǎn* 'sky-flower-plank'
cell	Lt *cella* 'small room'
chamber	Fr *chambre* 'room' < Lt *camera* 'vault, arched roof'
DOOR	OE *duru*, cognate to OCS *dvĭrĭ*, Lt *foris*
	• Fr *porte* < 'gate' < 'passage' • Ch *mén* 'gate' ‖ 'mouth'
floor	OE *flór* < 'flat'
	• Lt *pavīmentum* 'beaten down' • Fr *plancher* 'board' • Sp *suelo* 'ground' • Ger *Boden* 'bottom' • Ch *dìbǎn* 'earth-slab'
hall	OE *heall* 'large roofed area' > 'lobby, passage'
kitchen	Lt *coquīna* nomn. of 'cook'
roof	OE *hróf*
	• Lt *tectum* 'covered' • Ir *ceann* 'head' • Cz *střecha* < 'prepare, build' • Qu *wasi-pata* 'roof top' • Ch *wū* ‖ 'house'
ROOM	OE *rúm* 'space'
	• Fr *chambre* < 'vaulted roof' • It *stanza* 'standing place' • Sp *cuarto* '¼' • Ger *Zimmer* 'timber', *Stube* 'heated room', cf. *stove* • Rus комната 'with fireplace' • Ch *shì* 'house'
stair	OE *stǽʒer* 'climber'
	• Fr *marche* < 'walk' • Sp *escalón* < 'ladder' • Ch *tī* 'ladder'
step	OE *steppan*
	• Fr *pas* < 'stretched' • Ch *bù* ' go, walk'
WALL	Lt *vallum* 'palisade wall'
	• Lt *mūrus* cognate to Skt *mi-* 'build' • Sw *vägg* < 'woven' • OCS *stěna* < 'stone' • Skt *prākāra-* 'front-shape' • Ch *chéng* < 'build'
window	Norse *vindauga* 'wind-eye'
	• Gk θυρίς dim. 'door' • Sp *ventana* 'wind' • OCS *okno* 'eye' • Skt *jāla-* 'net' > 'latticework'
+	*attic, basement, closet, vestibule, balcony, foundation*

For most of history, families generally lived in a room or two. Roman houses, at least for the well off, had small bedrooms, or sometimes just niches for beds. There was little sense of privacy; if you were wealthy, your house would be filled with a scrum of relatives, servants, and hangers-on. (Galileo borrowed the Latin term for the latter, *satellitēs*, for the moons of Jupiter.)

In medieval England you slept in the *bower* and did everything else in the *hall*. It wasn't till Renaissance times that single-purpose rooms became common. In aristocratic homes, husbands and wives often had separate rooms; the *boudoir* literally is a room to sulk in (*bouder*).

Though words like *room, house,* and *window* are almost universal, recall that the prototypes differ. Not all houses are separate; not all rooms are square; not all windows have glass. Doors may not be rectangular; in fact the Semitic letter D ▷ seems to have received its name and sound from the word *delet* 'door'; the letter is an icon of a triangular tent-flap. The hobbits' round windows and doors were picturesque but must have required sophisticated joinery.

In earlier English a *house* could be almost any kind of building (*work-house, public house (> pub), lighthouse, House of Parliament*); in modern usage it's generally restricted to residences.

German distinguishes the wall of a house (*Wand*) from that of a city (*Mauer*).

In Japanese, if you can stand on a roof it's an *okujō*, otherwise a *yane.* Swedish *tak* covers both 'roof' and 'ceiling'.

Outside Germanic, it's rare to have separate words for *house* and *home,* though there may be special expressions for *at home* (It *a casa,* Lith *namie,* Ir *ag baile*).

As we'll see under *Kinship,* p. 225, words for *house* are easily extended to the people living in the house (our *household*).

Furniture

bed	OE *bedd* < IE 'dug out' • Lt *lectus* < 'lie' • Lith *lova* 'board' • Rus постель < 'spread out'
chair	Gk καθέδρα 'down-sit' • Lt *sella* < 'sit' • OE *stól* < 'something set up' • Rum *scaun* < 'stool' • Lith *kréslas* 'armchair' < 'wooden frame'
curtain	Old Fr *cortine* uncertain
desk	late Lt *desca* 'table, platform' < Gk δίσκος 'heavy metal disk' • Fr *bureau* < 'tablecloth' • Sp *escritorio* 'writing place' • Ch *shūzhuō* 'book-table'
seat	Norse *sǽti* nomn. of 'sit'
table	Lt *tabula* 'board, tablet' • Gk τράπεζα 'four-footed' • Lt *mensa* 'measured' > 'portion' • Ger *Tisch* 'dish' • Rus стол < 'chair' • Ch *zhuō* 'high'
+	*bench, couch, stool, cradle, shelf, bathtub, toilet, stove, sink, refrigerator* *mattress, sheet, blanket, pillow, tapestry, carpet*

▸ See also *Containers,* p. 167.

Naming furniture, first ask whether there is any. The Southeast Asian style (also found in traditional Japan) is to keep the house empty. You sat or knelt on the floor, so no chairs were necessary. Even today, it's common in Japan to put out mattresses at night and put them away during the day.

A curious lexical gap in English is that we have no word for *a piece of furniture*. French does: *meuble,* etymologically a 'moveable'.

The simplest work surface is a flat board, which is the meaning of Latin *tabula,* which gave us *table* and *tablet.* There was also *mensa* 'table', which was extended to the activity associated with it, a 'meal'. A moneychanger worked at a table, so he was a *mensārius.* English *board* could also be used for furniture: *sideboard, cupboard.* Like *mensa* it was applied to food, as in *room and board.*

The Germanic **bankiz* must have originally been just a long board with supports; at a low height it could be sat on and gave us *bench*; a higher one was a work surface and (with a digression into Romance) gave us *bank.*

Naming furniture, the obvious method is to think about the function (sleeping, sitting, eating, etc.). Diminutives come in handy in differentiating sizes (*tablet, cabinet*). As always, functional etymologies may be obscured by borrowing (*couch* < Fr. 'lay down', *wardrobe* = 'guard clothing').

Toilet-related terms are likely to be euphemisms. *Chamberpot* is nicely generic. A *toilet* was originally a small cloth, then a dressing room, then the *lavatory* ('washing place'). Americans speak of the *bathroom,* causing confusion in England where the bathtub and toilet may be in separate rooms.

Americans love their *closets* ('small closed (area)'), but that's because we have too damn much stuff. In earlier times people used cupboards and chests, which kept the floor plan simple.

CLOTHING

belt
OE *belt* < Lt *balteus* 'belt, girdle'
- Gk ζώνη < 'gird' • Rum *curea* 'strap' • OE *gyrdel* poss < 'surround' • Ch *dài* < 'circumference'

boot
Fr *bote,* uncertain
- Lt *pēro pērōn-* < 'leather sack' • It *stivale* < 'pipe' • Breton *heuz* < 'stocking' • Dutch *laars* 'leather-stocking'

cloak
late Lt *clocca* 'bell-shaped (robe)' (verb: 'wear a cloak' > 'cover' > 'hide')
- Lt *toga* < 'cover' • OCS *plasti* 'sheet, layer' • OE *fel* 'hide' • Welsh *cochl* < 'hood'

cloth
OE *çlaþ* 'wrapping cloth', poss. < 'felting'
- Lt *textum* 'woven' • Fr *étoffe* < 'coarse fibers' • Dutch *laken* < 'loose' • OCS *sukno* 'spun' • Ch *liào* 'measure'

clothes
OE *cláðas* original plural of 'cloth'
- Lt *vestis* < IE **wes-* 'clothe, cover, wear' • It *abito* < 'have' • Sp *ropa* < 'booty' • ModE *garment* 'equipment' • Ir *éadach* < 'clothe' • Lith *drabužis* < 'rag' • Bulgarian *halina* < 'carpet'

coat
Fr *cote,* uncertain
- Gk χιτών < 'linen garment' • It *giacchetta* < 'coat of mail' • Sp *saco* 'sack' • Pol *surdut* < Fr 'over-all' • Skt *kañcuka-* 'bound' • Ch *shàngyī* 'over-clothes'

dress
Fr *dresser* < Lt 'direct' > 'make ready' > 'wear clothes' (> noun 'robe')
- Gk ἐνδύω 'enter in' • Fr *habiller* 'prepare' • Lith *apgerbti* < 'honor' > 'adorn' • OCS *oděti* 'put about' • Pol. *ubrać* 'put by' • Ch *chuān* 'pierce'

fashion
Fr *façon* < Lt 'doing, making'
- Fr *mode* 'manner' • Ch *liúxíng* 'prevail, spread'

hat
OE *hæt* < 'cover'
- Gk πέτασος 'spread out' • late Lt *cappa* 'head covering' • Sp *sombrero* 'shader'

naked
OE *nacod* < IE **nogʷ-*, cognate to Lt *nūdus,* Gk γυμνός
- Ir *lom* 'peeled' • OCS *golŭ* 'bald' • Ch *luŏ* poss. < 'red'

rag
Norse *rogg* 'strip of fur'
- Fr *chiffon* < 'piece' ‖ *chip* • Sp *trapo* < 'cloth' • Ch *mābù* 'wipe-cloth'

robe
Fr < Germanic 'booty'
- Ger *Talar* < '(to) the ankles' • Ch *zhì* < 'cut'

strip
ME *strippen* < Low German

WEAR
OE *earian*
- Fr *porter* 'carry' • Ch *chuān* < 'perforate'

wrap
ME *wrappe* uncertain

+ *sleeve, collar, shirt, blouse, pants, skirt, glove, shoe, stocking, sandal, poncho, loincloth, veil*

sew, spin, loom, weave, pin, needle, thread, dye

linen, cotton, silk, lace, leather, wool, velvet, hemp

In Japanese, the word for 'wear' depends on the garment. If you put it on your legs and feet it's *haku*; if it hangs from the shoulders it's *kiru* (*kimono* just means 'draped thing'); if it's a hat it's *kaburu*.

Similarly, Czech has different word for putting on or removing shoes (*obléknout si / svléknout si*) and other clothing (*obout si / zout si*).

Clothing is one of the most distinctive features of a civilization; a glance at clothes immediately conveys details of location, epoch, sex, class, and climate. So think twice about simply providing equivalents for all the English words!

See the *PCK* p. 169 for an introduction to cloth, clothes-making, and clothing types. Some questions to keep in mind:

- What are the sources of cloth? Which are cheap? Before the machine era, thin, close-woven fabrics were tedious to make and thus likely to be expensive.

- How much clothing is required? Not all lands are temperate.

  Extremes don't always behave as one might expect. E.g. in the desert heat, it's *cooler*, not warmer, to have a few layers. The long white robes of Arabs reflect the sun and trap cooler air near the body.

- Are there additional requirements of modesty? Recall that cultures don't always agree with Americans that the breasts and groin are the must-cover parts of the body.

- How much sex differentiation is there? Recall that female clothing is not always based on the dress. The contemporary West is historically unusual in relegating bright colors and ornamentation to women.

- Western fitted clothing is fairly complex (and wasteful of cloth). Wrapped or draped clothes are simpler and thus more characteristic of primitive technology.

- What's the furniture like? Western dresses and pants are designed for sitting in chairs and uncomfortable for sitting on the floor; kimono are the opposite. (One reason is the stiff encircling *obi*, which just gets in the way in a chair, but provides back support when you sit on the floor.)

There's an interesting tendency to borrow foreign terms with a much narrower meaning. A *sombrero* is a specific type of hat to us, but in Spanish it's just the word for 'hat'.[2] Similarly, *sake* in Japanese is any alcoholic drink; *mouton* in French is the animal, not just mutton.

Both cloth and clothing are valuable luxury goods, and a region or city may specialize in making certain types. *Damask, calico, muslin, denim, cashmere, madras, tulle, nankeen, fustian, jeans, jersey, dungaree* all come from place names.

Despite what a few video game designers seem to believe, premodern peoples generally didn't wear *bras* and *panties*. If they wore anything underneath their clothes, it was a lighter version of the outer garment. We have Roman frescos showing what we'd call a *bikini*. The top was actually a cloth wrapped several times round the chest, called a *strophium*.

---

[2] Except that a brimless hat or a bonnet are *gorros*.

COLOR

black
OE *blæc* poss. < 'burnt'
- Gk μέλας < 'dirty' • Ir *dubh* prob. < 'smoky' • Ger *schwarz* < 'dark' • Ch *hēi* < 'ink'

blue
Fr *bleu* < Germanic, prob. cognate to Lt *flāvus* 'yellow' < IE 'shine'
- Sp *azul* 'lapis lazuli' • Lt *cæruleus* < 'sky' • Ch *lán* < 'indigo'

brown
OE *brún*
- Sp *moreno* < 'black' or 'mulberry' • Ch *hèsè* 'coarse cloth color'

color
Lt *color* < 'cover'
- Gk χρῶμα < 'surface' • Croatian *boya* 'dye' • Rus цвет < 'flower' • Ch *sè* poss. < 'ruddy (face)'

gray
OE *græ3*
- Fr *gris* 'drunk' ‖ Ger *greis* 'old' • Ch *huīsè* 'ash-color'

green
OE *gréne* ‖ 'grass', 'grow'
- Gk χλωρός, OCS *zelenu* < IE, cognate to 'yellow' • Lt *viridis* prob. < 'sprout' • Ch *qīng* ‖ 'tree', 'pasture'

orange
Fr, from the fruit

pink
ModE 'type of carnation'
- Fr *rose* 'rose'

purple
Gk πορφύρα 'shellfish yielding Tyrian purple'

red
OE *réad* < IE, cognate to Lt *ruber*
- Rum *roşiu* < 'rose' • Ir *dearg* < 'dark' • Rus красный 'beautiful' • Pol *czerwony* < '(dye-producing) worm' • Ket *súlàm* < 'blood'

white
OE *hwít*, cognate to OCS *svĕtŭ* 'light'
- Fr *blanc* < Germanic 'brilliant' • Skt *çukra-* 'bright, pure' • Ket *táγàm* < 'snow'

yellow
OE *3eolu* < IE, cognate to OCS *žlĭtŭ*, Gk χλωρός 'green'
- Gk ξανθός poss. < 'gray' • Sp *amarillo* 'bitter' • Welsh *melyn* 'honey'

A *bear* is etymologically 'the brown one'. French *jaune* 'yellow' surfaces in English in *jaundice*, and *rouge* 'red' as a type of makeup.

The commonest way to name colors is via an exemplar. Only *red* can be clearly traced back to IE; *yellow* goes back to IE **ghel-* but the same root in other branches produced *green*. Old Chinese **tşʰaŋ* was *blue* or *green*; later it was divided into 苍 for the sky and 沧 for the sea, both pronounced *cāng*.

Berlin & Kay

Analyzing color terms cross-culturally, Brent Berlin and Paul Kay discovered that there's a pattern to what basic colors a language will name. The order is:

> black, white
> red
> yellow, blue, green
> brown
> purple, pink, orange, gray

Colors on one line are unordered. That is, if there are four color terms, they will be *black, white, red,* and one of *yellow, blue, green.* If there are seven, there will be all of these plus *brown.* And so on.

Two important caveats:

- **Basic** colors must be monomorphemic, not contained within another color (as *scarlet* is part of *red*), general in application (i.e. not *blond*), and common (so, *puce* is excluded).

- For cross-linguistic comparison we must use **prototypes**. Berlin and Kay's procedure was to have respondents pick the best match for each color from a set of 320 standard color chips. Languages disagree on the boundaries of colors, but they agree on the prototypes. E.g. if a language merges what we call blue and green, the prototype will not be turquoise or cyan, but focal blue or focal green.

English is on the high end for color distinctions, but famously Russian has two words for what we call *blue*— голубой is 'light blue', синий is 'dark blue'. Similarly Spanish has *celeste* and *azul.*

Lakota doesn't quite fit Berlin & Kay's pattern:

sápa	black
ȟóta	gray
sáŋ	off-white
ská	pure white
šá	red
lúta	bright red, scarlet
stáŋ	dark or purplish red
tȟó	blue, green
zí	yellow

žî	tawny
ǧî	brown

Hue/Saturation/Brightness

You can specify any color, for humans, with three parameters.

- **Hue** is where the color lives along the spectrum: *violet, blue, green, yellow, orange, red.*

- **Brightness** is luminosity— how much light there is. Think of it as dialing up the brightness knob on your monitor. You can also think of it as how much black is mixed with the color.

- **Saturation** is how much white is mixed into the color. A faded photograph is *desaturated. Pastels* are high-brightness, desaturated colors.

Some colors are defined by more than hue:

- *Pink* is desaturated red.

- *Brown* is orange with low brightness.

- *Olive* is a desaturated, somewhat dark green.

Primary colors

This section is based on *Color for Philosophers* by C.L. Hardin, which I highly recommend if you want more.

You may have been taught that there are three primary colors, and that these relate somehow to the three types of color receptors in our retinas. You may even have gotten the impression that these three colors are somehow inherent in the nature of light.

They're not. These are features of human vision, and besides, there aren't three primary colors, there are four!

In physics, light has only one parameter: energy.[3] Higher energy means shorter frequencies. Light ranges smoothly from radio waves to infrared to visible light to ultraviolet to X-rays— see p. 247.

---

[3] More accurately, there is a second parameter, called **polarization**. Our eyes aren't sensitive to it, probably because most light in nature is unpolarized. There are exceptions— e.g., light bouncing off water is polarized. Patterns in the sky made by polarization are used by some insects to orient themselves.

The three receptor types in our eyes respond to slightly different frequency bands. S (short) receptors respond most strongly to light of about 440 nm; M (medium) to about 540 nm; L (long) to about 560 nm. If the brain responded to these wavelengths directly, the primary colors would be deep blue, green, and greenish yellow. (Compare to the spectrum on the back cover.)

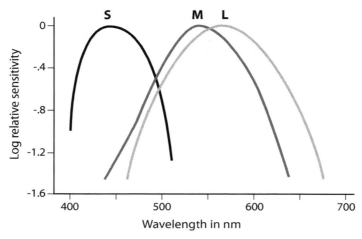

But it doesn't. It responds instead to **subtractions** of the basic inputs. As if by magic, subtracting one response curve from another gives you a much better picture of the overall frequency.

> **L - M** is the **red-green** signal.
>
>> If it's positive, we see *red*.
>>
>> If it's negative, we see *green*.
>
> **(L + M) - S** is the **yellow-blue** signal.
>
>> If it's positive, we see *yellow*.
>>
>> If it's negative, we see *blue*.

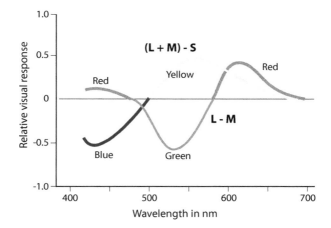

So these are the **four** primary colors. When the L - M signal is at its highest, you have focal red; when it's at its lowest, you have focal green, and so on. And these turn out to be the prototype colors selected by Berlin and Kay's subjects.

A corollary of this system (called **opponent-process** theory) is that you can see any gradation between red and green— but you can't have a color that's simultaneously red *and* green, as this would mean having an L + M signal that's negative and positive at the same time. Similarly, you can't see yellow *and* blue at the same time.

We can arrange hue in a neat circle, with a gradation of colors between blue and red— namely, the purples. These colors **don't live on the spectrum**! There is no single frequency of light that corresponds to purple. Rather, it's a combination of frequencies such that L - M is positive (it's red) and (L + M) - S is negative (it's blue).

Metamerism

You can create single-frequency colors in the lab. But most natural phenomena involve mixtures of colors.

What do you see when the frequencies are mixed? Whatever the receptor cells in your retina report. You can think of it as an averaging process— your eye reports "Well, there's a mess of frequencies coming in, but overall I'd say it's *this much* red-green and *that much* yellow-blue."

Thus, there's an infinite number of frequency combinations that will all trigger the same color response. We say that all those possibilities are **metamers**.

(The alternative would be to do frequency analysis, as a spectrograph does. Hearing works that way— you can distinguish multiple simultaneously played notes.)

Photo reproduction depends on metamerism, because it turns out that all you need to fool the eye are three frequencies. There's any number of possibilities, but computers have standardized on red, green, and blue, while printers use cyan, magenta, and yellow.

Why does red light plus green light produce a sensation of yellow? Let's work it out.

L - M is the red-green signal. Pure red would produce an L - M of some positive amount, call it $+x$. Pure green would produce $-x$. Red plus green thus produces $x - x = 0$. The red-green signal just isn't firing.

But what's the yellow-blue signal doing? We already know L and M are large and equal, so L + M is at its maximum. Pure green is at about the edge of the S response curve, and pure red doesn't trigger it at all— so S is minimal. So (L + M) - S will be very close to L + M— that is, we'll be pretty much maximizing the yellow response.

Red + green is far from the only way to produce yellow. A pure frequency of 580 nm will also produce the sensation of yellow. So will the wide bundle of frequencies from sunlight, minus some blue frequencies scattered by the atmosphere— which is why the sun looks yellowish. So will the complicated set of frequencies that bounces off an ear of corn.

Trichromats and variants

Organisms with three response curves are said to be **trichromats**. You can vary the number. If you have just two response curves you're a dichromat. Color blindness in humans is usually a defect in one of the color signal curves (usually the red-green one).

Our color cells don't respond well in low-light conditions— which means that at night, in the darkness, we see a desaturated world.

More interestingly, a species could have **more** color receptors. The Dzebyet, one of the species in my sf universe, are tetrachromats. One corollary is that their set of metamers is different from ours, so that simple systems of color reproduction aren't compatible. An RGB monitor can't produce an image that satisfies a Dzebyet.

It's easy enough to extend visual sensitivity into the **infrared** or the **ultraviolet**. To know what colors your creatures would *see*, however, you have to design the color response curves. At the least you're really adding primary colors in pairs, as you're creating a new opponent process signal.

Colored things

Colors of course can be used to name other things. E.g. 'white' underlies words meaning *blank, dawn, light, moon, silver;* it's used in English for 'white wine', '(egg) albumen', 'Caucasian', 'ultraconservative', 'snowy', 'with milk added.'

An alien would find our terms for skin color quite bizarre. Human skin color is due to varying concentrations of two pigments, the brownish *eumelanin* and the reddish *pheomelanin.* For Almea I gave humans a third pigment, a bluish *cyanomelanin*, allowing a wider and stranger color range.

CONFLICT

annoy	Old Fr *anuier* 'make odious to'
	• Sp *molestar* < 'burden' • Ger *ärgern* 'worsen' • Ch *nǎo* < 'trouble, turbid'
argue	Fr *arguer* < 'prove, accuse'
beat	OE *béatan,* uncertain
bother	ModE uncertain
brave	It *bravo* 'gallant brave'
	• Lt *animōsus* 'spirited' • Fr *courageux* < 'heart' • Sp *valiente* 'worthy' • Welsh *gwrol* 'manly' • Dutch *dapper* < 'weighty' • Sw *modig* < 'fierce, angry' Cz *statečný* 'standing firm' • Skt *çūra-* 'heroic, powerful'
comfort	Lt *confortāre* intensive of 'strengthen'
defeat	Fr *défaite* 'undone'
	• Gk ἥσσα 'be weaker' • Lt *clādes* 'disaster' • Sp *derrota* < 'broken apart' • Ir *díomua* 'un-victory' • Ger *Niederlage* 'laying down (of arms)' • Cz *poražka* 'smiting' • Ch *zhànshèng* 'battle-win'
defend	Lt *dēfendere* root obscure but also seen in 'offend'; ‖ *bane*
	• Rum *apăra* < 'prepare' • Ir *cosain* < 'exert' • Sw *försvar* < 'rebut' • Cz *braniti* 'fight' • Rus защитить 'behind shield' • Ch *fáng* 'dike'
fight	OE *feohtan* poss. < 'pull hair' (same derivation in Sp *pelear*)
	• Lt *pugnāre* 'hit with fists' • Sp *luchar* < 'wrestle' • Ir *comhraic* < 'meet' • Ger *kämpfen* < 'battle' • OCS *pĭrěti* 'strike' • Ch *dòu* 'quarrel'
free	OE *fréo* < Germanic 'dear', distinguishing family from slaves
	• Lt *līber* prob. < 'of the people' • Ir *saor* < 'good man' • OCS *svobodĭ* < 'self, kin' • Ch *zìyóu* 'self-proceeding'
frighten	ModE causative of 'fear'
hate	OE *hete,* cognate to Old Ir *cais* 'love/hate' poss. < 'care'
	• Lt *odium* poss. < 'disgust' • Rum *ură* < 'shudder' • OCS *nenavistĭ* 'not see' • Skt *dviṣ-* < 'separation, discord' • Ch *hèn* ‖ 'quarrelsome, obstinate'
hero	Gk ἥρως
	• Ch *xióng* < 'male'
hit	OE *hyttan* < Norse 'meet, reach'
	• Fr *frapper* imitative • Breton *dourna* 'hand' • Lith *ištikti* 'hit the mark' • Ger *schlagen* 'slay'
lose	OE *losian* 'perish, destroy' > 'be deprived of'
	• ModGk χάνω < χάος 'abyss' • Lt *āmittere* 'let go' • Ger *verlieren* 'for-loose' • Lith *pamesti* 'throw away' • Rus терять < 'rub' • Ch *shí* ‖ 'escape'

oppose   Fr *opposer* 'put against'
- Ch *fǎn* 'turn'

peace   Lt *pax pāc-* < 'fastened'
- Ir *síocháin* 'stable rule' • Sw *fred* ‖ 'friend', 'dear' • OCS *mirŭ* ‖ 'dear', 'mild' • Pol *pokój* 'rest' • Skt *saṁdhi-* 'putting together' • Ch *píng* 'level'

protect   Lt *prōtegere* 'cover the front'
- Ger *schützen* < 'earth wall' • Ch *hù* ‖ 'prevent'

protest   Lt *prōtestārī* 'attest forward (i.e. in public)'
- Ch *kàngyì* 'resist-proposal'

resist   Lt *resistere* 'stand back'
- Qu *chuchupakuy* benefactive of 'harden' • Ch *dǐ* 'push away'

safe   Lt *salvus* 'uninjured, healthy' < 'whole'
- Gk σῶς prob. < 'strong' • Fr *sûr* < 'without care' • Sw *trygg* 'true, trustworthy' • Skt *akṣata-* 'un-hurting' • Ch *ān* 'calm, peaceful'

save   Lt *salvāre* 'make safe'
- ModGk γλυτώνω 'let loose' • Sw *frälse* 'free' • Ger *retten* < 'drive' • OCS *sŭpasti* 'pasture' • Skt *tāraya-* causative of 'cross, escape' • Ch *jiù* ‖ 'help', 'prepare'

strike   OE *strícan* 'go, wander' > 'stroke, handle' > 'hit'

struggle   ME uncertain

suspect   Lt *suspectus* 'looked under'
- Ir *drochamhras* 'ill-doubt' • Sw *misstänka* 'mis-think' • Ger *argwohn* 'expect bad'

threat   OE *þréat* 'throng' > 'pressure' > 'intent to harm'
- Lt *minax mināc-* < 'jutting out' • Breton *gourdrouz* 'big noise' • Ger *drohen* < 'punish' • Lith *grumoti* 'thunder' • OCS *groziti* 'fright, horror' • Ch *hè* 'scare'

trap   OE *treppe* uncertain
- Fr *piège* < 'shackle' • Ch *jǐng* 'pit'

trick   Fr *tricher* < Lt *trīcarī* 'trifle, play tricks'

triumph   Lt *triumphus* 'victorious general's procession'
- Ch *shènglí* 'win-gain'

victory   Lt *victōria* 'overcome, conquer'
- Gk νίκη < 'abase' • Breton *trec'h* 'stronger' • Ger *sieg* < 'might, hold' • OCS *pobĕda* < 'compel'

violent   Lt *violens*
- Ger *gewalttätig* < 'power' • Ch *qiáng* 'strong'

warn   OE *warenian*
- Fr *prévenir* < 'come before', *alerter* • Ch *jiè* < 'guard (against)'

win   OE *winnan* 'work, fight'

+   *accuse, criticize, insult, gossip, quarrel, bold, rash, embar-*
       rass, irritate, revenge, torture, overthrow, betray

> ‣ The genteel fight with *Law* (p. 235) and the powerful with *War* (p. 383).

Fighting would seem to be a basic concept, going back to our animal heritage. However, note the simple spatial metaphors in *oppose, resist, protect.*

There's not much difference between *strike* and *hit*— the AHD defines them in terms of each other— though *beat* adds a frequentative meaning. Most languages have multiple words in this area, concentrating on the sound (*knock, thump*), the tool (*hammer,* Fr *heurter* 'ram', Norse *lyósta* 'hit with a spear'), or the seriousness (*smite, slay*). I've skimped on the etymology because original meanings are hard to come by. E.g. Greek τύπτω is cognate to Sanskrit 'hurt', Latin 'be stunned', OCS 'palpitate'— there's not much to say about the IE meaning except that it was tactile and unpleasant.

Spanish has a useful word *amolar* (literally 'grind') for anything annoying the kids are doing. Where in English you have to choose between "Shut up!" or "Stop that!" or "Leave that alone!", you can just say *¡Deja de amolar!*

CONTAINERS

bag
ME *bagge*

bottle
Fr *bouteille* < Lt dim. 'vessel'
• Ch *píng* 'water jug'

box
OE *box* < Gk πύξος 'boxwood'
• Sp *caja* < 'chest' • Ch *dú* < 'hollowed out'

chest
Gk κίστη 'box, chest'
• Fr *coffre* < Gk κόφινος 'basket' • Ger *Truhe* < 'tree'

CLOSE
Lt *claudere* 'shut'; as adj, 'near' < idea of the gap between being closed off
• Fr *fermer* 'firm' • Sp *cerrar* < 'bolt' • Welsh *cau* < 'enclosure' • Ger *zumachen* 'make to' • Rus закрыть 'beyond-cover' opposite открыть 'open' • Ch *guān* < 'bar'

collect
Lt *colligere* 'gather together'
• Ger *sammeln* < 'together' • Fr *rassembler* 're-assemble' • Lith *rinkti* < 'hand' • OCS *sŭbĭrati* 'carry with' • Ch *shōu* 'gather, harvest'

contain
Lt *continēre* 'hold together'

content
Lt *contentus* 'contained = satisfied with what one has'
• Ch *nèiróng* 'in-hold'

cover
Lt *cooperīre*, intensive of 'cover, conceal'
• Gk στέγω 'roof' • Welsh *gorchuddio* 'hide over' • Latvian *segt* 'fasten'

empty
OE *æmetiȝ* 'at leisure'
• Lt *vacuus* < IE • Ger *leer* < 'gleaned' • Dutch *ledig* 'free' • Rus пустой < 'desert' • Ch *kōng* < 'hollow'

fill
OE *fyllan* < Germanic causative of 'full'

full
OE *full* < IE, cognate to Lt *plēnus*
• ModGk γεμᾶτος < 'press'

gather
OE *gadrian* 'unite, come together'

group
Fr *groupe* 'mass, knot' > 'set of figures in a painting' > 'any group'
• Ch *qún* poss. ‖ 'swarm', 'all'

include
Lt *inclūdere* 'shut inside'
• Ger *einschließen* 'close in' • Ch *bāo* 'wrap'

individual
Lt *indīviduālis* 'indivisible' > 'inseparable' > 'whole, single'
• Ger *einzeln* < 'one' • Ch *gè* 'bamboo stalk' > 'item'

key
OE *cæȝ* uncertain
• Lt *clāvis* < 'peg' • Ir *eochair* 'open' • Lith *raktas* 'pick'

lock
OE *loc* < Germanic 'enclose' or 'hole'
• Gk μοχλός 'bar' • Lt *sera* < 'joiner' • Sw *lås* 'metal plate' • OCS *zamka* 'move through'

member	Lt *membrum* 'limb, part'
	• Ch *yuán* < 'circle'
OPEN	OE *openian* poss. < 'up'
	• Lt *aperīre* < 'unshut' • Ger *aufmachen* 'make up' • Rus открыть 'uncover'
pack	Dutch *pak* uncertain
pocket	dim. ME *poke* < Frankish *pokka* 'bag'
	• Sp *bolsillo* dim. 'purse' • Sw *ficka* 'stuck on' • Cz *kapsa* < 'chest' • Ch *yīdài* 'clothes-pouch'
shut	OE *scyttan* 'move a bolt to lock' ‖ *shoot*
+	*basket, jar, cage, shell, barrel, bucket, sack, cabinet, cupboard, chest*

Babies spend a lot of time learning that things can go into other things, and then be taken out. According to George Lakoff, this early bodily experience is abstracted to concepts, and forms the basis of our ideas of categorization. Our urge to put one class of things inside another is an extension of that infantile fascination.

Evolution seems to share this fascination. Astronomy and geology may involve undifferentiated masses, but evolutionary advances often consist of creating *containers*: cells with cell walls; membranes that enclose the nucleus and organelles; tissues that cover the body, line the gut, or enclose internal organs; thick protective structures like shells, skulls, exoskeletons, and rib cages.

One corollary is that words for containers can double as terms for anatomical parts (*pelvis* 'basin') or simple animals (*tunica* 'tunic, wrapper' > *tunicate*).

Think about what your conculture's containers are made of. The first containers were probably plaited baskets, or purses made from animal skins. If you have a lot of clay, as in the early Middle East, you made pots. Glass is ancient, but glassblowing started around the 1st century. It wasn't till the age of porcelain and stainless steel that pots and plates weren't liable to flavor the food.

As with tools (p. 369), words may be defined by an earlier technology. E.g. an early 'lock' was a wooden bar with a peg to lift it, or a bolt driven through it to hold it in place. Thus words for *lock* and *key* may be based on *bar* and *peg*, as in Greek.

DIMENSIONS

expand	Lt *expandere* 'spread out'
entire	Fr *entier* < Lt *integrum* 'not touched' > 'whole' • Ger *vollzählig* 'full-counted' • Ch *zhēng* < 'orderly'
fraction	Lt 'breaking'
increase	Lt *incrēscere* intensive of 'grow' • Ger *zunehmen* 'take to' • Ch *zēng* 'add'
MUCH	abbr of *mickle* 'large'
whole	OE *hál* 'sound, healthy, complete' • Gk πᾶς 'every' • Lt *tōtus* prob. < 'packed full', *integer* 'untouched' • Skt *sakala-* '(has) all parts'

Quantifiers

ALL	OE *all*
ANY	OE *ǽniȝ* adjectivization of 'one'
EACH	OE *ǽlc*
EVERY	OE *ǽfre ǽlc* 'ever-each' • Rum *fiecare* 'whoever' • Lt *quisque* < 'who'
few	OE *féawe*, cognate with Latin *paucus* • OCS *malo* < 'small' • Ger *wenig* 'pitiable' • Ch *shào* < 'tapering, pointed'
MANY	OE *maniȝ*, cognate to OCS *mŭnogŭ* • Gk πολύς < IE 'full' • Fr *beaucoup* 'beautiful blow' • Ir *mórán* < 'large' • Breton *kalz* 'heap' • Skt *bahu-* < 'high, thick'
MOST	OE *mǽst*
nobody	ME 'no body'
none	OE *nán* 'not one'
NOTHING	OE *nán þing* 'no thing'
nought	OE *nówiht* 'not any-wight'
several	Lt *sēpar* 'separate'
SOME	OE *sum*
various	Lt *varius* 'changing, different, diverse'

For the basic quantifiers (and comparisons between logic and everyday language), see *ALC*, p. 41.

I think you could get by combining *few* and *several*, but all the languages I've looked at insist on making the distinction:

English	*few*	*several*
French	*peu*	*plusieurs*

Swedish	*få*	*flera*
Hindi	*kuch*	*kaī*
Arabic	*qalīl*	*`idda*
Mandarin	*hěn shǎo*	*jǐge*

And yet *several* only has this sense in modern English. (Previously the word meant 'separate, distinct'; the earlier term for an indefinite small quantity was *divers*.) In English, the difference may be one of attitude: *I have few friends* seems like a complaint, *I have several friends* is neutral or a boast.

Valuation

ALMOST	'all most'
ENOUGH	OE ʒenóʒ < 'suffice' < 'reach'
	• Lt *satis* 'sated' • Sp *bastante* < Gk 'endure' • OCS *dovolĭnŭ* < 'prefer'
EVEN	OE *efen* 'flat, equal'
indeed	ME 'in deed' = 'in action, really'
JUST	Lt *justus* 'righteous, lawful'
lot	OE *hlot* 'chance marker' > 'share' > 'quantity'
ONLY	OE *ánlíc* 'one-like'
scarce	Fr *échars* < Lt 'select out'
somewhat	ME 'some what'
SUCH	OE *swelc* 'so-like' > 'to that degree'
TOO	OE stressed form of 'to'
VERY	Lt *vērus* 'true'
	• Fr *très* < Lt *trans* 'across'

These are words that not only express a quantity, but a value judgment. Based on the frequencies, we can say that English speakers are more eager to judge than simply to state a quantity.

Linear extent

broad	OE *brád* < 'spread out' • Ch *kuān* 'vast, wide'
deep	OE *díop* < IE 'deep, bottom, hollow'
	• Lt *profundus* 'fore-bottom' • Rum *adînc* 'bent' (i.e. not flat) • Skt *gahana-* prob. 'immersed' • Ch *shēn* poss. ∥ 'low'
fat	OE *fǽtt* < Germanic 'fattened'
	• Ger *dick* ∥ *thick* • Ch *pàng* poss. ∥ 'dense (growth)'

HIGH	OE *héah* < 'heap, mound'
	• Gk ὑψηλός < 'above' • Lt *altus* < 'reared' • Ir *ard* < 'steep' • Lith *aukstas* 'grown'
LONG	OE *lang* < IE, cognate to Lt *longus*
	• Sp *largo* < 'abundant' • Ch *cháng* < 'stretched'
low	ME *lah* 'short'
	• Lt *humilis* 'ground', *bassus* uncertain • Ir *íseal* < 'under' • Ger *niedrig* 'downish' • Ch *dī* < 'bottom'
narrow	OE *nearu*
	• Lt *angustus* < 'distressed' • Fr *étroit* < 'drawn tight' • Ger *schmal* 'small' • OCS *těsnŭ* 'pressed'
shallow	ME *schalowe*
short	OE *sceort*
	• Lt *brevis* < IE • Fr *court* < 'cut off' • Lith *trumpas* 'crumbled'
tall	OE *ʒe-tæl* 'prompt' > ME 'proper' > 'handsome' > 'stout' > 'big'
	• Lt *procērus* 'front-grown'
thick	OE *þicce*
	• Gk παχύς < IE 'heap, much' • Fr *épais* < 'dense' • Lith *storas* < 'standing' • Rus толстый < 'swollen' • Skt *sthūla-* 'strong'
thin	OE *þynne* < IE 'stretched', cognate to Lt *tenuis*
	• Gk λεπτός 'peeled' • Fr *mince* < 'made small' • Sp *delgado* < 'delicate' • Lith *plonas* 'flat' • Ch *xì* 'small, fine'
wide	OE *wíd* poss. < 'gone apart'
	• Gk πλατύς < 'spread out' • Fr *large* < 'abundant' • Sp *ancho* < 'ample' • Ch *kuān* 'vast'

In Latin, both *altus* and *profundus* could refer to distance up or down— that is, to either height or depth. *Profundus* seems to have referred to *exceptional* height or depth.

It's a bit mysterious why English has two terms for large vertical extent. A man can only be *tall;* a number can only be *high;* mountains and buildings can be either. *High* can be also be used for a level (high prices, high vowels, a high platform). Spanish uses *alto* for both. French uses *haut—* except that tall people are *grand.* Mandarin uses *gāo—* but agrees with us that *short (ǎi)* and *low (dī)* are different.

For flattish objects (ties, planks, books, windows, belts, papers, blankets, noodles) we use *thick/thin* for the smallest dimension and *wide/narrow* for the next-smallest. But if the object is more cubical, it's quirkier: cabinets and cars are *narrow/wide;* people are *fat/thin. Narrow/wide* are also used for spaces that can be traversed: gaps, corridors, roads, rivers, balconies.

We can use *short* as the opposite of both *tall* and *long;* in Polish 'not tall' is *ramie,* and 'not long' is *krótki.*

Arabic uses *ṭawīl* for both 'tall' and 'long'.

We generally use *thick* for inanimate objects, but *fat* for animals or people. Mandarin distinguishes the thickness of flat or sheetlike things (*hòu*) from that of long or stick-like things (*cū*), as well as the fatness of people (*pàng*) and animals (*féi*).

In Japanese, noses are *high/low (takai/hikui)*, just like mountains; most European languages consider them as *large* or *long* instead.

Lakota separates out what to us are senses of 'thick', 'thin':

šóka	wide, of flat solid objects: boards, ice, books
šmá	dense, of a collective of small things: grass, trees, hair, snow
tkápa	viscous: soup, blood, mucus
akhíšoka	dense in growth: fur, leaves, hair
čhépa	fat: animals, people

Physical height is so easily equated with amount, quality, or virtue that we forget that it's a metaphor: *low integers, rising prices, High Elves, the upper classes, raise the tone of the discussion, fall into sin, a low blow, profound thoughts.*

We use width as a metaphor for variety— perhaps the underlying image is a bunch of things spread in front of us: *a wide variety, broad knowledge. Fat* is more negative: *fat chance.* A *fat paycheck* sounds like someone else's excessive take— ours is at best *ample.*

Distance

CLOSE	Lt *claudere* 'shut'; as adj, 'near' < idea of the gap between being closed off
distant	Lt *distans* 'stand apart'
FAR	OE *feor*
	• Gk μακράν 'long' • Sp *lejos* < 'loose' • Ger *weit* 'wide'
local	Lt *locālis* adjn. of 'place'
	• Ch *běndì* 'root-earth'
NEAR	OE *néar*, comparative of *nigh*
	• Gk ἐγγύς 'at hand' • Lt *prope* < 'in front' • Fr *près* < 'pressed (close)' • Sp *cerca* 'around' • Breton *tost* 'soon' • Skt *antikam* 'opposite'
remote	Lt *remōtus* 'removed'

Distance is the extent not of an object but of the negative space between two points; when it's vertical, we often use *high* instead. C.S. Lewis notes that to us the heavens are *out there;* for the medievals they were *up there*— their worldview was vertiginous.

Distance is a key metaphor for interpersonal relationships. A curious collocationary gap: relationships can be *distant* but not *far.*

Size

SMALL	OE *smæl*
	• Gk μῑκρός ‖ Lt *mīca* 'crumb' • Lt *parvus* < 'few' • It *piccolo,* Fr *petit* < babytalk • Ger *klein* < 'shiny' • OCS *malŭ* poss. < 'milled (finely)' • Ch *xiǎo* 'young'
area	Lt *ārea* 'open space'
	• Ger *Fläche* 'flats' • Ch *miànjī* 'face-amount'
big	ME 'strong, stout'
	• Gk μέγας, Lt *magnus* < IE • Rum *mare* 'male' • Sw *stor* <'standing' • Rus большой < 'strong'
enormous	Lt *ēnormis* 'out of the norm'
	• Ger *gewaltig* 'powerful' • Ch *jùdà* 'huge-big'
extend	Lt *extendere* 'stretch out'
giant	Gk γίγᾱς
	• Ger *Riese* poss. ‖ 'height, peak' • Ch *jù* < 'increase'
huge	ME uncertain
large	Lt *largus* 'abundant, copious'
LITTLE	OE *lýtel*
miniature	It *miniatura* 'illumination' < 'color with minium'
size	Fr *assise* 'sitting' > 'court' > 'standard' > 'magnitude'
	• Fr *grandeur* 'bigness' • Skt *māna-* 'measure' • Ch *dàxiǎo* 'big-little'
tiny	ModE uncertain
vast	Lt *vastus* 'empty, huge'

An alien looking at English might wonder why humans were so concerned with size. Surely we could get by with just two terms, *big* and *small.*

If your conpeople aren't human, their whole vocabulary will be geared to their size. Dragons, for instance, would either not make many distinctions among very small things (*dust, grains, sand, powder, gravel, pebbles*), or they'd refer to much larger things. To a cat-sized creature, *bushes* and *trees* are both mazes of vegetation far larger than oneself.

Our basic terms all refer to the human scale, which leaves us without a systematic way of referring to the enormous range of scales in the universe.

In case you'd like to build an absolute scale, here are the touristic highlights on the journey from the smallest to the largest known things:

Meters	Multiplier	Explanation
10^{-35}	1.62	Planck length— the order of magnitude of the strings in string theory; in quantum gravity, the scale where the structure of spacetime is dominated by quantum effects
10^{-22}	1	upper limit on electron size, based on observation in Penning traps (emphasis is on 'upper limit'; the theoretical size is zero)
10^{-15}	1	*femtometer (fm)— Danish 'fifteen'*
10^{-15}	.88	radius of the proton (thus, of hydrogen nucleus)
10^{-15}	8.45	diameter of gold nucleus
10^{-12}	1	*picometer (pm)— Sp 'a bit'*
10^{-12}	1 to 10	wavelengths of gamma rays
10^{-11}	3.1	radius of helium atom (smallest atom)
10^{-11}	2	typical wavelength for dental X-rays
10^{-11}	5	highest resolution achievable with an electron microscope
10^{-10}	2.6	radius of cesium atom (largest)
10^{-9}	1	*nanometer (nm)— Gk 'dwarf'*
10^{-8}	1.3	width of a bacterial flagellum
10^{-8}	2 to 30	size of a virus
10^{-8}	3.2	smallest commercial transistor as of 2010— 96 silicon atoms wide
10^{-7}	2	width of eukaryotic cilium
10^{-7}	2	highest resolution achievable with an optical microscope
10^{-7}	4 to 7	wavelength of visible light (violet to red)
10^{-7}	5 to 10	size of mitochondria (energy-producing organelles)
10^{-6}	1	*micrometer (μm)— Gk 'small'*
10^{-6}	1	typical size of a plant cell wall
10^{-6}	1 to 10	size of bacteria

10^{-6}	6 to 8	diameter of a human red blood cell
10^{-5}	1 to 10	size of eukaryote cells
10^{-4}	1.13	thickness of one page of this book
10^{-4}	1	width of a human hair
10^{-4}	1.2	size of human ovum
10^{-4}	3.5	size of a pixel on my computer monitor
10^{-3}	1	*millimeter (mm)— Lt 'thousand'*
10^{-3}	1	wavelength of shortest radio waves (shorter wavelengths belong to the infrared)
10^{-3}	2.5	size of a fruit fly (*Drosophila melanogaster*)
10^{-3}	7	smallest known frog (*Paedophryne amauensis*)
10^{-2}	1.79	width of a US dime
10^{-1}	1.52	width of this book (printed)
10^{0}	1	*meter— Gk 'measure'*
10^{0}	1.7	average height of humans
10^{1}	3.3	blue whale specimen— largest animal by weight
10^{1}	6	longest known dinosaur (*Amphicoelias*)
10^{2}	1.16	tallest known tree— a coast redwood in California
10^{2}	8.3	height of Burj Khalifa, tallest building as of 2013
10^{3}	1	*kilometer— Gk 'thousand'*
10^{3}	6.65	length of Nile (longest river)
10^{3}	8.8	height of Mt Everest
10^{4}	2.2	height of Mars's Olympus Mons, highest mountain on any planet
10^{6}	3.48	diameter of moon
10^{7}	1.28	equatorial diameter of Earth
10^{7}	4.2	height of geosynchronous orbit
10^{8}	1.1	diameter of smallest red dwarfs
10^{8}	1.43	diameter of Jupiter
10^{8}	2.998	*one light-second*
10^{8}	3.84	mean distance to moon
10^{9}	1.39	diameter of sun
10^{11}	1.5	distance to sun— 1 AU
10^{12}	2.3	NML Cygni, largest known star

10^{12}	4.50	mean radius of Neptune's orbit
10^{13}	1.85	distance of Voyager 1— farthest man-made object, launched 1977
10^{15}	7.5	outer boundary of Oort cloud (comets and other debris)
10^{16}	.946	*light-year*
10^{16}	3.09	*1 parsec— distance at which parallax due to Earth's orbit is 1 second of arc— 3.26 ly*
10^{16}	4.15	distance to Alpha Centauri A (4.37 ly)
10^{17}	2.3	farthest Agent Morgan travels from the Sun in *Against Peace and Freedom*
10^{20}	2.5	distance to center of galaxy
10^{21}	1	diameter of Milky Way (100,000 ly)
10^{21}	1.63	distance to Large Magellanic Cloud
10^{22}	2.4	distance to Andromeda (2.5 million ly)
10^{23}	1	diameter of Local Group (~ 54 galaxies including ours)
10^{24}	1.1	diameter of Local Supercluster (contains about a hundred clusters)
10^{25}	1.3	Sloan Great Wall— largest known collection of superclusters
10^{26}	8.8	diameter of observable universe (92 billion ly)— this is larger than the age of the universe (13.7 billion years) because the universe is expanding!

DIRECTIONS

BACK OE *bæc*

• ModGk ράχη < 'spine' • Lt *dorsum* poss. < 'turned down' • Sp *espalda* < 'shoulder' • Lith *nugara* 'mountain ridge' • Skt *pṛṣṭha-* 'stands out' • Ch *bèi* < 'carry on back'

bottom OE *botm* < IE, cognate to Lt *fundus*

• ModGk πάτος < 'floor' • Ir *bun* < 'stump, trunk' • OCS *dŭno* < 'deep'

center Gk κέντρον 'sharp point (of a compass)'

• Ch *zhōng* 'inside' (poss. oldest meaning)

direct Lt *dīrectus* 'put straight'

DOWN OE *of dúne* 'off the hill'

• Fr *en bas* 'in low' • Ch *xià* 'descend, low'

east OE *éast* < IE 'dawn'

• Gk ἀνατολή, Lt *oriēns* 'rising' • OCS *vŭstokŭ* 'running up (of the sun)' • Lith *rytai* 'morning' • Ch *dōng* prob. ‖ 'bright, awake'

flat Norse *flatr*

• Lt *plānus* < 'spread out' • ModGk πλακωτός 'compressed' • Ir *réidh* < 'open, rideable'

forward OE *foreweard* 'fore-direction'

front Lt *frons front-* 'forehead'

• Ket *kúpkà* 'beak-ward'

further OE *furðor,* comparative of 'fore'

LEFT OE *left* 'weaker'

• Lt *sinister* poss. 'more useful' • Fr *gauche* 'awkward' • Rum *stîng* 'weak' • Ir *clé* < 'oblique' • Sw *vänster* 'friendlier' • Ger *link* < 'limp, crawl' • OCS *lěvŭ* < 'bent'

level Lt *lībella* 'little balance'

middle OE *middel* < IE, cognate to Gk μέσος, Lt *medius*

• Breton *ekreiz* 'in center/heart'

north OE *norð* poss. < 'lower'

• Gk Βορέᾱς 'north wind' • Lt *septentriō* 'seven oxen' = Ursa Minor • Ir *tuaisceart* 'left-part' • Lith *žiemiai* 'winter' • Skt *uttarā-* 'upper' • Ch *běi* 'back' (i.e. when facing south)

RIGHT OE *reht* 'straight'

• Lt *dexter* < IE • Sw *höger* 'easy'

SIDE OE *síde* prob. < 'broad, long'

• Gk πλευραί 'ribs' • Lt *latus* prob. < 'wide', *costa* 'rib' • Rum *parte* 'part' • Rus сторона < 'region' < 'spread' • Avestan *arəδa-* 'half' • Ch *piān* < 'oblique'

south   OE *súð* poss < 'sunny'

• Gk νότος < 'rain' • Lt *merīdiēs* 'mid-day' • Ir *deisceart* 'right-part' • Avestan *paurva-* 'in front' • Ch *nán* poss. < 'sunny side'

straight   ME *streʒt* 'stretched'

• Lt *rectus* < 'directed' • Gk ὀρθός 'upright' • Ger *gerade* 'quick' • OCS *pravŭ* < 'forward' • Ch *zhí* 'straight, right' ‖ 'real'

top   OE *top* 'top' < 'tuft of hair'

• Gr ἄκρος 'highest' • Fr *dessus* 'above' • Ger *Oberfläche* 'upper surface'

UP   OE *upp*

west   OE *west* poss. < 'down'

• Gk ἑσπέρα 'evening' • Lt *occidēns* 'perishing' • Breton *kuzheol* 'sunset' • OCS *zapadŭ* 'fall behind' • Ch *xī* < 'go down'

+   *horizon, vertical, oblique, parallel, perpendicular*

We take for granted what are called **egocentric** terms like *left* and *right*. But there's another way— use **geographic** coordinates all the time, as in this Australian language:

> In fact, Guugu Yimithirr doesn't make any use of egocentric coordinates at all. The anthropologist John Haviland and later the linguist Stephen Levinson have shown that Guugu Yimithirr does not use words like "left" or "right," "in front of" or "behind," to describe the position of objects. Whenever we would use the egocentric system, the Guugu Yimithirr rely on cardinal directions. If they want you to move over on the car seat to make room, they'll say "move a bit to the east." To tell you where exactly they left something in your house, they'll say, "I left it on the southern edge of the western table." Or they would warn you to "look out for that big ant just north of your foot." Even when shown a film on television, they gave descriptions of it based on the orientation of the screen. If the television was facing north, and a man on the screen was approaching, they said that he was "coming northward."

> —Guy Deutscher, "Does Your Language Shape How You Think?", *New York Times*, August 26, 2010

Speakers must be conscious of the cardinal directions at all times; children begin referring to them at age 2 and have fully mastered the system by age 8. This is a rare real-life instance of what Benjamin Lee Whorf talked about in *Language, Thought, and Reality*: people *thinking differently* because of their language.

Are there always four **cardinal directions**? Living on the planet, they're fairly natural: the sun rises in the east and sets in the west; go far enough north and south and the climate changes. There's no natural phenomenon that corresponds to heading 60° off of east. However, many cultures (including China) include *center* as a cardinal direction, for a total of five.

Flying or swimming creatures, or people living in a space habitat, would naturally consider *up* and *down* just as important as the horizontal directions. Navajo includes them, giving a set of six cardinal directions, with associated colors and animals.

Finnish can be said to have eight cardinal directions, as its words for northeast, southeast etc. are not compounds— e.g. north is *pohjoinen*, east is *itä*, and northeast is *koillinen*. Sanskrit associates gods with the eight directions, so northeast is *Ishanadisha* 'Ishana's direction'. The ancient Greeks did the same, though with specialized gods; northeast's was Καικίας.

To Indo-Europeans *north* is the direction of cold, *south* that of heat; a civilization in the southern hemisphere (such as those of Almea) will have the opposite associations.

Could your planet's sun rise in the west? Well, you can declare that it does, but why do you call that direction *west*? Directions are ultimately related to planetary rotation, and it's best to think of the position of sunrise as determining *east*. (Unless you define *north* as pointing to the north magnetic pole! But the magnetic poles have flipped many times in the earth's history. See the *PCK* p. 44.)

(But a *moon* can rise in the west: Phobos does, as it orbits Mars faster than the planet rotates.)

Some regions have a strong **geographical orientation** which may not align with the compass points— e.g. toward/away from the coast, or upstream/downstream relative to a great river.

In Quebec, the St. Laurent notionally goes west to east... even though it actually flows northeast. The road system and farming plots are oriented according to the river. In Montréal, the river happens to flow south to north, so if a *Montréalais* is going *sud*, that's everyone else's east!

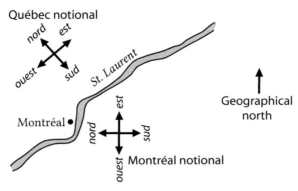

In addition *monter* 'ascend' is used for going either upriver or away from the river, and *descendre* is used for going downriver or back to the river.

The spatial directions also give metaphors for **time**. English speakers think of time as advancing like a man walking. Thus the future is *ahead*, the past is *behind* us. (In a flat pictorial representation, like a comic strip, however, the future is to the *right*.) In Aymara, the past is ahead and the future is behind us; in Chinese time moves from above us downward. In Kuuk Thaayorre, which has the geographic orientation described above, time runs from east to west (presumably imitating the sun).

Many etymologies reflect an idea that **right/left** correlates to good/bad. Bad news for lefties, but the Romans did warn us they were *sinister*. Chinese *yòu/zuǒ* don't derive from this metaphor, but they exemplify it: derivations of *yòu* mean 'friendly' and 'support, honor', while *zuǒ* is also 'evil, vicious'.

The use of left and right to refer to the **political spectrum** dates to the *Assemblée Nationale* during the French Revolution, where royalists sat on the right side, from the point of view of the presiding officer; sitting on the right was the place of honor. For a conlanger the lesson is that almost any minor attribute or symbol may be used to characterize a political group.

EFFORT

accomplish Fr *accomplir* 'make complete'

adventure Fr *aventure* 'about to happen'
• Ch *màoxiǎn* 'risk-danger'

attempt Lt *attemptāre* 'stretch to'
• Gk ζητέω 'seek' • OE *onginnan* 'begin' • Dutch *trachten* < 'consider' • Cz *snažiti se* < 'effort' • Ch *shì* < 'apply, use'

cause Lt *causa* 'plea, excuse' > 'give reasons' > 'make happen'
• Gk αἰτία 'responsibility' • Breton *abeg* 'the ABC' • Ger *Ursache* 'original-strife' • Cz *přičina* 'do near' • Ch *yǐnqǐ* 'guide-start'

control Fr *contrôle* 'counter-role = duplicate register'
• Ger *beherrschen* 'rule by' • Ch *jiǎn* ‖ 'lessen, restricted'

danger Lt *dominium* 'lordship' > 'power to hurt'
• Lt *perīculum* 'attempt' > 'risk' • Welsh *enbydrwydd* 'in-pitness' • Rus опасность < 'guard' • Ch *wēi* 'high, steep'

difficult Lt *difficilis* 'not easy'
• OE *earfeðe* 'toilsome' • Ger *schwer* 'heavy' • Ch *nán* ‖ 'suffer, ill'

easy Fr *aisier* 'put at ease'
• Gk εὔκολος 'good-turning' • Lt *facilis* 'doable' • Dutch *gemakkelijk* 'comfortable' • OCS *udobĭ* 'proper' • Rus лёгкий 'light' • Ch *yì* ‖ 'good'

effect Lt *effectus* 'worked out' < 'out' + 'make'
• Ger *Wirkung* 'working' • Ch *guǒ* 'fruit'

effort Fr *effort* 'out' + 'strong'
• Ch *nǔ* 'exert' < 'tense'

fail Fr *faillir* 'be lacking, miss'

force Fr *force* 'strength'

labor Lt *labor* 'labor, hardship'
• Ger *Mühe* < 'trouble, vex' • Ch *láo* 'toil'

mighty OE *mihtiʒ* 'strong'

mistake Norse *mistaka* 'take wrongly'
• Gk ἁμαρτία 'miss the mark' • Lt *error* < 'go astray' • Ger *Versehen* 'oversight' • Pol *błąd* < 'fornicate' • Rus ошибка < 'beat down' • Ch *cuò* poss. < 'mix-up'

order Lt *ordo ordin-* 'row, series, order'
• Ch *xù* < 'continue'

practice Gk πρακτικός 'active (knowledge)'
• Ger *üben* < 'perform, work' • Ch *xí* 'repeat' ‖ 'be accustomed to', 'learn'

result
: Lt *resultāre* 'leap back'
: • Ger *Ergebnis* 'begin-giving' • Ch *guǒ* 'fruit'

risk
: It *risco* uncertain

strong
: OE *strang* < 'stiff'
: • Lt *rōbustus* 'oaken', *fortis* poss. < 'hold' • Gk δυνατός 'powerful' • Sw *mäktig* < 'able' • Skt *balin-* < 'large'

succeed
: Lt *succēdere* 'go under' > 'take the place of'
: • Fr *réussir* < 'go out' • Ch *chénggōng* 'finish-merit'

task
: Lt *taxa* 'tax' > 'imposed fee' > 'imposed work'

trouble
: Fr *troubler* 'make turbid' > 'disturb'

train
: Fr *traîner* 'draw, drag'

TRY
: Fr *trier* 'sift, sort'
: **Test**: Gk πειράω prob. < 'go through' • Lt *temptāre* 'feel', *probāre* 'approve' • Fr *essayer* < 'balance' • Skt *parīkṣ-* 'look around' • Ch *cháng* 'taste'

weak
: ME < Norse *veikr* 'pliant, weak'
: • Lt *infirmus* 'not firm' • Fr *faible* < 'weepable' • Ir *lag* 'slack' • Ch *ruò* ‖ 'soft, tender'

+
: *compel, challenge, excel, fallible, accident*

‣ See also *Work,* p. 393.

We have a large number of words expressing the concept, or complaint, that actions take work. Directly or metaphorically, actions require strength (*force, effort*) or at least stretching (*attempt*) or strenuous movement (*result*).

If you have the strength to do something, you can do it— *might* 'power' is the source of our auxiliary verbs *may/might*.

ELEMENTS

air	Gk ἀήρ 'wind', cognate to Lt *ventus*, OE *wind* • OE *lift* < 'loft, ceiling' • OCS *vŭzduchŭ* 'up-breath' • Ch *qì* < 'anger'
earth	OE *eorþe* • Lt *terra* < 'dried' • Rum *pamînt* 'floor' • Ir *talamh* < 'surface' • Skt *pṛthivī-* 'wide'
fire	OE *fýr* < IE 'fire (inan.)' • Lt *ignis* < IE 'fire (anim.)' • Fr *feu* < 'fireplace' • Sw *eld* 'burn'
metal	Gk μέταλλον 'mine' • Ch *jīn* also 'gold' poss. < 'bright'
stone	OE *stān* < IE 'stiff, solid' • OCS *kamy* < 'edged' prob. ‖ *hammer*
WATER	OE *wæter* • Lt *aqua* < IE 'running water' • Skt *jala-* ‖ 'drip' • Ch *shuǐ* < 'what flows'
wood	OE *widu* 'tree, copse' • Lt *lignum* < 'collected' • Sp *madera* 'material'

▸ See also *Substances*, p. 342, and *Metals*, p. 261.

A system of **elements** can be useful for your people's cosmology, as well as a productive generator of terms and metaphors. Early philosophers are also likely to apply the elements to medicine (p. 242) and temperament (p. 274).

The old **European** and Indian system was

> *earth*
> *air*
> *fire*
> *water*

The incorruptible heavens were sometimes given their own fifth element, *quintessence* or *ether*. *Akasha* has a similar place in Hindu cosmology.

Luc Besson suggested that the fifth element was love, or in particular Milla Jovovich. But more soberly, the elements are divisions of matter; see *Spirit* for ways of categorizing the immaterial world.

The **Chinese** system:

木	*mù*	wood
火	*huǒ*	fire
土	*tǔ*	earth
金	*jīn*	metal
水	*shuǐ*	water

The **Verdurians** (or more precisely their ancestors the Cadinorians) came up with seven elements, which were neatly linked to seven intelligent species as well as to seven temperaments:

ur	clay	men	practicality
për	rock	elcarî	determination
mey	water	iliu	benevolence
endi	wood	icëlanî	delicacy
gent	metal	gdeonî (giants)	calm
tšur	fire	ktuvoks	energy
šalea	air	vyožî (spirits)	intellectuality

Mešaism, also from Almea, had a more open-ended system. The major deities were each associated with a substance (as well as an animal and a landmark or planet).

Axunašin	*totem*	*element*	*landmark*
Meša	hawk	air	planet Išira
Evonanu	carp	water	lake Van
Inbamu	lion	fire	the sun
Welezi	fox	diamond	planet Vereon
Xivazi	whale	water	the ocean
Moun	leopard	wood	the forests
Jenweliz	elk	emerald	planet Hírumor
Meidimexi	beetle	earth	planet Vlerëi
Ušimex	wolf	gold	planet Caiem
Emouriz	bear	jade	planet Imiri
Nejimex	eagle	silver	moon Iliažë
Nejimexi	owl	iron	moon Iliacáš
Nejimez	swallow	mercury	moon Naunai
Axun	snake	water	river Xengi

Once chemistry gets going, the list of elements is likely to multiply. Antoine **Lavoisier** came up with the following list, in the late 1700s:

light, caloric (heat), oxygen, azote (= nitrogen), hydrogen, sulfur, phosphorus, charcoal, muriatic radical, fluoric radical, boracic radical, antimony, arsenic, bismuth, cobalt, copper, gold, iron, lead, manganese, mercury, molybdena, nickel, platina, silver, tin, tung-

sten, zinc lime, magnesia, barytes (barium oxide), argilla (alu-mina), silex (silica)

The periodic table

Finally you get the revolution of **Mendeleev,** who realized that the known elements could be arranged by atomic number and according to periodic repetitions (1865). He left holes in the table to make the patterns line up, a boldness that was rewarded by the subsequent discovery of germanium, gallium, and scandium.

The number of elements ceased to be open-ended— though s.f. writers stayed for decades in a Lavoisierian mode, inventing new elements at will.

Elements in the same **column** share appearances and behavior, thanks to having a similar electron arrangement (p. 295). E.g. all the elements in the first column have a single unmatched electron in their outer shell, which means they easily form compounds with elements hungering for a single electron.

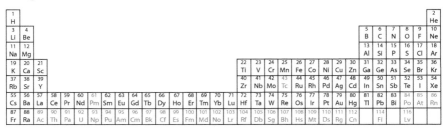

OK, that's a little hard to read. For quantum mechanical reasons, as you get more electrons you get more *kinds* of shells, which means you get more elements per row. The diagram above shows this nicely, but for ease of reading we normally move the rare earths to the bottom of the diagram:

1 H																	2 He
3 Li	4 Be											5 B	6 C	7 N	8 O	9 F	10 Ne
11 Na	12 Mg											13 Al	14 Si	15 P	16 S	17 Cl	18 Ar
19 K	20 Ca	21 Sc	22 Ti	23 V	24 Cr	25 Mn	26 Fe	27 Co	28 Ni	29 Cu	30 Zn	31 Ga	32 Ge	33 As	34 Se	35 Br	36 Kr
37 Rb	38 Sr	39 Y	40 Zr	41 Nb	42 Mo	43 Tc	44 Ru	45 Rh	46 Pd	47 Ag	48 Cd	49 In	50 Sn	51 Sb	52 Te	53 I	54 Xe
55 Cs	56 Ba		72 Hf	73 Ta	74 W	75 Re	76 Os	77 Ir	78 Pt	79 Au	80 Hg	81 Tl	82 Pb	83 Bi	84 Po	85 At	86 Rn
87 Fr	88 Ra	¶	104 Rf	105 Db	106 Sg	107 Bh	108 Hs	109 Mt	110 Ds	111 Rg	112 Cn		114 Fl		116 Lv		

*	57 La	58 Ce	59 Pr	60 Nd	61 Pm	62 Sm	63 Eu	64 Gd	65 Tb	66 Dy	67 Ho	68 Er	69 Tm	70 Yb	71 Lu
¶	89 Ac	90 Th	91 Pa	92 U	93 Np	94 Pu	95 Am	96 Cm	97 Bk	98 Cf	99 Es	100 Fm	101 Md	102 No	103 Lr

The table is divided into sectors. Their names refer to their state at room temperature; any element can of course be a solid, liquid, or gas at the right temperature. The structure refers to the outermost electron shell (p. 295).

Column	Structure	Description
1	$..s^1$	**Alkali metals** (except for hydrogen, a gas). All produce a huge explosion in contact with water. Reactivity increases as you go down the table.
2	$..s^2$	**Alkali earth metals**
13 - 16	$..p^{1-4}$	Divided in three: On the top right, the **nonmetals** On the bottom left, the **ordinary metals** On a diagonal in between them, the **metalloids**
17	$..p^5$	**Halogens**— highly reactive and rather nasty elements; reactivity decreases as you go down.
18	$..p^6$	**Noble gases**— with full electron shells, these gases almost never combine with other elements.
3 - 12	$..d^n$	**Transition metals**— a confusing name as they include all the common metals.
* ¶	$..f^n$	**Rare earths**

Rare earths is a term that's outlived its accuracy; some are not rare at all. The top row is the **lanthanides**, the bottom the **actinides**. Chemists spent a happy few decades in the 19th century disentangling these elements, which are all very much alike. These series represent filling out the **f** orbitals— but they all have the higher-energy 6s (lanthanides) or 7s (actinides) shell filled, which is why they are so similar chemically.

As atomic weight increases, there's a greater chance of spontaneous nuclear decay— **radioactivity**— the atom throws off a particle of helium, or otherwise splits. Some radioactive elements, like uranium, can last for a few billion years; the really high numbers are only stable for minutes or less, which is why it's not likely your sf unobtainium will ever be found up there.

Naming the elements

The elements discovered in the 19th century and later are named, rather arrogantly, after nations and famous physicists. To make up for this, four of them are named for the same tiny village in Sweden.[4]

Concultures on other planets, or in the future, could do better. Below is a list of the elements with their year of discovery and some basic facts to help in naming. For more, including beautiful pictures, I recommend Theodore Gray's *The Elements*. To get a feeling for the elements without risk of explosions, read Oliver Sacks's delightful *Uncle Tungsten*.

A few element symbols are non-transparent:

Fe	iron	Lt. *ferrum*
Na	sodium	Ger. *natrium* from the compound *nitre*
K	potassium	Ger. *Kalium*— cf. *alkali*
Sb	antimony	Lt *stibium* (used for stibnite or kohl)
Sn	tin	Lt *stannum*
Pb	lead	Lt *plumbum*
Cu	copper	vulgar Lt *cuprum* < *Cyprus*
Ag	silver	Lt *argentum*
Hg	mercury	late Lt *hydrargyrum* 'water-silver'

If a color isn't given, it's silvery. Pure elements are very boring in color— the interesting colors are all from compounds.

Where half-lives are given, it's for the most stable isotope.

---

[4] Really they're named for a mine near the village. Lanthanides are very hard to separate, so if you have a sample with one, you've pretty much got them all.

▸ See *Substances*, p. 342, for notable compounds

| 1 | H | hydrogen | 1766 | 75% of all matter; lightest gas; powers sun's nuclear energy; part of water and most organic compounds; foundation of acid/base chemistry |

Alkali metals

3	Li	lithium	1817	soft metal; floats on water; highly flammable and reactive; used in batteries and as a mood stabilizer
11	Na	sodium	1807	a soft metal, but naturally occurs only in compounds, including salt, feldspar, and sodas
19	K	potassium	1807	silvery metal but oxidizes black and explodes in water; essential nutrient (eat bananas!); potash is a common fertilizer
37	Rb	rubidium	1861	discovered from a purplish emission line; used in atomic clocks and fireworks
55	Cs	cesium	1860	gold-colored; melts in your hand, explodes in water; used to define the second
87	Fr	francium	1939	radioactive metal, naturally occurring but with a half-life of just 22 minutes

Alkali earth metals

4	Be	beryllium	1797	hard metal; hardens other metals in alloys; good aerospace material; component of some gems, e.g. emerald; dust is very toxic
12	Mg	magnesium	1808	strong light metal, very flammable
20	Ca	calcium	1808	light quickly-oxidizing metal; calcium carbonate makes up shells and Dover's cliffs; blackboard chalk is calcium sulfate; essential nutrient, crucial for bones
38	Sr	strontium	1808	used to harden aluminum alloys; strontium aluminate is nicely phosphorescent
56	Ba	barium	1808	slightly orangish light metal, quickly oxidizing (one use is getting oxygen etc. out of vacuum tubes); barium sulfate is used in medical imaging
88	Ra	radium	1898	radioactive metal used for glowing watch dials as well as other ill-advised products; half-life 1600 years

Nonmetals

6	C	carbon		hard clear crystal (diamond) or soft black rock (graphite); 4th most abundant element in universe and 2nd-most in human body; basis of organic chemistry including fossil fuels; easily produced in impure form as charcoal
7	N	nitrogen	1772	a gas, 78% of air; lots of useful compounds, incl. ammonia, saltpeter, nitric acid, many fertilizers
8	O	oxygen	1773	a gas, 21% of air; 3rd-most abundant element in universe and most abundant in Earth's crust; essential for respiration and combustion; forms water with H; most metals occur in crust as oxides
15	P	phosphorus	1669	pure white phosphorus is nasty explosive stuff; red is safer and is used to ignite matches; phosphates are an essential fertilizer
16	S	sulfur		a yellowish crystal, the smell of hell (Biblical *brimstone*); sulfides stink up rotten eggs and onions; sulfuric acid used widely in industry
34	Se	selenium	1818	transparent crystal; used in photocopiers and other products; a micronutrient (Brazil nuts are high in it)

Metalloids

5	B	boron	1808	black crystal or brown powder; formed by cosmic ray bombardment rather than in stars; best known compound is borax
14	Si	silicon	1824	in pure form, a bright metal; its oxide is sand, and other compounds form much of the Earth's crust; major component of computer chips
32	Ge	germanium	1886	metal, helped vindicate Mendeleev; used in early transistors; used in fiber optics
33	As	arsenic	1250	metal with notoriously toxic compounds; important in semiconductors
51	Sb	antimony	900	more brittle and crystalline than metals, yet hardens lead for fonts or bullets; popular with the alchemists; quite toxic
52	Te	tellurium	1782	used in DVDs and solar cells; rather smelly
84	Po	polonium	1898	radioactive; used in antistatic brushes

Ordinary metals

13	Al	aluminum	1825	light and strong, suitable for aerospace or the kitchen; oxide (corundum) forms a hard protective coating; common in crust; conducts heat well
31	Ga	gallium	1875	silvery metal, melts at just above room temperature; important in semiconductors and LEDs
49	In	indium	1863	named for its indigo emission line; very soft; heavily used in LCD screens
50	Sn	tin		an ancient metal, non-rusting but prone to crystallize in cold weather; alloys copper to form bronze; no longer used for cans and soldiers
81	Tl	thallium	1861	a reddish metal, highly toxic
82	Pb	lead		soft, dense grayish metal; used for centuries in pipes, fonts, and bullets; protects against radiation; added to glass to increase sparkle; also toxic
83	Bi	bismuth	1753	slightly reddish metal; highest-numbered stable element— except it's not *quite:* it decays with a half-life a billion times longer than the age of the universe
114	Fl	flerovium	1994	radioactive, half-life 1 min
116	Lv	livermorium	2000	radioactive, half-life 61 ms

Halogens

9	F	fluorine	1886	pale yellow gas, very reactive; compounds used for refrigerants and to reduce tooth decay; component of Teflon and Prozac
17	Cl	chlorine	1810	pale yellow, highly toxic gas; used in disinfectants; forms table salt, bleach, and hydrochloric acid
35	Br	bromine	1826	liquid (but quickly evaporates); mostly found as salts
53	I	iodine	1811	black solid that boils into a lovely purple vapor; a strong early disinfectant; a nutrient that prevents goiter
85	At	astatine	1940	radioactive; appears briefly as uranium or thorium decays

Noble gases

2	He	helium	1868	24% of matter; lighter than air; forms from hydrogen fusion in normal stars, or from radioactive decay

10	Ne	neon	1898	5th most abundant in universe but on Earth found mostly in air; glows reddish-orange in electrified tubes (other colors are not neon)
18	Ar	argon	1894	1% of air; used with nitrogen to fill light bulbs; glows bright blue in electric tubes
36	Kr	krypton	1898	once used in light bulbs; glows dark blue in electric tubes; as it's inert, Superman's "kryptonite" is particularly unlikely
54	Xe	xenon	1898	glows violet in electric tubes; used in arc lighting; strangely, it forms compounds, mostly with fluorine
86	Rn	radon	1900	radioactive gas; quick-decaying but common because it's produced by natural uranium and thorium

Transition metals

21	Sc	scandium	1879	rarely localized and thus expensive to collect; strengthens aluminum nicely
22	Ti	titanium	1791	non-rusting, extremely strong; its oxide is a major component in paint; non-allergenic, so it makes good body implants
23	V	vanadium	1801	yellowish metal; most important in forming hard steel alloys
24	Cr	chromium	1797	key ingredient in stainless steel and most 'silverware'; 'chrome' in cars is a thin electroplated layer; oxide is bright green
25	Mn	manganese	1774	slightly yellowish metal; used in steel alloys; black oxides are an ancient pigment
26	Fe	iron		a heavy metal, black in pure form; pure or in alloyed form (steel), the foundation of industry; also an important nutrient; makes blood red
27	Co	cobalt	1735	grayish metal; used to make tough steel alloys; its compounds make blue or purple pigments
28	Ni	nickel	1751	nickel-colored (but the coin is only 25% Ni); widely used to plate iron to prevent rust; nickel-iron alloys resist high heat, thus used in jet engines
29	Cu	copper		reddish metal; alloyed with tin to form bronze, or zinc to form brass; highly electrically conductive, thus used in wiring
30	Zn	zinc		slightly dull; zinc anodes used to protect iron from rust; now used for US penny
39	Y	yttrium	1843	used in lasers and superconductors

40	Zr	zirconium	1789	strong and hard, used to contain nuclear fuel; oxides make both abrasives and fake diamonds
41	Nb	niobium	1801	resists corrosion even when very hot, so used in rocket engines; good for jewelry due to safety and pretty anodized colors
42	Mo	molybdenum	1778	in pure form, resists stress well, but mostly used to strengthen steel
43	Tc	technetium	1937	first artificial element; lowest-atomic-number radioactive element; used for medical imaging
44	Ru	ruthenium	1844	darkish gray, often used to plate jewelry; used as a catalyst and alloying agent
45	Rh	rhodium	1803	very shiny, so used in plating jewelry; used in catalytic converters
46	Pd	palladium	1803	yellowish metal, used in catalytic converters and for plating as it doesn't tarnish
47	Ag	silver		the best reflector (i.e. it's shiny) but tarnishes easily; best electrical conductor
48	Cd	cadmium	1817	used for non-rusting bolts and Ni-Cd batteries; its sulfide is a bright yellow pigment
72	Hf	hafnium	1923	a small but key component in plasma torches
73	Ta	tantalum	1802	used in capacitors
74	W	tungsten	1783	strong at high temperatures and cheap, thus used in light bulb filaments; very dense, thus used to weight darts; tungsten carbide is harder and tougher than steel; also good for radiation shielding
75	Re	rhenium	1925	costly; used in Ni-Fe alloys in jet turbines
76	Os	osmium	1803	slightly bluish, very hard; densest of elements; costly; was used for phonograph needles
77	Ir	iridium	1803	costly and very dense; used in spark plug tips; forms alloys with platinum
78	Pt	platinum	1735	withstands heat and acids; important in oil refining; costly, so it's used in tiny amounts in e.g. electrodes
79	Au	gold		gold-colored; non-corroding, thus shiny forever; excellent electrical conductor
80	Hg	mercury		a liquid, so dense that lead and steel float in it; used for tooth fillings and (formerly) batteries; a deadly but very slow toxin
104	Rf	rutherfordium	1964	half-life 1 hour
105	Db	dubnium	1967	half life 28 hours
106	Sg	seaborgium	1974	half-life 2 min
107	Bh	bohrium	1977	half-life 61 s

108	Hs	hassium	1984	half-life 10 s
109	Mt	meitnerium	1982	half-life 8 s
110	Ds	darmstadtium	1994	half-life 11 s
111	Rg	roentgenium	1994	half-life 26 s
112	Cn	copernicum	1996	half-life 9 min

Lanthanides

57	La	lanthanum	1839	slightly yellowish; used in lighter flints and to make sparks
58	Ce	cerium	1803	abundant (much more so than lead); slightly yellowish; catches fire when scratched
59	Pr	praseodymium	1885	used in glassblowers' lenses, which cut out the intense yellow light of molten glass
60	Nd	neodymium	1885	slightly bluish; an alloy with boron and iron makes powerful magnets; used in lasers
61	Pm	promethium	1945	the only radioactive lanthanide; used in some compact fluorescents
62	Sm	samarium	1879	used in magnets and medicines
63	Eu	europium	1896	used in compact fluorescents, and for the red in cathode-ray tubes
64	Gd	gadolinium	1880	used in medical imaging; curiously, magnetic when cold and non-magnetic when warm
65	Tb	terbium	1843	changes shape in a magnetic field— used for speakers
66	Dy	dysprosium	1886	used in high-intensity lighting
67	Ho	holmium	1879	concentrates magnetic fields; used in medical imaging and in lasers
68	Er	erbium	1843	a crucial component in lasers
69	Tn	thulium	1879	used in high-intensity lighting
70	Yb	ytterbium	1907	doping element in lasers
71	Lu	lutetium	1907	used in high-intensity lighting

Actinides

Note: all radioactive; above uranium, all artificial

89	Ac	actinium	1899	half-life 22 years; decays from radium; used in radiation therapy
90	Th	thorium	1829	a very abundant metal, used as nuclear fuel, in magnesium alloys, and to increase refractive index of lenses
91	Pa	protactinium	1918	half life 32,788 years
92	U	uranium	1789	abundant goldish metal; used as reactor fuel and in atomic bombs; very dense, good for e.g. armor-piercing bullets; once used in glass and glazing

93	Np	neptunium	1940	decays from americium, so it's found in smoke detectors; used to detect high-energy neutrons
94	Pu	plutonium	1940	the major component of today's atomic bombs; good power source for space probes
95	Am	americium	1944	used in smoke detectors (smoke interferes with the emitted helium atoms), as well as neutron probes
96	Cm	curium	1944	used to power space probes; also in X-ray spectrometers
97	Bk	berkelium	1949	half-life 1380 years
98	Cf	californium	1949	used in neutron activation analysis— it emits neutrons, which can penetrate almost anything, allowing remote detection of various things— gold, oil, explosives
99	Es	einsteinium	1952	half-life 1.3 years
100	Fm	fermium	1952	half-life 100 days
101	Md	mendelevium	1955	half-life 52 days
102	No	nobelium	1958	half-life 1 hour
103	Lr	lawrencium	1961	half-life 3.6 hours

EMOTION

afraid ME 'affrayed' = 'out of peace'

alarm It *all' arme* 'to arms'
- Ger *Wecker* 'waker' • Ch *jǐngbào* 'warn-report'

amuse Fr *amuser* 'cause to muse (stare stupidly)'

anger Norse *angr* 'trouble, affliction'
- Gk ὀργή 'mood', χόλος 'bile' (> Fr *colère*) • Lt *īra* < 'strength' or 'passion' • Ger *Zorn* < 'torn' • Sw *vrede* < 'twisted' • Latvian *dusmas* 'panting' • OCS *gněvŭ* prob. < 'rot' • Cz *zlost* 'evil' • Ch *fèn* prob. < 'swell, increase'

anxious Lt *anxius* 'troubled' < 'pressed'
- Ger *Angst* < 'narrow' • Ir *sníomh* 'spinning' • Welsh *pryder* 'care' • Lith *bailė* 'fear' • Ch *guànniàn* 'hang thought'

bitter OE *biter* < 'biting'
- Gk πικρός 'pointed' • Ir *searbh* prob. < 'sour' • Skt *tikta-* 'sharp'

bore OE *borian* 'pierce' (but 'be tedious' is ModE, uncertain)

calm Fr *calme* apparently < Gk 'great heat'

caution Fr. 'security' < Lt *cavēre* 'beware'

cheer Old Fr *chere* < Late Lt *cara* 'face' (> countenance > disposition > good mood)
- Fr *gaité* < Germanic 'impetuous' • Ch *gāoxìng* 'high mood'

confuse Lt *confūsus* 'poured together'

cruel Lt *crūdēlis* 'rough, bloodthirsty', from 'raw, bloody'

delight Lt *dēlectāre* frequentative of 'lure away'

desperate Lt *dēspērātus* antonym of 'hopeful'
- Ger *verzweifelt* 'for-doubted' • Ch *juéwàng* 'exhaust-hope'

disgust Fr *dégouter* 'taste bad'

dread ME *dreden*

eager Fr *aigre* 'sharp, sour'
- Ger *eifrig* 'zealous' poss. < 'bitter' • Ch *kěwàng* 'thirst-hope'

emotion Lt *ēmōtio* 'moving out'
- Gk πάθος 'suffer' • Lt *adficere* 'do at' • Skt *bhāva-* 'being, becoming' • Ch *qíng* < 'nature, attribute'

enjoy Old Fr *enjoier* 'in joy'

excite Lt *excitāre* frequentative of 'set in motion'

experience Lt *experientia* 'trial, test'
- Ger *erfahren* 'begin-drive' • Ch *jīng* < 'pass through'

fear OE *fǽr* 'peril' > 'emotion facing peril'
- Gk φόβος 'flight' • Lt *pavor* prob. < 'struck' • Fr *crainte* < 'shake' • Dutch *schrik* < 'jump' • OCS *strachŭ* < 'stiff'

FEEL   OE *félan* 'handle, touch' > 'perceive', prob cognate to Lt *palpāre*

• Gk ψηλαφάω < 'pluck' • Sw *känna* < 'know, perceive'

fierce   Old Fr *fers* 'untamed' ‖ *feral*

• Ch *xiōng* 'evil'

glad   OE *glæd,* possibly 'smooth' > 'bright' > 'cheerful'

grave   Lt *gravis* 'heavy'

happy   ModE 'by chance' > 'by good fortune'

• Gk εὐδαίμων 'good daemon' • Lt *fēlix fēlīc-* < 'fruitful' • Fr *bonheur* 'good omen' • Ir *sona* 'wellness' • Ger *glücklig* 'lucky' • OCS *blaženŭ* 'blessed'

horror   Lt *horror* nomn. of 'bristle, shudder'

joy   Fr *joie* < Lt *gaudium* 'joy, delight'

• Sp *alegría* < 'lively' • Welsh *dywenydd* < 'smile' • Ger *Freude* prob. < 'quick' • Avestan *šāiti-* < 'rest' • Ch *lè* ‖ 'music'

mad   OE ʒ*emæd* 'made insane'

• Gk μανικός 'furious, raging' • Lt *insānus* 'unsound', *dēmens* 'away-mind' • It *pazzo* < 'the patient' • Welsh *gwallgof* 'lack-sense' • Ger *verrückt* 'displaced' • Rus безумный 'without mind' • Skt *vātula-* 'windy'

misery   Lt *miser* 'wretched, unfortunate'

nervous   Lt *nervōsus* 'sinewy'

pain   Lt *pœna* 'penalty, punishment'

• Lt *dolor* prob. < 'split, burst' • Ger *Schmerz* < 'crush, bite' • Pol *ból* < 'sickness, pain'

passion   Lt *passio* 'suffering'

• Dutch *hartstocht* 'heart-pull' • Latvian *kaislība* 'inflammation' • Ch *jiqíng* 'violent emotion'

pity   Lt *pietas pietāt-* 'piety'

• Lt *misericordia* 'wretched heart' • Welsh *tosturi* < 'cruel' • Danish *medynk* 'with-distress' • Rus жалость < 'grief' • Ch *lián* ‖ 'kindness', 'love'

pleasant   Fr *plaisant* 'pleasing'

pleasure   Fr *plaisir* nomn. of 'please'

relax   Lt *relaxāre* 'loosen'

• Fr *se détendre* 'loosen up'

relief   Lt *relevāre* 'lift again'

sad   OE *sæd* 'sated' > 'firm' > 'solemn' > 'sorrowful'

• Lt *tristis* poss. < 'grim' • Ir *brónach* 'grief' • OE *unrót* 'unglad' • Ger *traurig* < 'gory' • Skt *viṣaṇṇa-* 'sitting apart' • Ch *bēi* 'unhappy'

satisfy Lt *satisfacere* 'do enough'
serious Lt *sērius* 'grave, serious'
    • Ger *ernst* ‖ earnest • Ch *yán* < 'lofty'
shame OE *scamu* poss. < 'cover'
    • Gk αἰδώς 'reverence, modesty' • Lt *pudor* poss. < 'repulsed'
    • Fr *honte* '< 'dishonor' • Sp *vergüenza* < 'awe' • OCS *studŭ* ‖
    'hate' • Ch *xiū* < 'dirty'
shock Fr *choc* uncertain
    • Ch *zhènjīng* 'shake-fear'
sorry OE *sáriʒ* 'pained', from 'sore'
startle ME *stertle* < 'start = jump up'
suffer Lt *subferre* 'bear under'
    • Ger *leiden* < 'go through' • Skt *duḥkha-* 'ill, unpleasant' • Qu
    muchuy 'lack' • Ch *zāo* < 'meet'
surprise Fr *surpris* < 'taken under'
    • Ger *überraschen* '(come upon) rapidly' • Ch *jīngqí* 'afraid-
    unusual'
terror Lt *terror* 'dread, alarm' < 'tremble'
    • Gk δεῖμα cognate to 'threat', 'hate'
weary OE *wériʒ* 'tired' (modern sense is stronger)
worry OE *wyrʒan* 'strangle'
    • Qu *nanachikuy* 'hurt oneself'
+ *apathy, coward, depression, despair, disappointed, grief,*
    lament, merry, panic, shy

Paul Ekman (in *Emotions Revealed*) organizes all emotions under six basic types, based on a study of cultures worldwide:

    anger
    disgust
    fear
    joy
    sadness
    surprise

In *Making Comics*, Scott McCloud illustrates these and, more interestingly, shows how the wider range of emotions are formed out of these by **degrees**—

Mild...			...Intense
stern	*indignant*	*angry*	*raging*
disdainful	*averse*	*disgusted*	*revolted*
concern	*anxious*	*fearful*	*terrified*

satisfied	*amused*	*joyful*	*laughing*
dejected	*melancholy*	*sad*	*grieving*
alert	*wondering*	*surprised*	*shocked*

or **combinations**:

	disgust	fear	joy	sadness	surprise
anger	*outrage*	*caged animal*	*cruelty*	*betrayal*	*WTF!*
disgust		*horror*	*eww, dude!*	*pain empathy*	*you ate it??*
fear			*desperate hope*	*devastation*	*spooked*
joy				*faint hope*	*amazement*
sadness					*disappointment*

Throw in combinations of milder emotions (*mild joy + mild sadness = pity*) and you can get close to a thousand variations. I don't know if anyone has created a conlang based on these ideas, but at the least it provides a path for providing many of the terms.

Visual artists can find more, including the muscles that underlie these expressions, in Gary Faigin's *The Artist's Complete Guide to Facial Expression.*

Many emotions come with variant terms which include, at no extra charge, the speaker's disapproval (*whiny, smarmy, cowardly, simpering, slack-jawed, hedonistic, tight-assed, self-pitying*) or, more rarely, approval or at least concern (*compassionate, noble, heroic, pleasant, innocent, pitiable*).

One approach to creating terms for emotions is to look at what they make you do— shudder, cry, run, cry, etc. Or use metaphorical actions or qualities: *excite* = poked, *relax* = loosen, *depressed* = pushed down, *grave* = heavy, *delight* = brightness.

▸ See also *Temperament, p.* 274.

EVENTS

act	Lt *actum* < *agere* 'drive, act, do'
	• Ger *handeln* < 'hand' • Ch *xíngdòng* 'walk-move'
active	Lt *actīvus*
AGAIN	OE *onȝeán* 'back'
	• Lt *dēnuo* 'anew' • Fr *encore* < 'at that hour' • Sp *otra vez* 'another time' • Ger *nochmal* 'still' + temporal suffix • Ch *zài* < 'repeat, twice'
agent	Lt *agens* 'actor'
always	ME *alles weis* 'all way's'
	• Gk ἀεί < 'lifetime' • Lt *semper* < 'one-day' • Fr *toujours* 'all days' • Ger *immer* 'ever more' • Cz *stále* < 'stand'
BEGIN	OE *biginnan*
	• Lt *incipere* 'seize in' • Fr *commencer* < 'enter with' • Ir *tosaigh* 'leading forth' • Sw *börja* 'carry' • Lith *pradėti* 'put ahead'
busy	OE *bisiȝ*
	• Fr *occupé* 'occupied' • Ger *beschäftig* 'making by' • Qu *ruwanayoq* 'has things to do'
cease	Lt *cessāre* frequentative of *cēdere* 'go, give up' (> *cede*)
	• Lt *dēsinere* 'put down' • Welsh *peidio* 'submit' • Ger *aufhören* 'obey off' • Latvian *beigties* < 'end' • OCS *prěstati* 'stand before' • Skt *uparam-* < 'rest'
chance	Fr < Lt *cadentia* 'falling = how things happen'
	• Ger *Zufall* 'to-falling' • Ch *yìwài* 'unexpected'
common	Lt *commūnis* 'bound together' ‖ Ger *gemeinsam*
	• Gk κοινός < 'with' • Pol *spólny* 'same side' • Skt *sādhāraṇa-* 'hold together' • Ch *tōng* < '(well) communicated'
complete	Lt *complētus* intensive of 'filled'
constant	Lt *constans* 'stand together (firmly)'
	• Ch *jīngcháng* 'experience-always'
continue	Lt *continuāre* 'hanging together = uninterrupted'
develop	Fr *développer* < antonym of 'wrap, roll up'
	• Ch *kāifā* 'open-send'
DO	OE *dón* 'put, act' < IE, cognate to Lt *facere*
	• Gk ἔρδω < 'work' • Ir *déan* < 'beget' • Bulgarian *pravja* < 'direct'

END   OE *ende*

     Spatial: • Lt *extrēmus* 'outermost' • Fr *bout* 'strike' • Ir *deireadh* 'remains' • OCS *konici* < 'begin' ='an end-point' • Ch *mò* 'tip' poss. < '(comes to) nothing'

     Temporal: • Gk τέλος 'completion' • Lt *fīnis* 'boundary' • Sw *slut* 'closing' • Avestan *θraošti-* 'grow to maturity'

engage   Fr *engager* 'in pledge'

event   Lt *ēventus* 'occurence' < 'come out'

     • Ger *Fall* 'fall' • Ch *shìbiàn* 'affair-change'

finish   Lt *fīnis* 'end'

     • Ger *aufhören* 'obey up' • Ch *jiéshù* < 'tie'

forever   ModE 'for always'

happen   ME 'occur by chance' < Norse *happ* 'chance'

     • Lt *accidere* < 'fall' • Fr *se passer* < 'step', *occurrir* < 'run for' • Cz *státi se* refl. of 'stand' • Sw *hända* < 'seize, concern'

interrupt   Lt *interrumpere* 'break between'

     • Ch *dǎduàn* 'hit-sever'

NEVER   OE *nǽfre* 'not ever'

     • Fr *jamais* 'ever' • Sw *aldrig* 'in a lifetime' • Ger *nie* 'not always' • Lith *niekad* 'not when'

normal   Lt *normālis* adjn. of 'carpenter's square' > 'pattern'

     • Ch *zhèngcháng* 'always straight'

occasion   Lt *occāsio* nomn. of 'fall toward'

occur   Lt *occurere* 'run against, meet'

often   ME derivation of OE 'oft'

     • Gk πολλάκις 'many' • Lt *sæpes* < 'crowded' • Fr *souvent* < 'right after' • Ger *häufig* 'in heaps' • Skt *asakṛt* 'not once'

ONCE   OE *anes* genitive of 'one'

opportunity   Lt *opportūnus* 'suitable'

pause   Gk παῦσις 'halt, cease'

proceed   Lt *prōcēdere* 'go forward'

process   Lt *prōcessus* nomn. of 'proceed'

rare   Lt *rārus* 'low density, scarce'

     • Ch *shǎoyǒu* 'few-have'

repeat   Lt *repetere* 'attack again'

stable   Lt *stabilis* < 'stand'

start   OE *styrten* 'leap'

     • Ger *anfangen* 'catch on' • Ch *chū* 'first'

steady   ModE adjn. of 'stand'

stop   OE *(for)stoppian* < Rom 'plug up' > 'block' > 'cease moving'
                    • Fr *arrêter* 'make rest' • Sp *parar* < 'make ready' • Ch *tíng* < 'settle, set up'

subject   Lt *subjectus* 'thrown under'
                    • Gk θέμα 'proposition' < 'placement' • Ch *tí* < 'raise'

+   *habit, vary, lazy, role, victim*

A very powerful metaphor for talking about events— so basic that we're hardly aware of it as such— is EVENTS ARE OBJECTS. This allows us to use our conceptual and linguistic tools relating to objects to talk about events— we can talk about a *threat* or a *talk* or a *beginning* as easily as we talk about a *book* or a *tree* or a *tongue.*

The idea of movement is used as well; see the etymologies of *occur, event, occasion, chance, subject.* The metaphor NON-VARIATION IS STANDING gives us *steady, stable.*

Another basic metaphor TIME IS SPACE, gives us expressions like *in the act* and *present,* and allows locatives (p. 250) to apply to times and events as well.

EXISTENCE

absent	Lt *absens* 'being away'
	• Ger *fehlend* 'missing' • Ch *quēxí* 'vacant seat'
appear	Lt *appārēre* 'come in sight to'
BE	OE *béon* 'become' < IE *bheu-*, cognate to Lt *fuī*, OCS *byti*; present *is, am, are* < IE **es-*; past *was, were* < IE **wes-* 'remain, dwell'
	• Sp *estar* < 'stand' • Ch *shì* < 'right' < 'this'
become	OE *becuman* < Germanic 'be come'
	• Gk γίγνομαι 'be born' • Fr *devenir* < 'arrive' • Ger *werden* < 'turn' • Sw *bliva* 'remain' • Ch *chéng* 'finish'
change	Lt *cambīre* 'exchange, barter'
	• Gk ἀλλάσσω < 'other' • Welsh *troi* 'turn' • Sp *mudar* < 'alter, change' • Ch *huàn* < 'turn (in a circle)'
create	Lt *creātus* 'produced, made'
	• Ger *schaffen* < 'carve' • Ch *zào* 'make, build'
destroy	Lt *dēstruere*, antonym of 'pile up, construct'
	• Gk καταστρέφω 'overturn' • Ger *vernichten* 'for nought' • OCS *razoriti* 'loosen apart' • Pol *niszczyć* 'make low' • Skt *nāçaya-* causative of 'perish, be lost' • Qu *qollochiy* 'cause disaster'
disappear	Fr *disparaître* antonym of 'appear'
evolve	Lt 'roll out'
exist	Lt *existere* 'stand out, step forth'
	• Ger *vorkommen* 'come forth' • Qu *kawsay* 'live' • Ch *zài* < 'be at, set up'
generate	Lt *generāre* 'beget'
origin	Lt *orīgo* 'rising, beginning'
	• Ger *Ursprung* 'origin-arising' • Ch *běn* 'root'
present	Lt *præsens* 'be before = be at hand'
vanish	Lt *ēvānescere* 'vanish out' < 'empty'

In Hebrew *bārā ʾ* 'create' specifically refers to creation *ex nihilo*, and thus can only be used of God. Everyone else has to *yāṣar* 'produce' or *ʿāśā* 'do, make'.

Spanish distinguishes 'being' something temporarily (*está borracho* 'he's drunk') and permanently (*es borracho* 'he's a drunk'). African-American English makes the same distinction by including or omitting *be*: *He drunk* vs. *He be drunk*, respectively.

Existence may be a simple concept, but it's not a simple word. Most of the English terms are from Latin, and involve the metaphor EXISTING IS STANDING, with the corollary COMING-TO-BE IS MOVING (HERE).

English *turn into* is a rather neat equation of 'moving in place' to 'becoming'.

The other obvious metaphor is COMING-TO-BE IS BIRTH, as in *generate* or Greek *genesis*. Note that Greek has a neat noun and verb (γίγνεσθαι) for 'come to be', which is awkward in English.

FOOD

bread
OE *bréad* < Germanic 'bit, morsel'
• Lt *panis* < 'food' • Latvian *maize* < 'barley' • Ch *miànbāo* 'flour-wrap'

breakfast
ME 'break fast' (like Sp *desayuno*)
• Gk ἄριστον 'early' • It *colazione* 'gathering' • Ir *céadphroinn* 'first meal' • Danish *frokost* 'early food' • Dutch *ontbijt* 'un-bite' • Lith *pusryčiai* 'half-morning' • Cz *snidane* 'eat with' • Ch *zǎocān* 'morning meal'

cook
Lt *coquus* 'a cook' < IE *pek^w-
• Rum *gǎti* < 'prepare' • OCS *variti* 'boil' • Qu *chayachiy* 'make arrive' • Ch *zuòfàn* 'do cooked rice'

cup
Lt variant of *cūpa* 'tub, cask'
• Fr *tasse* < Ar 'bowl' • Lt *pōculum* < 'drink'

dine
Fr *dîner* 'end one's fast'
• ModGk γεῦμα 'taste' • Lt *cēna* 'portion' • OE *æfenmete* 'evening meal' • Lith *pietūs* 'food' • OCS *obědǔ* 'eat' • Rus ужин < 'noon' < 'south' • Ch *chīfàn* 'eat cooked rice'

drink
OE *drincan*
• Lt *bibere* < IE *$pō$- • Lith *gerti* < 'swallow'

eat
OE *etan* < IE *ed-, cognate to Lt *ēsse*
• Fr *manger* < 'chew' • Danish *spise* 'food' • Rus кушать < 'taste'

egg
OE *ǽʒ* < IE *$ōwo$, poss. ‖ 'bird' (cf. Lt *ōvum, avis*)
• Latvian *uola* 'pebble' • Lith *kiaušis* dim. 'skull'

food
OE *fóda* ‖ feed, fodder
• Fr *nourriture* 'nourishment' • It *vitto* < 'live' • Ger *Speise* < 'expenses' • OCS *brašĭno* 'grain' • Lith *maistas* < 'provide, live on' • Bulgarian *hrana* < 'protect' • Ch *shíwù* 'eat-thing'

fruit
Lt *fructus* '(what is) enjoyed'

knife
OE *cníf*
• Gk μάχαιρα 'fight' • Lt *culter* < 'cutter' • OCS *nožǐ* 'piercer'

lunch
ModE abbr. of 'luncheon' < perhaps Sp *lonja* 'slice, strip'
• Lt *prandium* prob. < 'early' • Fr *déjeuner* 'breakfast' • Sp *almuerzo* 'bite' • Norse *dagverðr* 'day-meal' • Rus завтрак 'tomorrow' • ModGk πρόγευμα 'before-dinner' • Ch *wufàn* 'noon-cooked.rice'

meal
OE *mǽl* 'repast, measure, occasion' < 'time'
• Gk δαίς 'portion' • Fr *repas* < 'feed' • Sp *comida* 'food' • Rus стол 'table' • Ch *cān* 'eat'

meat
OE *mete* 'food'
• Fr *viande* < 'life' • Ch *ròu* prob. < 'soft'

plate	Lt *plattus* 'flat'
	• Gk πίναξ 'board' • Fr *assiette* 'assigned (place)' • Rum *farfurie* 'porcelain' • Ger *Teller* < 'cut' • OCS *misa* < 'table'
tea	Fr *thé* < Middle Ch *ḍa* (Mandarin *chá*)
wine	Lt *vīnum*, cf. Gk οἶνος, Heb. *yayi*, uncertain
	• ModGk κρασί 'mixture' • Skt *madhu-* 'mead'
+	*coffee, milk, soda, cider, juice; poison*
	beer, ale, mead; ferment, brew
	fork, spoon, chopsticks, dish, kettle, bowl, pot, pan, oven
	cheese, honey, butter, sausage, gravy; butcher
	flour, dough, pastry, pasta, noodle, salt, sugar, spice
	candy, dessert, custard, pudding, cake, chocolate
	soup, broth, pie, sauce, stew

▸ See *Plants,* p. 301, and *Sensation,* p. 321, for flavors

It's worth spending some time thinking about how your people cook and eat. It tells you how they spend a good portion of the day, it has social and even spiritual ramifications, and it provides a sensual experience for the reader. I still remember C.S. Lewis's vivid descriptions of the meals served in Narnia.

(For more on basic cooking, see a good introductory cookbook. *The Joy of Cooking* has quite a lot of general noob-friendly information. A great introduction to the technology of cooking is Bee Wilson's *Consider the Fork.*)

Word variants

English doesn't have a common word for *eat **or** drink*, but Spanish does: *tomar.* You can *tomar* coffee, a pill, or breakfast.

In a premodern agricultural economy, the food you get in the largest quantity is grain, and it makes a good lexical stand-in for *food* or *meal*— as in "Give us this day our daily *bread.*" In Mandarin *chī-fàn* 'eat cooked rice' is simply to eat. (Mandarin likes verb + generalized object compounds— cf. *kàn-shū* 'read-book' for 'read'.)

Many languages don't bother to distinguish *meat* and *flesh* (e.g. It. *carne*, OCS *męso*).

Meals

How many meals are there in a day, and which is the chief one? People who do hard physical work generally prefer their main dinner to be at midday.

As habits change, words for a meal at one time frame shift to another— e.g. French *déjeuner* 'lunch' was originally *breakfast;* Russian ужин 'supper' was originally taken at noon.

What's the basic form of a meal?

- The oldest tradition is surely to gather round an animal, cooked or not, and grab off pieces.

- Put the meat in a pile on top of starch, such as rice or couscous. (The Argentine variant seems to be to skip the starch.)

- Serve big slabs of meat and let the diners cut off small pieces with knives and, as they get more civilized, forks.

- Cut the food up before cooking and eat with chopsticks.

- Wrap the food before cooking (in leaves, dough, or paper); this adds flavor and allows easy handling.

From the invention of agriculture till quite recently, how much meat you got correlated directly with social status. The majority of the population, till about 1800, lived at the subsistence level. In early medieval Europe, the poor had little meat but almost nauseating amounts of bread— three *pounds* a day per person, by one estimate.

Who does the cooking? In medieval Europe, chefs as a profession were men: cooking near an open fire was scorching and dangerous work. Bee Wilson points out that the first cookbooks written by and for British women were published at the same time the enclosed brick chimney and cast-iron fire grate were widely adopted, making the kitchen far safer.

Cooking

Cooking can be broadly divided into **dry heat** (cooking by exposure to heat, whether a fire or an oven) and **moist heat** (cooking with water or steam).

Dry heat

For centuries, in Western culture, there was an immense divide between *roasting* and *baking*. In the great houses these were done each in separate kitchens, with their own specialized equipment. You *roasted* food by sticking it on a *spit*, exposing it to open flame, and turning it. You *baked* it by putting it in an oven. Roasting was the technique *par excellence* for meat, baking for bread. The distinction largely evaporated in the 20th century with the adoption of the gas oven.

Grilling or *broiling* involves placing food directly on a grill or gridiron; the key difference from roasting is that only one side of the food is exposed to the heat at a time. Relatively short exposure to the grill, *toasting*, is appropriate for bread or cheese.

How did you make *crème brulée* without a blow torch? With a *salamander*, a long tool with a heavy lump of iron at the end. You heated it in the fire, then held it above the food, nicely broiling it.

Frying involves heating in a shallow pan; the high heat sears the outside of the food, sealing in juices. To *sauté* you agitate the pan (making the food inside 'jump'); to *stir-fry* you toss or stir the contents.

Deep-fat frying, as the name suggests, involves submerging the food in hot fat or oil. *Breading* absorbs more of the tasty fat... hey, who's hungry for KFC?

The Middle Eastern *tandoor* is a cylindrical clay oven, dating back three millennia, which (with far less fuel than the European open hearth) produces blistering temperatures, as high as 896° F. It can be equally be used for making bread or meat (and just one verb is needed, e.g. Arabic *khabaza*).

Chinese cooking relies heavily on a single type of knife, the cleaver-like *càidāo* ('vegetable knife'), and a single type of pan, the wok (*guō*). Chopping the food before cooking greatly reduces cooking time— a major advantage in a country where firewood is scarce. And of course the diner doesn't need a knife.

In Andean culture, large quantities of meat are cooked in a *pachamanka* or earth oven: stones are heated in a fire, meat is placed on top, and the whole thing is covered with grass and dirt and left alone while it cooks. The Polynesian *umu* is similar.

Moist heat

Boiling, cooking in boiling water, is notorious for producing bland foods. Most things taste better *simmered*, i.e. cooked in water just below the boiling point. *Poaching* involves either basting the food as it simmers or covering the pot, which produces a similar effect. *Stewing* is basically very long simmering. *Blanching* is done with boiling water in various ways, whose common element is shortening the exposure time.

Steaming lets steam do all the work, as in a double boiler, or the little bamboo containers used for dim sum.

There are combinations, as well; e.g. *braising* is browning in fat, followed by simmering in a closed pot.

Many languages don't differentiate *cook* and *boil*— e.g. German (*kochen*) and Russian (варить).

Sauces

French **sauces** are normally made as a coda to frying: remove the meat, leaving the pan brownings. Add butter, wine, or stock to dissolve these and create the sauce.

Asian sauces are diverse, but are often sweet-and-sour (combining soy sauce or fish sauce with sugar and vinegar) or salty-and-sour.

Classifying Chinese food

James McCawley's *Eater's Guide to Chinese Characters* offers the observation that many Chinese dishes are named with the formula *<cooking technique> <ingredient> <cutting technique>*.

炒	*chǎo*	stir-fried
炸	*zhá*	deep fried
煎	*jiān*	pan-fried
肉	*ròu*	meat (if no animal is specified, pork is understood)
牛	*niú*	beef
魚	*yú*	fish
雞	*jī*	chicken
蝦	*xiā*	shrimp
丁	*dīng*	cubed, diced
片	*piàn*	thin-sliced
絲	*sī*	shredded
塊	*kuài*	in bite-sized chunks
球	*qiú*	in strips that curl as they fry

With this information you can read dish names such as these:[5]

炒肉球　　炒牛肉絲　　　煎雞丁　　　　炸魚片

Preserving food

Premodern cooks faced the problem of **spoilage**. Raw meat spoils within hours at room temperature; cooking extends this a bit. To keep meat for longer, there are a few basic methods:

- Dry it out— that is, create *jerky*, from Quechua *charki*.

- Smoke it— most easily by hanging it above a fire. The smoke seals the outside layer of the meat, making it harder for bacteria to enter.

- Salt it. Nitrates (such as saltpeter) assist in killing bacteria and retaining the red color. Sugar may be added to improve the flavor.

- Freeze it, if you have the technology or live on an ice floe.

Vegetables can be preserved by **pickling**— soaking in salt brine, vinegar, or both.

Alcohol

Sometimes we just let the microorganisms win. **Fermentation** turns fruit juices into long-lasting wine, and milk into cheese. (It's interesting, or perhaps disturbing, that the mold used to ripen Roquefort is simple bread mold, and in fact in traditional cheesemaking the mold is collected by leaving bread to molder.)

In a premodern society, alcoholic drinks were far safer than the local water. There's some evidence that long-citified people develop a greater resistance to alcohol.

- Fruit **wines** (and *meads*, made of honey) depend on yeast (a fungus) turning sugar into alcohol. White wines are made by removing the skin just after crushing; red wines leave it in. The taste of wine is famously dependent on grape varietal, region, and other factors, so there are many ways your conpeople could divide up the concept.

---

[5] I've used traditional characters here, as they're what you're most likely to see on restaurant menus outside China.

- **Beer** starts with grains or other plants (in Europe, mostly barley). The starch is turned into a sugary liquid called *wort*, which is then fermented with yeast. Despite the extra step, beer is faster to make than wine.

  Hops (the ripened combs of a vine related to hemp) began to be added in medieval times, to impart a bitter flavor.

  A *lager* ferments mostly at the bottom of the tank, and at cooler temperatures; the process converts more of the sugar into alcohol, resulting in a less sweet beverage than *ales*, which are top-fermented.

  Rather than dividing beers by manner of production, French goes by color: *blonde, brune, blanche* ('blond, brown, white').

  Japanese **sake** is made with a similar process from rice, using a mold (*kōji*) to facilitate the breakdown of the rice starch. Traditionally the breakdown of starches to sugars was begun by chewing the grains, making use of the enzymes found in saliva.

- **Pulque** is produced from the sap of the agave plant.

  Chicha is widely made in Latin America from maize, **masato** from cassava.

- **Distillation** dates back about two thousand years; in Europe it was widely applied to wines starting in the medieval era (pioneered in the monasteries). The basic operation involves boiling a liquid and then collecting the condensate in another vessel; with alcoholic beverages the result is a great increase in the alcohol content.

  Wine can be mixed (*fortified*) with distilled wine for a in-between increase in alcohol content; examples are port, madeira, and sherry. Fortified wines last much longer than the regular kind.

GOVERNMENT

agent
Lt *agens* 'actor'

allow
Old Fr *alouer* 'make praise'
• Ger *erlauben* < 'approve' • Ch *yǔn* < 'trust'

authority
Lt *auctor* 'increaser = originator'

baron
Fr *baron* < 'man', i.e. the king's man

boss
Dutch *baas* 'master, uncle'
• Fr *patron* < 'protector' • Sp *jefe* 'chief' • Ch *gōngtóu* 'work-head'

captain
Fr *capitaine* < 'of the head = principal'
• [military] Ger *Hauptmann* 'main man' • [nautical] Ch *chuánzhǎng* 'ship-chief'

charge
Fr *charger* 'load a cart'

chief (tain)
Fr *chef* 'head'
• Ger *Haupt* 'main' • Ch *lǐngxiù* 'lead-sleeve'

command
Lt *commendāre* intensive of 'commit, charge' < 'put in s.o.'s hand'
• Gk κελεύω 'drive' • Ger *befehlen* 'grant' < 'bury' • Danish *byda* < 'awaken' • Ch *mìng* < 'name'

council
Lt *concilium* 'called together'

duke
Lt *dux duc-* 'leader'
• Ger *Herzog* 'army leader'

duty
Anglo-French *dueté* < *dû* 'owed'
• Lt *officium* 'make work' • Ger *Pflicht* < 'care' • Ch *yìwù* 'just matter'

elder
OE *eldra* 'older'

empire
Lt *imperium* 'command' < 'in-prepare'
• Ger *Kaiserreich* 'Caesar-realm' • Ch *dì* < 'god'

faction
Lt *factio* 'doing, making'
• Ch *zōng* 'clan'

free
OE *fréo* < Germanic 'dear', distinguishing family from slaves
• Lt *līber* prob. < 'of the people' • Ir *saor* < 'good man' • OCS *svobodĭ* < 'self, kin' • Ch *zìyóu* 'self-proceeding'

gentleman
ME 'well-born man'
• Sp *caballero* 'horseman' • Ger *Herr* 'lord' • Ch *jūnzǐ* 'son of a ruler'

govern
Lt *gubernāre* 'steer'
• Gk ἡγέομαι 'lead' • Pol *rządzić* < 'row, order' • Rus править < 'straighten'

king OE *cyning* ‖ *kin*
- Lt *rex rēg-*, Gallic *-rīx*, Skt *rāj-* < IE 'rule' • Welsh *brenin* < 'high' • OCS *kralĭ* < 'Charlemagne' • Ch *wáng* prob. < 'might, power' • Nahuatl *tlatoani* 'great speaker' • Sumerian *lugal* 'big man'

lady OE *hlǽfdíȝe* 'loaf-kneader'

lead OE *lǽdan* causative of *líðan* 'go'
- Lt *dūcere* 'draw, lead' • Fr *guider* < 'show' • Ir *treoraigh* < 'strong' • Welsh *tywys* < 'know'

LET OE *lǽtan* 'leave, allow'
- Fr *laisser* < 'relax' • Ch *ràng* 'concede'

lord OE *hláford* < 'bread-keeper'
- Gk κῦριος 'powerful' • Lt *dominus* < 'house' • OCS *gospodĭ* < 'guest-master' • Ger *Herr* < 'more venerable' • Ch *jué* < 'chew' = 'live off revenues'

majesty Lt *mājestās -tāt-* 'greatness'
- Ch *bìxià* 'steps to throne' + 'down'

manage It *maneggiare* 'use the hands'
- Fr *gérer* < 'carry' • Ch *lǐ* 'regulate'

master Lt *magister* < 'more'
- Skt *pati-* ‖ 'husband', 'able', Gk δεσπότης 'house-master' • Welsh *arglwydd* 'overlord'

mission Lt *missio missiōn-* 'sending'

nation Lt *nātio* nomn. of 'be born'
- Gk ἔθνος prob. < 'custom' • Old Ger *diot*, OE *þíod* < 'strong, swell, whole' • OCS *narodŭ* < 'generation' • Ch *guójiā* 'state-family'

noble Lt *nōbilis* 'famous' < 'known'
- Gk εὐγενής 'well-born' • Welsh *pendefig* < 'head' • Sw *ädling* 'estate-child' • Cz *šlechtic* < 'sort, kind' • Rus дворянин < 'court' • Ch *guì* 'precious'

office Lt *officium* 'doing before' = 'service, duty'
- Ru контора 'counting house' • Ch *bàngōngshì* 'manage-public-room'

peer Lt *pār* 'equal'

permit Lt *permittere* 'through' + 'let go' • Fr *laisser* 'relax' • Ger *erlauben* < 'trust' • OCS *povelěti* < 'will, order' • Skt *anujñā-* 'recognize'

politics Gk πολῑτικός 'of citizenship'

power Old Fr *poër* < Lt *posse* 'be able'
- Ger *Kraft* ‖ craft • Ch *lì* 'strength'

preside   Lt *præsidēre* 'sit before'
- Ger *Vorsitz* 'fore-sitting' • Ch *zhǒngtǒng* 'chief-unite'

prince   Lt *princeps princip-* 'principle' < 'take first', calqued in Ger as *Fürst* • Ir *flaith* 'ruler' • Welsh *tywysog* 'leader' • OCS *kŭnęzĭ* < Ger 'king' • Ch *wángzi* 'king-child'

queen   OE *cwén* < 'woman, wife'
- Danish *dronning* fem. of 'master' • Lt *rēgīna* fem. of 'king'

rank   Fr *rang* 'row, rank'
- Sp *fila* < 'thread' • Ch *děng* < 'step' < 'rise'

responsible   Fr 'able to respond'

royal   Fr *royal* < Lt adjn. of 'king'

rule   Lt *rēgula* 'stick, bar'
- Gk ἄρχω 'begin' = 'be first' • Lt *regere* 'direct' • Ger *herrschen* < 'lord' • OCS *vlasti,* cognate to *wield* • Skt *çās-* 'command' • Ch *zé* 'model, norm'

serve   Lt *servīre* < 'slave, servant'
- Lt *ministrāre* < 'lesser' • Ger *dienen* < 'slave' < 'rush, run' • Rus слуить < 'retainers' • Ch *pú* < 'child'

sir   Lt *senior* 'elder'
- Ger *Herr* 'lord' • Ch *xiānsheng* 'firstborn' (> Japanese *sensei*)

slave   Fr *esclave* < 'Slav'
- Lt *servus* poss. 'guardian' • Old Ir *dóir* 'bad-man' • OE *þrǽl* < 'oppress' • Lith *vergas* 'misery' • *rabu* 'work, trouble' • Pol *niewolnik* < 'unwilled' • Skt *dāsa-* 'non-Aryan' • Ch *nú* poss. < 'woman', or 'pressed (into service)'

support   Lt *supportāre* 'carry under'
- Ch *yǎng* 'rear'

throne   Gk θρόνος 'elevated seat'
- Ch *bǎozuò* 'treasure-seat'

+   *usurp, tyrant, assembly, bureau, embassy, ministry*

coronation, accession, diplomacy, treaty, tax

hierarchy, underling, align, vote, elect, intrigue, conservative, loyalist, reformer, radical

crown, flag, vassal, estate, appoint, steward

▸   For creating governments, see the PCK, p. 127.

Words for bosses lean on the metaphor AN ORGANIZATION IS A BODY, with the leader as head: *chief, captain, chef, headman, capo,* Russian глава, Mandarin *tóumù,* German *Hauptmann* 'captain'. In traditional societies the head guy was likely to be old, thus *elder, senior, sir, señor, monsignor.* Latin had the pair *magister/minister,* literally 'greater/lesser'; the first gave us *magistrate, master, maestro*, while the second is used directly in religion and government.

If you're a small neighbor of a major empire, you may get extra legitimacy by accepting a title from the emperor, or simply adopting it yourself, as the Germans took *Kaiser* and the Russians царь from Caesar, or as Europeans took *admiral* from the Arabs. Greek βασιλεύς 'king' seems to be taken from an unknown, non-IE people in the region. A huge number of our political terms (*elect, vote, census, consul, dictator, republic, empire, prince, Senate, plebeian, fascist*) are borrowed from the Romans.

Metaphors for ruling include steering a ship (*govern*), using the hands (*manage*), guarding something (*lord, steward*), or applying a standard (*rule*). More democratic states prefer the metaphor of *service*, already present in the idea of serving the king.

A natural metaphor for *power* is *strength*, as in Greek κράτος and Mandarin *quán* (etymologically 'fist'). French *pouvoir* and English *might* both share the idea of *ability*.

Seeking to adequately express the awe due one who can dispose of your life at will, language in the presence of monarchy resorts to hyperbole (e.g. extended titles claiming lands one does not in fact rule), indirection ('His august and imperial majesty'), and metonymy (*the throne, the crown, Westminster*). These may be used to derive further political terms— e.g. *coronation* for a king's investiture.

Though monarchs are likely to have distinctive headgear, you might consider something besides a crown; in Verduria the emblem of authority is a sash.

Nobility

Western aristocracy originates in getting a land and a title from the king in return for military service. This can be seen as an indictment of medieval monarchy: the institutions and wealth no longer existed to allow large standing armies and central control of a large country, to say nothing of a continent. A noble estate was as large a domain that could be competently managed, and sufficed to support a small but well-trained cavalry.

Of course, it was also a devil's bargain, as the nobles always wanted sovereignty, while the king wanted greater control. Nobles with private armies could and did go to war against the king.

In England, a charismatic monarch (Henry VII, Elizabeth I) could make the system work— though only with dubious expedients such as confiscating and selling church lands, or creating new titles for profit— but the end result was simple: the kings lost and Parliament won.

Thus the feudal nobility, geared for war, gave way to a landed aristocracy which preferred to sit back and collect rent, and ruled the country in uneasy alliance with the major city merchants.

A true feudal nobility was not large, and could be decimated by civil war. Henry IV's first Parliament included 97 Lords; in 1603 there were just 59. The peerage ballooned in the age of aristocracy: 186 Lords under Charles I; nearly a thousand under Victoria.

There's always churn in a noble system, feudal or aristocratic. Old estates decline; new families rise. As this goes against the ideology of a class that rules by inherent worth, it has to be somewhat hidden.

Important questions about a noble system:

- How far down the family tree does noble status go? The English system is strict about this (only the title-holder is 'noble', though heirs might get courtesy titles). Continental systems were more generous, with the result that anywhere from 1% to 15% of the population had noble status.

- What are the inheritance rules? Can women inherit? It's not always the case that the eldest son inherits.

In Western culture we've internalized the notion of patrilinearity— inheritance through the father. We still inherit family names this way, which encourages us to reify our names in a way that makes little genetic sense. (Without looking them up, can you list all the surnames of your great-grandparents?)

In pop culture (e.g. *Assassin's Creed* or *Les visiteurs*) we easily swallow a character looking exactly like his ancestor of 10 generations ago, as if DNA too were patrilineal.

Of course, an actual aristocracy increases the family resemblances by marrying cousins. In any case, the point is that by changing inheritance rules, you create different feelings for what a family is and how power works, even among non-nobles.

Ranks

The traditional European noble ranks are these:

king	OE *cyning*
prince	Lt. *princeps princip-* 'first'
duke	Lt. *dux duc-* 'leader'
marquis	'frontier (lord)'
count/earl	Lt. *comes comit-* 'companion' / OE *eorl*
viscount	Fr. 'under-count'
baron	Germanic 'warrior, free man'
knight	OE *cniht*

The ranks should mostly be taken as a rough guide to the size and importance of the estate. (Only rarely did a lower noble actually hold his estate from a higher.)

In Britain *prince* is restricted to the royal family, but elsewhere it may be a title in itself— e.g. Monaco is still a principality. German distinguishes *Prinz* 'monarch's son' from *Fürst* 'monarch who is not a king'.

Islamic nobility

The Islamic empires inherited and adapted the models of the more competent Byzantine and Persian states; they had neither nobles nor feudalism in their European forms.

There were two ways to become a large landowner:

- A grant of the right to collect taxes on land, in lieu of payment for governmental or military service.

- Tax farming, in which the grantee collected taxes and remitted a portion to the state.

Unlike Western lords, the landowners had no rights over the inhabitants beyond collecting taxes; they did not dispense justice or grant sub-fiefs.

In theory both arrangements were revocable and non-inheritable, but the landowners naturally tried to move in the direction of heritability and freedom from responsibility, while the state tried to exert more control. A change of regime often allowed the state to reacquire and redistribute the land.

If in Europe it can be said that the bourgeois took power from the aristocrats, in the Middle East the victors were the rulers, who used modern weapons and communications to actually make good on their age-old claims to absolute power.

China

From Hàn times at least, China has generally been able to maintain a powerful centralized system. Titles were granted by the emperor, but these were largely honorific.

Rather than relying on hereditary nobles, China relied on the imperial examination system— an exhaustive training in the ancient classics, producing a highly and uniformly educated ruling class. This was far more meritocratic than the European system, but was far from democratic— existing officials were the best placed to give their sons the necessary extensive schooling.

Ministries

The cabinet of George Washington's administration (1789-97) consisted of:

> Secretary of State
> Secretary of the Treasury
> Secretary of War
> Attorney General
> Postmaster General

The Navy was separated out in 1798; the next additions were Interior (1849), Agriculture (1889), and Labor/Commerce (1903).

The **British** cabinet system evolved out of the Privy Council, high officials who advised the monarch and could be entrusted with affairs of state. The later Stuarts relied on a secret subset of the Council— secret because what Parliament didn't know about, it couldn't supervise. This useful group became the Cabinet.

When George I arrived from Hanover, he had neither the ability nor the interest to run the British government; power effectively devolved to the Cabinet and was closely integrated with Parliament. Normally the leader of the House of Commons was also head of the Cabinet.

The members under Sir Robert Walpole (1730-42) show the typical, endearing British constitutional muddle; they are a mix of what are recognizable governmental ministries and age-old feudal offices.

Chancellor of the Treasury	taxation, borrowing, customs, mint, excise
Southern Secretary	both internal and external affairs, restricted geographically
Northern Secretary	

Lord Chancellor	administration of courts
Lord President of the Council	sinecure
Lord Privy Seal	sinecure
First Lord of the Admiralty	navy
Master-General of the Ordnance	artillery, engineering, fortifications, logistics
Paymaster of the Forces	received and disbursed military expenditures
Lord Steward	part of Royal Household
Lord Chamberlain	ran the Royal Household

The term *prime minister* was used in Walpole's time, but it was something of an insult. It only became official in the 19th century.

The Commander-in-Chief of the army was not a cabinet position (and in fact the position was vacant during Walpole's ministry). The administration of the army was in the hands of the War Office; military policy was however generally coordinated by the Northern and Southern Secretaries. If this sounds inefficient, well, Britain is an island— traditionally it neglected its army until well after a war started.

The **Chinese**, from the Táng dynasty, divided the executive into six ministries (*bù*):

吏	*Lì*	Personnel	appointments and ranking
戶	*Hù*	Revenue	taxation, treasury, census
禮	*Lǐ*	Rites	state ceremonies, foreign affairs, imperial examinations
兵	*Bīng*	Defense	war, including fortification and couriers
刑	*Xíng*	Justice	court and penal system
工	*Gōng*	Works	construction projects, roads, canals, gathering of resources

Xurno, one of the countries of Almea, is ruled by artists. It has nine ministries, each of which is supervised by one of the nine Salons (p. 127).

ministry		*responsibilities*	*overseers*
Lujidax	treasury	treasury, coinage, language	poetry
Šeledaus	customs	customs, excise, foreign ministry	music
Ešaudo	building	roads, buildings, fortifications	sculpture
Cívlex	army	defense and war	gymnastics
Midzudo	justice	criminal courts	drama
Besčeyséy	couriers	trade, post, maps, patents, civil law	weaving

Lučasú	engineers	irrigation, canals, ports, coast guard	painting
Zendzudo	education	culture, education	dance
Zezunas	registry	property registry, property law, re-cords; astronomy and cartography	prose

For a modern list, let's look at the **French** *conseil de ministres* (as of 2013), which is headed by the *premier ministre*:

Affaires étrangères	foreign affairs
Éducation nationale	national education
Justice	justice
Économie et Finances	economy and finance
Affaires sociales et Santé	social matters and health
Égalité des territoires et Logement	terriorial equality and housing
Intérieur	interior
Écologie, Développement durable et Énergie	ecology, sustainable development, and energy
Redressement productif	productive recovery
Travail, Emploi, Formation professionnelle et Dialogue Social	labor, employment, professional training and social dialog
Défense	defense
Culture et Communication	culture and communications
Enseignement supérieur et Recherche	higher education and research
Droits des femmes	women's rights
Agriculture, Agroalimentaire et Forêt	agriculture, food industry and forestries
Réforme de l'Etat, Décentralisation et la Fonction publique	state reform, decentralization, and public service
Outre-Mer	overseas departments
Sports, Jeunesse, Éducation populaire et Vie associative	sports, youth, popular education and community life
Commerce extérieur	foreign trade
Artisanat, Commerce et Tourisme	crafts, commerce, tourism

GRAMMAR

Articles

THE	OE *þe* prob. < 'that'
A	OE *án* 'one'

Comparatives

MORE	OE *mára*
MOST	OE *mǽst*
least	OE *lǽst* superl. of 'less'
less	OE *lǽs* 'littler'

Conjunctions

also	ME *all swa* 'all so'
AND	OE *and* < Germanic 'abutting, facing'
BECAUSE	ME 'by cause'
BUT	OE *be-útan* 'without, outside'
else	OE *elles* 'other'
however	ME 'how ever'
IF	OE *ʒif*
nor	ME abbr of 'nother'
OR	OE *ár* 'ere'
THEN	OE *þanne*
therefore	ME 'there fore'
THOUGH	OE *al þaʒ*
thus	OE *ðus*
WHILE	OE *hwíle* 'at the time'
unless	ME 'on less'

Deictics

THAT	OE *þæt* neuter demonstrative
THIS	OE *þis* neuter demonstative
THERE	OE *þǽr*
HERE	OE *hér*

Modals

CAN	OE *cunnan* 'know' > 'know how' > 'able'
	• Lt *posse* 'be able' • Rus мочь 'might, power' • Ch *huì* < 'understand'
COULD	OE past tense of 'can'

MAY	OE *maȝan* 'can' < 'be mighty'
	• Lt *licet* 'is permitted' < 'be for sale' • Ch *ke* 'bear' > 'able'
MIGHT	OE *miht* 'strong' > 'able' > 'possible'
MUST	past tense of *mót* 'may, must'
	• Fr *devoir* 'owe', *falloir* 'be needed' < 'lack' • Sw *bör* < 'be suitable' • ModE *have to,* cf. late Lt (inf.) *habere*
ought	OE past tense of *áȝan* 'owe'
perhaps	ME 'by chance'
shall	OE *sceal* 'owe, ought to'
SHOULD	OE *sceolde* past tense of 'shall'
WILL	OE *willian* 'intend, wish'
WOULD	OE *wolde,* past tense of 'will'

Particles

AS	OE *all-swá* 'all-so'
instead	ME 'in place (of)'
NO	OE *nó* 'always not'
NOT	ME abbr. of 'nought'
rather	OE *hraðor* 'faster'
SO	OE *swa*
THAN	OE *þanne* originally same as 'then'
whatever	ME 'what ever'

Contrastives

ANOTHER	ME 'one other'
either	OE *ǽȝhwæðer* 'always' + 'which of two'
neither	OE *nauðer* 'not whether'
OTHER	OE *óðer*

Pronouns

I	OE *ic*
THOU	OE *þú* singular 2nd person pronoun
HE	OE masculine of pronominal *hi-* ‖ *here*
SHE	OE *sío* feminine demonstrative
IT	OE *hit,* neutral of pronominal *hi-*
WE	OE *wé*
YOU	OE *éow,* accusative of 2p pronoun *ȝe*
THEY	Norse demonstrative *þeir*
self	OE *self*

Interrogatives

WHEN	OE *hwanne*
WHERE	OE *hwǽr*
whether	OE *hwæðer* < Germanic 'which other'
WHILE	OE *hwíle* 'at the time'
WHO	OE *hwá*
HOW	OE *hú*
WHY	OE *hwí* instrumental of 'what'
WHAT	OE *hwæt*
WHICH	OE *hwelc*

▸ For prepositions, see *Locatives,* p. 250.

This section is mostly just a place to store all the grammatical words from the Fantasy Frequency List. For how to write a grammar, see the *Language Construction Kit* and *Advanced Language Construction.*

Something to note from the etymologies, though: despite English's rampant borrowing, *none* of the basic grammatical words come from Romance, and just one word is borrowed at all (*they*).

At the same time, it's interesting that such common words as *because* and *not* are as late as Middle English. And lack of borrowing doesn't mean lack of change; the pronominal system has been revamped, the past tenses of modals were reinterpreted as new verbs, and of course a huge mass of inflectional morphology has been discarded.

Sources of grammatical words

Grammarians distinguish **form words**, required for the grammar, from **content words**, the bulk of the lexicon. But note that form words very often derive from content words. This is easiest to see in the case of modals, which can derive from ordinary verbs of volition *(will)*, possibility and knowledge *(can)*, and motion *(je vais..., I'm gonna).*

It's hard to derive a deictic from anything but another deictic. But pronouns can easily derive from other words— e.g. Japanese *boku* 'I' was originally a word for 'servant' (and was borrowed from Chinese to boot); Portuguese *você* 'you' was once a polite phrase *vossa mercê* 'your mercy'. French *on,* once an indefinite pronoun and now commonly used for 1st person plural, derives from *homo* 'man'.

Germanic and Romance definite articles derive from demonstratives, while indefinite articles derive from the word 'one'. French *mais* 'but' derives from the adverb *magis* 'more', while *pas* 'not' derives from the noun 'step'.[6] Mandarin words for 'and' include *hé* 'union' and *gēn* 'follow'.

All this is how grammaticalization works. A construction made up of content words gets used so much that it simplifies and formalizes, becoming a clitic and then an inflection.

Words about grammar

One fun exercise is to create words *referring to* grammar. You might not have any, of course, if your people don't have a tradition of writing grammars. Most people don't.

Most of our grammatical terminology derives from Latin and Greek, e.g.

noun	Lt 'name'
verb	Lt 'word, speech'
adjective	Lt 'adding'
gender	Lt 'type'
case	Lt 'falling'; the metaphor is DECLINING NOUNS IS FALLING, which also gives us the term for *oblique* roots as well as the term *declension*
form	Lt 'shape'
grammar	Gk 'of letters'
dialect	Gk 'through-speaking' = 'discourse'
accusative	Lt 'of accusing', after a Greek word which did mean 'accuse' but also 'affect'— it was the case of the 'affected' thing
dative	Lt 'of giving', another calque on Greek
alphabet	Gk 'alpha' + 'beta'
dictionary	Lt 'speech collection'

While the Sanskrit grammarians had very accurate phonetic terms, this was not an area where the Greeks shone. The unaspirated/aspirated division was characterized as ψιλόν 'smooth, plain' / δασύ 'rough'. They described the voiced consonants as μέσα 'intermediate' between these, which suggests that they did not understand the mechanism of voicing. Our modern phonetic terms, though built on Greco-Latin roots, are mostly borrowed from anatomy.

---

[6] This originated in expressions like *Je ne vais pas* 'I won't go a step'. This was extended to any verb; then in the modern spoken language *ne* could be omitted, leaving *pas* as the marker of negativity.

Another approach is to name sounds after exemplars— e.g. Spanish *seseo* for the practice of pronouncing c/z as [s], and *ceceo* for the hypercorrection of <s> to [θ]. This invites confusion in later centuries— e.g. we have the contemporary terms for the four Middle Chinese tones— *píng* 'level', *shǎng* 'rising', *qù* 'departing', *rù* 'entering'— but as these terms were chosen to illustrate the tones (i.e. *píng* had *píng* tone), their descriptive quality was poor and the actual phonetics of the tones has been lost.

For naming inflected forms, we normally enumerate the morphemes, e.g. *first person singular present indicative*. A rather neat alternative (used in Hebrew and Arabic) is to use a special word and inflect that. E.g. for Spanish we might invent the word *vangar*; then the 'first person singular present indicative' could simply be named the *vango* form. Of course, this would break down if a particular ending was used in multiple ways.

Peter Daniels extended the model of *alphabet* to name other writing systems by their prototypical first elements, e.g. *abjad* for a consonantal system, *abugida* for system where the glyphs stand for a consonant plus a default vowel, with diacritics used to indicate different vowels.

Letters of the alphabet

There are two obvious ways to name letters of the alphabet:

- By the *acrophonic* principle: the name starts with the sound the letter represents. This was how the Semitic consonantal system worked— e.g. ⌃ *gīmel* is named for *gāmāl* 'camel', and Ϙ *qōp* is 'ape'.

- By pronouncing just the sound. This works fine for vowels and even fricatives; with stops it's convenient to append a vowel. This is largely how the Romans named their letters, and we've inherited the system.

If you're borrowing the alphabet, you can borrow the names, as Greek did: *gīmel* became γάμμα. The words were arbitrary in Greek, but preserved the acrophonic principle. Greek innovated the vowels, arguably by accident. Trying to understand what *ʔālep* was for, without grasping the nature of the glottal stop, the Greeks might understandably have concluded that the letter meant /a/, thus creating ἄλφα.

The letters οὖ [o] and ὦ [o:] merged in the 3C, so they were distinguished as ὂ μικρόν 'little O' and ὦ μέγα 'big O'.

KINSHIP

ancestor	Lt *antecessor* 'fore-goer'
	• Gk πρόγονοι 'previous birth' • Ir *sinsear* 'elders' • Ch *zǔ* 'moved on'
aunt	Lt *amita* 'father's sister'
brother	OE *bróðor* < IE **bhrāter-*, cognate to Lt *frāter*
	• Gk ἀδελφόσ 'same womb' • Sp *hermano* < 'full, true' • Ch *dìdi* < '(next in) order'
daughter	OE *dohtor*
	• Lt *fīlia* < 'suck' • Ir *iníon* 'in-born' • Ch *nǔér* 'female child'
family	Lt *familia* 'household' < 'servant'
	• Gk οἶκος 'house' • Cz *rodina* < 'birth' • Ch *jiā* 'house(hold)'
father	OE *fæder* < IE **pətér-* from babytalk *pā*
grandmother	ME 'grand' < Lt *grandem* 'full-grown'
	• OE *ealdmódor* 'old-mother' • Sw *farmor, mormor* 'father-mother' etc. • Ch *zǔmǔ* 'generation before parents' + 'mother'
husband	OE *húsbonda* 'house-freeholder'
	• Gk ἀνήρ 'male' • Lt *spōnsus* 'promised' • Rum *soţ* 'companion' • OCS *sǫprǫgǔ* 'yoked' • Skt *pati-* 'master', *bhartar-* 'bearer'
marry	Lt verbn. of *marītus* 'married'
	• Lt *nūbere* prob. < 'veil' • Fr *épouser* verbn. of 'spouse' • Sp *casarse* 'make a house' • OE *weddian* 'pledge' • Dutch *trouwen* 'trust' • Lith *vedu* 'lead' • Cz *vdáti se* 'be given' • Ch *hūn* 'in-laws'
mother	OE *módor* < IE **māter-* from babytalk **mā*
parent	Lt *parentēs* '(one who) produced'
	• OE *ealdras* 'elders' • Sp *padres* pl. of 'father' • Ch *fùmǔ* 'father-mother'
sister	OE *sweostor* < IE **swesor-*
	• Ch *mèi* ‖ 'woman'
son	OE *sunu*
	• Lt *fīlius* < 'suck' • Ch *ér* 'child'
uncle	Lt *avunculus* 'mother's brother'
wife	OE *wíf* 'woman' poss. < 'wrapped'
	• Lt *uxor* < 'accustomed to' • Dutch *gade* 'companion' • Ch *àiren* 'lover'
+	*clan, dynasty, heir, grandfather, cousin, nephew, niece engagement, bride, groom, elope, dowry/bride-price, monogamy, divorce, in-law, step-*

▸ See also *Love*, p. 257.

In Finnish, 'mother' is *äiti* for humans, *emo* for animals. English sometimes uses *dam* for animal mothers.

Irish lacks a good term for *(nuclear) family*. *Clann* (source of *clan*) means 'offspring' and thus excludes your spouse; *muintir* is the extended family or even 'the locals'; and *teaghlach* is those living under one roof, i.e. *household*.

Kinship terms are often used outside the family— cf. *father* for priests, *brother/sister* for monks, nuns, and fellow activists. Family terms also provide names for classification systems (a *sister* category, a *daughter* language). Geeks created the useful term *grand-boss* for one's boss's boss.

In some churches, children have *godparents* who guarantee their religious education. The OE was *godsibb;* it was extended to friends, then narrowed to female friends, then to those who engaged in idle talk— modern *gossip*.

We use *child* as either *boy/girl* or *son/daughter*, but some languages have a term for 'son or daughter' (only), e.g. Gk τέκνον.

Languages with gender systems can (but don't always!) easily create gendered kinship terms with their ordinary morphology: Spanish *hermano/hermana, primo/prima, tío/tía, suegro/suegra*.

All languages have **babytalk** versions of the kinship terms, mostly using the easiest consonants for babies (labials and dentals) plus the easiest vowel /a/. Examples: *Momma, Papa*, Quechua *mama* 'mother', Gk πάππος 'grandfather', Gothic *atta* 'father', Gk νάννα 'aunt', Chinese *māma* 'mother', Georgian *deda* 'mother'. Occasionally these are messed up by sound change, e.g. Japanese *haha, chichi* 'Mom, Dad' from **papa, *titi*.

People terms

adult   Lt *adultus* 'grown up'
      • Qu *kallpayoq* 'having vigor' • Ch *chéngnián* 'complete years'

baby   ME *babi* uncertain
      • Gk νήπιος 'unwise' • Sp *criatura* 'creature' • Ger *Säugling* 'suckling' • Lith *kūdikis* 'small' • OCS *otroče* dim. 'child'

boy   ME uncertain
      * Lt *puer* < 'small' • Fr *garçon* 'servant' • Sw *gosse* 'boar' • OCS *otrokŭ* 'not speaking'• Cz *holek* 'beardless' • Skt *bāla-* prob. 'strong' • Ch *shăonián* 'few years'

child OE *cild* 'baby'
 • Scots *bairn* 'born' • Lt *infāns* 'not speaking' • Welsh *plentyn* 'sprout' • OCS *dětĭ* 'suckling' • Ch *zǐ* < 'come forth, be born'

crowd OE *crúdan* 'press, push' > 'throng together' > 'mass of people'
 • Lt *multitūdo* 'muchness' • Fr *foule* < 'pound cloth' • Lith *minia* < 'trample' • Ch *qún* 'herd, group', poss. ‖ 'all'

fellow OE *féolaȝa* 'lay down property', i.e. 'partner'

female Lt *fēmella* dim. 'woman'
 • Ch *nǚ* poss. ‖ 'sister'

folk OE *folc* 'people' < IE, cognate to *populus*

girl ME *gurle* 'young person (of either gender)'
 • Welsh *hogen* 'suckling' • Sw *flicka* 'ragged' • Skt *kanyā-* 'young' • Ch *nǚháizi* 'female-child'

human Lt adjn. of *homō homin-* 'human'

kid Norse *kið* 'goatling'

maid ME abbr. of 'maiden'
 • Ch *nǚpú* 'woman-servant'

male Lt *masculus* 'male person'

MAN OE *man* 'person, human'
 Human: Lt *homō homin-*, OE *guma* < 'earthly' • Farsi *mard* < 'mortal'; OCS *člověkŭ* 'householder' • Gk ἄνθρωπος poss. 'male-like' • Ch *rén* poss. < 'kin' or 'mind'
 Male: Lt *vir*, OE *wer* poss 'strong' • Gk ἀνήρ < 'strong, master' • Rum *barbat* 'bearded' • OE *wǽpnedman* 'weapon-person' • Ch *nán* < 'young male'

PEOPLE Fr *peuple* < Lt *populus* < IE, cognate to OE *folc*
 • Gk δῆμος 'district' • Ir *daoine* 'persons' • Welsh *gwerin* 'crowd' • Lt *gens gent-*, Skt *jana-* < 'beget' • Ch *mín* ‖ 'human'

person Lt *persōna* 'mask'

WOMAN OE *wífmon* 'woman-person'
 • IE *g^wenā-* > Gk γυνή, OCS *žena*, OE *cwene* • It *donna* 'lady'
 • Lt *fēmina* 'one who gives suck' • Lith *moteris* 'mother' • Skt *nārī-* feminization of *nar-* 'male'

I've placed the general terms for **people** here, as they make the same sex/age distinctions and words easily move back and forth between general and kinship terms (e.g. French *fille* = 'daughter, girl'). Also note the narrowing of OE *guma* 'man' to *(bride)groom*.

English *man* is ambivalent between *human* and *male*, but many languages distinguish them— e.g. Latin *homō* vs. *vir*, Gk ἄνθρωπος vs. ἀνήρ, OE *man* vs. *wer*. (A *werewolf* is a man-wolf.) Or the words may be related: Mandarin uses the transparent *nánrén* 'male-person' for 'a male'.

Words for 'man' and 'woman' are often the normal terms for 'husband' and 'wife'. English *wife* was originally just 'woman'— indeed, *woman* is from OE *wífmon* 'woman-person'.

Buck notes that words for 'woman' are particularly subject to attitudinal shifts. OE *cwén* 'queen' is an elevation of the IE word for 'woman'. Danish *kone* is 'wife', but Swedish *kona* is a woman of loose character. German *Weib* 'woman, wife' was for a long period seen as derogatory, replaced by *Frau*; it has regained respectability but only in the sense of 'woman'. English writers at times have seemed to have a horror of the word *woman*, substituting *lady* or *female* or *girl;* perhaps in recompense feminists seized on the word.

Systems of kinship terms

You may know that languages vary in kinship terms, but never have paid it much attention... surely most languages work like English. Well, no.

In 1871, Lewis Henry Morgan proposed a classification of kinship systems that's still a good place to start. He named them, in good Lakoffian fashion, after exemplars.

Hawaiian

This system is both very common and very simple. Each generation has just two terms, for males and females.

- Your parents' generation are all *father* and *mother*.
- Everyone else in your generation is *brother* or *sister*.
- The next generation is all *son* or *daughter*.

The system is exemplified below by Hawaiian itself. Males are triangles, females are circles; the ego is marked with a star.

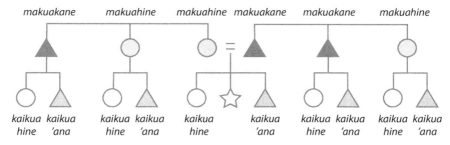

The use of the same names doesn't mean that there are no behavioral differences— you know who your biological mother is. But the names have behavioral consequences too— e.g. you can't marry a *brother* or *sister.*

This kinship system correlates with *ambilineal descent.* Essentially, you choose whether to belong to your father's or mother's kin group (*ramage*). Your siblings don't have to make the same choice. Plus, when you get married, you have the option of joining either of the ramages available to your spouse.

Ramages own land, so this is a good system for small groups (e.g. island populations) to combine the advantages of permanent ownership and flexible redistribution of land.

Eskimo

This system isn't much more complicated; within each generation, it distinguishes your direct ancestors/descendants and more remote relatives. No distinctions are made based on whether the relatives is on the mother's or father's side.

- Your parent's siblings are either *aunt* or *uncle.*

- Outside the nuclear family, everyone in your generation is a *cousin* (often differentiated by sex, as in French *cousin/cousine*).

- Outside the nuclear family, the kids are *niece* or *nephew.*

If it wasn't obvious, English falls in this class. So do many Western European languages, as well as the !Kung and the Eskimo/Iñupiaq/Yup'ik. It seems to correlate with the dominance of the nuclear family— remoter relatives and remoter marriage ties are less important.

On the whole Indonesian falls in this class, but it goes further than English in eliminating sex differences: *saudara* = brother/sister, *anak* = son/daughter, *cucu* = grandson/granddaughter, *keponakan* = nephew/

niece. On the other hand, there are also terms for an older sibling of either gender (*kaka*) and a younger one (*ade*).

Sudanese

If the Hawaiian system minimizes terms, this one maximizes them. The basic idea is that everyone gets their own term.

- Paternal and maternal aunts and uncles are distinguished.
- Up to eight types of cousins are distinguished,
- Brothers' and sisters' children have separate terms.

Latin is a good example.

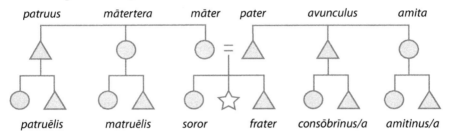

Let's look at the whole set of terms:

Generation	Term	Gloss
Parents	*māter*	mother
	pater	father
	mātertera	mother's sister
	patruus	mother's brother
	avunculus	father's brother
	amita	father's sister
Yours	*soror*	sister
	consōbrīnus/a	*avunculus*'s children
	matruēlis	*mātertera*'s children
	frāter	brother
	patruēlis	*patruus*'s children
	amitinus/a	*amita*'s children
Children	*fīlius/fīlia*	son/daughter
	sōbrīnus/a	sister's children
	fratruelis	brother's children

Other examples include Old English, Arab, Turkish, and Chinese. It tends to occur in patrilineal cultures (i.e. those where descent is reckoned from the father) with a strong class division.

You might think that the Romance languages would retain the Latin system, but they simplified it into a bilateral system. Look to see where French *oncle, tante, cousin* came from. *Neveu/nièce* are stranger: they derive from *nepos/neptis*, originally 'grandchildren'; new terms for grandchildren were invented (*grand-fils, grand-fille*). As you can see, English jettisoned its own terms outside the nuclear family and borrowed those of French.

Chinese kinship

Morgan was delicately multicultural for a 19th century thinker, but it's a bit odd to relegate East Asian culture to a footnote on "Sudanese", especially as it has a major extra complication: different terms by relative age. Here are the Mandarin terms:

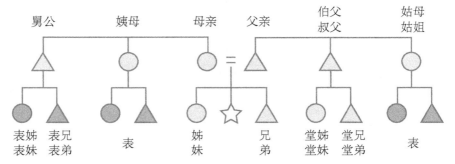

The diagram looks far neater labeled in Chinese, sorry. Here are the terms in the **parental** generation, left to right:

舅公	*jiùfù*	mother's brother
姨母	*yímǔ*	mother's sister
母亲	*mǔqīn*	mother
父亲	*fùqīn*	father
伯父	*bófù*	father's elder brother
叔父	*shūfù*	father's younger brother
姑母	*gūmǔ*	father's elder sister
姑姐	*gūjiě*	father's younger sister

The terms in the second row are all based on these words:

兄	*xiōng*	older brother

弟	*dì*	younger brother
姊, 姐	*zǐ, jiě*	older sister
妹	*mèi*	younger sister

The cousins are mostly named by prefixing these words with 表 *táng*, e.g. 表兄 *tángxiōng* 'male cousin older than oneself'. But the children of one's paternal uncle (*bófù* or *shūfù*) are prefixed with 堂 *biǎo*.

The terms above are replaced by reduplicated diminutives in everyday speech— e.g. *māma, bàba, mèimei, gēge* 'Mom, Dad, (younger) sis, (older) bro'.

In Korean, the words for siblings (which indicate relative age, as in Chinese) are used for 'friend'.

Bifurcate merging

Morgan defined three more systems, but they all look the same at the parents' generation, so let's first look at that.

- The same term is used for *father* and *his brother* (paternal uncle).
- The same term is used for *mother* and *her sister* (maternal aunt).
- There are distinct terms for the remaining aunt and uncle.

(The first two points are the merger; the third is the bifurcate part.)

In the next generation,

- *Brother* and *sister* are used for the children of anyone labeled *father* or *mother*.

This may be easier to understand looking at the diagram on the next page.

The three remaining systems differ in what the remaining cousins are called— the *consōbrīnus* and *amitinus* nodes.

Iroquois system   The same terms are used for both remaining cousins.

Omaha system   There are separate terms for the *amitinus* cousins.

For the *consōbrīnus* cousins, the female is called *mother*, the male is called by the same term as his father, the *avunculus*.

Crow system There are separate terms for the *consōbrīnus* cousins.

For the *amitinus* cousins, the male is called *father*, the female is called by the same term as her mother, the *amita*.

The Latin and Chinese systems are just extra-precise; this one may blow your mind. In the Omaha system, there are three nodes labeled *mother*, which to us are very different roles: mother, (maternal) aunt, and cousin (daughter of maternal uncle). The use of the same term across generations is called *skewing*.

The Omaha system correlates with patrilineal descent, and the mirror-image Crow system with matrilineal descent. Note that more distinctions are made in the 'more important' lineage.

An example of an Omaha system is **Dani**, from New Guinea. Because of skewing, we can't separate the terms by generation.

Term	Gloss
akoja	mother, or her sister, or her brother's daughter
ami	mother's brother, or his son
opaije	father, or his brother
he-opaije	father's sister
oe	son of any *akoja/ami* (i.e. brother, some cousins)
oe-etu	daughter of *akoja/opaije* (i.e. sister, some cousins)
ejak	child of *he-opaije* or *oe-etu*
abut	child of *oe*

The terms may be more understandable in terms of the rules for patrilineages. Here the black nodes mark a male ego's patrilineage, and gray that of his maternal uncle. White ones are neither.

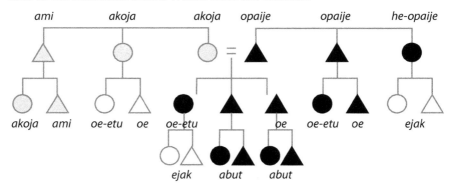

All the males in gray are *ami*, all the females *akoja*.

A man refers to his own children as *abut*, and his wife refers to them as *ejak!* From the above diagram, we can see that *abut* means children within one's own patrilineage, *ejak* those in another. For a woman, her own children don't belong to her patrilineage but to her husband's, so they are *ejak*.

Marriage

Morgan's systems don't address the additional terms introduced by marriage. In English we're used to forming terms by adding *in-law*, but often there are specific terms. E.g. Spanish offers:

suegro	father-in-law
suegra	mother-in-law
yerno	son-in-law
nuera	daughter-in-law
cuñado	brother-in-law
cuñada	sister-in-law
concuñado	sister-in-law's husband
concuñada	brother-in-law's wife

KNOWLEDGE

actual   Lt *actuālis* 'of action'
      • Ger *wirklich* < 'work, act' • Ch *xiànshí* 'reveal-real'

argue   Fr *arguer* < 'prove, accuse'

certain   Lt *certus* 'determined'
      • Gk βέβαιος 'firm' • It *sicuro* 'free from care' • Ir *cinnte* 'fixed' • Ger *sicher* 'safe' • Rus верный 'faithful' • Skt *asaṅçaya-* 'undoubtful' • Ch *bǎwò* 'grasp firmly'

check   Fr *eschec et mat* 'checkmate', ultimately Farsi 'the king is dead'
      • Ch *héduì* 'inquire-correct'

clear   Lt *clārus* 'bright, clear, manifest'

compare   Lt *comparāre* 'pair together'
      • Ch *bi* < 'associate' < 'follow'

correct   Lt *correctus* 'made straight'

describe   Lt *dēscrībere* 'copy off, write down'
      • Ch *miáoxiě* 'sketch-write'

discover   Fr *découvrir* antonym of 'cover'

examine   Lt *exāmen -min-* 'means of weighing'
      • Ger *untersuchen* 'seek under' • Ch *jiǎn* < 'measure, control'

explain   Lt *explānāre* 'smooth out, flatten'
      • Gk ἐξηγέομαι 'lead the way' • Lt *explicāre* 'unfold' • Dutch *verklaren* 'make clear' • Cz *vysvětliti* 'illuminate' • Ch *jiě* < 'loosen, untie'

fact   Lt *factum* '(something) done'
      • Ger *Tatsache* 'act-thing' • Ch *shìshí* 'matter-real'

false   Lt *falsus* 'deceived'
      • Ger *unwahr* 'untrue' • Ch *jiǎ* < 'simulate'

guess   Norse *gissa*
      • Fr *deviner* 'predict' < 'divine' • Ger *schätzen* 'estimate' < 'treasure'

idea   Gk ἰδέα 'look, form, kind' < 'see'
      • Lt *nōtio* < 'know' • Ger *Begriff* < 'understand' • Ch *yì* < 'think'

KNOW   OE *cnáwan* < IE, cognate to Lt *nōscere*, OCS *znati*
      • Gk οἶδα < 'see', cognate to *wit* • Fr *savoir* < 'taste'

maybe   ModE 'may be'

possible   Lt *possibilis* 'doable' < 'can (do)'

probable   Lt *probābilis* 'provable'

prove   Lt *probāre* 'test, try, demonstrate'

REAL   Lt *reālis* 'of things'
         • Ger *echt* < 'lawful' • Ch *zhěn* 'true'

reason   Lt *ratio* 'account, number, matter'
         • Gk λόγος 'word' • Rus разум 'separate-mind' • Ch *lǐ* 'regulate' poss. < 'divide in sections'

RIGHT   OE *reht* 'straight'
         Gk δίκαιος 'customary' • Lt *justus* 'lawful' • Ir *cóir* 'true' • Ch *zhèng* 'straight'

sure   Lt *sēcūrus* 'safe, secure' < 'without care'
         • Ch *kěndìng* 'agree-fixed'

test   Lt *testa* 'pot' > 'metallurgical vessel'

true   OE *tréowe* 'faithful, loyal'
         • Gk ἀληθής 'not forgotten' • Lt *vērus* < IE, cognate to OCS *věra* 'belief' • Sw *sann* < 'actual, existing' • Rus правда < 'straight'

wrong   late OE *wrang* < Norse 'awry, unjust'
         • Fr *tort* < 'twisted' • Ger *unrecht* 'unright' • Ch *cuò* poss. 'mix-up'

+   *genuine, fake, error, theory, science, topic*

    ‣ For perception and reasoning, see *Mind,* p. 263.

In Dutch, *leren* means both 'teach' and 'learn'. English *learn* used to be ambivalent too, but this is now non-standard.

Japanese *oshieru* is 'teach', but where the subject in English must be of at least middling importance, *oshieru* can be used for the simplest of data— you can *oshieru* someone your phone number.

Many European languages have two words for 'know'— one (Fr. *savoir*, Ger. *wissen*, Gk. οἶδα) for knowing things or skills, one (*connaître, kennen,* γιγνώσκω) for knowing or having experience with people or places. French also has the useful word *ignorer* 'not know, not be aware of'.

Education

class   Lt *classis* 'division of the people'

educate   Lt *edūcāre* 'lead out'
         • Ger *erziehen* 'begin-drag' • Ch *jiàoyù* 'teach-cultivate'

instruct   Lt *instruere* intensive of 'build, pile up'

learn   OE *leornian* < 'come to know' ‖ *lore*
         • Gk μανθάνω < 'think' • Lt *discere* < 'receive' • Fr *apprendre* 'seize' • OCS *učiti sę* refl. of 'teach' • Ch *xué* ‖ 'awaken'

school	Gk σχολή 'leisure'
	• Lith *mokykla* 'teach' • Ch *xiào* < 'enclosure'
study	Lt *studēre* 'strive, study'
	• Gk μελετάω 'care, attend to' • Ch *xué* 'learn'
teach	OE *tæcan* 'show' > 'impart'
	• Gk διδάσκω < 'plan' • Lt *dōcere* < '(make) receive' • It *insegnare* < 'mark, adorn' • Breton *kelenn* 'lesson' • Ger *lehren* < 'cause to know' • OCS *učiti* < 'accustomed to'
+	*lesson; university, professor*

The words for schools are an opportunity to design an educational system. (Note that medieval societies aren't likely to have a general system; schools were for the elite.)

- English uses the same word till age 18, then branches into *university, seminary, (military) academy.*

- French distinguishes secondary schools as *lycées. Lycée* and *academy* take their names from particular ancient institutions: Aristotle's Lyceum and Plato's Academy. (Both were gardens rather than buildings.)

- In El Salvador, you take grades 1-6 in an *escuela* and 7-11 in an *instituto*— unless all grades are in the same place, a *colegio.*

LAW

authority | Lt *auctor* 'increaser = originator'

court | Lt *cohors cohort-* 'farmyard' > 'attendants' • Ch *tíng* < 'court-yard'

Noble: • Pol *dziedziniec* 'inheritance' • Breton *lez* < 'fortified place'

Law: OE *þing* 'assembly' • Sw *rätt* 'law' • Rus суд < 'judg-ment'

fair | OE *fæʒer* 'beautiful' > 'unblemished' > 'unbiased'
• Ger *gerecht* 'straight' • Ch *gōng* ‖ 'equal, middle'

fine | Fr *fin* 'finished'

harm | OE *hearmian*
• Gk βλάπτω 'hinder' • Lt *nocēre* < 'kill', *damnum* < 'loss' •
OCS *vrěditi* 'wound' • Ch *hài* ‖ 'cut'

judge | Fr *juge* < Lt *iūdex* 'law-speaker'
• Gk δικάζω < 'justice, right' • Ger *urteilen* 'divide' • Sw *döma*
< 'set down' • Lith *spręsti* 'measure' • OCS *sǫditi* 'put to-
gether' • Skt *nirṇī-* 'lead out' > 'find'

JUST | Lt *justus* 'righteous, lawful'

law | OE *laʒu* '(things) laid down'
• Gk νόμος 'custom' < 'distribution' • Lt *jūs jūr-* ‖ 'swear', *lex*
lēg- prob. < 'collect' • Fr *droit* < 'straight, right' • Ir *dlí* 'right,
duty' • Ger *Gesetz* 'placed' • Dutch *wet* < 'know' • OCS
zakonŭ 'starting point' • Skt *dharma-* 'justice, order' • Ch *fǎ* <
'pattern, rule'

obey | Lt *obœdīre* 'hear toward'
• Ir *géill do* 'do pledge' • Skt *anuvṛt-* 'go after' • Qu *kasuy* <
'pay attention' • Ch *fú* < 'lie down'

police | Gk πολῑτεία 'citizenship'
• Fr *gendarmes* 'armed men' • Ch *jǐngchá* 'warn-inspect'

prison | Fr *prison* < 'seizing'
• Gk εἰκτή 'shutting in' • Fr *geôle* < dim. 'cage'• Latvian *cietums* < 'hard' • OCS *temĭnica* 'darkness' • Rus тюрма <
'tower' • Ch *yǔ* ‖ 'control'

rule | Lt *rēgula* 'stick, bar'
• Gk ἄρχω 'begin' = 'be first' • Lt *regere* 'direct' • Ger
herrschen < 'lord' • OCS *vlasti,* cognate to *wield* • Skt *çās-*
'command' • Ch *zé* 'model, norm'

steal | OE *stelan*
• Gk κλέπτω prob. < 'hide' • Fr *voler* 'fly' • Lith *vogti* < 'wander' • OCS *krasti* prob. < 'heap up' • Ch *tōu* < 'loosen'

swear | OE *swerian* 'make an oath'

+   *contract, license, summons, writ, subpoena*
                     suit, plaintiff, innocent, guilty, testimony, witness
                     punish, exile, execute, jail, dungeon, torture
                     crime, thief, pirate

▸   See the *PCK's* section on Law. p. 136.

Latin distinguished three types of law: *fas* is divine law, or what is permitted morally— its antonym *nefas* is sin or wickedness, and gives us *nefarious*. *Jūs* is right or authority, or fairness— the origin of our *justice*; something which is *injūrius* is unfair— a wrong, an *injury*. Finally a *lex* is a specific written law (and gives us *law* and *legal*).

Lex could also be contrasted with *mōs* 'custom', more familiar in its plural *mōres*. A judge could decide based on the immemorial practice of a community, its *mōs*.

The notion of *common law* started out similar to *mōs*, but now means 'precedent'— in a primitive system you can refer to custom, but in a mature one it's safer to refer to previous decisions. The continental *civil law* system is based on codified law with little reliance on precedent.

Suppose you heard of a conculture which divided law like this:

- There are two sets of laws and courts— Law 1 and Law 2.

- Both deal with property— indeed, a given piece of land has separate Law 1 and Law 2 titles, not necessarily held by the same person. One reason Law 2 is useful is because it allows the concept of *trusts* (ownership of land by one person, use by another).

- Law 1 courts can only award monetary damages. Law 2 courts can order or forbid a particular action.

- Only Law 1 cases involve a jury trial. Law 2 cases are entirely at the discretion of the judge.

- If you don't like a Law 1 ruling, you might seek to overturn it using Law 2.

Sounds a bit confusing and unmotivated, doesn't it? In fact I'm describing the English division of *Law* (Law 1) and *Equity* (Law 2). Equity developed as a corrective to law— cases were appealed to the king, who had the Lord Chancellor decide them according to his own notion of justice. This became codified into a parallel legal system, the Court of Chancery— Dickens's *Bleak House* is a satire of it. The UK and the US

have both partially merged Law and Equity, but the distinction still exists.

Where Americans have *lawyers,* the British have *barristers,* who argue in
court, vs. *solicitors* who offer legal advice and prepare cases, and who
can only appear in lower courts.

Another way of dividing law is between God and Caesar. In medieval
Europe, the church naturally disciplined its own clerics, but church law
also handled marriage and wills in general, and the disputes arising out
of them.

LIFE AND HEALTH

alive OE *on lífe* 'on life'

born ME participle of 'bear'

creature Lt *creātūra* 'something created'

dead/death OE *déad*, OE *déaþ*

die ME *dēӡen*
· Lt *morī* poss. < 'crush' · OE *sweltan* < 'burn', *steorfan* < 'stiff' · Farsi *marg* < 'destroy'

grow OE *grówan*
· Lt *crescere* ‖ 'create' · OE *weaxan* 'grow, increase' · OCS *rasti* prob. < '(get) high' · Ch *zhǎng* < 'tall, long'

heal OE *hǽlan* 'make whole'
· Gk θεραπεύω 'attend' · Lt *sānāre* 'make well' · Fr *guérir* < 'ward off' · Sw *bota* 'betterment' · Rus лечить < 'remedy' · Ch *yù* < 'suffer'

ill Norse *illr* 'wicked'
· Ch *bìng* poss. < 'warm'

kill ME *culle* 'strike, hit'
* Lt *necāre* < *nex* 'violent death' · Fr *tuer* < 'extinguish' · ModGk σκοτώνω 'darken' · Qu *wañuchiy* 'cause to die'

LIFE/LIVE OE *libban* < 'be left'
· Gk ζήω, Lt *vivēre* < IE · Rum *trai* < 'last' · Ir *mair* 'remain' · Ch *shēng* < 'come to exist'

medical Lt *medicālis* adjn. of 'heal'
· Ger *ärztlich* 'doctor-like' · Ch *yào* poss. < 'purify'

patient Lt *patiens* 'suffering'

recover Lt *recuperāre* 'regain'
· Ger *wiederfinden* 'find against' · Ch *xúnhuí* 'seek-return'

sick OE *séoc*
ModGk ἄρρωστος 'weak' · Fr *malade* < Lt 'bad state' · OE *ādl* 'fevered' · Ger *krank* < 'twisted' · OCS *bolĭnŭ* < 'evil' · Skt *vyādhi-* 'displacement'

survive Lt *supervīvere* 'live above'
· Ger *überleben* 'over-live' · Ch *xìngcún* 'happy-preserve'

treat Fr *traiter* 'drag' > 'manage, act'

+ *funeral, decay, rot, mold, mortal*

doctor, nurse, hospital, drug, pill, surgery, cure

disease, stroke, scurvy, epilepsy, diarrhea, nausea, arthritis, cancer

wound, bruise, rash, fever, wart, pimple, blister, pockmark

English *live* has the sense 'reside', but this is often a different verb— e.g. Mandarin *zhù* vs. *shēng* 'produce, give birth, be alive'.

In languages with a well-used causative, like Quechua, *kill* is simply 'cause to die' (*wañuchiy*).

Medicine

English *healthy* is related to *hale, whole*; health is oneness. Latin *salvus* (source of *salubrious, save,* and Spanish *salud*) has the same etymology. Swedish *frisk* is 'fresh' but also 'well, healthy'. Russian здарове combines 'well' and 'firm'. Avestan has the melancholy *abanta-* 'not sick'.

Healer is straightforward; *medic(al), medicine* derive from Lt *medeor* 'heal'. A *doctor* is anyone with an education, literally a 'teacher'; a *physician* is one who has studied 'nature'; apparently this study interested non-scholars only when they were sick.

Try thinking up some of the treatments your conpeople might use. You'd might as well be creative, because premodern medicine was almost entirely claptrap.

Diseases

The diseases and conditions are a chance to do some conworlding— what diseases attack orcs and elves? Or if they're human, do they share the same microorganisms as our world?

Here's a list of major disease agents and parasites, organized by taxonomic group (p. 114). If just one italicized name is given, it's a genus.

AIDS	virus	human immunodeficiency virus (*Lentivirus*)
chicken pox	virus	*Varicellovirus*
common cold	virus	*Enterovirus rhinovirus* (most often)
herpes	virus	*Simplexvirus* spp.
influenza	virus	orthomyxoviruses
measles	virus	*Morbillivirus*
mononucleosis	virus	Epstein-Barr virus *Lymphocryptovirus*
polio	virus	poliovirus (*Enterovirus*)
rabies	virus	*Lyssavirus*
smallpox	virus	*Variola major*

anthrax	bacterium	*Bacillus anthracis*
bacterial pneumonia	bacterium	*Streptococcus pneumoniae* etc.
botulism	bacterium	*Clostridium botulinum*
cholera	bacterium	*Vibrio cholerae*
gonorrhea	bacterium	*Neisseria gonorrhoeae*
leprosy	bacterium	*Mycobacterium* spp.
plague	bacterium	*Yersinia pestis*
salmonella	bacterium	*Salmonella* spp.
strep throat	bacterium	*Streptococcus pyogenes*
syphilis	bacterium	*Treponema pallidum*
tetanus / lockjaw	bacterium	*Clostridium tetani*
tuberculosis	bacterium	*Mycobacterium tuberculosis*
typhoid fever	bacterium	*Salmonella enterica*
urinary tract infection	bacterium	most often *Escherichia coli*
yeast infection	fungus	*Candida albicans*
amoebic dysentery	protist	*Entamoeba histolytica*
Chagas disease	protist	*Trypanosoma cruzi*
malaria	protist	*Plasmodium* spp.
toxoplasmosis	protist	*Toxoplasma gondii*
tapeworm	platyhelminthes	*Taenia solium* (pork), *T. saginata* (beef), etc.
schistosomiasis	platyhelminthes	*Schistosoma* spp.
guinea worm	nematode	*Dracuncula medinensis*
hookworm	nematode	*Ancylostoma duodenale*
roundworm	nematode	*Ascaris lumbricoides*
river blindness	nematode	*Onchocerca volvulus*
flea (human)	arthropod	*Pulex irritans*
head and body lice	arthropod	*Pediculus humanus*
pubic lice	arthropod	*Pthirus pubis*
scabies	arthropod (mite)	*Sarcoptes scabiei*
tick	arthropod	*Ixodida* order

If your culture hasn't invented the microscope, only the worms and arthropods will have names (but they will be ancient ones). But the diseases will have names, likely based on their symptoms.

Theories of medicine

A theory of medicine will not only add to your belief systems and cultural practices, but it'll generate words and idioms, even after the theory is abandoned.

The ancient and medieval theory of **humors** (literally 'moistures') is an example. Medical conditions were described in terms of the under- or overabundance of the humors, which themselves were combinations of the four elements (p. 183). Bloodletting or emetics might be prescribed for a supposed surplus of one humor.

blood	*fire + water*
choler	*fire + earth*
phlegm	*water + air*
melancholy	*earth + air*

Choler is bile or gall, created in the liver and stored in the gall bladder. It was assumed to produce anger— biliousness— or impudence (*what gall!*).

Melancholy is 'black bile', said to be made in the spleen— though there is no such substance; the spleen mostly filters blood. It was traditionally associated with sadness and depression (as in French writers' *le spleen*), but more recently with irritability and anger— *vent one's spleen*.

> ‣ Humors were applied also to temperaments; see p. 274.

Chinese medicine starts with the complementary forces of 阴 *yīn* and 阳 *yáng*. *Yáng* is associated with fire, the masculine, the sky, and with the qualities of speed, hardness, and focus. *Yīn* is associated with water, the feminine, the earth; it's said to be slow, soft, and diffuse. The solid lines of I Ching hexagrams are *yáng*, the broken ones *yīn*.

In medicine, *yīn* is associated with heat, *yáng* with cold; these are supposed to be in balance. A lack of *yīn* can be diagnosed by feelings of heat, insomnia, dry mouth, dark urine, or a rapid pulse; a lack of *yáng* by feelings of cold, clear urine, diarrhea, pale tongue, and a weak pulse. There are medicines for reinforcing either component.

In addition the five elements are associated with a taste and with certain organs:

mù wood	sour	liver, gall bladder, eye
huǒ fire	bitter	heart, small intestine, tongue
tǔ earth	sweet	spleen, stomach, mouth
jīn metal	acrid	lung, large intestine, nose

shuǐ water   salt   kidney, bladder, ears

气 *qì* is etymologically 'breath', and developed into a concept of energy or life force. The Huáinán Masters (-2C) taught that the universe produces *qì*; clear and fast (*yáng*) *qì* produced heaven and the sun; heavy and slow (*yīn*) *qì* produced the earth and water. *Qì* is believed to circulate invisibly within the body; various disorders are caused by blocked or unbalanced flows of *qì*.

Qìgōng 'cultivation of *qì*' is a set of practices of breathing, slow motion, and meditation, which conceptually produce a harmonious flow of *qì*; it's a component of *Tàijíquán* (Tai Chi) and many schools of martial arts. Bodily *qì* is considered *yáng*, balanced by the *yīn* fluids: blood (*xuě*) and all other bodily fluids (*jīnye*). *Qì* moves about in the earth and in structures; *fēngshuǐ* is largely concerned with managing this flow.

There are complicated relationships between the organs, bodily functions, and various posited qualities. As an example, the liver (*gān*) is a *zàng* organ— the concept relates to *qì* and blood, as opposed to the *fǔ* organs which relate to digestion. The liver governs the free flow of *qì*, stores blood, opens into the eyes, governs the tendons, and reflects in the nails. A dysfunctional liver results in anger, headaches, a bitter taste in the mouth, blurry vision, or jaundice. The liver is the seat of the *hún* portion of the soul (p. 314).

For ancient **Axunai**, I created a system based on three physical elements (*kie*)— water, earth, and wood. Each had their spiritual analog (*šeč*), a pair of attributes, and associated drives:

body	*spirit*	*attributes*	*drives*
water - *mii*	**female** - *zimun*	youth, harvest	love, hatred
earth - *suz*	**male** - *gumun*	night, planting	creativity, destruction
wood - *gule*	**light** - *silirti*	age, day	wisdom, honor

On the medical level, there were bodily substances (*kimini*) associated with the nine possible combinations of the bodily and spiritual elements:

	female	*male*	*light*
waters	blood	semen	urine
earths	liver, brain, etc.	muscle	heart
woods	ovaries	testicles	bone

An elaborate medicine and psychology were elaborated from this basis, proceeding from the idea that disorders were caused by an overabundance or a weakness of one of these nine combinations.

LIGHT

bright	OE *beorht*, cognate to Skt *bhrāj-* 'shine'
	• Lt *lūcidus* 'light' • Ger *hell* < 'clear, loud'
brilliant	Fr *brillant* 'shining'
DARK	OE *deorc* poss < 'hidden'
	• OE *mirce* 'flickering' > 'twilight' • Gk σκότος 'shade' • OHG *tuncha* < 'hazy' • Ch *àn* < 'deep black'
dim	OE *dim*
dull	ME 'stupid' > 'blunt'
fade	Old Fr *fader*
flash	ME imitative
	• Fr *étinceler* < 'spark' • Ch *shǎn* < 'blaze'
gleam	OE *glæm* 'brilliant light' > 'subdued light' ‖ *glimmer*
glow	OE *glówan* ‖ *glass*
LIGHT	OE *léoht*, cognate to Lt *lux lūc-*, Gk λευκός 'white'
	• Gk φῶσ ‖ Skt 'shine' • Ch *guāng* 'bright'
pale	Fr *pâle*
	• Ger *blaß* < 'bald' • Ch *dàn* 'insipid'
radiate	Lt *radiāre* 'emit rays'
ray	Lt *radius* 'staff, rod, ray'
	• Ger *Strahl* < 'arrow' • Ch *guāngxiàn* 'light-thread'
reflect	Lt *reflectere* 'bend back'
	• Ger *zurüchwerfen* 'throw back' • Ch *fǎnyìng* 'back-shine'
shadow	OE *sceadu*
	• Gk σκιά ‖ 'shine', both poss. < 'faint light' • Lith *pavėsis* < 'windy'
shine	OE *scínan*
	• Gk λάμπω < 'fire' • Lt *lūcēre* < 'light' • It *brillare* < 'whirl' • Ch *zhào* < 'bright'

Generally, we like light. It's homey and safe, especially at night. Thus it easily makes a metaphor for intelligence (*brilliant*) and morality (Jesus: "I am the *light* of the world"). The Dark Lord is the one without people skills.

It might be different for dwarves and drow, whose eyes are adapted to dark interiors and who could be expected to find the sun overpowering. For undersea dwellers *light* would mean *up*. Sapients based on other species might value another sense more— the canine equivalent of a *brilliant* man would be *one whose nose finds trails nodog else does.*

Fire

burn	OE *beornan*
	• Lt *ardēre* < 'dry' • Ir *loisc* < 'light' • OCS *goréti* < 'hot' • Ch *shāo* < 'kindling'
burst	OE *berstan*
explode	Lt *explaudere* 'clap out' = 'drive off the stage' > 'expel with force'
fire	OE *fȳr* < IE 'fire (inan.)'
	• Lt *ignis* < IE 'fire (anim.)' • Fr *feu* < 'fireplace' • Sw *eld* 'burn'
flame	Lt *flamma*, prob. ‖ *flag-* as in 'blaze'
	• Rum *flacără* dim. 'torch' • Skt *jvala-* < 'blaze, glow'
heat	OE *hǽtu*
smoke	OE *smoca*
	• Lt *fūmus* < IE ‖ 'shake', 'rush' • Ger *Rauch* prob. < 'spew out' • Ch *xūn* ‖ 'vapor', poss. 'steam'

Fire is more ambivalent, because it burns. It protects and it destroys. Thus it's an attribute of both God (the Burning Bush) and the Devil (the flames of Hell).

Chemically, fire is a fast form of oxidation (as opposed to slow forms like rust). A flame is simply hot gas and ash which is emitting light.

Radiation

To the physicists, light is electromagnetic radiation. You can think of this in two ways:

- As a moving wave, composed of electric and magnetic components oscillating in sync, but at right angles to each other. The difference between the maxima of the waves is the *wavelength* λ; the speed of oscillation is the *frequency* f. The waves have typical wave effects such as diffusion (which you can see in the fuzzy edge of a shadow) and interference when passed through narrow slits.

- As a particle, the photon, with a given *energy*. You can build a detector that will catch individual photons, and see that they're units at a particular location— you never catch part of a photon, or find it smeared out over space.

These pictures are both true, which causes endless confusion. Part of the problem is that we think in metaphors (p. 92), and metaphors of water waves and billiard balls are both misleading. We really need a new metaphor. Till then, read Richard Feynman's *QED* for the best way of thinking about quantum behavior.

Wavelength and frequency are related by the formula $c = f\lambda$ where c is the speed of light in vacuum, 299,792,458 m/s.

Grab yourself some light with a wavelength of 400 nm (to human eyes that's a lovely dark blue).

$$f = c/\lambda = 2.998{*}10^8 \text{ m/s} / 4{*}10^{-7} \text{ m} = 7.49{*}10^{14} \text{ /s}$$

The unit of frequency really is "per second", but we conventionally turn this into Hertz, producing the final answer of 7.49 THz. Blue light is really really small (the size of a mitochondrium, p. 173) and oscillates very very quickly.

If you try various frequencies you'll see that the longer the wavelength, the slower the oscillation.

The energy of a photon is given by *hf*, where *h* is Planck's constant, $4.1357{*}10^{-15}$ eV*s. For that blue light photon,

$$E = hf = 4.1357{*}10^{-15} \text{ eV*s} * 7.49{*}10^{14} \text{ /s} = 3.10 \text{ eV}$$

So the higher the wavelength, the more energetic the light. Light can be energetic enough to be dangerous—gamma rays are ionizing, which means they knock electrons off atoms, messing up chemical bonds and causing damage. This can be good or bad— radiation therapy is used to kill cancer cells, but high doses of gamma rays can also *cause* cancer.

For convenience we divide up the electromagnetic spectrum and assign names:

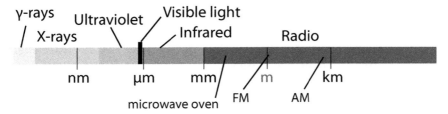

▸ For more see *Color*, p. 157.

For **imaging** things, you want the wavelength of light to be far smaller than the object. Visible light works great for the human scale, and is useful though fuzzy at the level of cells. Higher wavelengths offer more resolution, but as they're also more energetic— they can disturb or damage what you're looking at. For better pictures we turn to electrons, which have a wavelength 100,000 times smaller than visible light.

You could be forgiven for thinking *cosmic rays* are radiation. In fact they're mostly single protons and alpha particles (= helium nuclei), with some electrons and higher-weight nuclei.

LOCATIVES

frame	OE *framian* 'be profitable' > 'prepare' > 'shape' • Fr *charpente* < 'cut wood' • Sp *armazón* 'equipment'
gap	OE *gap* 'chasm' ‖ *gape* • Fr *trou* 'hole', *ouverture* 'opening' • Sp *brecha* 'break'
locate	Lt *locāre* verbn. of 'place'
occupy	Lt *occupāre* 'seize toward'
PLACE	Gk πλατεῖα 'broad way' • Lt *locus* poss. < IE 'set up' • Ir *ionad* < 'ground' • Danish *sted* < 'stand' • Ger *Stelle* < 'put' • OCS *město* prob. < 'post' • Farsi *gāh* < 'go' • Ch *dìdiǎn* 'earth-spot'
position	Lt *positio* 'putting, placing'
scene	Gk σκηνή 'tent, stage'
space	Lt *spatium* • Ch *jiān* 'interval, opening'
surround	Lt *superundāre* 'overflow' < *unda* 'wave' • Sp *rodear* < 'turn, wheel' • Ch *wéi* < 'go around'

The word for a *location* often derives from the act of putting or placing something (Lt *locus, position,* Old English *stów,* found in some place names, such as *Bristol*). Mandarin *dìfāng* is 'earth-direction'. The word *place* itself is generalized from a particular type of place— Gk πλατεῖα, a street or open area, from 'broad'.

Adpositions

ABOUT	OE *on-bútan* 'on without'
above	OE *a bufan* 'on atop'
across	ME 'on cross'
AGAINST	ME *aʒeines* genitive of 'again'
ahead	ModE 'at head'
along	OE *and-lang* 'long-facing'
amid	OE *on middan* 'in middle'
among	OE *on ʒemang* 'on mingling'
apart	Fr *à part* 'at the side'
AROUND	ME 'on round'
aside	ME 'on side'
AT	OE *æt*
AWAY	OE *on weʒ* 'on (one's) way = gone'
BEFORE	OE *beforan* 'by front'
BEHIND	OE *behindan* 'by back'

below	ME 'by low'
beneath	ME 'by under'
beside	ME 'by side'
between	OE 'by twin'
beyond	OE 'by yon'
BY	OE *bí* 'near'
DOWN	OE *of dúne* 'off the hill'
	• Fr *en bas* 'in low' • Ch *xià* 'descend, low'
during	participle of Fr *durer* 'last' < Lt 'harden'
except	Lt *exceptus* 'taken out'
FOR	OE *for*
forth	OE *forð* < Germanic 'fore' + a suffix
FROM	OE *fram*
IN	OE *in*
inside	ModE 'inner side'
INTO	OE 'in to'
OF	OE *of* root sense 'away (from)'
OFF	ME variant of 'of'
ON	OE *an*
onto	ME 'on-to'
OUT	OE *út*
outside	ME 'outer side'
OVER	OE *ofer*
overhead	ME 'over head'
since	OE *siððan* 'after that'
THROUGH	OE *ðurh*
TO	OE *tó*
TOWARD	OE *tóweard* 'to-direction'
UNDER	OE *under*
UNTIL	Norse 'up to' + 'to'
UP	OE *upp*
UPON	ME 'up on'
upper	ME comparative of 'up'
WITH	OE *wið* earliest meaning 'against'
within	OE *wiþinnan* 'with in'
WITHOUT	OE *wiþútan* 'with out'

I've listed all the prepositions from the frequency list here, whether they're strictly locative or not. This is convenient, but as we'll see, non-locative senses often derive from locatives anyway.

As with the grammatical words (p. 220), it's notable how little borrowing there is in this area.

Locatives often derive from body parts— e.g. *beside*, *behind*, Swahili *mbele* 'in front of' < 'breasts'.

Chinese prepositions derive from verbs— e.g. *kào* 'depending on' < 'lean against'.

Space expressions are normally extended to time using the TIME IS SPACE metaphor. Languages differ in the imagined direction of time; see *Directions* (p. 177). An expression like *in summer* is straightforward: the summer is a stretch of time, and the event falls inside it. *I'll see you in three hours* is stranger— the meeting takes place *after* the interval. But the original meaning was presumably 'within, no later than'.

Many of our prepositions are compounds, transparent (*inside, onto*) or not (*but* 'by out', *between* 'by the two'). French *dedans* represents a double application of this process: *de dans* = 'of inside' where *dans* itself derives from vulgar Latin *de-intus* 'of inside'. English *above* is just as bad: it was originally *a bufan* 'at above', where *bufan* derives from *be ufan* 'by above' (cognate to *up*). Expressions like *in front of* are probably on their way to becoming prepositions (perhaps Future English *mfruna*). The winner here is Spanish *en adelante* 'henceforth', from *in* + *ad* + *de* + *in* + *ante*.

Continuing the fusing process, adpositions can become case affixes.

Locatives are extended metaphorically to other uses, but this process is notoriously variable between languages. Some pitfalls just in French:

	literally...	but English would use...
dans trois heures	in three hours	after
aux yeux bleus	to blue eyes	with
à genou	to knee	on the knees
à bicyclette	to bicycle	by
mal à l'estomac	pain to the stomach	in
de loin	of far	from
traiter de voleur	treat of thief	as a
(partir) sur les 5 heures	(leave) on the 5 hours	(go) at 5 o'clock
un sur dix	one on ten	out of
arriver de nuit	arrive of night	at

par tout le pays	by all the country	throughout
commencer par le début	begin by the start	with
par le nord	by the north	from
dans les 50 F	in the 50 francs	around
en avion	in plane	by
en tyran	in tyrant	like a
contre 50 F	against 50 francs	(in exchange) for

French is also notorious for having complex rules for geographical location (*en France, au Mexique, à Paris*) and for the arbitrariness of whether you use *à, de*, or nothing at all after an infinitive.

English *with* has performed the neat trick of reversing its meaning! Its earliest sense was 'against', still used with *fight* and *contrast*.

French has the neat preposition *chez* 'at the home of', e.g. *chez sa tante* 'at his aunt's'.

The root meaning of Russian y is 'within reach, next to'; it can be used the same way as *chez* (у брата 'at my brother's'); it's also the normal way to express possession (У брата дом 'My brother has a house').

Some sets of locatives

Locatives vary widely between languages. **Quechua** has a very simple set, realized as case endings:

-ta	accusative	
-paq	dative	for (beneficiary), by (a time)
-pa	genitive	of
-manta	ablative	from, out of, about (topic)
-man	illative	to (goal or beneficiary)
-wan	instrumental	with, and
-rayku	causal	because of
-kama	terminative	as far as, until
-pi	locative	at, in, during
-nka	distributive	each
-pura	interactive	among, restricted to
-nta	transitive	through

Swahili relies heavily on the postposition *ya*, whose core meaning is 'of'— e.g. *milango ya nyumba* 'the doors of the house'. It agrees with its object: *vitu vya mfalme* 'the king's things'.

Expressions of the form *<locative> ya <noun>* correspond to our prepositional phrases: *chini ya mti* 'under the tree'. The locatives (in origin usually nouns) include:

chini	under
juu	on, over, about
nje	outside
ndani	in
nyuma	behind
mbele	in front of, beyond
katikati	in the middle of
zaidi	more than
kati	between, among
baada	after (time)
kabla	before (time)
baina	between, among
miongoni	among
kando	beside
mahali	instead of, in place of

In addition, there are locatives that use the particle *na* instead:

mbali	far from
karibu	near
pamoja	together with
sawa	equal to, the same as
tofauti	different from

Then there's *kwa* which is a **pre**position, used for place (*kwa mwalimu* 'to the teacher'), instrument (*kwa wino* 'with ink'), or manner (*kwa haraka* 'in a hurry').

Mandarin has a number of ways to form locatives, but I'll focus on two. First, there are a set of postpositions, normally used with the particle *zài* 'at'— e.g. *zài chéng wài* 'outside the city'.

lǐ	in, inside
wài	outside
shàng	on top of, above
xià	under, below
qián	in front of
hòu	behind, in back of
zhōng	in, among, between
páng	by, beside
dōng	east of (likewise the other directions)

zhèr	this side of
nàr	that side of
zuǒ	left of
yòu	right of

These may be combined with *-bian* 'side', *-mian* 'face', *-tou* 'head'— e.g. *zài fángzi hòumian* 'behind the house'.

In addition there are a set of **pre**positions, including those below. These derive from verbs, and it's useful to see their original meaning:

āi	next to	be next to
àn	according to	press
bèn	toward	go to
bǐ	compared to	compare
cháo	facing	face
chúle	except, besides	remove
cóng	from	follow
dǎ	from	hit
dāng	in front of	serve as
duì	to	face
gěi	for, by	give
gēn	with	follow
hàn	with	mix
jiě	from	untie, relieve
kào	depending on	lean against
lí	separated from	keep distance
nì	against	be opposed to
píng	according to	depend on
qǐ	from (time, place)	rise
shǐ	using, with	cause
tì	in place of	substitute for
xiàng	like	be like
yán	along	follow along
yī	according to	agree with
yú	to, for	be at

Russian prepositions often have a different meaning when used with different cases:

без	gen	without
через	acc	through, across, after (time)
для	gen	for
до	gen	up to, until
из	gen	out of

к(о)	dat	to, toward
кроме	gen	besides, except
между	instr	between
на	acc	(moving) onto, for (time)
	prep	(location) on
над	instr	above
о(б)	acc	against
	prep	about, concerning
около	gen	next to, near, about
от	gen	from, away from, from (a time)
перед	instr	in front of
по	dat	on, along, according to
под	acc	(moving) under
	instr	under
подле	gen	alongside
после	gen	after
позади	gen	behind
при	prep	in the presence of
с(о)	gen	from, off
	instr	with, using, in the company of
у	gen	near, at, *chez*
в(о)	acc	(moving) into, at (time)
	prep	(location) in
впереди	gen	in front of
за	acc	(moving) behind, during
	instr	for, after, (location) behind

LOVE

care	OE *caru* 'sorrow' > 'be concerned' > 'care for'
	• Fr *soin* < 'attend to' • Welsh *pryder* < 'take time' • Ger *Sorge* < 'sorrow, grief' • Cz *starati* < '(care for the) old' • Rus забота < 'alarm' • Ch *kānhù* 'guard-family'
companion	Fr *compagne* '(person one has) bread with'
	• Gk ἑταῖρος prob. < 'one's own' • Lt *socius* < 'follow' • Fr *camarade* < 'chambermate' • Welsh *cydymaith* 'fellow traveler' • Dutch *makker* < 'fit, equal' • Ger *Genosse* 'co-owner' • Rus товарищ 'waresman' • Skt *sahāya-* 'go with'
FRIEND	OE *fréond* < Germanic 'dear'
	• Lt *amīcus* < 'love' • Welsh *cyfaill* 'foster brother' • Sw *vän* < 'desire, love' • OCS *drugŭ* 'companion' • Farsi *dost* < 'take pleasure' • Ch *péng* < 'pair', *yǒu* < '(at one's) right'
hate	OE *hete*, cognate to Old Ir *cais* 'love/hate' poss. < 'care'
	• Lt *odium* poss. < 'disgust' • Rum *ură* < 'shudder' • OCS *nenavistĭ* 'not see' • Skt *dviṣ-* < 'separation, discord' • Ch *hèn* ‖ 'quarrelsome, obstinate'
LIKE	OE *lícian* < Germanic 'body' ‖ *lich*
loyal	Fr *loyal* < Lt 'legal'
love	OE *lufu* < IE, cognate to OCS *ljuby*, Skt *lubh-* 'long for' ‖ Lt *libīdo libīdin-* 'desire, lust'
	• Lt *amor* poss. < babytalk • Sp *querer* 'desire' • Rum *dragoste* < 'dear' • Sw *älskog* < 'nourish, bear' • Cz *láska* 'caress' • Avestan *zaoš-* < 'enjoy'
+	*affection, romance, date, flirt, boy/girlfriend, mate, partner*

> ▸ See also *Sex,* p. 327, and *Kinship,* p. 225.

I've found the ancient Greek fourfold division of love to be useful:

- στοργή— affection, love within the family
- φιλία— friendship, the most respectable of the loves to a philosopher
- ἔρως— romance, lust, what all those songs are about
- ἀγάπη— spiritual love, the type elevated by Paul

The latter was translated *cāritas* 'dearness' in Latin; thus *charity* in the KJV, since specialized to mere alms-giving. Amusingly, the English cognate is *whore* (cf. Buck §16.27).

Lakota traditionally had *kȟolá* 'male friend of a man' and *maškê* 'female friend of a woman', but no term for a friend of the opposite sex, which was considered improper.

In Korean, you refer to *friends* using kinship terms if they're older (e.g. *oppa* 'older brother of a girl'), *jingu* if they're the same age, otherwise simply by name.

'Friend' can be the basis for naming lovers, as in 'boyfriend/girlfriend' or French *petite amie*.

While retaining general *amar* 'love', Spanish uses *querer* 'want' for romantic love. Catalan uses *estimar* (cognate to 'esteem').

The optional terms given above are highly culture-specific. You can discover the terms you need by writing a little biography of a person from your culture. How do they get married? What activities are involved? What options do they have? Is marriage linked to love at all? What rituals are involved? How much freedom is there to hook up, or live together, outside marriage?

MEASUREMENT

count	Old Fr *cunter* < Lt *computāre* 'calculate' < 'think together'
inch	Lt *uncia* '1/12, ounce'
kilometer	Fr, from Gk 'thousand' + 'measure'
measure	Fr *mesure* < Lt *mētīrī* < IE, cognate to Gk μετρέω, OE *mæd* • Ch *chĭcùn* 'foot-inch'
meter	Gk μέτρον 'measure'
mile	Lt *mīlia* 'thousand (paces)' • Ch *lĭ* 'divide into sections'
number	Lt *numerus* poss. < 'share' • Gk ἀριθμός < 'reckon, order' • Ger *Zahl* < 'count, relate' • Skt *samkhyā-* 'add up' • Ch *shù* < 'what is counted'
rate	Lt *ratus* 'calculated; constant'
scale	Norse *skál* 'bowl'
total	Lt *tōtus* 'entire'
+	*ratio; accurate, calculate*

> ▸ See also *Dimension*, p. 169.

Readers will accept US units in fantasy, but this is one area where context will let you slip in terms from your conlang. If a character says "But Lord Nařo, Barakhún is two hundred *cemisî* away", it's clear that they're using unit of length for long distances. They won't know the exact distance, but they also won't care.

More subtly, you can calque the terms: "The ktuvok stood more than four strides tall and weighed more than four milletsacks."

Here's the system I came up with for Verduria:

Linear

eda - width of a scroll pen		.351 cm	.0014 in
mano - width of a hand	24 edî	8.42 cm	3.3 in
čima - length of a man's stride	9 manoi	.758 m	2.5 ft
proma - a unit used in racing, navigation, etc.	2 čimî	1.516 m	5.0 ft
cemisa - a thousand paces	1000 čimî	758 m	.47 mi
dënšadu - one day's ride by horse	80 cemisî	60.64 km	37.60 mi

Area

bařura - used to measure cloth, rooms, etc.	1 čima potë	.575 m^2	6.2 ft^2
meči - used to measure land		1.136 ha	2.8 acres

Volume

mika - smaller spoonful	1/2 miy	3.358 ml	0.7 tsp
miy - spoonful		6.716 ml	1.4 tsp
verae - liqueur glass	12 miî	80.6 ml	2.7 oz
ɗuro - flagon	5 veraî	.403 l	14 oz
lažna - wine-bottle	2 ɗuroi	.806 l	.21 gal
gemár - pitcher	5 lažnî	4.03 l	1.1 gal
luco - bushel	9 gemárî	36.27 l	9.9 gal
bečka - barrel	4 lucoi	145.1 l	38 gal

Weight

ris - the weight of a grain		60.71 mg	.94 grain
hecur - two sheets of paper	100 risî	6.071 g	.21 oz
süro - a standard cut of cheese	100 hecurî	.6071 kg	1.3 lb
cucuri - for weighing men and animals	10 süroi	6.071 kg	13 lb
pavona - cartload	288 cucurî	1750 kg	1.9 ton

Most of the units are based on homely exemplars, things premodern people are likely to have at hand. The multipliers are a bit miscellaneous— the neatness of the metric system doesn't appear before the scientific era.

A few terms (*proma, cucuri*) are restricted to particular domains; this is an imitation of terms like *furlong, dram, carat*.

METALS

gold   OE *gold* < IE derivation of **ghel-* 'yellow'
- Lt *aurum* prob. < IE 'reddish' • Ch *jīn* also 'metal' poss. < 'bright'

iron   OE *íren, ísen*, uncertain, but cognate to Celtic **īsarnom*
- Lt *ferrum* uncertain • Skt *ayas-* originally 'bronze' • Ch *tiĕ* < 'black'

lead   OE *léad*, cognate to Ir *luaidhe*
- Lt *plumbum*, Gk μόλυβδος loanwords but source uncertain

metal   Gk μέταλλον 'mine'
- Ch *jīn* also 'gold' poss. < 'bright'

silver   OE *siolfor*, uncertain, but cognate to OCS *srebro*
- Lt *argentum* poss. < IE 'bright, white' • Sp *plata* < '(silver) plate' < 'flat'

steel   OE *stýle*
- Fr *acier* < 'edge' • Ch *gāng* < 'hard'

tin   OE *tin*
- Lt *plumbum album* 'white lead' • Rus жесть 'hard'

+   *copper, zinc, bronze, brass, mercury*
forge, anvil, alloy, ore

> ▸ See also *Elements*, p. 183, and *Substances*, p. 342.

Few metals are available in pure form: basically **gold**, **silver**, **copper**, and **tin**. The rest are locked up in *ores*. The challenge of ancient metallurgy was to produce metals that were cheap enough to use for utensils, malleable enough to work, but strong enough to keep their shape. Gold and silver fail two of these tests, and even copper is too weak to make good swords and plows.

The key to unlocking ores is heat, and plenty of it. An open wood fire doesn't reach much above 550° C— not enough to melt most ores. A pottery kiln, however, can reach the melting point of **copper**, 1100° C. The development of the kiln, by the -35C, allowed copper metallurgy.

By the -30C, copper was combined with tin to form **bronze**, which was strong enough to make tools and swords. (Tin melts at just 250° C, so it's easily recovered from ores like cassiterite.) An alternative to tin is zinc, producing **brass**.

Iron melts at over 1500° C; with ancient technology such temperatures could be reached only by using a bellows, or by adding enough carbon (from charcoal) to lower the melting point.

Iron alloyed with carbon is *steel*. The simplest approach (developed by 1000 BC) is to heat iron with charcoal, then cool it in water, which creates a steel surface— enough to improve a blade considerably.

Add carbon in quantity (4%) and you have *cast iron*— too brittle for weapons, but still useful. The Chinese had developed this by 500 BC.

Pure steel has 0.5 to 1% carbon content and is much harder and stronger than iron. Crucible steel (formed by heating iron, glass, and charcoal in a clay jar— the glass bonded to impurities and floated to the top where it could be removed) was made in India (2C). Europeans could produce good steel by the 1500s, but it wasn't till the Bessemer process (1855) that steel could be produced cheaply and in quantity. (That's one reason you can't plausibly add steam boilers to a medieval society.)

Though steel is still our mainstay, we use plenty of other metals— see the *Elements* section for some of the major uses as well as modern alloys. There are cases where radioactive metals can be used: e.g. out in space where the radioactivity produces useful heat, or in bullets where the radiation poisoning is mostly happening to the enemy.

MIND

amaze — intensive of *maze* 'stupefy'
- Fr *stupéfier* 'make stupid' • Ger *verblüffen* < 'intimidate' • Ch *jīngqí* 'afraid-strange'

assume — Lt *assūmere* 'take to (oneself)'

astonish — Old Fr *estonnir* 'from thunder'

attention — Lt *attentio* 'stretch to'
- Ger *Aufmerksamkeit* 'up-notice' • Ch *zhù* < 'touch'

believe — ME *bileven* 'hold dear' (‖ *love* and Ger *glauben*)
- Gk πείθομαι 'be persuaded' • Lt *crēdere* < IE • Rus верить < 'faith' • Ch *xìn* prob. < 'trust'

brain — OE *brægen* poss < 'front of head'
- Lt *cerebrum* < IE *ḱer- 'head' • Gk ἐγκέφαλος 'in head' • OCS *mozgŭ* 'marrow' • Skt *mastiṣka-* 'skull'

choose — Fr *choisir* < Germanic 'try, test, prove'
- Sp *elegir* < 'pick out'

claim — Fr *clamer* 'cry out, appeal'

clever — ModE 'nimble with hands', poss. from 'claw'
- Fr *astucieux* < 'tricky'

commit — Lt 'put together'
- Ger *anvertrauen* 'trust on' • Ch *xǔnuò* 'much-promise'

concentrate — Fr *concentrer* 'draw to one center'

concern — Lt *concernere* 'sift together'

confuse — Lt *confūsus* 'poured together'

conscious — Lt *conscius* 'knowing with (others), privy to'
- Ch *yìshí* 'know idea'

consider — Lt *consīderāre* 'examine'; same obscure root as 'desire'
- Ger *nachdenken* 'after-think'

curious — Lt *cūriōsus* 'full of care or pains'
- Ger *neugierig* 'new-greedy' • Ch *hǎoqí* 'good-strange'

dare — OE *durran* < IE, cognate to Gk θάρσος 'courage'
- Lt *audēre* < 'eager' • Rum *cuteza* < 'play dice' • Ir *leomh* 'take in hand' • Ger *wagen* 'wager' • OCS *sŭměti* < 'courage'

decide — Lt *dēcīdere* 'cut off'
- Gk κρίνω < 'separate' • Ger *bestimmen* 'voice' • Sw *avgöra* 'do of' • Rus решать < 'release' • Ch *jué* < 'cut off'

desire — Lt *dēsīderāre* 'miss, long for', obscure root also in 'consider'
- Gk ἐπιθῡμέω < 'set heart on' • Sp *desear* < 'sit idle' • Rum *dori* < 'pain' • Ger *begehren* < 'eager' • OCS *želěti* < 'wish'

determine — Lt *dētermināre* intensive of 'set bounds to'

doubt   Lt *dubitāre* 'waver, hestitate'

• Gk ἀμφιβολία 'attacked on both (sides)' • It *amhras* 'disbelief' • Breton *mar* 'hesitation' • Ger *Zweifel* 'two-ness' • Lith *šaubas* 'shaking'

dream   ME (but must derive from OE as it is common Germanic)

• Lt *somnium* < 'sleep' • Rum *vis* 'sight'

expect   Lt *expectāre* 'look out'

forget   OE *forȝietan* < 'lose one's grip'

• ModGk ξεχάνω < 'lose' • Lt *oblīviscī* 'rub out' • It *dimenticare* 'from the mind' • Welsh *anghofio* 'disremember' • Sw *glömma* 'merry' > 'neglect' • OCS *zabyti* 'be behind' • Ch *wàng* 'lose, flee'

hesitate   Lt *hæsitāre* frequentative of 'adhere, stick'

hope   OE *hopa*, uncertain

• Gk ἐλπίς < 'wish' • Lt *spēs* prob. < 'success' • Ir *dóchas* < 'likelihood' • Rus надежда 'place oneself on' • Ch *jì* poss. < 'seek'

idea   Gk ἰδέα 'look, form, kind' < 'see'

• Lt *nōtio* < 'know' • Ger *Begriff* < 'understand' • Ch *yì* < 'think'

idiot   Gk ἰδιώτης 'private person = layman' > 'uninformed'

imagine   Lt *imāgināre* 'picture to oneself'

• Ch *xiǎngxiàng* 'think-image'

important   late Lt *importans* 'be weighty' < 'import, bring into'

• Ger *bedeutend* 'meaningful' • Ch *zhòngyào* 'heavy need'

indicate   Lt *indicāre* 'point out' < 'in' + 'say, make known'

intelligent   Lt *intelligens* < 'gather between'

• Ir *éirimiúil* 'talented' • Ger *verständig* 'understanding' • Rus умный 'mindful' • Skt *buddhi-* 'perceptive, aware' • Qu *umayoq* 'head-having'

intend   Lt *intendere* intensive of 'stretch'

interest   Lt *interesse* 'be between, matter'

LIKE   OE *lícian* < Germanic 'body'

main   OE *mæȝen* 'strong, mighty' > 'principal'

• Fr *principal* < 'first' • Ch *yào* < 'must'

major   Lt *mājor* 'greater'

MEAN   OE *mǽnan* 'intend, mean', cognate to Ger *meinen* 'think'

• Gk σημαίνω 'point out' • Lt *significāre* 'make a sign' • Ir *ciallaigh* < 'intelligence' • Welsh *ystyr* 'story' • Ger *bedeuten* < 'put in the vernacular' • Ch *yìsì* 'idea-think'

memory   Lt *memoria*

mental	Lt *mentālis* 'of the mind'
MIND	OE *ʒemynd* 'memory, thought', cognate to Lt *mēns ment-*
	• Fr *esprit* 'spirit' • Ger *Sinn* 'sense' • OCS *umŭ* < 'show, notice' • Cz *mysl* < 'thought' • Ch *xīn* 'heart'
mystery	Gk μυστήριον 'secret rite' < 'close (the eyes)'
	• Ch *shén* 'spiritual'
necessary	Lt *necesse* 'unyielding'
pick	ME ‖ *pike*
prefer	Lt *præferre* 'bear before'
prepare	Lt *præparāre* 'make ready beforehand'
ready	ME *rædiʒ*, from an OE verb 'put in order, prepare'
	• Lt *parātus* 'prepared' • Sp *pronto* < 'produced' • Ir *ullamh* 'at hand' • Ger *fertig* < 'journey' • Skt *kḷpta-* 'fitted'
realize	Fr *réaliser* 'make real'
recognize	Lt *recognōscere* intensive of 'come to know'
remember	Old Fr *remembrer* 'back to memory' < IE 'care, remember'
	• OE *ʒemunan* < IE, cognate to OCS *pomĭněti* • Fr *souvenir* < 'come down' • Sp *acordarse* 'harmonize' • Danish *huske* 'think' • Ger *sich errinern* < 'make within' • Ch *jì* 'record, regulate'
remind	ModE '(call) back to mind'
represent	Lt *repræsentāre* 'present again'
	• Ger *vertreten* 'step for' • Ch *dàibiǎo* 'substitute-show'
require	Lt 'seek again'
secret	Lt *secrētus* < 'divided off'
	• Gk κρυπτός 'hidden' • Ir *rún* 'rune, mystery' • Ger *geheim* 'domestic' > 'private' • OCS *tajĭnŭ* < 'furtive' • Ch *mì* < 'silent'
significant	Lt *significans* 'making a sign'
stupid	Lt *stupidus* 'stunned'
	• Sp *necio* < 'not knowing' • Ger *albern* < 'simple'
suppose	Fr *supposer* 'put under'
	• Ger *annehmen* 'take on' • Ch *cāixiǎng* 'guess-think'
THINK	OE *þyncan*, cognate to archaic Lt *tongēre* 'know'
	• Gk φρονέω < 'vitals' • Lt *cōgitāre* 'impel with' • Fr *penser* < 'weight' • Lith *galvoti* < 'head' • Rus думать 'judge, deem' • Ch *xiang* < 'observe'
understand	OE *understondan* 'stand under'
	• Gk συνίημι 'bring together' • Lt *comprehendere* 'seize with' • Sp *entender* 'stretch toward' • Breton *klevout* 'hear' • Skt *avagam-* 'come down to' • Ch *yù* poss. ‖ 'intellect'

wait	ME < Germanic 'guard' > 'lie in wait' > 'observe'
	• Fr *attendre* 'attend' • It *aspettare* < 'look at' • Sw *vänta* < 'hope for' • OCS *žĭdati* < 'desire'
WANT	Norse *vanta* 'lack'
	• Lt *velle*, cognate to *will* • Sp *querer* < 'seek' • Ch *yào* < 'must'
WILL	OE *willian* 'intend, wish'
wish	OE *wýscan* < IE
	• Fr *souhaiter* 'sub-vow'
wonder	OE *wundor* uncertain
	• Gk θαῦμα < 'sight' • Lt *stupor* 'numbness' • Fr *étonner* < 'thunder' • Welsh *rhyfedd* 'beyond measure' • Sw *förvåning* 'beyond expectation'
+	*personality, intellect, sane, cunning, naïve, wit*
	concentrate, discern; prejudice, bias, interpret, define
	predict, optimist, pessimist, nightmare, illusion
	alert, urgent, minor, sympathy, neurosis

Mandarin has a useful term *yǐwéi* which is used for a recently fixed misconception— e.g. "I thought you were coming (when it's now clear you're not)".

Metaphors of mind

However advanced our understanding of the physical world, it never helps us much with describing the mind. Whether we think in terms of the four elements or in terms of neurotransmitters, none of that explains what we think or feel. Even the basic level of language (objects, actions, and attributes) barely applies. Our senses can't look inside the brain, and the optimistically named *introspection* ('seeing inside') reveals nothing certain.

That is, our viewpoint is naturally and inevitably dualistic— even if we vehemently reject dualism as a philosophy.

We need to talk about the mind anyway, so naturally we reach for our basic mental tool— metaphor. Or rather, a whole set of metaphors.

- The mind is like a squabbling **group of people**. This was the basis for a huge literary genre of the Middle Ages, the allegory, but you can still hear it any day: *I should dump him, but my heart tells me not to. Don't listen to your fears. He's dominated by greed.*

The 19C notion of phrenology was an attempt to turn this into science. Though pure quackery, it offers insight into what people *thought* should be included in a science of mind.

Freud's *id, ego, superego* is a modernization of this, with a reduced cast of characters.[7] Paul used the idea of the 'old man' and the 'new man'[8] (cf. Ephesians 4:20-24), referring to the corrupt sinner in us and the newly emerging redeemed saint.

Marvin Minsky's *Society of Mind* and David Eagleman's 'team of rivals' (from *Incognito*) are also versions of this idea.

- The mind is like a **workshop** where ideas are manipulated by, um, the mental hands. To *attend* to something is to 'stretch toward' it; to *examine* it is to weigh it with scales; to *assume* is to take or receive. You *grasp* an idea or *turn it over in your mind*. You can *hold* it in English or French (*maintain*) or Latin (*tenet*). There is a mental stage with a mental observer who can *imagine* (form an image) of the work.

  As Daniel Dennett observes in *Consciousness Explained*, the notion of an internal homunculus who's presented with a TV-like image is very hard to eradicate, even in the writings of visual scientists. But it's nonsense; there is no homunculus, and if there were we'd be back at square one, having to explain *his* vision!

- The different **organs of the body** each contain a bit of mind. We still refer to the *heart* as the seat of love and value, localize lust in the genitals, and courage or sincerity in the *guts*. Cultures don't always make the same assignments! Galen considered the liver to be the seat of the passions. The Chinese located sadness

---

[7] Freud's terms were *Es, Ich, Über-ich* 'it, I, over-I'; his English translator Latinized them.

[8] Those are the usual English terms, but Paul actually used the sex-neutral ἄνθρωπος.

in the lungs, worry in the spleen, and fear in the kidneys. To the Hebrews, the intellect lived in the heart, the conscience in the kidneys, and anguish in the intestines.

- The mind is characterized or affected by the known **elements**. In medieval thought the elements within the body were expressed as the four *humors.*

- The mind is generally compared to the most complicated **mechanism** people were aware of. In medieval times this might be a clock; in the 18C a mill; today it's a computer. We say *the wheels are turning* to refer to decision-making; we complain that our knowledge of French is *rusty* or that we've *run out of steam*; in extreme cases we have a *breakdown.*

- Lakoff and Johnson draw attention to the **conduit metaphor**, used for language and meaning: we *put our thoughts into words,* we try to *get ideas across*; the listener may complain they didn't *come through* or had *little weight.* This is still a very live metaphor— even many linguists imagine that our mental message is constructed as a coherent whole (perhaps written in Mentalese), packed into language as a necessary medium, and reassembled in the listener's brain. As noted in the *LCK* (p. 132), meaning is much sloppier than this. It can't be reduced to a set of logical assertions, and the listener cannot be assumed to reconstruct 'the same message' at all.

- Arguments and belief systems are compared to **buildings**. They can be *well supported* or *shaky.* They have *foundations* and may *collapse.*

- Ideas can be consumed like **food**. We build them from *raw facts;* we *stew on them* or *ruminate* (= 'chew the cud'). We admire a *meaty* theory and *devour* a good book. If an idea is bad we just can't *swallow* it.

For more see Lakoff and Johnson's *Metaphors We Live By*: IDEAS ARE PLANTS, IDEAS ARE PRODUCTS, IDEAS ARE MONEY, IDEAS ARE FASHIONS, UNDERSTANDING IS SEEING, and more. What metaphors are used in the following examples?

> *He has a <u>sharp</u> wit but he wastes it on <u>dullards</u>.*

> *I <u>looked for</u> a reason but couldn't <u>find</u> one.*

> *The depression <u>hit</u> me, but I'm determined to <u>shake it off</u>.*

> *She's <u>full of energy</u>, but being with her makes me feel <u>drained</u>.*

Maintain a <u>healthy</u> skepticism, especially about <u>sick</u> ideas like that one.

You <u>drive</u> me crazy— I feel <u>lost</u> without you.

I can't <u>take my eyes off</u> her, and I could feel her eyes <u>on me</u> too.

The disciples couldn't <u>rise</u> to the occasion— they <u>fell</u> asleep.

The smell of the madeleine <u>brought up</u> memories from <u>deep</u> in his mind.

These metaphors can be used to construct mind-related words and expressions, and you can expand them into belief systems as well. Or invent your own: the mind could be likened to an army, or to a set of animals, or a dance, or a city, or a bureaucracy.

Theories of mind

How does the mind work? Building on these metaphors and our own experience, we need a theory of mind.

Julian Jaynes, reading ancient texts, had the intriguing notion that consciousness is relatively recent— less than 3000 years old. We interpret the voices in our head— thoughts and desires— as *ours*, even if we attribute them to hazy entities like 'the unconscious'. But the heroes of the Iliad and the Old Testament, according to Jaynes, did not report their inner life like this. They attributed those voices to the gods and were unable to consciously evaluate them— they could only obey or disobey. (See *The Origin of Consciousness in the Breakdown of the Bicameral Mind*.)

This may be wrong or exaggerated, but at the least it's a demonstration that people don't all have to have the same theories of mind. C.S. Lewis speaks of the process of *internalization* in the psychology of the West. To the 2C philosopher Apuleius, a *genius* was an individual daemon assigned to each human being as a 'witness and guardian'. Later this became the man's 'true self', and in modern times his talent or understanding.

Similarly, ancient men may have taken the stories of gods and heroes to be true for the same reason that we take them as untrue: that a poet or prophet was 'making them up'. To us, storytelling is an interior process and of course no guide to external truth. But to the ancients, how could a man produce an epic or a prophecy unless it was dictated by the gods, or the Muses (p. 127)?

For centuries people have debated the status of our conscious mind. The commonest idea, what I'd identify as the folk theory of mind, is that it's **us**. *You're the sovereign* within your own brain. Maybe parts of you are hidden to view (your memory isn't always reliable; no one really knows where a 'story' comes from; you don't choose who you're attracted to), but at the least *you* decide what to do. Law depends on this folk theory, holding you responsible for those decisions. So does language— the whole concept of persons and agency depends on it.

Calvinists, and many scientists, have the opposite view: the conscious mind is an **illusion** or an epiphenomenon. We're no more free than a clockwork mechanism; we just do whatever our brain tells us (or what God has predetermined).

We use this view as one part of our metaphorical toolkit (*I couldn't help myself; I didn't do it on purpose*), and it's our usual way of understanding sleep, unconsciousness, and mental illness. What would a conworld be like where this was the accepted view for all mental activity? Surely it shouldn't have personal pronouns, as there is no such thing as persons. Ideas like *will* and *sin* would be banished; law would probably be a subset of medicine.

What if both kinds of consciousness existed? Some of us are really here— there's *someone* that thinks and feels— but others only look and act as if they do; there's no one home. They're *philosophical zombies*. How would we tell? That might make for an interesting conworld too.

The sovereignty of consciousness seems to be losing ground. Things once seen as moral failings or unfortunate temperaments are now considered chemical states— addictions or an imbalance of neurotransmitters. Neurologists tell us, dismayingly, that when people are asked to make a decision to move their arm, the arm starts moving as much as a second before the subject reports their decision.

On the other hand, it's rash to make pronouncements about bits of the world we don't yet understand, and we don't yet understand the mind. Consciousness very likely has more surprises up its sleeve.

There's even more possibilities in an sf setting:

- What theory of mind would an insectile hive mind have? How about a symbiotic being— say, a sentient creature that has both a plant and animal part?

- How would it feel to integrate your computer (with its powers of calculation, simulation, and Internet access) into your brain?

Would those skills feel like 'part of you'? What if you could easily upgrade or replace them?

- There's a gulf between human beings— we can talk and touch but can't directly share minds. What if we could? Many sf writers have explored what telepathy would be like (Alfred Bester did it masterfully in *The Demolished Man*), but few have considered the linguistic consequences. Thinking is *like* talking inaudibly, but unlike speech it has multiple levels— fleeting impressions, assumptions, unstated 'real meanings' or images, background memories, the promptings of emotion. If all this was public, we'd need a shared way of analyzing and referring to these things. What does politeness look like if you can directly perceive a person's actual attitude? Are there mental techniques for restoring a certain privacy? What are the social effects if not everyone is telepathic, or if not everyone is observable?

  On the other hand, if you can read minds, perhaps the spoken language is radically simplified. E.g. Lee Killough's telepaths in *Deadly Silents* have no words for emotions, just the word 'feel' which invites another to probe your current feelings.

The same issues come up in fantasy if you allow magic. The world of Skyrim, where you can be charmed or frenzied or paralyzed by a spell that's readily sold in shops, raises troubling philosophical issues. Wouldn't it be rather terrifying to be subject to other's whims like that, and all the more so because no one ever seems to notice that they're under a spell?

Analysis

aim	Old Fr *esmer* < 'estimate'
arrange	Fr *arranger* '(put) to ranks'
case	Lt *cāsus* originally 'a falling'
character	Gk χαρακτήρ 'engraving tool'
	• Ger *Ruf* 'reputation' < 'call'
class	Lt *classis* 'division of the people'
	• Ch *jí* 'step, rank'
compare	Lt *comparāre* 'pair together'
	• Ger *vergleichen* 'be like for' • Ch *bi* < 'associate' < 'follow'
condition	Lt *condicio* 'compact = a speaking together'
	• Ger *Bedingung* < 'contract' • Ch *tiáojiàn* 'order item'
design	Lt *dēsignāre* 'mark out' > 'appoint'
	• Ger *entwerfen* 'throw away' • Ch *shèjì* 'arrange-plan'

detail   Fr *détailler* 'cut into pieces' > 'sell small pieces'
       • Ger *Einzelheit* 'singleness' • Ch *xìjié* 'small section'

differ   Old Fr *diférrer* 'carry apart, spread'
       • Ger *unterscheiden* 'under-divide' • Ch *bùtóng* 'not same'

general   Lt *generālis* 'of a genus' > 'universal'

kind   OE *ʒecynde* 'birth' > 'nature' (adjective: > 'of good nature')
       • Ch *lèi* < 'lineage', *wù* ‖ 'seed'

manner   Fr *manière* 'handling' < Lt 'of the hand'

match   OE *ʒemæcca* 'peer, one's like'

mess   Lt *missum* 'something sent' > 'serving' > 'quantity'

opposite   Lt *oppositus* 'put against'

order   Lt *ordo ordin-* 'row, series, order'
       • Ch *xù* < 'continue'

organize   late Lt *organizāre* 'furnish with organs, bring to life'

particular   Lt *particulāris* 'of a small part'

pattern   Fr *patron* 'model' < Lt 'protector', derivation of 'father'

plan   Fr 'drawing' < Lt 'flat'
       • Ch *móu* poss. < '(think) ahead'

problem   Gk πρόβλημα 'thrown forward' = 'a set task'
       • Ch *wèntí* 'question-topic'

program   Gk πρόγραμμα 'public written notice'

purpose   Lt *prōpōnere* 'put forward'
       • Gk πρόθεσις 'setting forth' • Ger *Absicht* 'by sight', *Zweck* 'peg' > 'target' • Pol *zamiar* 'measure' • Skt *artha-* 'reach'

puzzle   ModE uncertain
       • Fr *énigme* < 'obscurity' • Sp *rompecabezas* 'break-head' • Ch *nántí* 'difficult-topic'

range   Fr *ranger* < 'row, rank'

reason   Lt *ratio* 'account, number, matter'
       • Gk λόγος 'word' • Rus разум 'separate-mind' • Ch *lǐ* 'regulate' poss. < 'divide in sections'

relate   Lt *relātus* 'referred'

same   Norse *same*
       • Fr *même* 'self' • Sp *igual* 'equal' • Ger *gleich* < 'like' • Ch *tóng* 'together'

separate   Lt *sēparāre* 'prepared apart'
       • Gk σχίζω 'split' • Ir *scar* < 'cut' • Rus отделить 'divide off' • Skt *viyuj-* 'apart-join'

situation   Lt *situātio* derivation of 'position, site'
       • Ger *Lage* < 'lie' • Ch *xíngshì* 'appear-power'

sort	Lt *sors sort-* 'lot, fate, part'
state	Lt *status* 'standing' > 'condition'
	• Ch *zhuàng* 'shape'
system	Gk σύστημα 'organized whole', from 'set up' + 'with'
	• Ch *xìtŏng* 'connect-unity'
trick	Fr *tricher* < Lt *trīcarī* 'trifle, play tricks'
+	*example, similar, identical, chaos, abstract*
	nonsense, solve, riddle, goal, scheme, clue, code
	deduce, imply, induction, analyze, logic, fallacy

These are a particular type of mental tools— those we use to reason and analyze the world.

Etymologically, they rely heavily on physical **position**, **vision**, and **manipulation**. The main metaphor is that of the mental workshop: to think about an object, we bring it onto the mental table; we turn it around, take it apart, compare it to other things on the table. *Analysis* is 'loosening' something to break it down into its components; a *detail* comes from the similar metaphor of cutting things apart. A *deduction* is 'leading' the argument like a recalcitrant goat; to *imply* is to fold or wrap something— to involve or entangle it.

Latin *reor* 'think', the origin of *reason* and *ratio,* is a basic root; it also has the sense 'calculate' and may be cognate to Greek ἀριθμός 'number', so it may be a generalization from this particular kind of thinking. OE *þyncan* is 'seem, appear'— *methinks* didn't mean 'I think', but rather 'It appears to me'. It had a causative *þencan* which merged with it to give us *think*— so the basic idea is 'causing something to appear (to oneself)'. French *penser* is another tool metaphor: weighing something.

To the Greeks λόγος 'reason' was what distinguished humans from animals; note that it included morality as well as logic. The Word in John 1:1 is ὁ λόγος; marrying Hebrew spirituality to Greek rationality created a religion of wide appeal.

An important type of thinking is describing **classes** of things— their *kinds* or *nature*. To talk about the categories of things in the world is basically to analyze or study the world— in Verdurian, *kestora* 'the categories' is the name for natural philosophy. English *kind* took on the sense 'temperament', then 'good or proper temperament', leading to the narrower sense of 'compassionate, benevolent'.

The original sense of *class* was a division of the Roman people; this was easily extended to other divisions. The same semantic transformation applied to the adjective *classic* as to *kind*: from 'belonging to a class' the sense became 'belonging to the highest class', and thus 'the standards, the masterpieces'.

Temperament

A map of the soul is useful for understanding those infuriating creatures, our fellow humans, as well as for generating vocabulary.

To medieval Europeans, there were four bodily fluids, the *humors*, themselves combinations of the four elements. Your particular combination of humors was your *temperament* ('mixture'). Note the semantic drift: fine perception of people's temperaments was a *sense of humor*, revealing your particular temperament was *showing your temper*, and being cursed with a bad one was to be *ill-tempered*.

blood	*fire + water*	*sanguine*: pleasant, cheerful, though peppery
choler	*fire + earth*	*choleric*: angry and vindictive, neurotic
phlegm	*water + air*	*phlegmatic*: sluggish and dull
melancholy	*earth + air*	*melancholic*: withdrawn and brooding, stubborn in opinions, long in anger

Another way of describing personalities was by comparing them to the conventional characters of the planets:

Saturn	*saturnine*: melancholy and contemplative, the patron of disasters, sickness, accident, and age
Jupiter	*jovial*: like a king in repose, merry and festive, magnanimous and serene
Mars	*martial*: sturdy, hardy, and warlike
Sol	wise, noble, and fortunate, patron of theologians and philosophers
Venus	the source of beauty and love, survived by the crappy word *venereal*
Mercury	studious, but also associated with profit and action (modern *mercurial* has narrowed to 'volatile')
Moon	*lunatic*; wandering, including that of the mind

For **Verdurian**, I associated temperaments with the seven elements:

ur clay	*urise* - mortal, fallible; *urete* - down to earth, practical
mey water	*mese* - benevolent, wise, tender; happy, playful
ĝumë stone	*ĝumise* - strong, determined, patient
endi wood	*enil* - quiet, shy, timid
gent metal	*geteme* - strong, powerful, with the qualities of a leader

tšur fire   *mëril* - fiery, bold, energetic
šalea air   *šaleme* - intellectual, unwordly, ivory-tower

MOVEMENT

(a)rise
OE *rísan*
- Dutch *opstaan* 'stand up' • Lt *surgere* < 'guide under' • Fr *se lever* 'lift oneself'

accompany
Fr *acompagner* 'make companion'
- Ger *begleiten* 'lead by' • Ch *péi* < 'double'

advance
Fr *avancer* 'away before'
- Ger *vorrücken* 'fore-move' • Ch *qiánjìn* 'front-proceed'

approach
Fr *approcher* '(come) near to'
- Gk ζυνώνω 'join' • Sp *acercar* 'circle' • Ch *jìn* 'imminent'

arrive
Lt *adrīpāre* 'to the shore'
- Sp *llegar* < 'fold, turn' • Rum *sosi* < 'safe' • Ger *ankommen* 'come at' • Sw *nå* 'near' • OCS *prispěti* 'near-succeed'

bury
OE *burʒan*
- Fr *enterrer* 'into earth' • Ger *begraben* 'dig by'

camp
Lt *campus* 'field'

capture
Lt *captūra* 'seizure'
- Ger *fangen* 'catch' • Ch *bǔhuò* 'seize-get'

climb
OE *climban* 'rise by cleaving to a surface'

COME
OE *cuman* < IE *g^wem-*, cognate to Lt *venīre*
- OCS *priti* 'go to' • Qu *hamuy* 'go toward speaker'

crawl
Norse *krafla* < frequentative of 'claw, scratch'
- Fr *ramper* < 'climb' • Lith *ļisti* < 'slip' • Pol *szołgać się* '(touch the) forehead'

creep
OE *créopan*
- Lt *serpere*, Gk ἕρπω < IE

depart
Lt *dispertīre* 'divide' > 'separate' > 'move away'
- Gk ἀναχωρέω 'make room' • Fr *sortir* < 'cast lots' > 'predict' > 'escape' • Sp *salir* < 'jump' • Rum *pleca* 'bend'

descend
Lt *dēscendere* antonym of 'climb'

drag
dialectal variant of 'draw'

drift
ME nomn. of 'drive'

drive
OE *drîfan*
- Lt *agere* 'act, drive' • It *spingere* 'push' • Sp *manejar* 'handle' • OCS *gŭnati* < 'strike'

enter
Lt *intrāre*, verbn. of 'within'
- Ger *eintreten* 'walk in' • OCS *vuniti* 'go in' • Skt *viç-* < 'home' • Ch *rù* ‖ 'inside, sink'

FALL
OE *feallan*
- Gk πίπτω < 'fly' • Fr *tomber* imitative • Ir *titim* prob 'hit the ground' • OCS *pasti*, Skt *pad-* poss. < 'foot'

fast   OE *fæst* 'firm, fixed' > 'determinedly' > 'quickly'

• Lt *celer* < 'driven', *rapidus* < 'violent' • Ir *luath* < 'move' • Dutch *vlug* 'fly' • OCS *brĭzo* 'shortly' • Ch *kuài* 'happy'

float   OE *flotian* < IE **pleu-* found in words meaning 'float, swim, sail, rain'

• Ir *snámhán* 'swim' • Ch *fú* < 'raft'

flow   OE *flówan* ‖ 'float'

• Lt *fluere* < 'swell, burst' • Fr *couler* < 'drip' • Ir *rith* 'run' • Welsh *llifo* < 'pour'

fly   OE *fléoӡan* < IE ‖ 'float, sail'

• Lt *volāre* poss. < 'wing' • Ir *eitil* < 'feather' • OCS *poletěti* < 'jump, kick'

GO   OE *gán* (but past tense from *wend*)

• ModGk πάω 'withdraw' • Fr *aller* < 'walk' • Rum *merge* < 'sink' • Dutch *varen* < 'carry' • Ch *qù* 'get rid of'

guide   Fr *guide* prob. < Germanic ‖ *wit*

hop   OE *hoppian*

jump   ModE imitative

• Fr *sauter* < Lt 'dance', frequentative of 'jump' • Gk πηδάω ‖ 'foot' • OCS *skočiti* < 'shake'

leap   OE *hléapan*

leave   OE *lǽfan* < causative of 'remain'

• Gk ἀφίημι 'let go' • Fr *laisser* < 'loosen' • Ch *lí* < 'separate'

lift   Norse *lypta* < 'air'

march   Fr *marcher* 'trample'

• Ch *xíngjūn* 'walk-troops'

miss   OE *missan*

mount   Lt *mons mont-* 'mountain'

MOVE   Lt *movēre*

• Gk κῑνέω < 'go' • Fr *bouger* < 'bubble' • Welsh *symud* 'change' • OE *styrian* < 'disturb' • Cz *hnouti* 'bend'

pace   Lt *passus* 'step' < 'stretching (of the leg)'

• Ch *bù* 'walk'

pass   Fr *passer* < Lt 'step'

progress   Lt *progressus* 'movement forward'

pull   OE *pullian* 'pluck'

• ModGk τραβῶ < 'bull' • Lt *trahere* < IE • Ch *qiān* < 'rope'

quick   OE *cwicu* 'alive' > 'in motion' > 'fast'

race   Norse *rás* uncertain

• Fr *course* 'running'

raise Norse *reisa* < causative of 'rise' ‖ OE *rǽran* > *rear*
• Lt *tollere* < 'support', *levāre* < 'light' • It *alzare* < 'high' • Sw *lyfta* < 'air'

rapid Lt *rapidus* adjn. of 'seize, carry off'

remain Lt *remanēre* 'stay back'
• Fr *rester* 'rest' < 'stand' • Gk λείπομαι 'be left' • Qu *qepay* 'be after'

return Fr *retourner* 'turn back'
• Ch *huí* < 'revolve, go around'

ride OE *rídan*
• Ir *marcaigh* < 'horse' • OCS *jachati*, cognate to Skt *yā-* 'go' • Ch *qí* prob. < 'be carried'

RUN Norse *rinna*, replacing OE cognate *irnan*
• Gk τρέχω < 'wheel' • Lt *currere* ‖ 'vehicle' • Ger *laufen* ‖ 'leap' • OCS *tešti* 'run, flow' • Rus бежать prob. < 'flee' • Ch *zǒu* < 'quick'

rush Old Fr *russer* 'reject' > 'push out' > 'move quickly'

sink OE *sincan*
• Gk βυθίζω < 'depth' • Sp *hundir* < 'bottom' • Fr *plonger* < 'lead (weight)' • Ch *chén* ‖ 'immerse', 'drown'

slide OE *slídan*
• Lt *lābī* < 'loose, weak' • Sp *deslizar* < 'smooth' • Norse *skriðna* < 'crawl' • Ch *huá* 'slippery'

slip Dutch, Low German *slippen*

slow OE *sláw* 'obtuse' > 'slothful' > 'not fast'
• Lt *lentus* 'pliant' • Rum *încet* 'quiet' • Ir *mall* 'slow' • Ger *langsam* 'long-late' • OCS *mǫdǐnǔ* 'delay' • Ch *màn* ‖ 'extensive'

speed OE *spéd* 'abundance' > 'power' > 'quickness'

stay Lt *stāre* 'stand'
• Lt *menēre* 'remain' • Fr *rester* < 'stand back' • Sp *quedar* < 'be quiet' • Dutch *blijven* < 'be stuck'

stride OE *strídan* 'straddle, take long steps' poss. ‖ 'strive'

swim OE *swimman*
• Lt *natāre* < IE 'swim, bathe, wet' • Fr *nager* < 'navigate'

thrust Norse *þrýsta*

walk OE *wealcan* 'roll, toss'
• Fr *marcher* 'march' • Sp *caminar* < 'road' • Ger *gehen* 'go' • Ch *zǒu* < 'run'

wander OE *wandrian*
• Fr *errer* < Lt 'go astray' • Sp *vagar* < 'be empty, at liberty' • Ch *mànbù* 'flow-walk'

+   *abandon, exit, halt, stumble, sneak, squeeze*

Pursuit

avoid — Old Fr *avoider* 'empty out'
- Ger *vermeiden* < 'move away' • Sp *huir* 'flee' • Ch *bì* < '(go) obliquely'

escape — Fr *échapper* < '(get) out of a cloak'
- Ger *entfliehen* 'flee away' • Qu *urmay* 'fall' • Ch *táo* 'run away'

FIND — OE *findan*, prob. ‖ Skt 'path'
- Lt *invenīre* 'come upon' • Sp *encontrar* '(come) against' • Ir *faigh* 'seize under' • Welsh *caffael* 'get' • Ch *zhǎodào* 'seek-reach'

follow — OE *folȝian* < Germanic 'full-go'
- Lt *sequī* < IE • Ir *lean* 'adhere' • Rus следить 'track'

hunt — OE *huntian* < 'seize, capture'
- Lt *vēnārī* < 'seek, strive for' • Fr *chasser* 'chase' • Gk θηράω < 'beast' .• OCS *lovŭ* 'hunting, booty' • Ch *liè* 'trample' • Ket *kəj* 'walk around'

press — Lt *premere*
- Gk πιέζω 'sit upon' • Latvian *spiest* < 'thick' • Rus дивать 'choke' • Ch *àn* 'cause to calm'

pursue — Lt *prosequere* 'follow forward'
- ModGk κυνηγῶ 'hunt' • OCS *goniti* 'drive, chase' • Skt *anudhāv-* 'run after' • Ch *zhuī* poss. ‖ 'track'

push — Lt *pulsāre*, frequentative of 'drive, beat'
- Lt *trūdere* < 'trouble' • Ir *sáigh* causative of 'sit' • Ger *stossen* 'strike' • Ch *tuī* 'push away, shove'

search — Fr *chercher* < Lt 'go around' ‖ 'circle'

seek — OE *sécan* ‖ 'scent', 'lead'
- Gk ζητέω < 'exert oneself' • Fr *chercher* 'circle' • Sp *buscar* < '(hunt) firewood' • Ir *lorg* 'track' • OCS *iskati* < 'seek, wish, ask' • Cz *hledati* < 'look at'

trace — Lt *tractus* 'trailing, dragging, drawing'

+   *chase, flee*

Paths and journeys

address — Fr *addresser* 'straighten'
- Ch *chēng* 'weigh'

COURSE — Fr *cours* 'a running'

journey — Fr *journée* 'day-ness'
- Ch *lǚ* ‖ 'stranger', 'lodging'

passage	Fr *passage* nomn. of 'pass'
path	OE *pæþ*, uncertain
	• Gk ἀτραπός 'trodden' • Ir *cosán* < 'foot' • Lith *takas* < 'run' • Ger *Steig* < 'climb' • Ch *xiǎolù* dim. 'road'
road	OE *rád* 'act of riding' > 'course'
	• Gk ὁδός < 'walk' • Lt *via* poss. < 'seek' • Fr *route* < 'broken' • Rus дорога < 'drawn out' • Skt *mārga-* 'animal (path)'
origin	Lt *orīgo origin-* 'rising, beginning'
	• Ch *běn* 'root'
track	Fr possibly a form of 'trace'
trail	ME 'drag' < likely Lt 'dragnet'
travel	Fr *travailler* 'travail'
	• Qu *illay* verbn. of 'absent' • Ch *lǚ* ‖ 'guest, stranger'
trip	Old Fr *treper* < Germanic 'tread, stamp'
visit	Lt *vīsitāre* 'go see' = frequentative of 'see'
	• Ger *besuchen* 'seek by' • Ch *fǎng* 'inquire'
WAY	OE *weʒ* 'path'
	• Gk τρόπος 'turn' • Lt *modus* < 'measure' • Fr *manière* 'handling' • Dutch *wijze* < 'appearance' • Lith *būdas* 'character' • OCS *obrazŭ* 'form' • Ch *dào* poss. < 'conducting thing'
+	*source, destination, explore, vacation*

Movement in place

bend	OE *bendan* < 'bend a bow' < 'bind, restrain'
	• Gk κάμπτω < 'bent, crooked' • Fr *plier* < 'fold' • Sw *kröka* < 'hook'
flitter	ME *flitten* ‖ 'flow, float'
roll	Lt *rotula*, dim. 'wheel'
	• Gk κυλίνδω < 'cylinder' • Lt *volvere* < IE 'roll, wind, wrap'
shake	OE *scacan* ‖ 'stir, leap, move'
	• Fr *secouer* < 'toss' • OCS *tręsti* 'tremble'
shift	OE *sciftan* 'arrange'
shiver	ME *chivere*, uncertain
shudder	ME < Germanic frequentative of 'shake'
spread	OE *sprǽdan* < 'sow, scatter'
	• Fr *étendre* 'strech out' • Ir *leath* 'wide' • OCS *rasypati* 'pour out'
stretch	OE *streccan* < 'stiff'
	• Lt *tendere* < IE **ten-* • Ir *sín* < 'throw out' • Ch *shēn* < 'pull'
swing	OE *swingan* 'scourge' > 'rush, throw' > 'move back and forth'

tremble	Lt *tremere*
TURN	Gk τόρνος 'compass' > 'turn in a lathe'
	• ModGk γυρίζω < 'round' • Sw *vända* < causative of 'wind'
twist	ME *twinn* 'combine two things' > 'weave' > 'wring'

English verbs of motion make a basic distinction between movement toward the speaker (*come, bring*) and away (*go, take*).

The array of motion verbs above is less intimidating once you realize that many of them are based on locatives— e.g. *enter, exit* derive from Latin *in, out*.

The manner verbs seem to have some sound symbolism going on— e.g. *hop, slip, jump, leap, flap* with their abrupt ending *-p*; or compare the similar-sounding *slip, slide, slither, slink, slog, slouch, sneak*. The *-er* of *clatter, flutter, wander, waver, shudder, clamber* as well as *glitter, mutter, slumber, flicker, chatter, twitter* is a frequentative.

Czech has different sets of movement words for walking, vehicles, and flight, e.g.

přicházet	arrive by foot
přijet	arrive by vehicle
přiletět	arrive by air

Russian adds a distinction between one-way movement (ходить) and two-way or habitual movement (ездить).

Spanish distinguishes *ir* 'go (to a place)' from *irse* 'go away, leave'.

In Hua, spoken in the mountains of New Guinea, motion words distinguish upward and downward movement.

The Siberian language Ket has an interesting array of verbs relating to movement along the river:

áɣà	move from riverbank to forest
ɔ́tà	move from water to riverbank
ígdà	move from forest to riverbank
étà	move upriver along the ice
átà	move downriver along the ice
éskà	move upriver by boat
tíɣà	move downriver by boat

Germanic movement verbs typically emphasize **manner,** Romance verbs **path**. Compare English *The girl ran down the stairs* with Spanish *La chica bajó corriendo las escaleras*— literally 'descended running'. Note the close variants of manner offered by English: *creep / crawl / slither, hop / jump / leap / spring, slip / slide / glide.*

English is somewhat rare in having a specialized verb *walk*; many IE languages just use the word for *go.*

Causatives are particularly useful here, and are often lexicalized: *cause to go = drive / impel, cause to jump = sauté, cause to rise = raise, cause to stand = build, cause to leave = expel.*

From *driving* animals we come to *drive* vehicles, but other languages may use different words— e.g. French *chasser / conduire.* In Russian you can править a horse or a car, but other forms of forcing movement are гнать.

Movement verbs are promiscuous metaphorizers. Some of the commonest:

- A ROUTE IS MOVEMENT: *the road goes to Vyat; the pectoralis muscle runs from the chest to the shoulder.*

- FUNCTIONING IS MOVEMENT: *the computer is running; what makes a steam engine go?*

- TIME IS MOVEMENT: *Time flies; we're halfway through the year.*

- NARRATIVES ARE JOURNEYS: *the author takes us from the slums to the penthouses; I can't get through this book; now we come to the climax.*

- CONVERSION IS MOVEMENT: *I started out as a fundie and ended up as an atheist.*

- TRANSFER OF POSSESSION IS MOVEMENT: *Alsace went to France; this watch came from my grandfather.* Note the dual meaning of *return* ('go back, give back').

- LEADERSHIP IS (CAUSED) MOVEMENT: *Can he move the party forward?* A contrasting framing is that *not* moving is good— *We need stable leadership; he knows how to hold firm.*

- BENEFICIAL CHANGE IS (FORWARD) MOVEMENT: *This country isn't progressing, it's backwards.*

Check an English dictionary for the many extensions of *run.* Another language won't reproduce this set! E.g. French *courir* matches the base meaning of 'fast ambulation', but different verbs are used for most of its extensions:

the river runs	*la fleuve coule*	flow
run for President	*être candidat à la présidence*	be
run for it!	*sauvez-vous!*	save
the dye ran	*la teinture a bavé*	dribble
the play is running	*la pièce se joue*	play
the machine is running	*la machine marche*	walk
my stockings ran	*mes bas ont filé*	slip, spin
run an article	*publier un article*	publish
it's run its course	*ça a suivi son cours*	follow
run a business	*diriger un commerce*	direct
run your fingers over	*passer les doigts sur*	pass
run a program	*exécuter un logiciel*	execute
I ran into Nicolas	*Je suis tombé sur Nicolas*	fall

It's always pleasant to look up a word in your lexicon and find you already have it. But sometimes, when you're using an extended or metaphorical sense, you should use a different or new lexeme anyway.

NATURE

cave(rn) Lt *cava* 'hollow (places)'
• Qu *chinkana* 'place to be lost' • Ch *dòng* 'hole, pierce'

cloud OE *clúd* 'rock, hill' > 'mass of stuff'
• Lt *nebula* 'mist, cloud' • OCS *oblakŭ* 'covering' • Danish *mulm* 'darkness' • Ch *yún* poss. < 'swirl'

country Old Fr *contrée* 'what's opposite = view, landscape'
Land: • Fr *pays* < 'rural district' • OCS *strana* 'side' < 'spread' • Skt *visaya-* 'sphere of activity' • Ch *guó* < 'boundary'
Countryside: Lt *rūs rūr-* 'space' • Fr *campagne* < 'fields' • Cz *venkov* < 'outside' • Rus деревня 'village' • Ch *nóngcūn* 'agriculture-village'

desert Fr *déserter* < Lt frequentative of 'abandon, forsake'
• Ger *Wüste* 'wastes' • Ch *shāmò* 'sand-pasturage'

farm Lt *firmus* 'fixed' > fee, rent > agricultural land
• Ger *Bauernhof* < 'build, cultivate' + 'yard' • Ch *nóngchǎng* 'agriculture-field'

field OE *feld* < IE 'flat, spread out', cognate to *plānum*, поле
• Lt *campus* < 'curved', *ager* < 'pasture' • Sw *mark* 'boundary' • Lith *laukas* 'open' • OCS *niva* 'lowland' • Avestan *karšū-* 'plowed'

fog ME 'grassy, mossy' > 'fleshy' > 'murky' > 'misty'
• Fr *brouillard* < *breu* 'broth' • Ch *wù* ‖ 'dark'

forest Lt *foris* 'outside' (as opposed to fenced in)
• Gk δάσος 'thick' • Rum *pădure* 'swamp' • Ir *coill* collective of 'wood' • OE *wald* 'wilderness' • Skt *araṇya-* 'distant' • Lith *girė* cognate to OCS *gora* 'mountain' • Ch *lín* 'crowd'

freeze OE *fréosan*
• Lt *gelāre* < 'ice'

garden Norman *gardin* < Germanic 'yard'
• Lt *hortus* 'enclosure' • Danish *have* < 'hedge' • Rus сад < plant' • Avestan *pairidaēza-* 'wall about', source of *paradise* • Ch *yuán* prob. < 'encircling (wall)'

ground OE *grund* 'bottom, base, earth'
• Gk πέδον < 'foot' • Lt *solum* 'base, sole' • Ch *dìmiàn* 'earth-face'

hail OE *haʒol*

hill OE *hyll* < IE 'raise, high', cognate to Lt *collis*
• Sp *cerro* 'nape' • Welsh *bryn* 'swelling' • Cz *pahorek* 'dim. mountain' • Gothic *hlains* < 'bend' • Dutch *heuvel* 'hump'

ice OE *ís*
• Gk κρύσταλλος < 'frost, crust' • Lt *glacies* < 'icy cold'

LAND OE *land* ‖ Welsh *llan* 'enclosure'

mountain   Rom 'mountain region' < Lt *mons mont-* < IE 'project' as in *prom<u>in</u>ent*

    • Gk ὄρος < 'high, raised' • Norse *fjall* 'rock' • Bulg *planina* < '(high) plateau' • Skt *parvata-* 'rugged, knotty'

nature   Lt *nātūra* 'birth, character'

    • Ch *zìrán* 'by itself'

peasant   Fr *paysan* 'countryman'

plain   Lt *plānum* 'flat'

    • OE *emnet* < 'level, even' • Ir *má* 'expanse' < 'big'

rain   OE *reʒn* <IE 'wet'

    • Lt *pluvia* <'flow, swim' • Skt *varṣa-* <'water'

sky   Norse 'cloud'

    • Ch *tiān* prob. < 'top'

snow   OE *snáw*, cognate to Lt *nix niv-*

    • Gk χιών < 'winter' • Rum *zăpadă* 'fallen'

storm   OE *storm*

    • Fr *orage* < 'breeze' • Sp *tempestad* < 'weather' • Ch *fēngbào* 'wind-violent'

valley   Lt *vallis*

    • OE *dæl* < 'bent, curved' • Gk κοιλάς 'hollow' • Ir *gleann* 'river bank' • Skt *upatyakā-* 'beneath (the mountain)'

wild   OE *wilde*

    • Ch *yě* < 'grassland'

wind   OE *wind*, cognate to Lt *ventus*, Gk ἀήρ 'wind'

    Gk ἄνεμος 'breath' • Ch *fēng* also 'air'

WORLD   OE *weorold* < Germanic 'man age' > 'lifetime, era'

    • Ir *domhan* 'foundation' • OE *middan-geard* 'mid-yard' • Lith *pasaulis* 'under-sun' • OCS *svĕtŭ* 'light' • Skt *bhū-* 'existence' • Ch *shì* 'generation'

yard   OE *ʒeard* < Germanic 'enclosure'

    • Gk αὐλή < 'sleep place' • Lt *cohors cohort-* 'enclose together' • OCS *dvorŭ* 'door (to public place)' • Skt *aṅgana-* 'walking' • Ch *yuàn* < '(en)circle'

+   *plateau, canyon, cliff, volcano, meadow, glade*

    jungle, savanna, swamp, glacier

    plow, sow, harvest, crop

    mist, drought, lightning, thunder, rainbow, sleet

‣   For water features, see *Water*, p. 389.

See p. 65 on how we came to have a word for Everything (*nature*), and how it's normally used in a demoted sense, generally meaning the non-human geography or just the biology of our own planet.

We used to live in 'nature', so you might expect terms for geographical features to be basic, but often they're not. An obvious way to derive terms is by shape (*cavern* = hollow, *plateau* = flat). To an agricultural society the notable thing about the wild is that it's uncultivated— *desert, jungle, forest* all had this basic meaning, and later specialized to particular ecological zones.

Americans, I think, have an image of *farms* as wrested from the primordial waste by individual settlers, but the etymology is a reminder that rural life has always been bureaucratized, and most often dominated by large landowners, the actual workers being not much more than serfs. The semantic progression from *villa* to *villain,* or of *churl* from 'man' to 'serf' to 'boor', is also instructive on the social status of those who actually worked the land.

Do we really need the separate terms *land, country, nation*? Mandarin calls them all *guójiā*. However, it has separate terms for 'land' as real estate (*tǔdì*) and 'country' as rural areas (*xiāngcūn*).

NUMBERS

ONE	OE *án* < IE **ʔey-* 'this one'
TWO	OE *twá* poss. < IE **dew-* 'further'
THREE	OE *þrí* poss. < IE **ter-* 'even further'
four	OE *féower* poss. < IE **mey-* 'lessen'
five	OE *fíf* ‖ Hittite *pankus* 'whole'
	• Inuit *tatleman* < 'right hand' • Ojibwe *nanan* '(one hand) gone' • Bacairi *ahage ahage tokale* 'two two one' • Choctaw *talhhaapih* 'the first hand finished'
six	OE *sex*
seven	OE *seofon*
eight	OE *ahta* poss. IE dual of 'four', cf. Avestan *ašti-* '4 fingers'
nine	OE *niʒon* poss. ‖ IE 'new'
ten	OE *tíen*
	• Shasta *tsec* 'man' • Unalit *kolin* 'upper body' • Wintun *pampa-sempta* 'two hands' • Piro *pamole* 'tribesman' • Zuñi *astemthla* 'all the fingers' • Gabrieleño *wehes-mahar* 'two-five'
twelve	OE *twelf* 'two left'
twenty	OE *twentiʒ* 'two tens'
	• ME *score* 'notch' • Takelma *yapamis* 'one man' • SW Pomo *tca-hma* 'four-five' • Jibaro *mai náwi amúkahei* 'I have finished both feet' • Yucatec *kal* prob. < 'tie'
hundred	OE *hundred* < Germanic 'hundred-count'
thousand	OE *þúsend* IE 'multitude'
	• Fox *negutimakakw* 'one box'
million	It *milione* augm. of 'thousand'
	• Ch *băiwàn* 'hundred-myriad' • Kwakiutl *tlinhi* 'uncountable'
both	OE *báðar*
couple	Lt *cōpula* 'band, connection'
double	Lt *duplus* 'two-full'
dozen	Fr *douzaine* < 'twelve'
pair	Lt *pār* 'equal'
quarter	Lt *quartārius* 'fourth part'
FIRST	OE *fyrst* 'foremost' ‖ Lt *prīmus*, Gk πρῶτος
	• Ger *erst* 'earliest' • Ch *dìyī* 'order-one'
second	Lt *secundus* 'following' > '2nd' > '2nd division by 60'
single	Lt *singulus* 'one, individual, separate' ‖ 'simple'
third	OE *þridda*
twice	OE *twiʒes* combining form of 'two' + genitive ending

twin   OE < combining form of 'two'

Before agriculture and trade, people can readily get by without roots past *two*. Even such simple systems can be extended by concatenation: 3 = 'two-one', 4 = 'two-two', etc. I've researched number systems extensively, but found only two languages which are claimed to have no numbers at all: Pirahã and Yumbri. When people feel a need to count higher, they may simply borrow the words from the nearest major power— e.g. many Peruvian languages borrowed numbers from Quechua.

Though the early Indo-Europeanists cheerfully reconstructed IE numbers up to 100, each family has its own pattern, and the proto-language probably only counted to 10. The etymologies for 1-9 above follow the suggestions of Winfred Lehmann in *Theoretical Bases of Indo-European Linguistics*. The reconstructed 'hundred', *$k\d{m}tóm$, from 'ten-ten', was used for 120 in Germanic, and may have simply been used for a very large number.

Similarly, ancient Hebrew ʔelep 'thousand' was often used simply for a large number— which makes better sense of Samson's claim to have killed an ʔelep of men with the jawbone of a donkey (Judges 15:16).

Languages often name **numbers** with reference to finger-counting; see the derivations given for 5, 10, 20.

The Wede:i of Almea use base 6, with a fist for 1, one finger for 2, two fingers for 3, all fingers extended for 6, leading to the written numbers ۰ — = Ⅲ Ⅲ Ⅰ . The other hand is used to count the sixes, allowing the Wede:i to count to 36 with the two hands.

Almeans have just four toes, which leads some of its cultures to use base 18. You don't need different anatomy to consider alternate bases; earthly languages often use base 5, 10, or 20, but bases 2, 4, 6, and 12 are attested. Even in English we have words for base 12: *dozen, gross.*

In the Indo-Pacific language Kewa, you start counting on the hand, but continue along the arm and up the body till you reach *rikaa* 'between the eyes' = 24.

Chinese and Greek have a word for '10,000'— *wàn*, μῡριάς. Hindi, and thus Indian English, have words for 100,000 (*lakh*) and 10 million (*crore*).

Sometimes number words are borrowed only for a particular domain— e.g. Quechua uses the Spanish numbers only for the hours of the day; compare also *ace, deuce, trey* which apply only to cards.

Mathematics

add	Lt *addere* < 'give to'
	• Fr *ajouter* < 'put next to' • Ger *hinzuzählen* 'count away to' • Ch *jiā* < 'attach'
subtract	Lt *subtractus* 'drawn under'
multiply	Lt *multiplicāre* 'fold many times'
divide	Lt *dīvidere* frequentative of 'divide, separate'
	• Ger *teilen* 'share' • Ch *fēn* 'part, divide'
equal	Lt *æquālis* 'even, equal'
odd	abbr of Norse *odda-maðr* 'angle-man' = 'third man'
even	OE *efen* 'flat, equal'
number	Lt *numerus* poss. < 'share'
	• Gk ἀριθμός < 'reckon, order' • Ger *Zahl* < 'count, relate' • Skt *samkhyā-* 'add up' • Ch *shù* < 'what is counted'
REAL	Lt *reālis* 'of things'
complex	Lt *complexus* 'folded together'
	• Ger *vielschichtig* 'many-layered'
whole	OE *hál* 'sound, healthy, complete'
	• Gk πᾶς 'every' • Lt *tōtus* prob. < 'packed full', *integer* 'untouched' • Skt *sakala-* '(has) all parts'
fraction	Lt *fractio* 'breaking'
+	*negative, exponent, infinity, logarithm, sine, cosine, integrate, differentiate*

Mathematics is technology, and so all the mathematical words are derived, not basic roots. This is another area where we retain some Arabic roots, such as *algebra, algorithm*. The Arabs also passed along *zero* from the Hindus; *ṣifr* means 'empty.' *Cipher* was also used for the Arabic numerals as a set, leading to the sense of 'symbolic character' and thus 'substitution code'.

If you work out your own mathematical notation, you might (especially if your language is SOV) consider postfix notation. If you avoid ternary operators, this lets you get rid of parentheses and rules for operation order: e.g. (5 + 3) × (8 - 2) becomes 5 3 + 8 2 - ×.

What's your favorite denominator? Dividing things in 10 matches the decimal system, but we often pick a simpler number (1/2, 1/3) or a more divisible one (8 for ounces, 12 for inches, 60 for minutes/seconds).

PHYSICAL ACTIONS

attract
Lt *attractus* 'drawn to'
• Ch *xīyǐn* 'inhale-guide'

balance
Lt *bilanx* 'two-scaled (balance)'

beat
OE *béatan*, uncertain

bind
OE *bindan* ‖ bound, band, bend
• Lt *vincīre* < 'fold' • Sp *atar* < 'make fit' • Ch *kǔn* < 'beat'

bore
OE *borian* 'pierce' (but 'be tedious' is ModE, uncertain)
• Gk τετραίνω < 'turn, rub' • Lt *forāre* < 'strike' • Fr *percer* < 'beat through' • Ir *toll* 'hole' • Rus буравить < 'auger (the tool)' • Ch *zuān* ‖ 'sharp, thorn, pierce'

break
OE *brecan*, cognate to Lt *frangere*
• ModGk οπάζω < 'pull, tear' • Fr *casser* < 'shake' • Sp *quebrar* < 'rattle, crack' • Welsh *torri* 'cut, break'

cut
ME *cutte*, possibly Norse
• Fr *couper* < 'hit' • Sp *corta* 'shorten' • Welsh *torri* 'cut, break' • Ch *qiè* < 'joint'

divide
Lt *dīvidere* frequentative of 'divide, separate'
• Ch *fēn* 'part, divide'

hurt
Fr *heurter* 'knock, strike'
• Qu *nanachiy* 'cause pain' • Ch *shāng* poss. ‖ 'sick'

join
Fr *joindre* < IE 'join', cognate to *yoke*
• Gk συνάπτω 'fasten with' • Ir *ceangail* 'bind' • Ger *fügen* 'fasten' • OCS *sŭčetati* < 'crowd' • Ch *hé* also 'shut'

knock
OE *cnocian* imitative

link
Norse *hlenkr*
• Fr *maillon* < 'mail (armor)' • Ch *huánjié* 'bracelet-knot'

mar
OE *merran* 'spoil, hinder'

mix
Lt *mixtus* 'mixed'
• ModGk ἀνακατεύω 'upside-down' • Sw *blanda* < 'make turbid' • Ch *hùn* < 'chaos'

snap
Dutch *snappen*

stir
OE *styrian*
• Fr *remuer* < 'change' • Sp *revolver* 'revolve' • Ch *jiǎo* 'disturb'

tear
OE *teran* < IE **der-*
• Gk σπαράσσω prob. imitative • It *stracciare* 'pull apart' • Fr *déchirer* < 'scrape off' • Dutch *scheuren* < 'notch, cut' • OCS *rŭvati* 'tear off, pluck' • Ch *sī* < 'cleave'

whip
ME uncertain

wound | OE *wund* poss. < 'pierce'
• Gk τραῦμα < 'rub' • Fr *blessure* < 'livid' • Sp *herida* 'struck' • Ir *créacht* < 'scab' • Sw *sår* < 'pain, injury' • OCS *rana* <'tear' • Ch *shāng* < 'suffer, hurt'

+ *tie, connect, knot, web*

chop, rip, peel, stab, sting, dig, spoil, damage

▸ See also *Bodily actions,* p. 144, and *Movement,* p. 276.

If you were simulating the world in a new graphics engine, you'd spend your first months working out 3-D modeling and camera positioning, and then work on texturing, lighting, and fancy substances like smoke and water. The verbs in this category would offer a particular challenge, as they either divide one object into pieces, or combine multiple objects into one, both of which complicate your data structures. (Even the verbs of damaging add new things to the model, such as a scar or dent.)

With such transformations, a word can take the point of view either of the single component:

> *The log broke in two.*

> *This sandwich is made out of bread, Serrano ham, cheddar, and arugula.*

or the multiple components:

> *These sticks all broke off that tree.*

> *Take the flour and add milk, eggs, and salt.*

Words for connection are naturally extended to human relationships as well as more ethereal links, such as those mediated by electricity or gravity. Words for damage are even more broadly useful— consider how *cut* can refer to budgets, acerbic wit, film editing, interruption, disinheritance, or tailoring.

What could be simpler than *break*? Yet, as Takao Suzuki points out, *break* translates to a number of Japanese words: *kowasu, waru, oru, kiru, yaburu, sakeru, kowareru, kudaku...* it's a nest of confusion for speakers of either language trying to learn the other.

- *Oru* divides an object in two by application of a force— twigs and bones *oru*. But the two parts need not come apart: wires and knees *oru* too, but in English we need to use *bend*.

- If a force separates things into pieces, you can use *kiru*— e.g. a power line may *kiru* due to high winds. But you can *kiru* with a knife, too; in that case English uses *cut*. If you catch your coat on a nail and it rips, that's *kiru* too, but we have to say *rip* or *tear*.

- *Oru* is normally fracturing or breaking off, but when you *oru* paper you simply *fold* it (it's the root of *origami*).

- In the sense of 'destroy, make worthless', you'd use *kowasu*.

In French there is substantial overlap between *rompre, casser,* and *briser.* You can use any of the three for bones, thread, or a marriage. But as Myriam Bouveret and Eve Sweetser show, there are specializations:

- *Rompre* is often used for long thin objects, especially when the breakage destroys the original object or disconnects something. Thus you can *rompre* a stick or a baguette, but almost never a teacup. Metaphorically, a dialog can be *rompu* but not *cassé* or *brisé.*

- *Casser* is often used for machines that stop working: computers, televisions, bicycles, and files can get *cassés.*

- *Briser* is preferred when the object shatters into many pieces— mirrors, teacups.

Even the overlaps turn out to involve different frames. To *rompre un mariage* refers to ending the legal and especially the religious bond. To *casser un mariage* is used of civil divorce— it's more neutral, meaning that the marriage is simply dissolved. And *briser un mariage* is generally used when a third party interferes with the couple.

The difference between *hurt* and *damage* is largely based on the objects— animates vs. things. Spanish uses *dañar* for both— cognate to *damn*, which has specialized to spiritual damage.

PHYSICS

cold	OE *cald* ‖ *cool*, Lt *gelidus* 'icy'
	• Gk ψῦχρός < 'blow, breathe' • Breton *yen* < 'ice' • Pol *zimny* 'wintry' • Cz *studený* poss. < 'congeal'
cool	OE *cól*
	• Ch *liáng* < 'cold'
energy	Gk ἐνέργεια 'in-work'
	• Ch *néng* < 'capable'
gravity	Lt *gravitas* 'heaviness'
	• Ch *yǐnlì* 'drawing power'
heavy	OE *hefiʒ* 'weighty' < 'lift', cf. *heave*
	• Lt *gravis* < IE • Sp *pesado* 'weighed' • Latvian *smags* < 'laborious' • OCS *tęzĭkŭ* < 'pull' • Ch *zhòng* ‖ 'double'
hot	OE *hát*
	• Lt *calidus* prob. cognate to *cold* • Welsh *brwd* < 'boil' • Skt *usna-* 'burn'
LIGHT	**Radiation**: OE *léoht*, cognate to Lt *lux lūc-*, Gk λευκός 'white'
	• Gk φῶσ ‖ Skt 'shine' • Ch *guāng* 'bright'
	Not heavy: OE *léoht*, cognate to Lt *levis*, OCS *lĭgŭkŭ*
	• Ir *éadrom* 'not heavy' • Latvian *viegls* 'lively' • Ket *béjìŋ* < 'wind'
mass	Lt *massa* 'lump, mass' poss. < Gk μᾶζα 'barley cake'
material	Lt *māteriālis* 'of matter'
	• Ch *liào* < 'measure'
matter	Lt *māteria*
	Ch *wùzhì* 'substance-nature'
physical	Gk φυσική 'of nature'
warm	OE *wearm*, cognate to Gk θερμός 'hot'
weigh	OE *weʒan* 'bear, lift' > 'balance in a scale' > 'be heavy'
+	*atom, molecule, proton, neutron, electron, photon*

▸ See *Light,* p. 246, and *Elements,* p. 183.

The division of *matter* and *energy* comes late; previously people thought in terms of the *elements*, or of matter vs. *soul* (p. 314).

To Aristotle, ὕλη **'matter'** was merely raw material, simply what gives a thing existence; what makes it a thing is μορφή 'form' or 'organizing principle'. To us, a lump of bronze turned into a statue has simply been restructured, but to Aristotle its μορφή has changed, from 'lump' to 'statue'. With living things, the μορφή of the body is the soul.

Newton talked about *massa* (he was writing in Latin) as the quantity of matter. For the purposes of working out the laws of motion and gravity, that was all that was needed, and the important property of matter was inertia, its ability to resist changes in velocity. The more modern formulation is that inertia *is* mass.

The idea that all the elements were 'really one thing', rather than a hundred separate things, was hinted at by Mendeleev's periodic table, but wasn't solidified till the atomic nucleus was understood.

As for **energy**, physics began by investigating velocity, which has always been a bit disreputable philosophically— at a particular moment *something* distinguishes an arrow in motion from an arrow at rest, but it wasn't easy to see what— the matter making up the arrow is obviously the same.

The 19C was a process of enumerating new types of energy, then reducing them to one thing. William Rankine invented the term *potential energy* and explained its relation to kinetic energy. Kelvin explained *heat* in terms of the motion of molecules. Maxwell unified the previously disparate concepts of light, magnetism, and electricity.

Finally Einstein showed that mass and energy were convertible into each other. Energy isn't a thing, it's an attribute of things. A better fundamental division would be between particles with mass (like electrons and quarks) and those without (like photons and neutrinos).

The main point here is that your conlanging here depends on your people's theories of the universe— and using our opposition of *matter* and *energy* for a medieval or sf society is anachronistic.

Electromagnetism

If you have an sf world, or perhaps magic that interfaces at a deep level with reality, you might want to know what science thinks the universe is like. (Or you might not. Much sf and comics are still written as if it were 1904, when scientists could still discover six new forces or substances before tiffin.)

A huge swath of phenomena— light and optics, magnets, chemistry, the elements, heat— in fact, everything but gravity and radioactivity— is explained by **quantum electrodynamics**, memorably explained by Richard Feynman in *QED: The Strange Theory of Light and Matter*.

Almost everything can be explained with just three actors:

- The photon, the smallest packet light comes in

- The electron, a particle of -1 charge

- The proton, a particle of +1 charge

A number of protons, from one to a hundred-odd, clump together in the nucleus. The number determines what element you've got. Normally they attract the same number of electrons.[9] This 'attraction' is a matter of exchanging photons.

Electric derives from Gk ἤλεκτρον 'amber', a great generator of static electricity. The Chinese, very sensibly, re-used the word for 'lightning', 电 *diàn*. An *ion* is from ἰόν 'going', because these were the units that *went* towards an electrode. An *electron* was an 'electric ion'— Chinese uses 电子 *diànzǐ* 'little lightning'. The *-on* was generalized to other particles: *photon* < 'light', *proton* < 'first'.

An early metaphor for electricity was a fluid, thus terms such as *flux, flow, current.*

Energy states

You might think that the protons somehow produce the properties of an element, but from the point of view of chemistry, the nucleus is mostly just an inert sack that electrons gather round.[10] The properties of the elements are the results of their electron structure.

Physicists originally pictured atoms as little solar systems with electrons orbiting the nucleus. Designers still love to draw atoms like this to invoke the Space Age— usually lithium because three orbits make a pretty picture. But it's entirely wrong.

Electrons have *energy levels*, which have whole numbers starting with 1. To jump up one level takes energy— the electron absorbs a photon. To move down a level it loses energy— it emits a photon.

With more energy the electron can move farther from the nucleus, but thanks to Werner Heisenberg we *can't say exactly where*. We can calculate a density plot of the **probability** of finding an electron at each location in space, though. This plot looks different for each energy level.

---

[9] There are exceptions— e.g. metals, where the outermost electrons aren't tied to an atom, but smear out over the substance. Ions (atoms with extra or missing electrons) also persist happily dissolved in water.

[10] The *mass* of the neutrons can be important chemically, however.

Here are simplified representations of the probability density for the four types of orbitals:

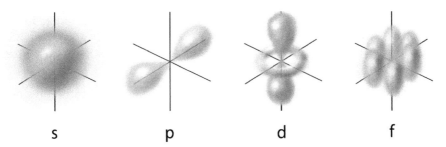

| s | p | d | f |

Think of these pictures as telling you "Welp, we've cornered the varmint; the electron is somewhere in there." Though it's worse than that, really— the probability density drops off sharply outside this shape, but it never drops to zero!

Roughly speaking,

- s orbitals are shaped like spheres.
- p orbitals are shaped roughly like a dumbbell, with lobes pointed in the x, y, or z direction.
- d orbitals mostly have four lobes, and can be oriented five possible ways.
- f orbitals mostly have six lobes, oriented seven possible ways.

The names derive from spectral lines: *sharp, principal, diffuse, fundamental*. At high enough energies you get g and h orbitals.

The pictures get more complicated at higher energies— e.g. the higher s orbitals contain multiple spherical shells.

Filling in shells

Picture a staircase with some burly men on it. Only two men can fit on one stair. More men keep coming in from the top; they can only move to the topmost unoccupied stair.

The energy levels work like this as electrons are added. The energy levels are filled from the bottom, and if a level already has its two electrons, no more will fit— the next electron takes the next level. (The two electrons in each shell differ in *spin*, which can only take two values, conventionally -1/2 and +1/2.)

Electrons fill the orbitals in a particular order:

1s 2s 2p 3s 3p 4s 3d 4p 5s 4d 5p 6s 4f 5d 6p 7s 5f 6d 7p

That gives us the information to list the elements by their outermost shells:

1s H																	1s He
2s Li	2s Be											2p B	2p C	2p N	2p O	2p F	2p Ne
3s Na	3s Mg											3p Al	3p Si	3p P	3p S	3p Cl	3p Ar
4s K	4s Ca	3d Sc	3d Ti	3d V	3d Cr	3d Mn	3d Fe	3d Co	3d Ni	3d Cu	3d Zn	4p Ga	4p Ge	4p As	4p Se	4p Br	4p Kr
5s Rb	5s Sr	4d Y	4d Zr	4d Nb	4d Mo	4d Tc	4d Ru	4d Rh	4d Pd	4d Ag	4d Cd	5p In	5p Sn	5p Sb	5p Te	5p I	5p Xe
6s Cs	6s Ba	**4f**	5d Hf	5d Ta	5d W	5d Re	5d Os	5d Ir	5d Pt	5d Au	5d Hg	6p Tl	6p Pb	6p Bi	6p Po	6p At	6p Rn
7s Fr	7s Ra	**5f**	6d Rf	6d Db	6d Sg	6d Bh	6d Hs	6d Mt	6d Ds	6d Rg	6d Cn	7p Fl		7p Lv			

The two cells with **f** orbitals (lower left, boldfaced) are actually a sequence of 14 elements each, the *lanthanides* (57 to 71) and the *actinides* (89 to 103).

The chemical behavior of an atom is predominantly due to its *valence number*— the number of electrons in its outer *s* and *p* shells. The basic principle is, shells just wanna be filled. If two atoms can share electrons so as to fill their s-p shells, they do so, forming a *molecule.*

- The rightmost column has a full s shell and (past helium) a full p shell. They're happy as is and almost never react with other elements— these are the noble gases.

- Elements with valence 1 (leftmost column) have a single electron in the outermost s shell.

- Elements with valence 7 (just left of the noble gases) need just one electron to fill the p shell.

- Do you see a match there? The atoms sure do. A valence-1 atom like sodium (Na) happily donates its extra electron to chlorine (Cl). Now you've got Na-, a negative ion, and Cl+, a positive ion. Each is happy with its shell configuration, but as one is negative and one is positive they attract each other, forming NaCl, which is ordinary table salt.

- An atom can bond with more than one partner. Oxygen has valence 6— it wants two electrons to fill its p shell. Hydrogen can just offer one... but we have *lots* of hydrogen. *Two* hydrogen atoms can thus fill oxygen's need for two electrons, forming H_2O.

- Elements of valence 4 have the most opportunities for bonding with other atoms— they can bond with one to four atoms, making them nature's building blocks. The most reactive element in this column is the first one, carbon (C), which forms ten million different compounds, far more than any other element.

Things get more complicated with the d and f orbitals— see the web resources page for more.

The particle zoo

The nucleus is more than just a store of protons, of course. For one thing, it also contains a bunch of neutrons, which are electrically neutral and thus irrelevant to electron structure, though they do add mass to the nucleus.

When you throw particles at each other, you get more exotic particles... by now there are hundreds of known particles. However, most of these turn out to be made of smaller subcomponents, *quarks*. This allows a simple listing of the building blocks of the universe.

Fermions have half-integer spin (odd multiple of ½), and all have antiparticles. They come in three tiers of increasing mass, though ordinary matter is composed only of the first tier:

electron	e-neutrino	up quark	down quark
muon	μ-neutrino	charm quark	strange quark
tau	τ-neutrino	top quark	bottom quark
-1	0	2/3	-1/3

The last row gives the electric charge. Quarks also have a different type of charge related to the strong force, called *color*, though this has nothing to do with visible color.

The four forces are mediated by **bosons**, which have integer spin:

Photon	Electromagnetism
W , Z	Weak
Gluon	Strong

The recently discovered Higgs boson, which generates mass, is a boson of spin 0.

The strong force

Now we can build the nucleons, with the correct electric charge:

up	+	up	+	down	=	proton
+2/3		+2/3		-1/3		+1
up	+	down	+	down	=	neutron
+2/3		-1/3		-1/3		0

The three quarks in a proton or neutron are held together by the strong force, so named because it's the strongest of the four fundamental forces, 100 times stronger than electromagnetism (but it also drops off very fast with distance).

Just as charge involves electrons and the nucleus flinging photons at each other, the strong force is mediated by *gluons*.

The strong force is very powerful at the quark level, binding the quarks very closely together— if you try to pull them apart, the energy applied actually goes into an explosion of new particles.

The strong force also holds the nucleus together, though less closely. The nucleons don't exchange gluons but pions, combinations of a down quark and a down antiquark.

The weak force

The weak force allows changes between quark flavor— e.g changing a down to an up quark. A free neutron (one outside any atomic nucleus) will experience this, becoming a proton (and emitting a W boson, which itself quickly decays) with a half-life of about fifteen minutes.

This can happen in the nucleus, though it takes great energy. This can be generated by whacking it with a proton, but quantum fluctuations can also generate the energy spontaneously. This is called *beta decay* and is one form of radioactivity.

In the sun, free protons (i.e. hydrogen atoms) are constantly knocking into each other. Normally they form a diproton which immediately breaks back into two protons. But sometimes we see this process:

- One proton changes via the weak force into a neutron, producing deuterium (and a photon).

- Deuterium combines with another proton to form ^{3}He.

- Two ^{3}He atoms collide, producing a stable ^{4}He atom and two free protons.

This is hydrogen fusion, which is what makes the sun shine, and slowly convert its hydrogen into helium. For more listen to the *They Might Be Giants* song "The Sun".

PLANTS

bush	Norse *buskr*
	• Fr *buisson* dim. 'wood' • Ch *guànmù* 'irrigation-tree'
flower	Lt *flōs flōr-* ‖ *bloom*
	• Gk ἄνθος, uncertain • OCS *cvĕtŭ* < 'bloom, shine' • Skt *puṣpa-* 'thrive'
fruit	Lt *fructus* '(what is) enjoyed'
grass	OE *græs* ‖ 'green', 'grow'
	• Gk πόα < 'fat' • Lt *grāmen -min-* prob. < 'fodder' • Lith *žolė* 'green' • Skt *tṛṇa-* < 'stalk'
plant	Lt *planta* 'sprout'
	• Gk φυτόν < 'grow' • OE *wyrt* < 'root, plant' • OCS *sadŭ* < 'set'
rose	Lt *rosa*, prob. ‖ Gk ῥόδον, Armenian *vard*
	• ModGk τριαντάφυλλο 'thirty-petals'
stick	OE *sticca* < Germanic 'pierce' (which also led to the verb)
	• Fr *bâton* poss. < 'carry' • Ch *bàng* < 'club'
tree	OE *tréow*
	• Lt *arbor* poss. < 'high' • Welsh *coeden* singular of 'woods' • Ch *shù* < 'to plant' • Ket *óks* nomn. of 'stick out'
+	*weed, stalk, stem, leaf, petal, seed, twig, thorn, stump, trunk, root, branch, log*

In Swedish a leaf is a *blad* on the tree and a *löv* once it's fallen off.

Plant parts provide terminology for similarly-shaped objects— *leaf* for paper and knives, *trunk* for columns. Any sort of process can use the metaphor of plant growth: *the seeds of conflict; establish a branch plant; the fruits of our labor*. *Root* is probably used metaphorically far more than literally— as in linguistics, where it refers to a morphological base form.

It's a little lazy that the staples of most fantasy worlds are potatoes, carrots, and wheat. It's not hard to at least suggest local variation— e.g. in Arcél, on Almea, the food crops are *stripcorn, streff, hardroot,* and *teng bean*, and the textile crops are *truca* and *petay*. These are the mix of borrowings and calques that a terrestrial observer might come up with.

The botanical view

▸ For more on taxonomy, see *Animals*, p. 114.

Plants are characterized by cell walls with cellulose and the production of energy from sunlight using chlorophyll.

The overall classification looks something like this:

1 Glaucophyta— a small group of blue-green algae

2.1 Rodophyta— red algae

2.2 Viridiplantae— green plants

The overall divisions of the green plants are:

Chlorophyta	'green plants'	some green algae
Charophyta	'stonewort plants'	stonewort
Marchantiophyta	after a genus	liverwort
Anthocerotophyta	'flower horn plants'	hornwort
Bryophyta	'moss plants'	moss
Lycopodiophyta	'wolf foot plants'	club moss
Pteridophyta	'fern plants'	fern, horsetail
Cycadophyta	'palm plants'	cycad
Ginkgophyta	'ginkgo plants'	ginkgo— one species
Pinophyta	'pine plants'	conifers— pine, cedar, cypress, fir, juniper, larch, redwood, spruce, yew
Gnetophyta	after a genus	small, diverse set of woody plants
Angiospermae	'receptacle seeds'	flowering plants— the vast majority of plant species

Reading this list, your first question will undoubtedly be "What's a *wort?*" It's the OE word for 'plant', cognate to the Norse word that gave us *root*, and is often used for medicinal herbs.

The flowering plants were traditionally divided into *monocots* and *dicots*, based on whether there are one or two embryonic leaves; the flowers of monocots also typically have three petals, dicots four or five. However, it turns out that dicots don't form a neat class. Most of them are now grouped as the *eudicots*; the biggest defectors are the Magnoliidae (named for the magnolia).

There are over 400 families of plants; here are the family assignments for a number of well known plants. (The etymologies are boring— most derive from the commonest examples, e.g. *fabaceae* = 'beans'.)

Eudicots

Ranunculaceae   delphinium, clematis, buttercup

—Caryophyllales—

Caryophyllaceae	carnation, pink (source of the color name), baby's breath, chickweed
Cactaceae	cactus, peyote

—Asterids—

Balsaminaceae	impatiens, balsam
Ericaceae	cranberry, blueberry, azalea, rhododendron, heather
Theaceae	tea, camellia
Ebenaceae	ebony, persimmon
Boraginaceae	comfrey, forget-me-not, borage, heliotrope
Solanaceae	nightshade, potato, tomato, eggplant, tobacco, chili pepper, henbane, boxthorn, mandrake, petunia
Convolvulaceae	morning glory, sweet potato
Rubiaceae	coffee, quinine, madder, gardenia
Oleaceae	olive, ash, lilac, jasmine, forsythia, privet
Lamiaceae	mint, basil, rosemary, sage, savory, marjoram, oregano, thyme, lavender, teak, catnip
Apiaceae	carrot, celery, cilantro, cumin, dill, fennel, poison hemlock, parsley, parsnip, silphium, Queen Anne's lace, anise
Araliaceae	ivy, ginseng
Asteraceae	aster, marigold, daisy, dahlia, zinnia, dandelion, lettuce, sunflower, artichoke, chrysanthemum, ragweed

—Rosids—

Euphorbiaceae	cassava, rubber tree, spurge, poinsettia
Violaceae	violet, pansy
Linaceae	flax
Fabaceae	bean, pea, chickpea, peanut, alfalfa, clover, carob, mesquite, tamarind, licorice, gorse, kudzu, lupin
Fagaceae	oak, chestnut, beech, chestnut
Betulaceae	birch, alder, hazel, hornbeam
Juglandaceae	walnut, pecan, hickory
Rosaceae	apple, plum, cherry, peach, apricot, almond, raspberry, strawberry, rose, rowan, hawthorn
Cannabaceae	hemp, hops
Ulmaceae	elm
Rutaceae	orange, lemon, lime, grapefruit, kumquat, rue

Cucurbitaceae	cucumber, pumpkin, watermelon, squash
Sapindaceae	maple, horse chestnut, lychee, guarana, soapberry
Brassicaceae	cabbage, broccoli, cauliflower, turnip, rapeseed, radish, horseradish, mustard, watercress, woad
Malvaceae	okra, cotton, cacao, kola, durian, mallow, baobab

Monocots

Amaryllidaceae	onion, garlic, chive, leek, amaryllis
Arecaceae	palm, rattan, coconut, açaí, raffia
Poaceae	grass, wheat, barley, oats, rye, maize, sorghum, millet, bamboo, rice, reed, sugarcane
Iridaceae	iris
Liliaceae	lily, tulip
Musaceae	banana, plantain
Orchidaceae	orchid, vanilla
Asparagaceae	asparagus, hyacinth, bluebell

Magnoliids

Lauraceae	laurel (bay), cinnamon, camphor, avocado
Magnoliaceae	magnolia
Myristicaceae	nutmeg (and mace)
Myrtaceae	myrtle, clove, guava, allspice, eucalyptus, mangrove
Piperaceae	black pepper, betel
Vitaceae	grapevine (source of wine)

The functional view

Botanical classification is sometimes illuminating— e.g. it's interesting that so many garden herbs belong to the Lamiaceae family— but for most purposes we use an informal classification based on what the plant is good for. Or bad for.

Food

grain	grassy plants where we eat the small seeds
fruit	plants with large fruit (that we eat)
bean	plants where the seed comes in a pod
nut	plants with a hard edible shelled seed
herb	small plant used for flavor or medicine
vegetable	basically, any other plant we eat

Wood

hardwood	wood from angiosperms— often but not always harder than evergreen wood; contains microscopic pores
softwood	wood from conifers; lacks those pores

Harmful

weed	plants that invade fields. To some extent this is an ecological niche: some plants are adapted to colonizing bare earth, e.g. after a fire
poison	weaponized plants— what harms their own predators, such as insects, often harms us big things as well

And...

textile crops	plants used for cloth, e.g. cotton, flax, hemp
flowers	botanically, this would be any angiosperm, but in ordinary language it's reserved for small decorative plants
ground cover	the garden center's term for grass alternatives

Size and climate

Another classification is by **size**: big plants are *trees*, medium-sized woody ones are *bushes* or *shrubs*; small soft ones are *grasses* and *herbs*.

Plants can also be classified by **climate**— indeed, the type of plant cover is used to indicate what climate zones are alike, alongside latitude, temperature, and rain patterns.

rain forest	hot, wet, highly biodiverse tropical forest
savanna	tropical areas with a long dry season, covered by scrub and isolated trees
desert	dry areas with no trees; typical vegetation is shrubs and cactus
Mediterranean	subtropical but very dry; mostly shrubs and hardy trees like olives and cedars; most of our food grains evolved in this area
temperate forest	the natural ground cover of temperate regions, dominated by a mix of angiosperms and conifers; the best farmland is cleared forest
grassland	semi-arid regions covered by grass

taiga	cold areas dominated by conifers
tundra	arctic deserts, with frozen ground and no trees, dominated by shrubs, grasses, moss, and lichen

For more see the *Biology* chapter of the *PCK*.

Corn words

As Adam Smith pointed out, few careers require so much specialized and localized knowledge as farming— and in few is that knowledge so little valued by outsiders.

Farmers will have a wide variety of terms related to growing, harvesting, processing, and eating plants. As an example, here's some of the Quechua terminology relating to corn (maize):

aha	chicha, alcoholic drink made from corn
atupa	a type of corn disease
chala	dried leaves of corn
chamcha	milled grain
chochoqa	dried corn kernels
choqllo	corn cob
chukcha	corn silk (also the general term for hair on the head)
chullpi	a type of sweet corn with wrinkled kernels
kalchay	cut down corn
kamcha	toasted corn (also, *hamka* or *qamka*)
kukmu	stubble, pieces of corn stalk remaining in the ground after harvest
kulli	the deep red or purple color of some corn and the chicha made of it
lawa	soup made from corn (or other) flour
muti	hominy, boiled corn
p'anqa	leaves covering the cob
pallpa	a crust of moist sod used to cover corn
panqa	corn husk
paraqay	white; a color used only for corn and oca
parwa	unthreshed grain (esp. of corn)
qarampa	corn husk
qominta	humita— ground corn tamale, cooked with spices in the husk
qoronta	tassel or corn silk
sara	general word for corn; in Peruvian Spanish, also refers to corn starch
sara haku	corn flour
sinqa	point of a corn kernel

sura	germinating corn
tanku	cooked corn bran
tipiy	to husk corn
ullihu	bud of corn
urwa	sterile corn
wiñapu	sprouts of corn used to make chicha
wiru	corn stalk

And I can't resist mentioning *tusa*, a Cuban term for a cigar rolled in corn leaves.

POSSESSION

accept   Lt *acceptāre* 'toward-take'

bear   OE *beran,* Lt *ferre,* Gk φέρω < IE **bher-*

belong   ME *bilongen* intensive of 'long'
   • Fr *appartenir* < 'be attached to' • Ger *gehören* < 'obey'

bring   OE *bringan,* cognate to Celtic words meaning 'lead'
   • Sp *traer* < 'pull' • Breton *digas* 'send to' • Ch *nálái* 'carry-come'

carry   Old Fr *carier* '(convey by) cart'
   • Fr *lever* 'lift' • Ger *tragen* < 'drag' • OCS *nesti* < 'reach' • Ch *yùn* 'revolve'

cast   Norse *kasta* 'throw' > 'put into shape' > 'cast metal'

catch   Norman Fr *cachier* 'chase' < Lt 'captive'

drop   OE *dropa;* as verb, 'fall in drops' > '(cause to) fall'

fling   Norse **flinga*

GET   Norse *geta* < IE 'seize'
   • Lt *parāre* 'prepare' • Fr *obtenir* < 'hold for' • Rum *căpăta* < 'seize' • Ir *faigh* < 'find' • Dutch *krijgen* 'strive, exert' • Ger *bekommen* 'arrive at' • Cz *dobyti* 'be up to' • Ch *jiě* < 'connect'

GIVE/GIFT   OE *ʒiefan,* cognate to Ir *gabh* 'take'
   • Lt *dare* < IE **dō-*

grab   ME possibly Dutch

grasp   ME *graspen* ‖ 'grope'
   • Gk ἁρπάζω < 'hook' • Lt *prehendere* < 'hold/get before' • Fr *saisir* < 'claim' • Dutch *vatten* 'pack' • Gothic *fahan* < 'fasten'

grip   OE *gripe* ‖ 'gripe'
   • Ch *jǐnwò* 'tight-grasp'

guard   Fr *garde* < Germanic, surviving as 'ward'
   • Ger *wachen* 'be awake' • Ch *wèi* < 'encircle'

HAVE   OE *habban* 'hold, possess' < IE 'seize'
   • Gk ἔχω cognate to 'gain, be victorious' • Lt *habēre* < 'hold' • OCS *iměti* 'take'

HOLD   OE *haldan* 'guard, keep, hold'
   • ModGk βαστῶ 'carry' • Lt *tenēre* < 'stretch, last' • Ger *halten* < 'pasture'

KEEP   OE *cépan,* uncertain; earliest senses 'seize, seek, observe'
   • Gk φυλάσσω 'guard' • Lt *servāre* 'serve, protect, watch' • Ger *bewahren* < 'beware' • Lith *saugoti* 'care for' • Ch *bǎocún* 'protect-preserve'

lack   OE *lac* 'defect, fault'
   • Fr *manquer* < 'defective' • Ch *quē* < 'break, splinter'

load	OE *lád* 'way, journey' > 'conveyance' > 'burden'
lose	OE *losian* 'perish, destroy' > 'be deprived of' • ModGk χάνω < χάος 'abyss' • Lt *āmittere* 'let go' • Ger *ver-lieren* 'for-loose' • Lith *pamesti* 'throw away' • Rus терять < 'rub' • Ch *shí* ‖ 'escape'
NEED	OE *níed* 'constraint, necessity' • Fr *besoin* 'by care' • Sp *faltarse* 'lack' • Sw *behov* 'use' • Ir *riachtanas* 'attaining' • OCS *nevolja* 'unwilled' • Ch *xū* 'await'
OWN	OE *áʒnian* < 'owe'
pack	Dutch *pak* uncertain
possess	Lt *possidēre* 'sit' + (uncertain) 'power' or 'onward' • Gk κέκτημαι 'have aquired' • Ir *sealbhaigh* < 'property' • Ger *besitzen* 'sit by' • Rus владеть 'rule' • Ch *suǒyǒu* 'place-have'
put	OE *putian* 'thrust' • Lt *pōnere* 'put down' • Fr *mettre* < 'let go', *poser* 'make rest' • Ger *setzen* causative of 'sit' • OCS *položiti* causative of 'lie' • Ch *fàng* ‖ 'throw'
receive	Lt *recipere* 're-take'
remove	Lt *removēre* 'move back'
send	OE *sendan* causative of 'travel, go' • ModGk στέλλω 'equip, arrange' • Lt *mittere* 'throw' • It *mandare* < 'commit' • Fr *envoyer* < 'on the road' • Ger *schicken* 'prepare' • OCS *sŭlati* poss. < 'offer' • Qu *apachiy* 'make carry' • Ch *sòng* 'escort'
set	OE *settan* causative of 'sit'
stick	OE *sticca* < Germanic 'pierce' (which also led to the verb)
TAKE	OE *tacan* 'grasp' • Fr *prendre* < 'seize' • Rum *lua* < 'lift' • Rus брать < 'collect' < 'bear' • Ch *lǎn* < 'gather'
throw	OE *þráwan* 'turn, twist' • Gk βάλλω < '(let) fall' • Fr *jeter* < frequentative of Lt *iacere* • Sp *tirar* 'draw' • Cz *hazeti* < 'aim at' • Skt *kṣip-* < 'swift'
+	*property, inherit, suffice, abound, deliver, garbage*

Having

You might think that *possession* was a very basic concept, but normally it's derived from something even simpler.

- Location, as in Russian: У меня яблоко 'The apple is near me', or So (a Nilo-Saharan language): *Mek Auca eo-a kusin* 'Clothes aren't in Auca's home' = 'Auca has no clothes'. Compare French *c'est à moi*, literally 'it's at me'.

- Direction— the idea being that if something is headed your way, you have it: Quechua *wasi tiyapuwan* 'a house is toward me' = 'I have a house'.

- Holding or carrying: Spanish *Tenemos un coche* 'We hold a car' = 'We have a car.'

- Seizing or capturing (if you grabbed it, it's yours): Cushitic *Ani mín k'awa* 'I seize a house' = 'I have a house'.

There are also derivations from 'rule, have power over'— e.g. Welsh *meddu*, Russian владеть, and possibly Latin *possidēre*. It's hard to say whether ruling or possessing is more abstract. Perhaps the first, as dominating another goes back to our primate heritage, and makes a good analogy for our power over our own belongings.

A very easy transition is from possessing things to feeling obligations. We say *I have to work*, French *j'ai à travailler,* and as we've seen (p. 95) a similar Latin expression led to the Romance future tense.

Another easy transition is from possession to experience. If you simply allow people to own their own actions— *I have 'I ran'*— you're most of the way to a perfect: *I have run*. American English has recreated this with *get*, as in *I got to drive the tank.*

A German friend didn't quite master these two developments, writing on a postcard "I have to spend a couple of days on this beautiful island"— turning an expression of gratitude into one of obligation!

Needs and wants

If you don't have it, you want it and you need it... no surprise that words wander between these meanings; the original sense of *want* was 'lack'. French *manquer* 'lack' is from Latin *mancus* 'defective'; along with Spanish *faltar* this suggests blaming the object because it's not in our possession.

French *besoin* 'need' is related to Frankish **sunjôn* 'be concerned with'— again, it's natural to be preoccupied with what you're lacking. The fact that French has gone for centuries without a proper verb corresponding to this noun is a good demonstration that not all languages are as happy to verb nouns as English is.

Transfer

In English, *bring* (like *come*) implies movement toward the speaker (*Bring me ale!*); if the movement is away you're supposed to use *take* (*Take this empty cup!*). Irish *beir* is used for carrying things regardless of direction, and Irish English applies this to *bring*: "Bring the bottle with you when you go."

Czech *dát* covers both 'give' and 'put'.

RELIGION

bless OE *blóedsian* 'mark with blood' > 'consecrate'
• Lt *benedīcere* 'speak well of' • Ger *segnen* 'sign (the cross)' • Latvian *svetīt* < 'holy' • Skt *svasti-* 'well-being' • Ch *zhùfú* 'wish-benefit'

curse OE *cursian*, poss. < 'wrath'
• Gk καταράομαι 'pray against' • Lt *maledīcere* 'say ill of' • Rum *blestema* < 'blaspheme' • Sw *förbanna* < 'forbid' • Ger *verfluchen* < 'strike, blow' • Latvian *lādēt* 'revile' < 'bark' • Ch *mà* 'scold'

damn Lt *damnum* 'damage, hurt'

demon Gk δαίμων 'minor deity'
• Welsh *cythraul* < 'contrary' • Ger *Unhold* <'unmerciful' • OCS *běsŭ* 'fright' • Skt *rakşas-* 'injury' • Old Persian *daiva-* < 'god'

devil OE *déofol* < Gk διάβολος 'slanderer, traitor' < 'throw across'
• Rum *drac* 'dragon' • OE *féond* 'enemy' • Hebrew *Šātān* 'adversary'

fate Lt *fātum* '(what was) spoken'
• Ch *yùn* 'revolve'

fortune Lt *fortūna* ‖ *fors fort-* 'chance'
• Gk τύχη 'happening' • It *ventura* 'coming to' • Cz *štěstí* 'share' • Ch *mìngyùn* 'life-turn'

ghost OE *gást* 'soul, spirit', cognate to words for 'frighten, fury'
• Gk σκιά 'shade', φάντασμα 'appearance' • Lt *mānes* < 'good' • Fr *revenant* 'returning' • Ir *taibhse* 'showing' • Breton *bugelnoz* 'night child' • Norse *draugr* 'deceit' • Ger *Gespenst* 'enticement' • Pol *strach* 'fear' • Skt *pitaras* 'ancestors' • Ch *guǐ* poss. < 'terrorizer'

god OE *god* poss. < IE '(what is) invoked'
• Gk θεός uncertain • Lt *deus*, Gk Ζεύς, Norse *Týr* ‖ 'day', 'shine' • OCS *bogŭ* poss. < Scythian 'lord, dispenser' • Skt *sura-* < 'spirit' • Lushai *pa-tʰian* 'father above'

hell OE *Hel*, a goddess, 'the hider'
• Gk ἄδης poss. < 'unseen' • Lt *infernus* 'underground' • Cz *peklo* 'pitch' • Skt *naraka-* 'nether' • Hebrew *Gēihinnōm* a valley associated with child sacrifice • Ch *dìyù* 'earth prison'

luck Dutch *luk*
• Fr *chance* < 'falling' • Sp *suerte* < 'drawing of lots, prophecy, fate' • Ch *hǎoyùn* 'good-fate'

magic Gk μαγικός < Persian *maguš* 'priest'
• Fr *sorcellerie* < 'oracle, lot' • Sp *hechiceria* < 'doing' • Ir *draíocht* 'druidism' • Ger *Zauberei* poss. < 'red lead' • Sw *svartkonst* 'black art' • Ch *móshù* 'demon-skill'

offer Lt *offerre* 'bring before, present'
- Ger *bieten* ‖ bid • Qu *munachiy* 'make want' • Ch *tígōng* 'propose-supply'

pray Old Fr *preier* < Lt *precārī* 'entreat'
- Gk εὔχομαι < 'speak, vow' • Rum *ruga* 'ask for' • Danish *bede* < 'request' • OCS *moliti sę* < 'tender, soften'

priest OE *préost* < Gk πρεσβύτερος 'elder'
- Gk ἱερεύς 'holy' • Lt *sacerdos -dōt-* 'sacred-doer' • Old Ir *drui* 'know true' • Breton *beleg* 'staff' • Lith *kunigas* 'master' • Skt *hotar-* 'invoke' • Ch *shénfù* 'god-father'

religion Lt *religio -giōn-* < 'scruple'
- Gk θρηκεία 'rites, worship' • Ir *creidamh* 'belief' • Dutch *godsdienst* 'God-service' • OCS *věra* 'faith' • Skt *mārga-* 'way' • Ch *jiào* 'teaching'

soul OE *sáwol*
- Gk ψῡχή, Lt *anima*, Skt *ātman-* < 'breath' • Latvian *gars* 'steam' • Ch *pò* < 'aspect of the moon' ‖ 'white'

spirit Lt *spīritus* 'breath' (like Gk πνεῦμα)

temple Lt *templum* 'consecrated place'
- Gk νᾱός 'dwelling', ἱερόν 'holy' • OCS *chramŭ* 'house' • Old Persian *āyadana-* 'place of worship'

witch OE *wicce* uncertain
- Gk φαρμακίς < 'drug, spell' • Lt *striga* < mythical bird • Fr *sorcière* < 'oracle' • Welsh *rheibes* 'ravager' • Breton *boudig* 'mumbler' • Lith *ragana* 'seer' • Rus ведьма 'knower' • Ch *wū* poss. < 'deceive' or 'dance'

wizard ME 'wise one'
- Fr *enchanteur* < 'sing against' • Rum *fermecător* < 'drug, poison' • Lith *žynys* < 'know' • Ch *nánwū* 'male witch'

worship OE *weorðscipe* 'worthiness'
- Gk προσκυνέω 'kiss (the ground)' • Lt *venerārī* < 'pray to Venus' • Ger *verehren* intensive of 'honor' • OCS *pokloniti sę* 'bow down' • Pol *wielbić* 'magnify' • Ch *chóngbài* 'high-salute'

+ *angel, idol, holiday, prophecy, sacrifice, festival, ceremony, abstinence, heaven, omen*

cleric, monk, hermit, shaman, disciple, pilgrim, atheist

lore, enchant, spell, taboo, blasphemy

‣ For creating religions, see the Religion chapter in the *PCK*.

Latin *religio* 'piety, religion' is of uncertain etymology, possibly related to *religāre* 'bind'. Mandarin *zōngjiào* is roughly 'sect-teaching'; note that in East Asia there is much less idea that one must choose a single belief system.

Hebrew neatly distinguishes *ʾĕlōah* 'the Hebrew God', *ʾĕlīl* 'a god besides the Hebrew God', and *ʾēl* 'either God or a god'.

The majority of Christian religious terms derive from Greek, the language of the early church— even Hebrew terms such as *Sabbath, Messiah* passed through Greek. (If they were direct loans they'd be *Shabbath, Mashiah.*) In some cases the word was borrowed so early that it doesn't look very Greek: e.g. *church* < κῡριακόν 'of the Lord', *priest* < πρεσβύτερος 'elder', *bishop* < ἐπίσκοπος 'overseer'. Words associated with a religion acquire some of its numinous power, and adherents may be reluctant to change them; note that Chinese, normally highly resistant to phonetic borrowings, made an exception for Buddhist terms (e.g. *nirvana* > *nièpán*).

Personally, I find it jarring when highly Judeo-Christian terms are used for other religions— e.g. in a translation of Ovid's *Metamorphoses* where a god is offered *hosannas*. It's like they took up a collection in *dollars*. So I'd appreciate it if you use more general terms (e.g. *priest* for a leader), or conlang terms (*aďom*), or English calques (*godspeaker*).

Souls

There's an obvious gulf between our internal and external life, and between a dead body and a living one. We can't explain it all, but we can name it; the immaterial part is the *soul*. (Or if that sounds too religious, the *mind*; see p. 263.)

Paul distinguished ψῡχή 'soul' as the Old Person, the unredeemed portion of humanity, as opposed to πνεῦμα 'spirit', the New Person, the redeemed, perfect portion created through Christ. It might have been useful to continue the idea of 'good spirit, bad soul', but this wasn't really pursued— though it's why we speak of the Holy Spirit and not the Holy Soul.

To medieval Europeans (and Wilkins, p. 73), there were three types of soul (*anima*):

- Vegetable Soul, associated with nutrition, growth, and reproduction. All life has this, and it's the only kind of soul possessed by plants.

- Sensitive Soul, or Sensuality, which adds sensation and movement. Animals share this with humans. Sensation included not only the five senses (p. 321) but the faculties of memory, instinct, retention in the mind, cogitation, and the amalgamation of sensory inputs into a perceived whole.

- Rational Soul, which adds reason— understanding and morality. Philosophers in turn divided this into *intellectus*, which grasps truth instantly and holistically, and *ratio*, which must proceed step by step.

But how does the soul affect or control the body? The medieval habit of mind was to invent a *tertium quid*, something in the middle that is neither, but which can serve as an intermediary. This was the *spirit* or *spirits*. Galen divided these into *natural spirits* (found in the veins), *vital spirits* (in the arteries), and *animal spirits* (in the nerves). Alchemists considered the liquids they derived from distillation to be *spirits*, e.g. *spirit of salt* (hydrochloric acid); thus our own *spirits* for distilled liquors.

More loosely, and less usefully, *spirit* was also used as a synonym for *soul*. The Germanic *ghost* is a synonym, now narrowed to apparitions of the dead (once the body is gone, the *soul / ghost* is what's left; its transparency and ability to move through doors are tokens of immateriality). Note *Holy Ghost*, the earlier term for *Holy Spirit*.

In **Chinese** thought, there are two types of soul, *hún* and *pò*. Axel Schuessler defines 魄 *pò* as the 'vegetative or animal soul', responsible for growth and life, cognate to other words meaning 'last quarter of the lunar month' and 'be white'; 魂 *hún* is the 'spiritual soul' which produces the personality. *Hún* leaves the body after death, while *pò* stays with the corpse.

They are inevitably associated with *yīn/yáng*: *hún* is *yáng* (light and bright), *pò* is *yīn* (heavy and dark). *Hún* is seated in the liver, *pò* in the lungs.

As with *spirit/soul*, there were other interpretations. Some people didn't bother to distinguish *hún* and *pò*, while some Daoists suggested that there are three types of *hún* and seven *pò*.

Ecclesiastical hierarchy

Few religions are centrally organized. If yours is, you may wish to refer to the Roman Catholic hierarchy:

pope   head of church

cardinal		bishop who can participate in papal elections
primate[11]		once had authority within a particular country (now honorary)
archbishop	*archdiocese*	oversees a large area with multiple bishops
bishop	*diocese*	oversees multiple priests; only a church with a bishop is a cathedral
priest	*parish*	ordained by a bishop; responsible for pastoral care for one congregation
deacon		reintroduced by Vatican II; can assist with but not perform mass; not required to be celibate

In early church history there were multiple *patriarchs* responsible for large regions; the Pope was the patriarch of Rome. With the Great Schism, the leaders of Eastern Orthodoxy retained the title, as do Eastern churches in communion with Rome. The head of the Church of England is the monarch.

A *vicar* is etymologically a substitute (cf. *vicarious*) or representative. In the Roman church there are several types of vicars, but the commonest is a priest assisting the *pastor* (principal priest) of a parish. In the Anglican church a *rector* received both greater tithes (grain) and lesser (other produce), while a *vicar* received only lesser tithes; the distinction is now merely historical.

Religious orders are organized separately. They are led by a *superior general*; an *abbot* is in charge of a particular monastery (Gk μονάζειν 'live alone'). Monks and nuns live communally, and take solemn vows of poverty, obedience, and chastity. They start as *postulants*, then become *novices*. Monks in many orders may be ordained as priests. *Monks* and *nuns* are cloistered; *friars* and *sisters* are those who go out into the world for ministry.

---

[11] This sounds amusing today, but of course the ecclesiastical sense precedes the biological. Both derive from Latin *prīmum* 'first'.

SHAPE

Objects

band	Fr *bande* < Germanic 'binding'
	• Ger *Gurt* < 'gird' • Ch *dàizi* dim. 'belt'
bar	Fr *barre* uncertain
beam	OE *béam* < Germanic 'tree'
	• Gk δοκός 'support' • Lt *trabs* < 'build, dwell' • Fr *poutre* < 'mare' (prob. from carvings at end of beam) • Welsh *trawst* < 'across' • Ir *sail* 'willow'
block	Fr *bloc* < Germanic
board	OE *bord*
	• Lt *planca* < 'flat' • Lith *lenta* 'linden' • OCS *dŭska* < 'plate'
circle	Lt dim. *circus* 'circle' ‖ 'curved'
	• Gk κύκλος 'wheel' • OCS *krągŭ* 'ring, circle' • Ch *yuán* 'round, turn, encircle'
cross	Old Ir *cros* < Lt *crux cruc-*, poss. ‖ Norse *hryggr* 'back, ridge'
	• Gk σταυρός 'stake' • OE *ród* 'rod' • OCS *krĭstŭ* < 'Christ' • Ch *shízì* 'ten (+)-character'
figure	Lt *figūra* 'shaping, forming'
	• Ch *túxíng* 'draw-shape'
form	Lt *forma* 'form, shape'
	• Gk σχῆμα 'holding', μορφή uncertain, εἶδος < 'appearance' • Ger *Gestalt* 'put in place' • Lt *stāvs* 'standing' • Cz *tvar* < 'make' • Ch *xíng* < 'model'
globe	Lt *globus* 'ball'
heap	OE *héap*
	• Sp *montón* < 'mount' • Ch *duī* < 'mound'
line	Lt *līnea* 'flaxen thread'
	• Ger *Strich* < 'line, way, stroke' • Ch *háng* poss. < 'go, road'
object	Lt *objectus* 'thrown before' = 'presented'
	• Ger *Gegenstand* 'stand against' • Ch *wù* 'sort, class'
panel	Lt *pannellus* 'small cloth'
pile	Lt *pīla* 'pier, pillar'
POINT	Lt *pūnctum* 'pricking, dot, point'
	• Gk ἀκμή 'edge' • Breton *beg* < 'beak, hook' • Ger *Spitze* < 'spit, spike' • Pol *koniec* 'end' • Ch *jiān* 'sharp'
post	Lt *postis* 'door, door-post'
ring	OE *hring*, cognate to OCS *krągŭ* 'circle'
	• Gk δακτύλιος < 'finger' • Lt *ānulus* dim. *ānus* • Fr *bague* < 'berry' • Rus кольцо < 'circle' • Ch *huán* < 'surround'
row	ME *ráw*

shape OE ʒesceap poss. < 'hewed out'
- Ch *xíng* < 'model'

square Old Fr *esquare* < 'make square' < Lt *quattuor* 'four
- Gk τετράγωνον 'four-cornered' • Ir *cearnóg* < 'corner' • Sw *fyrkant* 'four-edge' • Ch *fāng* 'side, region'

stick OE *sticca* < Germanic 'pierce' (which also led to the verb)
- Fr *bâton* poss. < 'carry' • Ch *bàng* < 'club'

strip ME *strippe* < Low German

THING OE *þing* 'assembly, matter, thing'
- Gk πρᾶγμα 'doing' • Lt *rēs re-* 'property' • Fr *chose* < 'cause' • Ir *ní* < 'someone' • Welsh *peth* 'piece, part' • Lith *daiktas* < 'point, sticking up' • Pol *rzecz* 'saying, matter' • Skt *vastu-* < 'dwell'

tube Lt *tubus*

+ *triangle, cube, ball, pyramid, dome, pole, rod, column, ribbon, lump*

Attributes

area Lt *ārea* 'open space'
- Ch *miànjī* 'face-amount'

bare OE *bær*
- Fr *nu* 'naked' • Ch *chì* < 'red'

firm Lt *firmus*
- Ger *hart* ‖ *hard* • Ch *dìng* < 'settle'

hollow OE *holh* ‖ 'hole'
- Lt *cavus* < 'curved' • Sp *hueco* prob. < 'empty' • Rus вогнутый 'bent in'

loose Norse *louss* ‖ *less, lose*

rough OE *rúh* < 'hairy'
- Gk τραχύς 'stirred up' • It *ruvido* < 'wrinkled' • Sw *ojämn* 'uneven' • Cz *drsný* < 'gritty'

round Fr *rond* < Lt *rotundus* 'wheel-shaped'
- Gk στρογγύλος < 'twisted' • OE *sin-wealt* 'always rolls' • OCS *kruglŭ* 'circular' • Cz *kulatý* < 'ball'

sharp OE *scearp* < IE 'cut'
- Lt *acūtus* < IE 'edge, tip' • ModGk μυτερός < 'snout' • Rum *ascuţit* < 'whet'

smooth OE *sméðe* uncertain
- Lt *lēvis* < IE 'slippery, slimy' • Ir *mín* 'gentle' • Breton *kompez* 'equal' • Ger *glatt* prob. < 'shiny' • Skt *sama-* < 'same' • Ch *huá* 'slippery'

solid	Lt *solidus*
	• Ger *fest* 'firm, fixed' • Ch *gùtĭ* 'firm-body'
stiff	OE *stíf*
tight	Norse *þéhtr* 'tight, dense, solid'
	• Fr *étroit* 'narrow', *raide* 'stiff' • Ch *jĭn* < 'tie, twist'
+	*blunt, volume*

Portions

base	Gk βάσις 'stepping' < 'go'
	• Ger *Grundlage* 'ground-site' • Ch *dĭ* < 'bottom'
bit	OE *bita* 'bite' > 'fragment'
	• Sp *pedacito* dim. 'piece'
corner	Old Fr *cornier* < 'horn' = 'angle'
	• Gk γωνία prob. < 'knee' • Lt *angulus* 'angle' • Fr *coin* < 'wedge' • Sp *esquina* 'spine' • Ger *Winkel* < 'turn, bend', *Ecke* 'edge'
crack	OE *cracian*
	• Fr *fente* 'split' • Ger *Knall* 'sharp sound'
edge	OE *ecg* < Germanic 'edge, point' < IE 'sharp'
	• Lt *ōra* < 'mouth' • It *filo* 'thread' • Ger *Schneide* 'cut' • Breton *dremm* 'face' • Ch *dāokŏu* 'knife-mouth'
feature	Old Fr *faiture* 'making'
	• Ger *Zug* 'pulled, drawn' • Ch *tèsè* 'special color'
fold	OE *fealdan*, cognate to Lt *plicāre* 'fold, bend'
	• Sp *doblar* 'double' • Sw *vika* < 'move, yield' • Cz *skladati* 'lie with' • Ch *zhé* 'overlay'
hole	OE *hol* 'a hollow place'
	• Gk ὀπή < 'eye' • It *buco* < 'empty' • Ir *poll* 'pool' • Ger *loch* < 'enclosed' • Rus дыра 'torn'
limit	Lt *līmes līmit-* 'boundary'
	• Ch *jiè* poss. < 'guard against'
mark	OE *mearca* 'boundary, sign'
part	Lt *pars part-*
	• Gk μέρος 'share' • Ger *Teil* < 'divide' • OCS *čęstĭ* 'bite'
piece	Fr *pièce* uncertain
scar	Old Fr *escare* 'mark from a burn' < Gk 'hearth'
	• Ch *shānghén* 'injury-mark'
scrap	Norse *skrap* 'scrapings'
spot	ME uncertain
surface	Lt *superficiēs* 'under-face'

tip	ME *typpe* poss. < Germanic
	• Fr *bout* < 'hit' • Sp *punta* 'point' • Ch *jiān* 'sharp'
+	*wrinkle, flaw, rim*

The shape words are very useful for building other words— they can name building materials, machine parts, clothing details, bits of anatomy, portions of a chart.

The attributes too: we can speak of a *rough* character, a *firm* commitment, a *tight* schedule.

As ever, many of these metaphorical extensions are obscured by being made in Latin or Greek: *asperity* = roughness, *lubricate* = make smooth, *apex* = tip, *radius* = rod, *margin* = edge, *punctual* = like a point, *cycle* = circle, *stele* = slab, *acme* = tip, *sclerotic* = hardening.

In Czech, an inside corner is *kout,* an outside corner *roh.*

Simple shapes make good icons, and thus can represent nations or ideologies— consider how the *cross* is associated with Christianity, and thence with war (*crusade*). The typographical dagger † is not a cross but an ὀβελίσκος ('little roasting spit'), used in ancient times to mark spurious passages in a text.

SENSATION

appear	Lt *appārēre* 'come in sight to'
aware	OE *ȝewær* 'wary'
hide	OE *hýdan*
	• Gk κρύπτω 'cover, hide' • Fr *cacher* < 'squeeze (into a small space)' • Sp *esconder* < 'build, hide' + 'away' • Ger *verbergen* for-keep' • Sw *dölja* < 'confuse' • Ch *cáng* 'store'
ignore	Lt *ignōrāre* 'not know'
	• Ch *bùlĭ* 'not recognize'
note	Lt *nota* 'mark'
observe	Lt *observāre* 'look toward, watch'
perceive	Lt *percipere* 'seize through'
	• Ger *empfinden* 'find out' • Cz *číti* < 'notice'
reveal	Lt *revēlāre* 'unveil'
SEEM	Norse *søma* 'fitting, seemly'
	• Gk φαίνομαι 'made to appear' • Fr *sembler* < 'pretend to be' • Sw *synas* 'show oneself' • Ger *scheinen* 'shine' • Ch *kànlái* 'look-come'
sense	Lt *sentīre* 'feeling'
	• Ger *Sinn* < 'go, travel' • Ch *jué* 'wake up'
smell	ME *smellen*, uncertain
	• Lt *olēre* < IE • ModGk μυρίζω < 'ointment' • Sw *lukta* < 'air' • Ger *riechen* < 'smoke, steam', cf. *reek* • OCS *vonjati* 'breathe in'

Hearing	
echo	Gk ἠχώ prob. ‖ 'sound'
	• Ger *Wiederhall* 'against-sound' • Ch *huíshēng* 'return-sound'
HEAR	OE *híeran*, poss. cognate to Gk ἀκούω
	• Lt *audīre* < 'ear' • Fr *entendre* < 'stretch toward'
listen	OE (Northumbrian) *lysna* < IE, cognate to OCS *slušati*
	• Gk ἀκροάομαι 'sharp ear' • Qu *uyariy* < 'face' • Swahili *sikiza* 'make hear'
loud	OE *hlúd* < 'heard'
	• Lt *clārus* 'clear' • Fr *fort* 'strong' • Sw *hög* 'high' • Rus громкий 'thunderous'
noise	Fr *noise* 'clamor, outcry' uncertain
quiet	Lt *quiētus* 'having come to rest'
	• Rum *liniştit* < 'mild' • Welsh *llonyd* < 'cheerful' • Dutch *rust* 'rest' • OCS *tichu* 'even' • Skt *çānta-* < 'weary' < 'toil'

silent   Lt *silens* 'being silent'
- Sp *callar* < 'slacken' • Ger *schweigen* < 'cease' • Latvian *klusēt* < 'listen' • Ch *mò* ‖ 'black'

sound   Lt *sonus*
- Ir *foghar* < 'cry out' • OCS *zvonŭ* poss. imitative

Sight

blind   OE *blind* poss < 'dark'
- Lt *caecus* prob. < 'squinting' • Fr *aveugle* 'without eyes' • Gk τυφλός < 'murky' • Ch *shīmíng* 'lose bright'

gaze   ME uncertain

glance   ME 'glide off, pass over'
- Fr *coup d'œil* 'hit of eye' • Ger *Blick* < 'flash, shine' • Ch *yíkàn* 'one-look'

image   Lt *imāgo imagin-* 'imitation, likeness'
- Ch *xiàng* < 'resemble'

LOOK   OE *lócian,* uncertain
- It *guardare* < 'guard' • Sp *mirar* < 'wonder' • Ger *schauen* < 'show' • Ch *kàn* ‖ Tibetan 'know'

notice   Lt *nōtus* '(something) known'

SEE   OE *séon,* poss. cognate to Lt *sequor* 'follow'
- Gk ὁράω < 'watch' • Lt *vidēre* < IE, cognate to 'wit'

sight   OE *ʒesihð* nomn. of 'see'

stare   OE *starian*
- Sp *mirar fijamente* 'look at fixedly' • Ch *níngshì* 'concentratè-look'

view   Fr *vu* 'seen'

visible   Lt *vīsibilis* 'seeable'

vision   Lt *vīsio* nomn. of 'see'

watch   OE *wacian* variant of 'wake'

Taste

bitter   OE *biter* < 'biting'
- Gk πικρός 'pointed' • Ir *searbh* prob. < 'sour' • Skt *tikta-* 'sharp' • Ket *qə́làŋ* < 'bile'

sweet   OE *swéte* < 'pleasant'
- Lt *dulcis* uncertain • Ir *milis* < 'honey' • OCS *sladŭkŭ* 'seasoned' • Ch *tián* poss. ‖ 'lick' • Ket *hílàŋ* < 'birch sap'

taste   Old Fr *taster* < Lt frequentative of *taxāre* 'touch, feel'
- Lt *gustāre* < IE • Sw *smaka* < 'pleasing' • Skt *ras-* < 'juice'

+   *salty, delicious, bland, spicy, sour*

               transparent, deaf, distract, stink

Mandarin uses the same word (*kàn*) for 'reading' books and 'watching' TV. And in Quebec French, you 'listen' (*écouter*) to the TV.

French *sentir* is also used for 'smell'— thus English *scent*— while Italian *sentire* is used for 'hear'. Welsh *clywed* is principally 'hear' but also refers to any of the senses but sight. English *wit*, originally 'mind', was also used for the senses.

English uses *smell* for both perceiving or having an odor, but Lithuanian distinguishes *uost* vs. *kapėti*. Latin distinguishes *gustāre* 'taste something' vs. *sapere* 'have a flavor'.

> ‣   For touch, see *Bodily actions,* p. 144.

Human senses

The idea of **five senses** goes back to the ancient Greeks, though there was then disagreement over the number. Aristotle considered taste to be a form of touching, while Plato named "heat and cold, pleasure, pain, desire" as senses.

Neurology would add at least *proprioception* (the sense of where your limbs are, and their movement), *nociception* (pain), *thermoception* (heat and cold— there are different receptors for each), and *equilibrioception* (balance).

The basic **tastes** (*sweet, sour, salty, bitter*) correspond to different types of taste buds on the tongue. **Umami** does not have a good English equivalent (though *savory* has been suggested), and indeed its Japanese discoverer, Kikunae Ikeda, simply named it 'delicious taste'. Monosodium glutamate gives a good wallop of *umami*; it's also strong in cheese, soy sauce, fish and shellfish, cured meats, tomatoes, and mushrooms.

If you're tempted to derive 'sweet' from *sugar* (< Arabic *sukkar*), note that most premodern peoples didn't have access to sugar cane.

It used to be taught that each taste was localized to one part of the tongue, but this is not true— all five receptor types are found all over the tongue.

The five taste receptors are not the whole story, though. There are other receptors in the mouth:

- **Spiciness** is a sort of pain reception; it responds exquisitely to capsaicin from chilis and piperine from black peppers.

- Certain chemicals can trigger the cold receptors, producing the **cool** sensation of mint, menthol, and camphor.

- An **astringent** sensation in the lining of the mouth is caused by tea, red wine, rhubarb, and some unripe fruit.

- Some receptors are sensitive to a **metallic** taste.

In addition, taste is deeply tied to **smell**, which is why foods taste blander when you have a cold. Smells resist classification simply because there are several hundred kinds of receptors. Each is specialized to respond to a particular type of molecule.

In Czech, there's no neutral word for 'smell'— it's either pleasant (*vůně*) or bad (*smrad, zápach*).

Our sense of **touch** is primarily a measurement of pressure; it should really be divided from the sense of **itchiness** which is communicated by different nerves.

In addition to the external senses, there are **internal senses**. There are nerves that respond to stretching of the lungs, fullness of the bladder or rectum, CO_2 levels in the brain, dilation of blood vessels, etc. And Plato was not wrong— feelings of hunger, thirst, or sexual excitement can be described as senses.

People can have lacks or **deficits** of the less recognized senses. Oliver Sacks describes a patient whose sense of balance was damaged; he walked at an angle, completely unaware that something was wrong. (He was outfitted with a sort of spirit level attached to his glasses, which allowed him to optically compensate for his lack of equilibrioception.)

Responsiveness to all the senses follows a **power law**. This is widely known for sound, because of the *decibel* scale. If a sound is roughly 3 times louder than another, the loudness differs by 10 dB. But as Stanley Smith Stevens found in the last century, this is how all our senses work, and even our perception of value— e.g. if people are asked to think of how happy they'd be to have a free gift of $1000 they estimate that they'd be twice as happy as that if they got not $2000 but $4000.[12]

Another way of putting it is that our senses are finely tuned to relative difference, and lousy at detection of absolute magnitudes. It's easy to create sensory illusions to show this.

---

[12] For more see William Poundstone's *Priceless*; his subject is prices but this turns out to involve a lot of psychology.

Exotic senses

If your conpeople are **nonhuman**, they may have interesting new senses. For an overview, see Howard C. Hughes, *Sensory Exotica*.

- Humans are notoriously bad at smell— though Richard Feynman points out that this is in part because our noses are up so high, and we just don't bother to use them. E.g. he was able to detect by smell which book on a bookcase was touched by another person. He had to admit, however, that his dog was better at it, since the dog could not only find his trail on the carpet but know which way he'd gone.

- Mammals really have two senses of smell, responding to different chemicals. In humans, most molecules are detected by the olfactory epithelium, at the top of the nasal cavity; but a few are detected by the vomeronasal organ in the lower nostril. The VNO is specialized to detect pheromones, chemicals produced by members of the same species, though snakes use them to detect prey. Whether humans have pheromones or even a functional VNO is unclear.

- Our vision is adapted to the portion of the electromagnetic spectrum that the sun most strongly emits. Naturally, species adapted to other stars will have vision corresponding to their output spectra.

- Birds and bees can see well into the ultraviolet. Flowers have co-evolved to display brightly in the ultraviolet.

- Many animals can see into the infrared, which is particularly useful as all bodies turn thermal energy into light, and at ordinary earthly temperatures this means the infrared.

- Birds and many invertebrates can sense magnetic fields (*magnetoception*). They usually perceive the direction rather than the polarity of the field— which is good since the polarity of the Earth's magnetic field periodically flips. There are bacteria which sense the direction of the field; as the lines of magnetic force always lead into the earth, this lets them find the sea floor.

- Flies have taste receptors on their feet, which allows them to taste whatever they're standing on.

- Bats gain a picture of the space around them, in the dark, via *echolocation*— emitting high-pitched sounds and listening to the echoes. Dolphins do the same in the water.

- The lateral line of fish detects electric currents (*electroreception*), which allows sensing of prey and other fish.

- Some fish go further, emitting a weak electric current and detecting changes in the resulting magnetic field. Other fish have lower electric resistance than water, which increases the local field intensity; inanimate objects usually have higher resistance, which reduces the local field. The current can also be used for social communication.

  These electric fields are small, but some fish, like electric eels, can generate a high-current wallop than can kill a horse. (Not their usual prey.)

- Bacteria can respond to gradients of various chemicals, allowing them to move toward food and away from irritants.

- A radiation sensor would be useful in post-apocalyptia, as well as in outer space.

SEX

sex	Lt *sexus* poss < 'cut' = 'a division'
	• Gk γένος 'kin, race' • OCS *polŭ* 'half' • Pol *płeć* 'flesh' • Ch *xìng* 'nature, property'
fuck	ModE uncertain
	• Gk ὀχεύω < 'master' • Lt *coīre* 'come together' • OE *swífan* 'sweep, sway' • Ger *beischlagen* 'sleep by' • Lith *pisti* < 'strike, push' • Qu *satiy* 'insert' • Ch *gàn* 'work'
+	*fondle, orgasm, pregnant, erotic; chaste, virgin, prude*
	homosexual, lesbian, gay, transgender
	adultery, perversion, rape, prostitute, harem, woman-izer, orgy, bondage

Fuck of course occurs in the textual corpus mostly as an expletive, but it's a convenient place to list words for having sex. Like words for the genitals, words for sex tend to be highly marked for register.

English lacks an all-purpose transitive which can be used for 'have sex with' for both sexes. *Fuck* can be used this way, but it's still highly charged; for Verdurian I supplied the neutral *rašir*.

Sexual vocabulary is interesting in part because so little of it is purely descriptive. Merely to name the act of sex requires choosing an attitude: clinical (*sexual intercourse*), euphemistic (*make love, come together*), vulgar (*fuck, screw*), or misogynistic (*tap that ass*). Your culture's terms should reflect its (various) attitudes.

You also have to decide what your culture considers acceptable, perverse, or criminal.

- In pre-modern societies, disease, the risk of pregnancy, and the desire for a clear inheritance put free love into disrepute.

- The contemporary view of oral sex as normal and minor is surely possible only due to modern good hygiene.

- On the other hand, where marriages are arranged, people still fall in love, and their affairs will be adulterous. Attitudes to this may be complicated; an example is Malory's *Morte D'Arthur*, where Lancelot's affair with Guenever is simply characteristic of a heroic knight. (Indeed, when Arthur is made aware of challenges to her virtue, his response is spectacularly regressive: she's condemned to death unless her champion defeats the accuser.)

- Though rape is normally viewed as a crime, most premodern societies are highly male-dominant, so the crime was viewed as one against the woman's husband or family rather than against her.

What are the local standards of modesty? At a first approximation, people wear less clothes in hot climates. At a second approximation, people tend to maintain their standards even when moving into a new climate zone. Thus you get descendants of Spaniards wearing three-piece suits in the Amazon, and Mennonites sweltering in wool coats in Paraguay.

On homosexuality, see the *PCK*, p. 165. Note that our terms are all modern— which doesn't mean the practice is modern, just that earlier ages didn't conceptualize sexual acts and orientations as we do.

In the future, possibly anything goes. In my sf world, the Incatena, sex changes are routine, which makes nonsense out of most present-day moralisms and even earnest debates about evolutionary psychology. But why stop there? It's easy to imagine modified bodies allowing new sexes, new sex acts, and new perversions.

When devising sexual terms, recall that people often have a titillating eye on foreign cultures. Words like *harem, seraglio, concubine, geisha, courtesan,* even *orgy* evoke an Orientalist fantasy; *bondage, beau, massage, lingerie, demimonde, coquette, madam* (of a brothel), and even *passion, romance, paramour* are reminders that for the English, the French were viewed as a little too expert in matters of love. Who can your conculture blame illicit practices on?

Sexual slang is notorious for creating traps for foreigners... for instance, to call a woman *bonne* (literally 'good') in French is highly vulgar— it's like saying she's good in bed.

SIN

admit	Lt *admittere* 'send to'
	• Gk ὁμολογέω 'same-reason' • Fr *avouer* < 'vow' • Norse *játa* 'yes' • Ger *gestehen* 'stand' • Cz *uznati* 'recognize' • Skt *svīkr̥-* 'make one's own' • Ch *rèn* < 'know'
anger	Norse *angr* 'trouble, affliction'
	• Gk ὀργή 'mood', χόλος 'bile' (> Fr *colère*) • Lt *īra* < 'strength' or 'passion' • Ger *Zorn* < 'torn' • Sw *vrede* < 'twisted' • Latvian *dusmas* 'panting' • OCS *gněvŭ* prob. < 'rot' • Cz *zlost* 'evil' • Ch *fèn* prob. < 'swell, increase'
kill	ME *culle* 'strike, hit'
	* Lt *necāre* < *nex* 'violent death' • Fr *tuer* < 'extinguish' • ModGk σκοτώνω 'darken' • Qu *wañuchiy* 'cause to die'
lie	OE *lуȝe*, cognate to OCS *lōža*
	• Gk ψεῦδος 'false' • Lt *mendācium* < 'defect', *mentīrī* < 'mind' • Welsh *celwydd* 'hide knowledge' • Skt *asatya-* 'untrue'
MEAN	OE *mǽnan* 'intend, mean', cognate to Ger *meinen* 'think'
murder	OE *morðor* < 'death'
	• Gk φόνος < 'kill, strike' • Lt *nex nec-* 'violent death' • Ir *dúnmharú* 'man-killing' • Welsh *llofruddiaeth* 'red-handedness' • Cz *vražda* < 'enemy' • Ch *móushā* 'plan-kill'
proud	OE *prút* 'boastful, lordly' < Old Fr *prod* 'valiant' < Lt 'be useful'
	• Lt *superbus* adjn. of 'over' • Sp *orgulloso* < 'distinguished' • Fr *fier* < 'fierce' • Ir *mórálach* < 'large' • Dutch *trotsch* < 'stubborn' • Ger *stolz* < 'strut' • Rus надменный 'blown up' • Skt *garvita-* 'heaviness' • Ch *jiāo* < 'tall'
shame	OE *scamu* poss. < 'cover'
	• Gk αἰδώς 'reverence, modesty' • Lt *pudor* poss. < 'repulsed' • Fr *honte* '< 'dishonor' • Sp *vergüenza* < 'awe' • OCS *studŭ* ‖ 'hate' • Ch *xiū* < 'dirty'
+	*sin, guilt, tempt, corrupt, fraud*
	honest, confess, forgive, pardon, excuse
	villain, bully, sadist, brute, bastard, malice
	lust, avarice, greed, sloth, gluttony
	assassin, strangle, drown, slaughter

C.S. Lewis pointed out in *The Abolition of Man* that all cultures have a similar set of basic moral values. Fortunately for conworlding, though, there are still interesting differences.

- How many wives are permitted? What's the attitude toward homosexuality? How different is sexual morality for men and for women? Are marriages arranged, and by whom?

- Are the worst crimes offenses against persons (e.g. murder), or against property (e.g. theft)?

- Is it more important that a criminal offer recompense to his victim, that he be punished, or that he repent his crimes?

- Urbanites are generally more tolerant of diversity; on the other hand, urban life creates whole new categories of crime: disputes over land; fraud and false advertisement; harassment by lawsuit; monopoly exploitation; copyright violation.

- Premodern agricultural states (but not hunter-gatherers or nomads) are big on authority. Rulers are to be obeyed even when they're lunatics; savants advise matching one's belief system to the state's; fathers may have life-or-death powers over even adult children.

  A modern civilization is by contrast much more interested in justice and individual freedom. Earlier cultures might value 'freedom', but found it self-evident that only a fraction of society deserved it.

- How far can the individual pursue personal wealth and fulfillment? In many cultures the chief economic unit is the extended family. And there have been cultures where social mobility is actively prosecuted (mostly as a ham-handed attempt to keep up production in a time of decline).

- Is the material world a positive good, or a worthless snare? If you value only the spiritual world, that may affect your view of trade and rich men (exploitative Mammon-worshippers!), politics (vanity and foolishness), sex (disgusting animality), self-mortification (a valuable aid to focusing on the spiritual), and capital punishment (bodily life isn't worth much).

- Though everyone is against 'cruelty', what's viewed as cruel varies by culture. Earlier cultures found it completely normal to punish people with grotesque mutilations. And for millennia, after all, the most powerful social class was that trained to carve each other up with sharp blades.

  Though there was always an ethos to go along with this, it's still the behavior of schoolyards and chimpanzee troupes: it's good to be physically powerful and quick to violence. (Malory's heroes are explicitly described as "big and strong", and even the best of his knights occasionally brutally kill a relative or a woman— and that's to say nothing of the horses they go through.)

- Which of our own everyday actions will look inexcusably horrible to our descendants? Many would say war, or carnivorism, but I'd suggest it's our offenses against sustainability. Destroying the ecosphere, or even using up its resources, is a sociopathic crime against the future.

It can be useful to attempt to **categorize sins** according to the values of your conculture. (See the discussion in the *PCK*, pp. 207-210.) This not only gives you a good set of words, but helps work out your culture's belief system.

A neat derivation: the Ket word for 'guilty' is *saʙan* 'without a squirrel'; the Ket paid their taxes to the tsar in furs, so it was bad to have none.

SOCIETY

agree	Fr *agréer* 'make pleasing'
alien	Lt *aliēnus* 'of another (place)' • Ger *ausländisch* 'outlandish' • Ch *wàilái* 'come from outside'
alone	ME 'all one' • Lt *sōlus* poss. < 'by oneself' • Ir *amháin* 'no more' • Danish *blot* 'bare' • Cz *toliko* 'so much' • Ch *dú* dialectal 'one'
barbarian	Gk βάρβαρος 'babbler', imitative • Ch *yí* an ethnic name
civilize	Fr *civiliser* 'turn into citizens' • Ch *wénmíng* 'writing-bright'
colony	Lt *colōnia* from 'farmer, cultivator' • Ch *zhímíndì* 'breed-people-place'
community	Lt *commūnitas -tāt-* 'fellowship', from 'common' • Qu *ayllu* '(theoretical) lineage' • Ch *shè* 'god of soil'
company	Fr *compagnie* '(people one has) bread with' • Ch *gōngsī* 'public-office'
confident	Lt *confīdens* intensive of 'trust' • Ger *überzeugt* 'with evidence' • Ch *xìnxīn* 'believe-heart'
crowd	OE *crúdan* 'press, push' > 'throng together' > 'mass of people' • Lt *multitūdo -din-* 'muchness' • Fr *foule* < 'pound cloth' • Lith *minia* < 'trample'
dwell	OE *dwellan* 'delude, stun' > 'hinder, delay' > 'abide'
explore	Lt *explōrāre* 'search out'
faction	Lt *factio* 'doing, making' • Ger *Splittergruppe* 'splitter-group' • Ch *zōng* 'clan'
favor	Lt *favor* 'show goodwill, side with' • Ger *Gunst* 'benevolence' • Ch *hǎoyì* 'good-idea'
gentle	Rom 'of good family' < Lt *gentīlis* 'of the same clan'
group	Fr *groupe* 'mass, knot' > 'set of figures in a painting' > 'any group' • Ch *qún* poss. ‖ 'swarm', 'all'
join	Fr *joindre* < IE 'join', cognate to *yoke* • Gk συνάπτω 'fasten with' • Ir *ceangail* 'bind' • Ger *fügen* 'fasten' • OCS *sŭčetati* < 'crowd' • Ch *hé* also 'shut'
native	Lt *nātīvus* 'by birth' • Ger *eingeboren* 'born in' • Ch *běnguó* 'origin country'
neighbor	OE *néahʒebúr* 'near-dweller' • Lt *vīcīnus* < 'quarter, village' • Welsh *cymydog* 'live near' • OCS *sǫsědŭ* 'sit with'

party	Fr *parti* 'divided'
	• Ch *dǎng* < 'category' < 'equal'
patient	Lt *patiens* 'suffering'
	• Ger *geduldig* < 'tolerate' • Ch *nàixīn* 'enduring heart'
PEOPLE	Fr *peuple* < Lt *populus* < IE, cognate to OE *folc*
	• Gk δῆμος 'district' • Ir *daoine* 'persons' • Welsh *gwerin* 'crowd' • Lt *gens gent-*, Skt *jana-* < 'beget' • Ch *mín* ‖ 'human'
populate	Lt *populāre* verbn. of 'people'
public	Lt *pūblicus* 'of the people'
	• Ger *öffentlich* 'openish' • Ch *gōng* < 'palace'
reside	Lt *residēre* 'sit back'
	• Lt *habitāre* frequentative of 'have' • Ir *áitrigh* 'place' • Breton *chom* < 'shelter from heat' • Ger *wohnen* < 'seek, gain' • ModE *dwell* < 'delay' • OCS *žiti* 'live' • Ch *zhù* < 'stop (moving)'
settle	OE *setl* 'sitting place'
society	Lt < *socius* 'companion'
	• Ger *Gesellschaft* 'comradeship' • Ch *shè* < 'god of soil'
stranger	Fr *étranger* < Lt *extrāneus* 'external, foreign'
	• Ch *qí* ‖ 'irregular', 'put aside'
together	OE 'to' + *gador* 'together'
unite	Lt *ūnīre* 'make one'
	• Ch *hé* < 'join, close with a lid'
+	*league, gang, tribe, organization, solitary*
	foreign, newcomer, immigrant, refugee
	appreciate, mercy, benevolent

▸ See *Conflict* (p. 164), *Government* (p. 211), *Sin* (p. 329), *War* (p. 383)

Most primates are social animals, so it's no surprise there are lots of terms for human interaction. It can be wondered, in fact, whether sentience can develop in solitary animals. Though predation requires smarts, the most complicated things we deal with are other people.

I've covered how to create societies and cultures in the *PCK*, so I won't add much here.

English, like all major languages, derives from conquering cultures, and thus has many words for expanding at the expense of unluckier peoples (*settle, populate, civilized, colony, barbarian*). The process, and the vocabulary, would look different for the people losing their territory— or for species that are less territorial.

Social relationships

accord	Lt *accordāre* 'to heart'
admire	Lt *admīrāri* 'wonder at'
	• Ch *qīnpèi* < 'respect'
agree	Fr *agréer* 'make pleasing'
assist	Lt *assistere* 'stand at'
contact	Lt *contactus* 'touched together'
convince	Lt *convincere* intensive of 'vanquish'
glory	Lt *glōria*
	• Gk δόξα 'expectation', κῦδος 'perception' • Ger *ruhm* prob. < 'call, cry' • OCS *slava* 'fame' ‖ 'word' • Ch *guāng* < 'extensive'
guide	Fr *guide* prob. < Germanic ‖ *wit*
help	OE *helpan*
	• Gk ἐπικουρέω 'run with' • Lt *adjūtāre* poss. ‖ 'please', *auxilior* < 'augment' • Fr *assister* < 'stand by' • Ir *cabhraigh* < 'bear with' • OCS *pomošti* < 'be able' • Ch *zhù* < 'hoe together'
honor	Lt *honor*
	• Gk τῑμή 'value, price' • Old Ir *oineach* 'face' • Sw *heder* 'clear, shining' • OE *weorðscipe* 'worthiness' • Lith *garbé* 'praise' • OCS *čĭstĭ* 'reckoning' • Skt *māna-* 'opinion, thought' • Ch *zūn* ‖ 'sacrifice', 'ancestors'
impress	Lt *imprimere* 'press into'
invite	Lt *invītāre* 'invite, entertain'
meet	OE *métan*
	• Gk ἀναντάω < 'face to face' • It *incontrare* < 'against' • Ir *casadh* < 'turn' • Ger *treffen* 'hit' • OCS *sŭrěsti* < 'find' • Ch *yù* < 'pair'
propose	Fr *proposer* 'put forward'
respect	Lt *respectus* 'looked back'
shame	OE *scamu* poss. < 'cover'
	• Gk αἰδώς 'reverence, modesty' • Lt *pudor* poss. < 'repulsed' • Fr *honte* < 'dishonor' • Sp *vergüenza* < 'awe' • OCS *studŭ* ‖ 'hate' • Ch *xiū* < 'dirty'
support	Lt *supportāre* 'carry under'
	• Ger *stützen* < 'post, stud' • Ch *yǎng* 'rear'
trust	Norse *traust*

+   *host, guest, introduce*

      benefit, advantage, worldly, cynical

      inspire, praise, merit, famous, reputation

These are terms largely relating to how unrelated members of a community think of each other, or interact with each other. For negative reactions, see *Conflict*; for verbal interaction, see *Speech*.

Terms for bodily action (*touch, link, bear, support, press*) are good building blocks for social interaction.

Customs

custom	Old Fr *costume* < Lt intensive of 'be wont to, used to'
	• Gk ἔθος, Ger *Sitte* < 'one's own' • It *usanza* 'usage' • Ir *nós* < 'known' • Ch *sú* poss. 'common, vulgar'
greet	OE *grœtan* 'approach, address'
	• Fr *accueillir* < 'collect' • Ch *zhù* < 'wish < 'pray'
manners	Fr *manière* 'handling' < Lt 'of the hand'
please	Lt *placēre* < 'flatten'
	• Gk ἀρέσκω 'be fitting' • Sp *agradar* < 'agreeable' • Portuguese *gostar* < 'taste' • Ger *befallen* 'fall to' • Rus нравится 'character'
polite	Lt *polītus* 'polished'
	• Sp *cortés* 'courtly' • Ch *lĭ* 'ritual'
proper	Lt *proprius* 'one's own'
thank	OE *þanc* 'thought' > 'good will' > 'gratitude'
	• Gk χάρις, Lt *grātia* 'grace' • Fr *merci* < 'wages' • Breton *diolch* < 'prayer'
welcome	OE *wilcuma* 'desired guest', reanalyzed as 'well come'
+	*courtesy, tact, chivalry, faux pas, vulgar, rude, routine*

    ▸ On politeness, see the *LCK* p. 145, and the *PCK* p. 181.

Polite expressions such as *please, thank you, you're welcome, goodbye* are generally not roots, but entire phrases, usually quite worn down.

Playing games

game	OE *gamen* < Germanic, possibly 'with-man' > 'communion'
play	OE *pleʒan* 'move energetically'
	• Gk παίζω 'child' • Fr *jouer* < 'joke' • Sw *leka* < 'hop' • OCS *igrati* 'dance' • Ch *xì* ‖ 'joke', 'laugh'

race	Norse *rás* uncertain
	• Fr *course* 'running'
+	*sport, score, toy, doll, puppet, athletic, prize, card, maze, bet, compete*

The semantic space of *play* varies:

- French agrees with English on the wide range of 'play', but the case structure differs: you *joues à* a game, you *joues de* an instrument, and you *joues* a role, a note, or a card.

- In Swedish, you *spela* games, instruments, and roles, but children playing is *leka*.

- Finnish has *pelata* for games or sports, *soittaa* for music, and *leikkiä* for children playing.

- In Spanish, you use *tocar* ('touch') with musical instruments, and in Quechua *waqachiy* ('make cry').

- Japanese *asobi* is having fun or relaxing in general— it's the opposite of 'work'. You can even invite people to *asobi ni kuru* 'come to play' meaning 'come for a visit'.

- Northern English *laik* can also be glossed 'not work'; children *laik,* but adults who are *laiking* are striking or unemployed. French has *chômer* 'be unemployed'.

- In Mandarin, you must use specific verbs appropriate to the sport or instrument— you 'hit' a basketball, 'kick' a soccer ball, 'pull' a cello.

See Wittgenstein on *game* (p. 49). Note that languages don't have to agree that all of his examples are *games.*

Words for games make good metaphors for war, for business, for seduction (*make a play for her hand*). The very useful word *check,* in all its senses, derives from chess, as do *pawn* 'underling' and *rank and file.*

It wouldn't be a bad idea to come up with a few games and sports for your conculture. Baseball, for instance, supplies new meanings to *pitch, battery, walk, base, strike, ball, hit, tag, steal, home, bean.* More interestingly, it provides a rich set of metaphors: *umpire, strike out, screwball, big leagues, softball questions, out of left field, off base, hit a home run, cover all the bases, take a rain check, a ballpark figure, he threw me a curveball, did you get to third base with her?*

And to give equal time to the Brits, cricket gives us *hat trick, bowled over, sticky wicket, not cricket, stumped, hit for six.* And of course baseball terms such as *inning, single, run, umpire, out* started as cricket terms. *(Pitch* is different in cricket, though— it's a part of the field; throwing the ball is *bowling.)*

SPEECH

communicate	Lt *commūnicāre* 'make common'
	• Ger *mitteilen* 'share with' • Ch *tōngxùn* 'transmit-news'
converse	Lt *conversārī* 'turn about' > dwell
express	Old Fr *expresser* 'press out'
language	Fr *langage* < Lt *lingua* 'tongue'— cf. Gk γλῶσσα, OCS *językŭ*
	• Ger *Sprache* 'speech' • Qu *simi* 'mouth'
message	Fr *message* nomn. of 'send'
name	OE *nama*, Lt *nōmen*, OCS *imę*, Skt *nāman-* < IE
	• Lith *vardas* < 'word'
SAY	OE *secgan* < IE prob. 'point out'
	• Lt *dīcere* < 'point out' • Ir *abair* 'bring forth' • Lith *teikt* < 'bestow' • Rus сказать < 'show' • Cz *praviti* < 'guide, set right'
sign	Lt *signum* 'mark, token'
	• Gr σῆμα < 'observe' • Welsh *arwydd* 'see before' • OE *tácen* < 'point out' • Pol *znak* < 'know' • Ch *fú* 'tally' < 'add to'
signal	Rom derivation from 'sign'
	• Ger *Zeichen* ‖ *teach, token* • Ch *hào* < 'call out'
SPEAK	OE *sprecan* < 'crackle'
	• Gk λέγω < 'select' • ModGk μιλῶ < 'consort with' • It *parlare* < 'parable' • Sp *hablar* < 'story' • Sw *tala* < 'reckon, tell' • Dutch *praten* prob. imitative • Rus говорить < 'noise' • Ch *shuō* 'explain'
TALK	ME *talkien*, dim. 'tale' or 'tell'
TELL	OE *tellan* verbn. of 'tale'
term	Lt *terminus* 'boundary'
	• Ger *Ausdruck* 'out-pressing' • Ch *qīxiàn* 'period-limit'
VOICE	Lt *vox vōc-* 'voice, sound' < IE 'say'
	• Sw *röst* < 'loud talk'
WORD	OE *word*, Lt *verbum* < IE 'speak'
	• It *parola* < 'parable' • Fr *mot* < 'mutter' • Ir *focal* < 'name' • OCS *slovo* < 'hear' • Skt *çabda-* 'noise' • Ch *zì* 'compound character' < 'progeny'
+	*mute, dialect, accent, pidgin*

There may not be a word for 'language'; many languages make do with the word for 'speech' or 'tongue' (e.g. Lt *lingua*). Quechua uses *simi* 'mouth'.

We generally use *speak* when concentrating on the action, *say* when reporting the utterance; Greek uses λέγω for both. *Speak* and *talk* differ mostly in formality. *Tell* emphasizes the listener; French gets by with *dire à* 'speak to' for this— though it has a verb *raconter* for stories.

Speech acts

address	Fr *addresser* 'straighten' • Ch *chēng* 'weigh'
admit	Lt *admittere* 'send to' • Gk ὁμολογέω 'same-reason' • Fr *avouer* < 'vow' • Norse *játa* 'yes' • Ger *gestehen* 'stand' • Cz *uznati* 'recognize' • Skt *svīkṛ-* 'make one's own' • Ch *rèn* < 'know'
advise	Fr *aviser* 'make seen'
announce	Lt *adnuntiāre* 'bear news to' • Gk ἀγγέλλω < 'messenger' • Sw *kungöra* 'make known' • Latvian *sludināt* < 'rumor' • Ch *xuān* < 'spread, cast'
answer	OE *andswaru* 'swearing against' = 'legal rebuttal' • Lt *respondēre* 'pledge back' • Ir *freagra* < 'shout against' • Ger *antworten* 'against-word' • OCS *utŭvěštati* 'speak away'
argue	Fr *arguer* < 'prove, accuse'
bless	OE *blóedsian* 'mark with blood' > 'consecrate' • Lt *benedīcere* 'speak well of' • Ger *segnen* 'sign (the cross)' • Latvian *svetīt* < 'holy' • Skt *svasti-* 'well-being' • Ch *zhùfú* 'wish-benefit'
ASK	OE *áscian* < 'seek' • Lt *rogāre* < 'direct (oneself)' • Fr *demander* < 'entrust' • Sp *preguntar* 'test using a pole' • Danish *spørge* < 'track' • Ger *fragen*, OCS *prositi* < IE • Ch *wén* < 'hear'
assure	Fr *assurer* 'make safe'
CALL	Norse *kalla* • Lt *vocāre* < 'voice' • It *chiamare* < 'shout' • Fr *appeler* < 'drive to'
comment	Lt *comminisci* 'contrive, invent', from 'mind' • Ger *bemerken* 'notice by' • Ch *duǎnpíng* 'short-discuss'
complain	Fr *complaindre* < intensive of 'bewail' • Ger *beklagen* 'shout by' • Ch *bàoyuàn* 'embrace-spite'
curse	OE *cursian*, poss. < 'wrath' • Gk καταράομαι 'pray against' • Lt *maledīcere* 'say ill of' • Rum *blestema* < 'blaspheme' • Sw *förbanna* < 'forbid' • Ger *verfluchen* < 'strike, blow' • Latvian *lādēt* 'revile' < 'bark' • Ch *mà* 'scold'
declare	Lt *dēclārāre* intensive of 'make clear'

demand	Lt *dēmandāre* intensive of 'order, charge'
	• Ger *fordern* '(ask to come) forward' • Ch *xūqiú* 'need-seek'
describe	Lt *dēscrībere* 'copy off, write down'
	• Ger *schildern* 'paint' • Ch *miáoxiě* 'sketch-write'
discuss	Lt *discutere* intensive of 'shake, strike'
	• Ger *besprechen* 'speak by' • Ch. *lún* poss. ‖ 'advice'
explain	Lt *explānāre* 'smooth out, flatten'
	• Gk ἐξηγέομαι 'lead the way' • Lt *explicāre* 'unfold' • Dutch *verklaren* 'make clear' • Cz *vysvětliti* 'illuminate' • Ch *jiě* < 'loosen, untie' • Swahili *eleza* 'make intelligible'
inform	Lt *informāre* 'give form to'
	• Ger *benachrichtigen* 'by-for-righten' • Ch *tōngzhī* 'general-know'
insist	Lt *insistere* 'stand in'
	• Ch *jiānchí* 'solid-hold'
joke	Lt *jocus* 'joke, sport'
	• Fr *plaisanter* 'be pleasing' • Sp *broma* 'shipworm' • Ch *xiào-huà* 'laugh-talk'
lie	OE *lyge*, cognate to OCS *lŏža*
	• Gk ψεῦδος 'false' • Lt *mendācium* < 'defect', *mentīrī* < 'mind' • Welsh *celwydd* 'hide knowledge' • Skt *asatya-* 'untrue'
mention	Lt *mentio*, verbn. of 'mind'
question	Lt *quæstio* 'asking, inquiry'
	• Ger *Frage* < 'ask for' ‖ 'beg' • Ch *wèn* < 'hear'
reply	Lt *replicāre* 'fold again'
report	Lt *reportare* 'carry again'
	• Ch *bào* ‖ 'return, reply'
respond	Lt *respondēre* 'pledge back'
suggest	Lt *suggerere* 'carry under'
swear	OE *swerian* 'make an oath'
thank	OE *þanc* 'thought' > 'good will' > 'gratitude'
	• Gk χάρις, Lt *grātia* 'grace' • Fr *merci* < 'wages' • Breton *diolch* < 'prayer'
+	*mock, flatter, exaggerate, vow*

Speech acts are the activities that are accomplished or performed by speaking. The prototypical examples (as J.L. Austin points out) are statements that are inherent parts of a deed or ritual: *I pronounce you man and wife; you are hereby made a Fellow of our society; I'll name him Cuddles.*

But this is only a stepping stone to realizing that all utterances are **performative**. Grammarians talk about *statements, questions, imperatives,* as if language was used only to make statements of fact, ask questions, and give orders. These things are likely to be grammaticalized, but speech is used for all sorts of purposes: to reinforce relationships, to make jokes, to express emotions, to seduce, to praise. The speech acts listed above are only a sampling.

Manner

cry	Fr *crier* < Lt 'wail, scream'
	• Ch *kū* < 'lament' ‖ 'call out, shriek'
exclaim	Lt *exclāmāre* 'call out'
murmur	Lt *murmur* imitative
mutter	ME imitative
roar	OE *rárian* imitative
scream	ME *scræmen*
shout	ME *schoute* uncertain
	• Gk κράζω 'croak' • Lt *clāmāre* < 'call out' • Ger *schreien* < 'shriek' • OCS *kričati* 'wail'
sob	ME imitative
tone	Gk τόνος 'stretching, tension, pitch'
	• Ger *Klang* imitative • Ch *shēng* 'sound'
whisper	OE *hwisprian*
whistle	OE *hwislian* imitative
yell	OE ʒellan
+	*whine, irony, sarcasm*

The **manner** words deal with how the utterance (including non-linguistic ones) sounds, which in turn expresses the speaker's feelings or attitude. These may be merely descriptive, but often express speech acts, or judgments. E.g. *whisper* can suggest not only a low volume but secretiveness, even evil. *Whine* is often used as an unsympathetic description of any complaint.

Note the large number of imitative words in this domain; also consider *babble, prattle, jabber, howl, bark.*

Other things you can do with the mouth are also fair game for speech: you can *spit out* an epithet, *gasp* a cry for help, *breathe* a seductive remark.

SUBSTANCES

air Gk ἀήρ 'wind', cognate to Lt *ventus*, OE *wind*
• OE *lift* < 'loft, ceiling' • OCS *vŭzduchŭ* 'up-breath' • Ch *qì* < 'anger'

dirt Norse *drit* 'excrement'
• ModGk λερός < 'turbid' • Lt *sordēs* cognate to Ger *schwarz* 'black' • Sp *suciedad* < 'sap' • Danish *snavs* < 'food refuse' • Ger *Schmutz* < 'smut, filth' • Ch *ní* 'mud'

dust OE *dúst*; same IE root as Lt *fūmus* 'smoke'
• Ir *luaithreach* < 'ashes' • Lt *pulvis* 'dust, powder'

emerald Gk σμάραγδος
• Ch *lùbǎoshí* 'green-gem-stone'

glass OE *glæs* < Germanic ‖ 'shine, green, glow'
• Lt *vitrum* poss < 'woad' • OCS *stĭklo* < '(glass) vessel'

helium ModE 'sun element'

jewel Old Fr *joel* either from Lt 'joy' or 'play'
• Fr *bijou* < 'finger-ring' • Lt *gemma* 'bud' • Ir *seoid* 'valuable' • Breton *braoig* 'beautiful' • Ger *Kleinod* 'fine-possession' • Cz *drahokam* 'costly stone' • Ch *bǎo* 'precious'

marble Gk μάρμαρος probably from 'sparkling'

paper Gk ράπῡρος 'papyrus'
• It *carta* < 'sheet of paper' • Rus бумага < 'cotton'

powder Fr *poudre* < Lt *pulvis* 'dust'
• Ch *fěn* 'flour'

rock Old Fr *roque* uncertain
• Ir *carraig* 'rugged' • Sw *klippa* 'cliff' • Rus скала < 'split'

sand OE *sand*, cognate to Gk ψάμμος, Lt *sabulum* < IE 'crumble, crush'
• Rum *nisip* 'strewn' • Welsh *tywod* 'shore' • Lith *smėlis* < 'ground up'

silk Gk σηρικός 'of the Sēres (an eastern people)'

stone OE *stān* < IE 'stiff, solid'
• OCS *kamy* < 'edged'

stuff Old Fr *estoffe* 'equipment', uncertain

substance Lt *substantia* 'standing under'

tar OE *teru* prob. ‖ 'tree'
• Lt *pix pic-* also 'pitch' • Ch *jiāoyóu* 'burnt fat'

wood OE *widu* 'tree, copse'
• Lt *lignum* < 'collected' • Sp *madera* 'material'

> ▸ See *Metals*, p. 261, and *Elements*, p. 183.

Minerals and other substances are the prototype of things that require real-world knowledge to name. Names are generally based on

- surface properties (*saltpeter*)

- where they're found (*ammonia*)

- what you can do with it (*potter's ore*)

- how they're produced (*spirit of hartshorn*)

- what you were really looking for when you found it (*fool's gold*)

The old names are often quite charming (*the green lion, flower of zinc, butter of antimony, lunar caustic, copperas, orpiment, realgar*)— particularly when they're wrong; e.g. *black lead* isn't lead, and Paracelsus's *mercury of life* contained no mercury.

Then, of course, there's the modern chemical name, in the system introduced by Antoine Lavoisier, which you can't produce till you have a knowledge of chemistry at the 18C level.

This overview is organized historically, and peters out in the 19C, when the number of known substances explodes, and their names are generally just restatements of their chemical formula anyway.

For more see especially Robert Multhauf, *The Origins of Chemistry*. Wikipedia articles on the various substances often have a History section that's useful.

If you're trying to apply this to a conworld, consider:

- What's the overall technological level? Discovery may depend on the hottest temperatures that could be produced, or the strength of glassware or other containers.

- Who lives in the mountains, where the interesting minerals are likely to be mined?

- What was the first use? Metallurgy, painting, decoration, medicine? Each domain might think of the same substance differently.

Prehistory

The basic metals have been known since prehistory. In later times they were associated with the seven planets, and shared their symbols:

gold	sun	☉
silver	moon	☽

mercury	Mercury	☿
copper	Venus	♀
iron	Mars	♂
tin	Jupiter	♃
lead	Saturn	♄

Iron and manganese oxides were found in the caves of Lascaux, and used as pigments.

Flint or **silex** is a grayish hard stone, often with white incrustations, a very pure form of silicon dioxide. **Quartz** is a crystalline form, with many variations depending on impurities.

Natural glasses such as **obsidian** were long valued for making sharp weapons.

Clay is chemically a hydroxyl-bearing alumino-silicate with a sheet structure.

Earliest civilizations (Egypt, Mesopotamia)

Electrum is a naturally occurring alloy of gold and silver. The Egyptian name is *asem*.

Pottery was fired in pits ~ -70C and in kilns ~ -35C. The results depend on heat. Unfired clay is leather-hard but melts when exposed to water. *Low-fired* earthenware (e.g. fired in open campfires) is rather soft. At white heat, 1800° F, the sheetlike structure collapses and a hard, less porous *stoneware* is produced. And at 3000° the minerals melt into a semi-glassy state, forming a very hard, non-porous *porcelain*.

Salt is of course sodium chloride NaCl. It's not important for hunter/gatherers, but it is for agriculturalists (-60C).

Natron (Gk νίτρον = saltpeter; Egyptian *n-t-r*) is sodium sesquicarbonate Na_2CO_3. An alkaline salt, occuring naturally in dry lakes. In Egypt it was more important than ordinary salt. Along with salt and gypsum, used in embalming, cleansing, and preservation. Known as early as -50C.

Quite a few minerals later important in metallurgy were first used as **pigments**. The Egyptians used malachite and galena; later we have azurite, ochre, realgar, orpiment, stibnite. All these were obtained naturally rather than prepared chemically.

Copper was smelted from **malachite** (Gk 'mallow-like') starting ~ -40C, probably in Iran, which was rich in ores. The temperatures necessary are obtainable only with an air blast, and it seems areas of strong wind were used for furnaces (e.g. in Palestine and in Peru). Very likely metallurgy co-developed with pottery kilns. Malachite (hydrous copper carbonate) is a deep green, glassy mineral. The Egyptians used it as a pigment, notably for painting the eyes.

Gypsum [Gk γύψος] is hydrous calcium sulfate. Heated, it could be used as plaster, and was in Paris: thus **plaster of Paris**. Used as a plaster in Egypt before -34C.

Tinstone or **cassiterite** (Gk κασσίτερος 'tin') is the most common ore of tin— stannous oxide. It was known to the Phoenecians.

Bronze was smelted before -30C, probably in Iran. Bronze is an alloy of copper and tin; the latter was probably obtained from tinstone.

Lime (Calcium oxide, Lt *calx*) is an alkaline earth formed by roasting limestone or seashells; made by -25C in Babylonia. A brittle white solid, very caustic. Combined with clay and water, forms mortar. Also used in making glass and leather; and in the Middle Ages, soap and fertilizer.

Bitumen (Lt) is a type of pitch, occurring naturally in the Mideast, and used for plaster; it's basically a stew of hydrocarbons. **Naphtha** is a liquid form, which can also occur naturally.

Tar is a dark, oily substance produced by distilling wood, coal, or peat. It's used for its antiseptic properties and to protect wood. Further distillation produces **pitch**, used for waterproofing, caulking, and paving.

Steatite ('tallow-like stone') or **soap-stone** or **French chalk** is a heavy type of talc $Mg_3Si_4O_{10}(OH)_2$, grayish-green, soapy in feel. Used for writing, statues, lubrication, even as a soap. Powdered, it's **talcum powder**. *Talc* itself originally meant any shiny substance.

Artificial, non-transparent **glass** appears -25C; it's made from sand plus 2-10% lime and 15-20% soda or natron. The mixed ingredients, just before melting to form glass, are called **frit**, and this was also used (ground up) as a blue pigment— the first artificial pigment. Up to 1500 years earlier, glazed stones were produced (quartz or soapstone covered with soda or lime water and heated). Intermediate in technology is **faience**: heated quartz powder mixed with soda or lime water.

Charcoal was the usual source of carbon, a black porous substance formed by imperfect combustion of organic matter. If pure it's wholly carbon. Essential for making iron as it reduces the melting point. Also used for coloring and heating and in many (al)chemical operations. "Coal" originally meant charcoal but now implies mined coal. Earliest reference to it is in Egypt, -20C, but it was probably known earlier.

Alum (potassium aluminum sulfate) is a whitish transparent crystalline mineral salt, found naturally as a crystal efflorescence on rocks in rain-poor regions. Mordant for dyes, astringent (binding or constricting substance). Known in Egypt by -20C. Tended to be confused with vitriol.

Powdered sulfur plus lead, copper, or silver produced a blackened alloy named **niello** ('little black'), used for decoration (-8C); Homer mentions shields with colored designs produced from niello, gold, silver, and copper.

Glazes are applied to pottery about -15C.

Litharge (Gk 'stone silver') is lead oxide, PbO. It can be produced by exposing melted lead to a current of air; it's also produced in extracting gold and silver from lead ores. Gk μολύβδαινα from μόλυβδος 'lead', latinized as *molybdaena* or **plumbago**, a word later applied to graphite. Litharge was used along with antimony oxide to form **Naples yellow**, a yellow glaze, in Assyria, -8C.

Stibium— Gk στίβι, Lt *stibium*, Ar. *ithmid*, whence **antimony**. Originally used for antimony trisulphide, which in native form is **gray antimony**, later called **stibnite**, and when calcined and powdered, **black antimony** or **kohl** (the latter word is related to 'paint'). Used as a pigment. Antimony was used in the -7C to decolorize glass.

The Greeks

Identification of many of these substances is not always easy. Ancient terms may have given their names to different modern substances. And the ancients often confused similar substances, or gave different names to the same substance based on where it came from.

Greek **alchemy** was based on knowledge of metallurgy, dyeing, and medicine. Belief in the transmutability of metals was helped by a) philosophies which derived everything from the basic elements anyway, and b) none too firm a grasp on the differences between metals or on what exactly an alloy was.

The basic goal was to remove a property from a substance, creating a blank slate for adding others. E.g. lead is dense, soft, grey; gold is dense, soft, and yellow. All that should be necessary is to change the color!

Amid all this silliness, a real insight— or good guess— from Plato, who held that oxides were produced by the weathering of metal.

Sulfur (= **brimstone**) is a greenish-yellow substance found abundantly in volcanic regions. Occurs naturally as crystal. Highly flammable. "Flower of sulfur" is powdered sulfur.[13]

Cinnabar is red or crystalline mercuric sulphide, the most important ore of mercury. Because it was red, it was often used to make "gold". Known by 1612 to be made of 'quick-silver' and 'brimstone'. As a pigment, known as **vermilion** (the name comes from 'worm' but refers to cochineal) and valued for its scarlet color. Mercury can be formed from cinnabar by heating.

Orpiment or [**yellow**] **arsenic** (Lt *auri pigmentum*, Gk ἀρσενικόν) is trisulfide of arsenic As_2S_3: a bright yellow mineral which made a good pigment.

Realgar (Arabic *rehj al-ghār* 'powder of the cave'; Gk/Lt *sandaraca*), or ruby sulfur or red arsenic or red orpiment; arsenic disulfide, As_2S_2. Occurs as a native mineral; known as a poison.

White lead or **cerusse** or **calx of lead** is a lead carbonate and lead hydrate $PbCO_3 \cdot Pb(OH)_2$, used as a pigment and medicine (e.g. for eye ointments). Seems to have a waxy quality to it. White lead doesn't occur in nature; rather, it's created by corroding lead with vinegar.

Similarly *ios*, copper acetate, **verdigris** or **verdet** 'little green', was produced by corroding copper with vinegar. Used as a pigment and medicine.

Marble (Gk 'sparkling') is chemically a crystalline form of limestone.

The Romans

Petroleum ('rock oil', a hydrocarbon stew) has been known from ancient times— it's mentioned in Pliny. It occurs naturally on the surface in some rocks and bodies of water, especially in the Middle East. A cute later name was **Seneca oil**, from the Indian tribe which collected it.

Argentite or **silver-glance**, silver sulfide, was mentioned by Pliny.

Chalcopyrite is also mentioned by Pliny as a copper ore. It's an iron-copper mixture, normally found below the normal sources of malachite, which indicates deeper mining going on by this time.

---

[13] In medieval usage *flower* could be used for the best part of anything— the *flower of chivalry*. Refined grain was *flower (of wheat)*, now spelled *flour*.

Pyrites, mentioned by Pliny, could be used for chalcopyrite or for flint (hence its name, from 'fire'); but in modern times it's used for iron sulfide FeS_2, also called **fool's gold**. It's a very common mineral, a yellowish grey in color— to me it looks like nickel. In ancient times it was mined mostly to get the copper or gold nearby; today it's mined as a source of sulfur. Roasted, the sulfur is driven off and is recovered in water as sulfuric acid.

Galena (Lt) or **potter's ore** is the common lead ore, lead sulfide. The source for lead of course, but also used in glazing pots. Extraction is particularly easy: you can toss it in a campfire and pick up the lead fragments later.

Calamine or **cadmia** (zinc carbonate) was used, with charcoal and copper, to make **brass**, starting in Roman times. The zinc existed only as a vapor and was not yet known as a metal.

Minium was used for cinnabar or for lead oxide, used as a pigment. Multhauf identifies it as Pb_3O_4 and notes it can be obtained from litharge by further oxidation; it's not certain if this was realized in ancient times. Dioscurides knew it could be made by heating white lead, or from heating certain stones occurring with silver ore.

Vitriol (from 'glass') or **copperas** (from 'coppery water'): a protosulfate of copper, iron, or zinc. Generated from the weathering of pyrites; but run off with water except in special circumstances, as in mines. Three types:

- **Green vitriol**, or simply vitriol, or (confusedly) green copperas, proto-sulfate of iron, used in dyeing, tanning, and making inks (in alchemy called the "green lion"). Gathered from iron mines; later (16C) formed by weathering pyrite.

- **Blue** vitriol is of copper; it occurs in the drainage of copper mines, and is also called **chalcanthum** (Gk 'copper flower'); this term is also sometimes applied to the iron form.

- **White** vitriol is of zinc.

Potash is an alkaline substance formed by leaching the ashes of land plants and evaporating the solution in iron pots— thus the name. Used to make soap. Chemically this is a crude form of potassium carbonate.

An **alkali** is Arabic *al-qalīy* ('roasted'), originally the roasted ashes of certain marine plants, producing sodium carbonate, also in this sense **soda** or **soda ash**; used in making glass and soap. It later was used for any caustic substance which could make soap and neutralize acids.

Lye, sodium hydroxide, also **caustic soda**, is made from a precipitation reaction of lime and soda ash. Pliny lists it, made from lime and natron. As a strong base, it will dissolve grease and hair. It was at first (by the 3C) used only to make soap.

A **lodestone** ('way-stone') is a magnetic iron oxide. In ancient times often called *magnesia* 'Magnesian stone'

Pliny mentions **opium** (from a Gk dim. of 'vegetable juice'), though I'm not sure it was used in its present significance. The OED mentions the word from the 12C.

Distillation— boiling a substance and letting it condense in another vessel, removing impurities— was known in the ancient world, going back to -30C devices used for making perfumes. It was greatly improved in Alexandria, 1C; Maria the Jewess is credited with inventing much of the classical distillation apparatus, though Multhauf thinks it couldn't have been very effective if the alchemists never discovered alcohol or the mineral acids. Or it could be that the failure derives from an excessive interest in sulfur and the arsenic sulfides— the later alchemists were more interested in alums and salts.

Calcination is reduction of a solid to a powder via heat. This produced a **calx**, taken to be the essential form of the mineral, though actually it's usually an oxide.

Fluorspar is calcium fluoride CaF_2, of various colors, and usually crystallized. **Fluor** was first a term for a class of minerals, lighter than gems and used in smelting; and later applied to fluorspar in particular.

Manganese is a black mineral, manganese oxide, later called **pyrolusite**, used in glass-making. The name is a corruption of *magnesia* (which however meant either magnets or talc) and it's also called **black magnesia**.

In the 3C **gilding** was done by painting an object with gold **amalgam** (the term originally was any softened metal, but came to mean a compound with mercury). Heat then removes the mercury. Or, you dip the object in a molten alloy of lead and gold, then corrode it, which removes the lead. The latter process is older, and was also known in the Americas.

White arsenic, later called arsenolite and **flowers of antimony**, is arsenic trioxide As_2O_3. A white mineral, very poisonous. Obtained by roasting one of the arsenic sulfides, orpiment or realgar. Known to the Hellenistic alchemists, and used in the Renaissance as a medicine.

Arsenic, antimony, and bismuth are similar in properties, and all their compounds were not really disentangled till the 19C. The metals themselves were often mistaken for lead, and the oxides with sulfur.

China

1C: The **blast furnace** was known in China, 15 centuries before Europe. Used to produce high-quality cast iron, as opposed to the impure wrought iron produced in primitive furnaces.

By the 4C the Chinese could distill **alcohol** from wine; done in Europe in 12C.

Gunpowder is saltpeter, charcoal and sulfur, produced by 1050.

Saltpeter (potassium nitrate) or **niter** is found naturally as a white crystalline substance with a salty taste. Used in gunpowder and medicine. Lt *sal petræ* 'salt of stone', since it occurs as an incrustation on rocks. Also formed by evaporating certain earths containing animal refuse. Some historians say the Babylonians knew it, but the identification isn't supported by archeology. The Arabs and Europeans got it in the 13C.

Porcelain (clay of high glassiness requiring immense heat) was first made by the Chinese in the -1C, and European imitations appeared in the 16C.

Arabs

Arab medicine relied much more on mineral than on botanical preparations. Just about all the minerals known were used somehow— e.g. antimony was used for eye diseases.

The Arabs maintained that metals were a compound of mercury and sulfur (or abstract essences given these names). Lawrence Principe points out that this may have been based on observation: powdered iron and copper emit a sulfurous smell when burned, and melted tin and lead look much like liquid mercury. The fact that the common metals corrode or rust was also taken as evidence that they were compounds.

By the 9C the Arabs had *nusadir,* **sal ammoniac** (ammonium chloride NH_4Cl), from distilling hair with salt and urine. The OED says they used camel dung from the temple of Jupiter Ammon (thus the Latin name); it also occurs naturally in volcanic deposits (e.g. in the Tarim basin). A hard white opaque crystalline salt, useful in coloring and dissolving metals.

Borax is a white salt, sodium tetraborate; it occurs naturally in central Asia in saline deposits. **Tincal** is an unrefined form, greasy greenish or yellowish crystals, found in lakes or in the earth.

In the 9C it was discovered how to manufacture cinnabar from mercury and sulfur.

Antimony was isolated as an element. It's a flaky crystalline metallic substance, bluish white. Presumably made from black antimony or kohl, and originally called **regulus of antimony**. A regulus ('little king') is the purer or metallic part of a mineral, which sinks to the bottom of your crucible.

Mercury was sublimed with vitriol and salt by the Spanish Islamic alchemists to produce **corrosive sublimate** (mercuric chloride, $HgCl_2$). A white crystalline substance and a strong acrid poison. One use was to eat away dead flesh.

Medieval

Medieval alchemists were not so much interested in Galenic compounds, as in "essences" and "elixirs" formed by distillation.[14] The urge to decompose substances was instrumental in the development of chemistry.

In the 12C Europeans got round to distilling **alcohol**, called *aqua vitæ* 'water of life' or *aqua ardens* 'burning water'. Some identified it with *quintessence*, the fifth element. Gold dissolved in it produced potable gold, believed to have healing powers.

The **mineral acids** were known in Europe in the 13C, and revolutionized chemistry. They couldn't be produced till distillation apparatus was improved (for alcohol, cooling was key), and glassware was stronger!

- Nitric acid, HNO_3, **aqua fortis**, is a clear liquid with a very pungent smell and acrid taste. It separates gold and silver (and indeed dissolves silver, though not gold). Said to be isolated by Geber, who however is probably not the Arab Jābir but a European taking his name. Distilled from vitriol and saltpeter.

- Sulfuric acid H_2SO_4 was **vitriolic acid** or **oil of vitriol**. Distilled from vitriol or alum.

---

[14] A ξήριον was originally a healing powder, then an agent of transmutation. It was Arabized as *al-iksīr*, and came back to Europe as *elixir*.

- Hydrochloric acid (HCl) was **muriatic acid** or **spirit of salt**. From *muria* 'brine', formed by heating salt with a solution of sulfuric acid.

- **Aqua regia**, a mixture of hydrochloric and nitric acids, could dissolve gold (but not silver).

Sphalerite (from Gk 'deceptive'; the name is modern), **blende** (German 'deceptive'), or zinc sulfide is the most common ore of zinc. The disapprobatory names come because it resembles galena, but yields no lead.

Zinc or **spelter** (both words are obscure). A hard bluish-white metal, recovered by heating zinc ores with carbon, first done in India in the 13C, and in Europe in the 16C.

Red precipitate or **calx of mercury** or mercuric oxide (HgO) was first formed (13C) by gentle heating of mercury in air, or by the thermal decomposition of mercury nitrate. The alchemists' goal was to 'redden' mercury, presumably to turn it into gold. Later important in medicine, e.g. as an 18C treatment for syphilis.

Substances known to Chaucer:

> alkali, alum, argol, Armenian bole, arsenic, ashes, borax, brimstone, bull's gall, burnt bones, chalk, clay, dung, egg white, hair, iron scales, litharge, oil of tartar, prepared salt, quicklime, quicksilver, ratsbane, sal ammoniac, saltpeter, silver, urine, vitriol, waters albificated ('whitened'), waters rubificated ('reddened'), wort (a stage in producing beer), yeast

Armenian bole is more usually **bole armoniac**; a "soft friable fatty earth of a pale red color."

Argol is crude potassium bitartrate, the unpurified **cream of tartar**, which was used as a medicine (and, today, in baking powder). It's found caked on the sides of wine casks.

Salt of tartar is potassium carbonate, a transparent white powder $KClO_3$, used in making glass, pigments, ceramics, and soaps. It liquefies if exposed to air. A saturated solution of this is called **oil of tartar**. It was known in the 17C at least. (Potash has the same formula, so I suppose this is just a purified form.) It could also be produced by burning tartar (wine lees).

Black lead, also called **plumbago** and now graphite, is a grayish-black shiny substance, mostly carbon with a little iron, and used for drawing and for polishing iron.

Renaissance

Tin-glass, later called bismuth, a reddish-white metal, found pure and in ores (16C). Brittle and easily melted; similar to antimony. Used for alloys; oxides and salts used in medicine (often confused with antimony and arsenic). It occurs native, or in its common ores, bismuth oxide (Bi_2O_3) or **bismuth ocher** or **bismite** (yellowish white, earthy or flaky), and bismuth sulfide (Bi_2S_3) or **bismuth glance** or **bismuthinite** (a lead-grey lustrous mineral, hard to tell from stibnite, antimony sulfide).

Early 16C: **calomel** or **sweet precipitate**, mercurous chloride Hg_2Cl_2, produced. A yellowish-white powder much used in medicine (it's much less caustic than mercuric chloride). (The name means 'beautiful black' and has various explanations, the most likely referring to a stage in its manufacture.)

Cobalt was named for a demon, because of its uselessness and un-healthiness— it often contained sulfur or arsenic. The term first meant the ores of the metal. The most common ore is an arsenide of cobalt (CoAsS) called **cobalt glance**, **cobaltine**, **cobaltite** or **silver-white cobalt**— silvery but not silver, thus considered enchanted by kobolds.

Copper-nickel or **niccolite** or **nickeline**, a compound of arsenide and nickel was named for its disappointing resemblance to copper.

Wolfram is a tungstate of iron and manganese. It received attention mostly for the problem of separating it from useful metals like tin.

The word **tungsten** (Sw. 'heavy stone') or ponderous stone originally referred to calcium tungstate.

Paracelsus is a major name in the 16C; he focused on medical uses. An advance was to localize diseases; previously all diseases were problems of whole body. He had "three principles" of salt, sulfur, and mercury.

Paracelsus had a remedy he named **laudanum**, whose recipe is obscure. It was widely taken as, and came to mean, a less caustic preparation of opium.

He also obtained **butter of antimony**, antimony trichloride, by subliming antimony. He got its origin wrong, calling it **mercury of life**. Later we find other butters— all anhydrous chlorides.

A contemporary, Cordus, distilled **ether** (diethyl ether, $C_4H_{10}O$) from sulfuric acid and alcohol. It was sometimes (mistakenly) called **sulfuric ether**. Paracelsus's "sweet oil of sulfur" also seems to be ether.

Antimony (sulfide) was a popular remedy, often used as a purgative. The confusion of antimony with arsenic and the use of the latter by unscrupulous or uninformed physicians contributed to the disrepute and sometimes prohibition of antimony remedies.

Van Helmont (d. 1644) put emphasis on quantitative and careful methods— e.g. he grew trees in a jar, weighing the soil first, allowing him to conclude that only water was needed for growth. He didn't consider the air; still, it was a real experiment with an emphasis on control. He invented the word *gas*.

In the 17C, **spirit of hartshorn** was obtained from, oddly enough, harts' horns. This was an aqueous solution of ammonia; also called *aquila cœlestis* 'the celestial eagle'.

A spirit obtained from distilling urine (which seems to have been done as early as the 14C), was later (early 18C) called **volatile alkali**; it turned out to be ammonia itself.

1620: Sala synthesized sal ammoniac from 'volatile salt of urine' (ammonia) and 'spirit of salt' (hydrochloric acid).

1649: Elemental **arsenic** isolated. This can be done by reducing the oxide with **coke** (the impure carbon residue left by roasting coal— heating without air).

1661: Boyle's *Sceptical Chymist* attacks 4-element and Parcelsian doctrines, e.g. pointing out that not all substances can be divided into all 4 Aristotelian elements. The old theory of elements had to be destroyed before a new concept could emerge. He found that "syrup of violets" changed color when touched to an acid or a base— forerunner to litmus paper. Boyle also used the new air pump to investigate combustion; linked pressure and volume: Boyle's law.

1674: Mayow shows that a candle or a mouse removes the "nitrous part" of the air and loses pressure ("elasticity"). This did not refer to nitrogen but to another proposed simplification into overall principles, derived from the idea of gunpowder, hypothesized to cause lightning and combustion.

1675: Hennig Brand, an alchemist, extracts **phosphorus** from urine. (He boiled urine to a paste, then heated it, causing phosphorus to form by sublimation.) This produces **white phosphorus**, a waxy solid that burns (glowing blue-green) when exposed to air; it's quite poisonous. Roasting it produces the powdery, less toxic **red phosphorus**. It glows in the dark; thus the name ('light bringer'). At first it was considered just one of several glowing substances, such as **Bolognian phosphorus** or barium sulfide, which glows under calcination (1602), or heated nitrates or sulfides of calcium.

1675: **Epsom salts** (chiefly magnesium sulfate) isolated from the mineral water of Epsom. Seidlitz in Bohemia has similar salts.

1693: **Molybdena** referred to molybdenum disulfide, the principle ore of molybdenum, occurring in bluish-grey crystals. The name comes from a confusion with ores of lead; it also closely resembles graphite. Now usually **molybdenite**.

Crystalline ammonium carbonate was first called **salt of hartshorn** (attested 1698) and later called **smelling salts**.

17C: It's noticed that iron placed in copper vitriol "turns into copper": the solution becomes iron vitriol and copper precipitates. By the end of the century it's understood that copper and iron participles are exchanging places, and it's said that iron has a greater "affinity" for the acid.

17C: Various nitrates (of tin, mercury, copper, lead, silver, and calcium) produced. These were at first called vitriols; later, niters.

18th century

Chemists were interested in "elective affinities" and created tables showing what reacts with what. It wasn't yet realized that mass, temperature, and pressure have an effect too.

1702: **Narcotic salt of vitriol**, later boric acid H_3BO_3, distilled by Homberg from borax and vitriol. Springs of **sedative salt** discovered in Italy later in the century proved to be the same substance.

Stahl (d. 1734) created **phlogiston theory**. There were three invisible earths or elements; they formed secondary principles like gold, silver, and many calxes (=oxides); these in turn produced higher "mixts" like salts. He thought of oxidation not as a metal gaining oxygen but as a metal *losing* phlogiston. It was later noticed that calxes are heavier; some saved the theory by giving phlogiston negative weight! Stahl also distinguished inorganic and organic chemistry and thus nixed the old idea that metals grow in the earth like plants.

Jargon or **zircon**, a silicate of zirconium, was found in tetragonal crystals of various colors. Probably known for a long time in its place of origin, Ceylon.

1730s: Brandt isolates **cobalt**, a reddish-grey brittle metal, much like nickel.

1735: Platinum is isolated. It was discovered by the Spanish in the Americas, but seems to have been generally recognized as a metal only at this time.

Heavy spar or **barytes** or **barite** (words all referring to its density), barium sulfate. Used in medicine and later as a white paint.

Feldspar ('field shiny-metal') is the most abundant aluminosilicate (containing also potassium, sodium and calcium), the commonest form of aluminum. A white or pink quartzy mineral, pretty much omnipresent. (The principal rock of the Earth's crust is **granite**, composed of feldspar and quartz with some other minerals. The name is Italian ('grained') but the substance was undoubtedly known in ancient times.)

1754: Earth of alum, later called **argil** and then **alumina**; aluminum oxide. A white insoluble substance, the chief part of clay, and found crystallized as sapphire.

1754: Nickel is isolated from copper-nickel. A hard but malleable silvery-white lustrous mineral.

1754: Fixed air (carbon dioxide CO_2), made from alkaline substances by solution in acids or by calcination, was first isolated by Black.

1756: Black shows that potash is really a compound. Remove the CO_2 and you get a powerfully caustic substance, hard white and brittle, potassium hydroxide KOH, which is what chemists now mean by '**potash**'— also called **caustic potash**.

1758: Pitchblende, a native uranium oxide, was found in blackish pitch-like masses, sometimes crystalline. *Blende* is German 'deceit', because it looked like galena but wasn't.

1760s: "Fixed air" (CO_2) was shown to make plants thrive; in the 1780s plants were found to give off "dephlogisticated air" (O_2).

Lavoisier (d. 1794) revolutionized chemistry. He improved equipment, showed that demonstrations of "water turning to earth" was due to leaching of glass from the apparatus, understood the transition of water to vapor and thus the three states of matter. Understood oxidation as "fixing" of air (thus the increase in weight).

Priestly (d. 1804) performed experiments on air, producing over 20 "new airs", including what he called **dephlogisticated air** (oxygen), 1774; the Swede Scheele isolated it in 1772 and called it **fire air**.

1774: Manganese was isolated from its oxides (and now takes their name). It's grayish white and of almost no use in metallic form.

It was known that mercury could be produced from mercuric oxide just by heating, without charcoal (a difficulty for phlogistonism). The air produced is of course **oxygen;** Lavoisier invented the name (1778) on the ground that it was the key element of acids— incorrect as it turns out. But he produced a theory explaining oxidation, acid formation (oxygen reacting with nonmetals), and even the internal heat of organisms.

The non-respirable part of air (**nitrogen** 'niter-forming') was first called **azote** 'non-life-(supporting)' or **mofette**, which however is also a term for volcanic exhalations of CO_2.

1778: **Molybdenum** was isolated from molybdena. A brittle, hard to melt silver-white metal which rapidly oxidizes.

1782: **Tellurium**, a tin-white brittle substance, is found, occurring naturally in crystals.

1783: **Tungsten** isolated from calcium tungstate (previously called tungsten) and/or wolfram. A heavy grey metal.

Flower of zinc = zinc oxide; appeared in large quantities in the flues of brass furnaces.

1780s: **Water** determined to be hydrogen + oxygen. Several did the experiment but Lavoisier interpreted it correctly. In 1789, water was synthesized using an electric spark. He also produced a new theory of acids and largely generated today's system of naming elements and compounds (replacing a mishmash of names). He invented terms such as *sulfate* and *oxide* and defined *elements* as things that couldn't be decomposed further.

Another of his few mistakes: Lavoisier called chlorine **oxygenated muriatic acid**— muriatic acid being hydrochloric acid.

See p. 184 for Lavoisier's list of elements.

He didn't make the alkalis (potash and soda) elements— he suspected they were compounds, like ammonia. Davy indeed decomposed them in 1808.

Hydrogen was called **inflammable air**, produced when a metal was treated with an acid.

1785: Ammonia (NH_3) decomposed into nitrogen and hydrogen. Obtained from sal ammoniac, from which it takes its name.

1787: Guyton comes up with name **carbon**, from Lt *carbo* 'charcoal'.

1789: **Zirconium**, a black powder or a grayish crystalline substance, isolated from zircon.

1789: **Uranium** was isolated from pitchblende or other ores. A rare, heavy, grayish metallic element. Its radioactivity wasn't recognized for a century.

1791: **Titanium**, an iron-grey lustrous powder, isolated from **rutile** ('reddish') = titanium dioxide.

1792: Richter quantifies acidity/baseness by seeing how much of what substances neutralize others.

1797: **Chromium** isolated from its brilliantly-colored compounds. What we call chrome these days is usually chromium plating.

1797: Yttria or a yttrium oxide, a white powder obtained from **gadolinite**, a silicate of yttrium. Very soon decomposed into **yttrium**.

1798: **Beryllium** or **glucinum** isolated from its oxide, **glucina** ('sweetish') or **beryllia** (from the gem beryl).

19th century

Dalton (d. 1844) is known for the idea of **atomism**. He explained ratios of substances and their compounds as arising from the combination of integral numbers of atoms. He assumed the smallest integers first and thus first misinterpreted water as HO and ammonia as NH. This of course led to the wrong atomic weights, but the idea was good.

Dalton created a theory of static gases based on sizes of particles; this was superseded in 1850s by the kinetic theory of gases.

1800: Invention of **battery** or **pile**, literally a pile of zinc and silver disks. Many experiments with electrolysis followed.

Nitrous oxide (laughing gas) was investigated by Davy (1800s); it was used as an anesthetic in 1846.

1803: **Cerium** isolated, named after the recent discovery of Ceres. It was the first of the lanthanides, which are all so chemically close and hard to separate that it would take a century to isolate them all.

1808: Davy isolates **calcium** (a gold-like but highly oxidizing metal—expose it to air and you get lime), **strontium** and **barium** from alkaline earths. (Barium, a white metallic element, comes from **baryta**, the protoxide of barium; strontium from **strontia**, strontium monoxide.) Renamed oxymuriatic acid *chlorine*. He isolated **potassium** from potash, 1807.

1813: Berzelius introduces element abbreviations and subscripts; varied his system over time. In the 1840s Thomas Graham culminated a century of graphical experimentation by creating the chemical equation.

Berzelius also understood that two volumes of H to one of O are needed to synthesize water, and so corrects the formula for water to H_2O.

1815: Prout notices that atomic weights are all close to whole numbers and suggests that all "elements" are compounds of hydrogen.

1825: **Aluminum** was isolated by Wohler— another book says Oersted— by reduction of aluminum chloride with potassium dissolved in mercury.

1859: The spectroscope is invented; used to identify new elements like **thallium** and **rubidium**; and in 1868, based on the solar spectrum, **helium**.

1869: Dmitri Mendeleev noticed that the elements listed by atomic order displayed certain patterns, which led him to create the **periodic table** (p. 185). He boldly left gaps for elements that 'should' exist that hadn't yet been discovered; chemists vindicated him by duly finding them in nature.

> ▸ See *Elements*, p. 183, for the elements per se, and *Physics,* p. 293, for where the periodicity comes from.

TIME

abrupt	Lt *abruptus* 'broken off'
AFTER	OE *æfter* 'farther off'
age	Fr < late Lt **ætāticum* 'aginess' • Gk ἡλικία < 'same (age)' • Ger *alter* 'oldness' • Dutch *leeftijd* 'life-time' • OCS *vŭzdrastŭ* < 'growth'
ago	ME 'gone'
already	ME 'all ready'
ancient	Fr *ancien* < Lt *ante* 'before' • Ger *uralt* 'origin-old' • Ch *gŭ* < 'old'
brief	Lt *brevis* 'short'
century	Lt *centuria* 'a hundred (things)'
current	Lt *currens* 'running'
early	OE *árlíce* 'ere-like' • ModGk ἐνωρίς 'in time' • Fr *tôt* 'toasted' • Sp *temprano* 'timely' • Ger *früh* < 'before' • OCS *rano* 'morning' • Ch *zăo* prob. < 'begin, make'
elder	OE *eldra* 'older'
ever	OE *ǽfre* uncertain
final	Lt *fīnālis* 'of the end' • Ger *letzt* < 'laziest' • Ch *zuìhoù* 'most-behind'
fresh	OE *fersc* < Germanic • Ch *xiān* ‖ 'new'
future	Lt *futūrus* 'what is to be' • Ch *jiānglái* 'soon-come'
haste	Old Fr < Germanic 'violent, impetuous'
hurry	ModE, possibly imitative • Gk σπεύδω < 'press' • Fr *se dépêcher* 'dispatch oneself' • Ir *brostaigh* 'incite' • Latvian *traukt* 'strike down'
immediate	late Lt *immediātus* 'with no mediate' = 'directly' • Lt *statim* 'standing' • It *subito* 'suddenly' • Ir *láithreach* 'on the spot' • Sw *strax* 'straight' • Ger *sofort* 'so forth' • Rus тотчас 'that hour' • Ch *lì* 'stand'
instant	Lt *instans* 'standing in' • Ger *Augenblick* 'eye-glance' • Ch *shùnjiān* 'blink-interval'
LAST	OE *latost* 'latest' • Gk τελευταῖος 'end' • Lt *ultimus* 'beyondest' • Fr *dernier* < 'from behind' • OCS *poslědĭnĭjĭ* 'following' • Ch *chíjiŭ* 'hold-long'

late(r)	OE *late* 'slowly, in time, afterward'
	• Fr *tard* < 'slow' • Ir *deireanach* 'end' • Ger *spät* prob. < 'drawn out' • OCS *pozdě* < 'after'
meanwhile	ModE; 'mean' < Lt 'of the middle'
MOMENT	Lt *mōmentum* 'motion, balance, moment, influence'
month	OE *mónað* < 'moon' < 'measure'
NEW	OE *níwe*, cognate to Lt *novus*, Gk νέος, OCS *novŭ*
	• Ch *xīn* poss. ‖ 'alive, green'
next	OE *néahst* superlative of 'nigh'
NOW	OE *nú*, cognate to Lt *nunc*, Gk νῦν
	• Fr *maintenant* 'in the hand' • Sp *ahora* < 'this hour' • Breton *brema* 'time-here' • Rus теперь < 'first' • Ch *xiànzài* 'presently' < 'appearing'
OLD	OE *ald* < 'nourished, grown up'
	• Gk παλαιός < 'long ago, far away', ἀρχαιός 'beginning' • Lt *vetus* prob. < 'year' • Ir *críonna* 'wise' • OCS *starŭ* < 'big' < 'standing'
past	ME 'passed'
present	Lt *præsens* 'be before = be at hand'
soon	OE *sóna* 'immediately'
	• Gk τάχα 'quick' • It *presto* 'ready' • Fr *bientôt* 'well early' • Ir *go gairid* 'shortly' • Ger *bald* 'bold' • Ch *bùjiŭ* 'not long'
STILL	OE *stille* 'quiet' > 'unchanging' > 'continuing'
sudden	Lt *subitus* < 'go under'
swift	OE *swift* < 'swept'
TIME	OE *tíma*
	• Lt *tempus* prob. < 'stretch' • Lith *laikas* 'remainder' • OCS *vrěmę* < 'turning' • Ch *shí* < 'what is proceeding'
week	OE *wice* < 'change'
	• Lt *septimāna* 'of seven' • Welsh *wythnos* 'eight nights' • OCS *nedělja* 'no work' > 'Sunday' > 'week' • Ch *zhōu* 'circuit'
YEAR	OE ʒéar, cognate to Gk ὥρα 'hour'
	• Gk ἔτος < IE • Lt *annus* poss < 'go, wander' • Rus год 'period'
YET	OE ʒíet
young	OE ʒeong, cognate to Lt *juvenis*
	• Gk νέος 'new' • Rus моп党ой > 'tender' • Ch *qīngnián* 'green year'
+	*period, era, permanent, eternal, temporary*

It's common in European languages for *old* to be the opposite of both *young* and *new*. But Indonesian, to give just one example, has separate words for not-young (*tua*) and not-new (*lama*).

Ancient Egyptian had two words for 'always' or 'eternity'— *ḏt* for the unchanging, *nḥḥ* for the cyclical. Thus, the Nile always flows (*ḏt*) but the Sun always rises (*nḥḥ*).

How do you divide up time? Astronomy provides some benchmarks (days, months, seasons, years); this could get interesting if you have multiple suns or moons, or a slow-rotating inner planet.

Some novels and video games used invented day and month names— a relatively painless way to display your conlang, though don't count on readers to remember the order.

By the TIME IS SPACE metaphor, words relating to space can be applied to time (*short, long; close to 4:00; in summertime; over time*). But time can get its own words instead.

An sf society may routinely deal with multiple planets, and thus need a way of keeping apart multiple worlds' days and years. Charles Stross is fond of using *megaseconds* (11.57 days); a *gigasecond* is 31.7 years.

The day

afternoon	ME 'after noon'
dawn	ME prob. < Norse *dagn* 'day'
	• Gk ἕως, Lt *aurōra* < IE • It *alba* < 'white' • Sw *gryning* 'graying' • Ger *Morgenrot* 'morning red' • OCS *zora* 'shine' • Ch *límíng* 'much bright'
DAY	OE *dæʒ* poss. < 'heat, summer'
	• Lt *dīes*, OCS *dĭnĭ* < IE 'shine, heaven' • Old Persian *rauča* < 'light' • Ch *rì* 'sun'
evening	OE *æfnung* nomn. of 'move toward even', cf. Ger. *Abend*, cognate to *after*
	• Lt *vesper* < IE ‖ *west* • It *sera* < 'late' • Sp *tarde* < 'slow' • Ch *wǎnshàng* 'night-at'
hour	Gk ὥρα 'season, hour'
	• Sw *timme* 'time' • Ger *Stunde* < 'stand' • Pol *godzina* 'period'
minute	Lt *minūta* abbr. of 'first small part [division by 60]'
morning	ME *morwening* 'morn' + '-ing', cognate to words meaning 'dark' or 'light'!
	• Lt *mātūtinus* < goddess *Mātūta*, cognate to 'mature' • OCS *utro* < 'dawn' • Ch *chén* < 'stir'

NIGHT	OE *niht*, cognate to Lt *nox noct-*
second	Lt *secundus* 'following' > '2nd' > '2nd division by 60'
today	OE *tó dæʒ* 'to day'
	• Fr *aujourd'hui* 'to the day of today' • Ger *heute* < 'this day'
tomorrow	ME 'to morning'
	• Gk αὔριον < 'dawn' • Fr *demain* < 'of morning' • Breton *arc'hoaz* 'on again' • Ch *míngtiān* 'bright-day'
tonight	ME 'to night'
+	*dusk, noon, midnight, yesterday*

The day may start at any time, not just midnight; and there's nothing sacred about 24 hours, though this is a nicely divisible number.

Do the hours track with the sun (and thus vary in length by season) or are they fixed? Does everyone use local time, or standard time based on longitude? This may depend on clock technology, or even transportation— it was the railroad that drove the adoption of standard time.

Though the 60-fold division of hours into minutes and minutes into seconds dates back to Babylon, before accurate clocks were available ordinary people could hardly care much about them. The first mechanical clocks had only an hour hand.

The ancient Hindus applied the 60/60 pattern at the day level: i.e. a day was divided into 60 *ghaṭikas* (each 12 minutes long), the *ghaṭika* into 60 *palas*, the *pala* into 60 *vipalas*.

The Roman day was divided into 24 hours, which were simply numbered from dawn and dusk; e.g. *hōra secunda* was the 2nd hour. Early Christians prayed at the 3rd, 6th, and 9th hours after dawn— *tertia*, *sexta*, and *nōna*, which became the ecclesiastical *tierce, sext, nones*. The latter word gave us *noon,* with a curious shift earlier in the day.

English distinguishes *afternoon / evening / night* where Spanish has only *tarde / noche* (roughly separated by sunset). We can refer to the events of yesterday as 'last night', but in German if something happened *gestern Nacht* it woke you up. In Spanish *buenas noches* can be used as a greeting after dusk, but in French it has to be *bonsoir*; you say *bonne nuit* only when going to bed.

Latin American Spanish uses *ahora* for both 'today' and 'now'. Though as there is little urgency in the Latin American now, there's also *ahorita* meaning 'right now'.

Bengali uses the same word *kalke* for both 'yesterday' and 'tomorrow'— the meaning is clear from the tense used. And *poršu* means either the day before yesterday or the day after tomorrow.

The week

The **Babylonians** and Jews both used a seven-day week. The seven-day week is close to being a quarter of a lunar month— but not quite, as the lunar cycle is 29.53 days. The Babylonians added a day or two to the end of each month so that the next month, and week, began on a new moon.

The **Etruscans** had a week of eight days, inherited by the Romans; every eight days came the *nundinae*, the market day. The seven-day week began to be used in the early Empire, and was made official by Constantine.

The **Greeks** associated the days of the week with heavenly bodies and their associated gods, and the Romans and the Germanic peoples adapted the system to their own pantheons:

Greek	Roman	Germanic
Helios	Sol	Sun
Selene	Luna	Moon
Ares	Mercury	Tiw
Hermes	Mars	Woden (Odin)
Zeus	Jupiter	Thor
Aphrodite	Venus	Frige
Chronos	Saturn	(Saturn)

In the Romance lands, Christians renamed Sunday for the Lord (e.g. Italian *domenica*), and associated Saturday with the Hebrew Sabbath (*sabato*). The Portuguese, Greeks, and Slavs piously removed the references to pagan gods, simply numbering the days.

The **French** Revolution briefly used a ten-day week (*décade*), with the days named *primidi, duodi, tridi, quartidi, quintidi, sextidi, septidi, octidi, nonidi, décadi.* In the 1930s the Soviets tried a five-day and then a six-day week.

The **Chinese** week (*xún*) was ten days long; with a bit of wrangling three weeks fit into a month. A seven-day week was also used for astrology, probably influenced by Middle Eastern models:

sun	日	*rì*
moon	月	*yuè*

fire / Mars	火	*huǒ*
water / Mercury	水	*shuǐ*
wood / Jupiter	木	*mù*
metal / Venus	金	*jīn*
earth / Saturn	土	*tǔ*

On **Bali**, there are concurrent weeks of 2, 3, 5, and 7 days, giving a cycle of 210 days.

Dwiwara	Menga, Pept
Triwara	Pasah, Beteng, Kajeng
Pancawara	Paing, Pon, Wage, Keliwon, Umanis
Saptawara	Redite, Coma, Anggara, Buda, Wraspati, Sukra, Saniscara

As any fool can see, the day named *Pept Beteng Wage Redite* can only be the 113th day of the cycle.

(There are actually weeks of every length up to 10 days in the system, but as most of these numbers don't evenly go into 210, kludges are required.)

The **Maya** had a similar system (the *sacred round*) based on 13 and 20, giving a 260-day cycle. The 13 days were simply numbered, using the base 20 Mayan numbers:

hun	*ca*	*ox*	*can*	*ho*
wak	*uxac*	*waxac*	*bolon*	*lahun*
buluc	*lahca*	*oxlahun*	*canlahun*	*holahun*
waclahun	*wuclahun*	*waxaclahun*	*bolonlahun*	*kal*

The 20-day cycle had day names:

imix'	*ik'*	*ak'b'al*	*k'an*	*chikchan*
kimi	*manik'*	*lamat*	*muluk*	*ok*
chuwen	*eb'*	*b'en*	*ix*	*men*
k'ib'	*kab'an*	*etz'nab'*	*kawak*	*ajaw*

Thus the cycle starts with *hun imix'* (1 - 1) and ends with *oxlahun ajaw* (13 - 20). (The names are meaningful— e.g. *ik'* is 'wind, breath, life force', *b'en* is 'young maize', *ix* is 'jaguar'.)

Months

The word *month* is related to *moon*; thus months derive from the lunar cycle. The length of the lunar cycle (29.53 days) and the tropical year

(365.242 days) are designed to intrigue and ultimately frustrate calendar makers, who would really prefer whole numbers and neat fractions.

The ancient **Jews**, and **Muslims** to this day, strictly began a month when the new moon was spotted. When the lunar calendar diverged from the solar, the Jews inserted an extra month (or technically, repeated the last month, *Adar*). The Muslims simply define a year as 12 months (354 or 355 days) and let it drift through the seasons.

The earliest **Roman** calendar seems completely slapdash. It began with the vernal equinox (~ March 21), but contained only ten months (of 31 or 30 days). The first four were associated with deities (*Mars, Aprīlis, Maia, Jūno*), and the rest were numbered.

In 713 BC king Numa named January (after *Jānus*) and February (after a purifying ceremony). A leap month was intermittently added to keep the year in track with the seasons. Julius Caesar regularized the system, lengthening the months so that the year was 365 days long, with a leap day inserted every four years.

Augustus renamed *Quintilis* as *Julius* and *Sextilis* as *Augustus*. Other early emperors renamed some of the remaining numbered months, but none of these changes survived.

The **French** Revolution introduced new months and began the year on September 22, the date of the proclamation of the Republic. The season-specific suffixes are a nice touch.

vendémiaire	'grape harvest'
brumaire	'foggy'
frimaire	'frosty'
nivôse	'snowy'
pluviôse	'rainy'
ventôse	'windy'
germinal	'germination'
floréal	'flowering'
prairial	'pasture'
messidor	'harvest-giving'
thermidor	'heat-giving'
fructidor	'fruit-giving'

The Slavs (except the Russians) have their own nice earthy names for the months. Here are the Czech names:

leden	'ice'
únor	'toss about'
březen	'birch' or 'with young'

duben	'oak'
květen	'blossom'
červen	'red'
červenec	'redder'
srpen	sickle
září	'it shines'
říjen	'rutting (of deer)'
listopad	'leaf-fall'
prosinec	prob. 'pig (slaughter)'

The **Mayans** had a 365-day year, known as the *vague year* as it drifted away from the seasons. It was composed of 18 months of 20 days each (plus a 5-day special period, *wayeb*):

pop	*wo*	*zip*	*zotz'*	*zec*
xul	*yaxkin*	*mol*	*ch'en*	*yax*
zac	*ceh*	*mac*	*kankin*	*maun*
pax	*kayab*	*cumku*		

Combine the sacred round with the vague year— e.g. *4 Ajaw 8 Cumku*— and you have the *calendar round (baktun)*. These have a common multiple at 18,980, which produces a 52-year period. Now you number the *baktuns* to get the *long count*, starting in 3114 BC.

The **Almean** year has 328 days. The Verdurian calendar is as follows:

	days	*meaning*	*season*	
olašu	27	beginning	*demeča*	spring
reli	27	sowing		
cuéndimar	28	festival		
vlerëi	27	name of planet	*esta*	summer
calo	27	heat		
recoltë	28	harvest		
yag	27	hunt	*peleti*	fall
želea	27	calm		
išire	28	name of planet		
šoru	27	dark	*iveri*	winter
froďac	27	cold wind		
bešana	28	promise		

Almea has three moons, of which the largest, Iliažë, has a period of between 27 and 28 days. The Uytainese had cycles following both Iliažë and the second largest moon, Iliatál, used for different purposes— the first was used for civic and administrative schedules, the second for religion and trading.

The Xurnese never bothered with months, but numbered the days of the four seasons.

Seasons

spring   OE *spring* 'water spring' > 'source, origin' > '1st season'

Lt *vēr,* OCS *vesna* < IE • Fr *printemps* 'first season' • Ger *Frühling* 'earliness' • Dutch *voorjaar* 'fore-year' • Breton *nevez-amzer* 'new time' • Croatian *projeće* 'pre-summer' • Ch *chūn* < 'sprout'

summer   OE *sumor*

• Gk θέρος 'heat' • Lt *æstas* < 'fire' • Sp *verano* < 'spring' • OCS *žętva* 'harvest' • Ch *xià* 'great'

FALL   OE *fealle* 'a fall'

Lt *autumnus* uncertain • Ir *fómhar* 'under-winter' • Ger *Herbst* 'harvest' < 'gather' • Danish *eferaar* 'after-year' • Lith *ruduo* 'red' • Ch *qiū* poss. < 'end'

winter   OE *winter* poss. < 'watery'

• Lt *hiems,* OCS *zima* < IE • Ch *dōng* poss. < 'terminate'

season   Lt *satio* 'sowing'

We're used to the astronomical seasons being given priority, but seasons can be defined by climate or the agricultural year as well. As the environment takes time to heat up or cool down, the hottest period of summer and the coldest period of winter are some weeks after the solstice.

In India there are six seasons, of two months each: *Vasanta* (spring, moderate temperatures), *Grishma* (summer, very hot), *Varsha* (monsoon, hot and wet), *Sharad* (autumn, mild temperatures), *Hemant* ("winter"; rice harvest), *Shishir* (cold season).

In Swahili the seasons are *kiangazi* (when the sun is strongest, also *kaskazi* 'monsoon'), *masika* (heavy rains), *kipupwe* (cool season), and *vuli* (lesser rains).

Tolkien's Quenya also has six seasons: *tuile* 'spring', *laire* 'summer', *yávie* 'autumn', *quelle* 'fading', *hríve* 'winter', *coire* 'stirring'.

TOOLS

bolt	OE *bolt* 'crossbow bolt'
	• Fr *verrou* < 'little spit or broach'
brush	Fr *brosse* '(broom made of) small twigs'
	• Lt *pēniculus* dim. 'tail' • Sp *cepillo* dim. 'bough' • Rum *perie* < 'feathers'• Rus щётка 'bristle'
car	Lt *carrus* 'cart'
	• Gk ἅμαξα 'framework' • Fr *voiture* < 'transport' • Sp *coche* < Hungarian place-name *Kocs* • Lith *ratai* 'wheels' • Ch *chē* < 'chariot'
chain	Lt *catēna*
	• OE *racente* < '(part of) rigging' • Norse *hlekkir* 'links' • Lith *grandinė* 'rings' • Rus цепь 'stick to'
engine	Fr *engin* < Lt *ingenium* 'talent' < 'innate (quality)' < 'in birth'
	• Ch *fādòngjī* 'issue-move-machine'
equip	Fr *équiper* 'fit out a ship'
	• Ger *ausrüsten* 'prepare out' • Ch *bèi* < 'prepare'
handle	OE *handlian* verbn. of 'hand'
	• Fr *poignée* < 'fist' • Ger *Griff* < 'grab' • Ch *bǐng* < 'grasp' • Ket *dūl* 'something's pole'
hook	OE *hóc*
	• Lt *uncus* < 'bend' • Lith *kablys* 'hanger' • Ch *gōu* < 'crooked'
knife	OE *cníf*
	• Gk μάχαιρα 'fight' • Lt *culter* < 'cutter' • OCS *nožĭ* 'piercer'
lamp	Gk λαμπάς nomn. of 'shine'
	• OE *léohtfæt* 'light-vessel' • Lt *lucerna* < 'light' • Ch *dēng* poss. < 'high-legged vessel' < 'rise'
machine	Gk μηχανή 'contrivance'
	• Ger *Apparat* < 'preparation' • Ch *jī* poss. < 'joint' = 'with moveable parts'
mechanical	Late Lt adjn. of 'machine'
mirror	Fr *miroir* < 'something to look at'
	• Lt *speculum* < 'look' • Ir *scáthán* 'shade' • OE *glæs* 'glass' • Lith *veidrodis* 'show-face' • Ch *jìng* < poss. 'light-thing'
motor	Lt *mōtor* 'mover'
operate	Lt *operārī* 'work, labor'
prepare	Lt *præparāre* 'make ready beforehand'
ready	ME *rædiȝ*, from an OE verb 'put in order, prepare'
	• Lt *parātus* 'prepared' • Sp *pronto* < 'produced' • Ir *ullamh* 'at hand' • Ger *fertig* < 'journey' • Skt *klpta-* 'fitted'

rope	OE *ráp*
	Gk σχοῖνος 'reed' • Fr *corde* < Gk 'gut, string' • Sw *tåg* < 'pull' • Sw *lina* < 'linen' • OCS *vrŭvĭ* < 'twisted cord' • Cz *provaz* < 'bind'
scale	Norse *skál* 'bowl'
screen	prob. Old Fr. *escrin* < Ger 'grill' or Dutch 'windbreak' • Ger *Wandschirm* 'wall-shade' • Ch *píng* < 'protect'
string	OE *streng* ‖ Lt 'stretch' • Fr *ficelle* < 'little cord'
switch	Dutch 'whip, branch'
train	Fr *traîner* 'draw, drag'
use	Lt *ūsus* • Gk χρῶμαι 'need' • Fr *employer* < 'enfold' • Sp *servirse* 'serve' • Breton *ober gant* 'do with' • Danish *nyde* 'enjoy' • Ger *anwenden* 'turn to' • Cz *užiti* 'live through'
waste	Lt 'empty, desolate' • Sp *malgastar* 'spend badly' • Ch *làng* < 'disperse'
watch	OE *wacian* variant of 'wake'
wheel	OE *hweoʒol* < IE *k^wel-* 'turn', cognate to Skt *cakra-*, OCS *kolo*, Gk κύκλος 'ring' • Lt *rota* < 'run'
+	*abuse*
	boiler, pump, loom, mill, kiln, computer
	net, hinge, broom, sponge, scissors, towel, torch, comb, razor, napkin, umbrella, candle, ticket, lever, brake, fan, pipe, ladder, thread, sickle
	hammer, saw, screw, nail, chisel, pliers, wrench
	yoke, rake, hoe, shovel, axe, pitchfork, plow
	lens, clock, spectacles, gauge, telescope, microscope, thermometer
	wagon, sled, carriage, cart

▸ For ships, see *Water*, p. 389; for weapons, see *War*, p. 383

Some naming strategies for tools:

• Their use: *computer, boiler, razor* ('shaver'), *lever* ('lifter'), *pliers* ('folders'), *chisel, scissors, saw* (all from 'cut'), *candle* ('little shiner'), *rake* ('gatherer'), *hoe* (from 'hew'), *lamp* ('shiner'), *wrench* ('twister'), *mirror* ('looker').

- What they're made from: *sponge, glass, iron, broom, pen* ('feather'), *tin* (*can*).

- Their shape: *nail* (the 'fingernail' sense is primary), *lens* ('lentil'), *pencil* ('little tail'), *cannon* ('big tube'), *balloon* ('big ball'), (computer) *mouse*, *scale* ('bowl').

- The sound it makes: *drum, bomb, trumpet, clock, petard* ('farter', a type of bomb).

- A description: *gunpowder, telescope* ('far-seeing'), *dirigible* ('directable'), *submarine, spinning wheel, bicycle, vacuum tube, dishwasher*.

- The inventor or manufacturer: *zeppelin, macintosh* (jacket), *guillotine, daguerrotype, Gatling gun, Mason jar, diesel, Xerox, Kalashnikov, Luger, Petri dish*.

- In modern times, abbreviation— e.g. *radio*, from terms such as *radio-telegram*; *auto* from *automobile, cel* from *cellular telephone*— or acronyms, such as *laser, radar, PC*.

Words for tools are naturally applied to variants or similar items— e.g. cannon *barrels* started out resembling the ordinary kind. The new sense may become more common and replace the old:

- A *fan* was a winnowing tool, now used for ventilators.

- A *bolt* was a short thick arrow used in crossbows, now used for various fasteners.

- A *car* was a wagon or chariot, now used for automobiles.

- A *pipe* was the musical instrument (named for its sound), later applied to larger tubes.

- A *pencil* was originally a paint-brush.

Tools can be used as metaphors (*hammer out an agreement, carry a torch for someone, wear rose-colored glasses*), though they seem curiously underutilized. A few more are hidden by Latinization: *equilibrium* ('equal scales'), *concatenate* ('chain together'), *agglutinate* ('glue together'), *cardinal* ('hinging').

Words for tools and bits of hardware are likely to vary spectacularly between languages. As just one example, French assigns our *bolt* to six different words:

- You fasten a door or window with a *verrou*.

- A lock has a *pêne*.

- The thing that goes with a nut is a *boulon*.

- A roll of cloth is a *rouleau*.

- A crossbow fires *carreaux*.

- A shaft of lightning is an *éclair*.

Strings and cords

Logically, long flexible connectors would seem to need just one word, with size affixes. But we have quite an array. By size there's *cable, rope, cord, string, thread, filament*. If it's made of metal, we use *wire* rather than *string* or *thread*. A rope is made of several *strands* twisted together. A *lace* was once a loop or length of cording, but only survives in that sense in *shoelace* (and, with a detour into Spanish, *lasso*).

Spanish *cuerda* covers anything from a string to a rope, and is used in the technical sense of *cords* on a string instrument; a telephone cord is however a *cordón*.

Note some of the useful extensions: a *string* is anything that extends in a linear sequence; e.g. the programmer's *string* of characters. *Wired* goes from 'supplied with electricity (by wire)' to 'energetic'. A message transmitted by *cable* also takes that name. Animals with a *notochord* ('cord along the back') are *chordates*, the supercategory for vertebrates.

(A musical *chord* is a shortening of *accord* 'harmony' < Lt '(bring) to the heart'. The *h* is caused by confusion with Latin *chorda* 'string', itself from Gk χορδή 'gut'.)

Sailing ships had a dizzying variety of rope-related terms:

belay	coil a rope round a cleat to secure it
bight	the portion of a rope excluding the ends
brails	ropes fastened to the edges of a sail to truss it up
breast-fast	large rope to attach a ship to a wharf by its side
cable	a very thick rope, esp. that used to suspend the anchor
clew-lines	ropes connecting the lower edge of a sail to its yard, allowing it to be furled
cringle	a ring formed within one rope allowing another to be attached to it
dolphin	a mass of plaited rope round a mast to hold it up in case the ropes supporting it are shot off
downhaul	a rope fasted to the upper corner of a sail to allow it to be shortened or taken in

fag-end	the untwisted or frayed end of a rope
grummet	a circlet of rope used in place of a rowlock
guy	rope used to steady and guide something being hoisted or lowered
halyard	rope used to lower a sail, yard, flag, etc.
horse	a rope stretched under a yard as a foot-hold; also one that allows a sail to move
jeers	ropes used to hoist or lower the lower yards
lanyards	small ropes used to secure large ones (shrouds, stays)
lead line	rope with markers on it, used to measure water depth
lifts	ropes connecting the mast head with the ends of the yards
nippers	plier-like instrument for grabbing ropes; also, braided cordage wrapped round a cable to keep it from slipping
oakum	loose fiber made by untwisting old rope, used in caulking
painter	rope attached to the bow, used to hold the boat in place
pay out	allow a rope to run out by slackening it
pudding	plaited cording round the masts under the lower yards
reeve	pass a rope through a hole or block
rigging	all the ropes on the ship
rounding	rope wound around a cable to prevent chafing
rowse	to pull on a rope without the use of a tackle
sheet	rope fixed to the lower corner of a square sail
shroud	large ropes fixed to the head of the mast, relieving lateral strain
stay	ropes fixed to a mast, leading to other masts or to the side of the vessel
sternfast	a rope tying the ship's stern to the wharf
stoppers	short ropes knotted at the ends, used to suspend a weight or keep a cable in position
truss	a rope used to keep a yard close to the mast
whip	to bind twine around the ends of a rope to keep it from fraying
yarn	one strand of a rope— to spin a yarn is to make one of these, extended metaphorically to telling a tale.

Any technology your people rely on extensively is likely to generate such a list. This can be fun to work out for magic or future tech.

TRADE

account
Old Fr *acunt* 'calculate'
• Gk λογισμός 'reckoning' • Norse *tala* 'tale, number' • Ger *Rechnung* < 'right' • Rus счёт < 'count, read'

bank
It *banca* 'bench'
• Ch *yínháng* 'silver shop'

beg
ME *beggen*, uncertain
• Lt *mendīcāre* < 'defective' • Sw *tigga* < 'accept' • Rus просить < 'ask'

business
OE *bisiʒnis* 'busy-ness'
• Fr *affaires* '(things) to do' • Ger *Gesellschaft* 'comradeship' • Ch *shāng* < 'trade'

buy
OE *bycʒan*
Gk ἀγοράζω 'market' • Lt *emere* < 'take' • Sp *comprar* < 'prepare with' • Fr *acheter* < 'receive' • Ger *kaufen* < 'tradesman'

company
Fr *compagnie* '(people one has) bread with'
• Ch *gōngsī* 'public-office'

deal
OE *dǽlan*

display
Lt *displicāre* 'unfold'

due
Fr *dû* 'owed'
• Ger *fällig* 'fallen' • Ch *yīngfù* 'should-pay'

gain
Fr *gagner* < Germanic 'forage, secure food'
• Ger *gewinnen* < 'toil' • Ch *huò* 'catch, take'

interest
Lt *interesse* 'be between, matter'
Gk τόκος 'offspring' • Lt *ūsūra* 'use' • Ir *breis* 'increase' • Dan *rente* 'income' • Ger *zins* 'tax' • Lith *nuošimčiai* 'percentages' • Cz *úrok* 'term' • Qu *wachay* 'birth, fruit' • Ch *lì* 'advantageous' < 'sharp'

job
ModE uncertain

merchant
Lt *mercātor* 'trader'
• Gk ἔμπορος 'traveler' • Ger *Kaufmann* 'trade-man' • Lith *pirklys* 'buyer'

money
Lt *Monēta,* a name of Juno, in whose temple money was coined
• Lt *pecūnia* 'cattle' • Fr *argent* 'silver' • Sp *dinero* < name of a coin • Ger *Geld* < 'payment' • Ch *qián* < 'coin' < 'hoe(-shaped)'

offer
Lt *offerre* 'bring before, present'
• Ger *bieten* ‖ *bid* • Qu *munachiy* 'make want' • Ch *tígōng* 'propose-supply'

pay	Fr *payer* < 'pacify'
	• Gk ἀποδίδωμι 'give back' • Lt *solvere* 'release (a debt)' • Ger *zahlen* 'count' • Lith *mokėti* 'know how' • Rus платить < 'linen' • Skt *dā-* 'give' • Ch *fù* 'hand over' < 'store'
poor	Fr *pauvre* < Lt *pauper,* reduplication of 'little'
	• Gk πένης 'toiling' • Ir *bocht* 'broken' • Sw *fattig* 'taking little' • Ger *arm* 'miserable' • Pol *biedny* 'needful' • Skt *nirdhana-* 'no wealth' • Ch *qióng* 'extreme'
promise	Lt *prōmittere* 'sent forward'
	• Gk ὑπιςχνέομαι 'undertake' • Ir *geall* < 'pledge' • Sw *lova* < 'permit' • Ger *versprechen* 'for-speak' • Skt *pratijñā-* 'recognize' < 'know toward' • Qu *churakuy* 'put oneself' • Ch *nuò* 'agree'
refuse	Lt *refūsum* 'poured back'
	• Ir *eitigh* 'swear off' • Dutch *weigeren* < 'fight, resist' • OCS *otŭrešti* 'say away' • Skt *pratiākhyā-* 'tell back'
rich	OE *ríce* 'powerful, noble, wealthy'
	• Gk πλούσιος 'wealthy' • Lt *dīves dīvit-* < 'god' • Breton *prinvidig* 'princely' • OCS *bogatŭ* < 'share' • Qu *kapuqniyoq* 'with means' < benefactive of 'be' • Ch *fú* ‖ 'good fortune'
sell	OE *sellan* < causative of 'take'
	• Gk πωλέω prob. < 'come and go' • Lt *vendere* 'give a price' • Ger *verkaufen* 'for-buy' • OCS *prodati* 'give for' • Ch *mài* 'cause to buy'
share	OE *scearu* < Germanic 'division'
	• Fr *partager* verbn. of 'part' • Ch *jūnfēn* 'fair-divide'
show	OE *scéawian* 'look at'
	• Gk δείκῡμι ‖ Lt *index indic-* 'forefinger' • Lt *mōnstrāre* < 'portent' • Sw *visa* < 'wise' • Ch *gěikàn* 'give-look'
spend	Lt *expendere* 'hang out, pay'
store	Lt *instaurāre* 'renew, restore' > 'furnish'
	Shop: Lt *taberna* 'booth' • Fr *boutique* < 'storehouse' • Sp *tienda* 'tent' • Welsh *maelfa* 'gain-place' • Dutch *winkel* 'corner' • Danish *forretning* 'business' • Rus лавка 'bench'
trade	ModE < Low German 'track' > 'course' > 'way of life'
	• Gk ἐμπορεύομαι 'travel' • Lt *mercārī* 'market', *negōtiārī* 'affair' • It *trafficare* < 'put across' • Breton *kenwerza* 'with-sell' • Ger *handeln* < 'handle' • Cz *obchoditi* 'walk around'
treasure	Gk θησαυρός, uncertain
	• Rum *camoară* < 'vault' • OE *hord* < 'cover' or 'hidden' • Danish *skat* < 'property, money' • Rus клад < 'layer' • Ch *bǎo* ‖ 'value, price'

value	past participle of Lt *valēre* 'be worth'
	• Ger *Wert* 'price, splendor' • Ch *jià* 'price'
worth	OE *weorþ* 'price, value', uncertain
+	*affair, capital, coin, price, cost, fee, cheap, expensive*
	market, shop, festival, moneylender, counterfeit, partner
	luxury, alms, prosper, purse
	loan, rent, negotiate, mortgage, advertise
	file, ledger, profit, debit, credit, asset, liability, bill

▸ See the section on the Economy in the *PCK*, p. 140.

The biggest thing for conlangers to remember is that everything about capitalism is a technology. *Coins, markets, interest, insurance, accounting, banks, stocks, corporations* are all inventions, and once made their inventors the high-finance centers of their time. Names for these things would be borrowed from their languages, or calqued.

In the case of English, the source language is mostly French or Italian, sometimes hidden by Latinization. Note the homely origins of *bank*, cognate to *bench*; it was one the plank where the moneylender did his business. The word *interest* is an example of a financial metaphor applied to things of the mind: the original meaning is 'share, partnership'; one's financial concern was generalized to other forms of careful attention.

Where we have the cumbersome *stock exchange*, French has *bourse*, literally 'purse', said to be taken from the sign on an inn where some early traders met.

Prize is a variant of *price*; French still uses *prix* in both senses.

Finnish has one word, *lainata*, for 'loan' and 'borrow'; they're disambiguated by case.

Money systems

Even if a fantasy writer cheerfully shows his Europeanish peasants eating potatoes, with a fork, while giving grace to the Twelve Gods, he knows not to have them use dollars.

Many things have been used for currency— oil, cowrie shells, beads. In many societies **livestock** is the main gauge of wealth— the word *cattle* derives from 'capital', and Latin *pecūnia* 'wealth, property' derives from *pecus* 'livestock'. But advanced urban societies have always moved to

metal, which has the magic triplet of being valuable, durable, and portable.

Here's some historical currency systems. Non-English names are given in the singular.

In imperial **Athens**, all coins were silver:

1 δεκάδραχμος = 2.5 στατήρ = 10 δραχμή = 60 ὀβολός.

Hades had a one-ὀβολός entry fee.

The **Romans** could not avoid the perennial temptation to water down and thus inflate the currency; note the declining worth of the *denarius*:

Republic:

1 *dēnārius* (silver) = 4 *sestertius* (silver) = 5 *dupondium* (brass) = 10 *as* (copper)

Empire:

1 *aureus* (gold) = 25 *dēnārius* = 100 *sestertius* (brass) = 400 *as*

Under Diocletian:

1 *solidus* = 10 *argenteus* = 40 *nummus* = 1000 *dēnārius*

In **China**, the first emperor Shǐ Huángdì introduced a uniform copper coin, the *wén* (*cash*). They were of low value, and had holes allowing them to be strung on a thread— strings of 1000 were commonly used.

Later there was a silver coinage system, which persisted to the 19C. The English terms for the units derive from Malay.

1 *liǎng* (*tael*) = 10 *qián* (*mace*) = 100 *fēn* (*candareen*) = 1000 *lí*

The **Umayyad** caliphate has the silver *dirham* (the name comes from δραχμή), the silver *dinar* (parallel to the Byzantine *solidus*, but taking its name from the *dēnārius*), and the copper *fulus*.

Venice was the economic star of the late Middle Ages; the ducat (3.5 g of gold) was never devalued from 1284 to 1797, and was widely accepted throughout Europe.

1 *ducato* = 24 *grosso* = 32 *piccolo*

Charlemagne established the **French** system, though till the 13C only the *deniers* were actually minted:

1 *livre* = 20 *sou* = 240 *denier*

This was adopted by the **British**:

> 1 pound = 20 shillings = 240 pennies

These were made in *sterling* silver, which is 92.5% pure; the rest is copper. This is actually a plus, as pure silver is too soft to stand up to the wear and tear of being currency.

The coin ratios are obviously based on convenience, but if multiple metals are used, they're based on the relative abundance of the mined metals, which of course can change when a new source is found. Historically gold has been 10 to 20 times more valuable than silver.

Classical Islamic sources declare that 7 dinars (4.25 g) = 10 dirhams (3 g); this makes sense only if they're made of the same metal.

Some common **naming strategies** for coins:

- Composition: *aureus* = 'golden'
- Quantity: *dēnārius* = 'of 10', *doubloon* = 'double'
- Weight: *livre* = 'pound', στατήρ = 'weight'[15]
- Issuing authority: *ducat* = 'duchy'; *florin* = 'Florentine', *dollar* = 'from Joachimsthal', *euro*
- What they depict: *eagle, loonie*
- You can't go wrong with the name of a prestigious foreign coin— note the persistence of the Roman *dēnārius*.

Paper money was used by the Chinese from the 9C. The medieval Italian traders pioneered using personal letters of credit, which led to banks issuing banknotes payable to the bearer. European states began offering paper money around 1700.

The term **credit**, introduced into sf by E.E. Smith, is highly plausible— it recognizes that money, like language, is ultimately a social invention— though the idea of a futuristic credit being *universal* is I think naive. There is no such thing as universal value; things have different costs depending on location and people's differing and changing desires, and the ubiquity of computation allows these to be taken into account in increasingly sophisticated ways. In my sf universe, the Incatena, things don't have prices, they have pricing algorithms. At any given moment they will spit out a number which you can compare to the hopefully higher number emitted by your funding algorithm.

---

[15] Yet another derivative of 'stand'.

VALUATION

Quality

awful	OE *eʒefull* 'full of dread'
	• Fr *affreux* < 'terror' • Ch *kěpà* 'can-fear'
bad	ME *badde* 'worthless' prob. < 'effeminate'
	• Gk κακός ‖ κακκάω 'shit' • Lt *malus* poss. < 'deceive' • Rum *răŭ* < 'defendant' • Breton *gwall* < 'defect' • Sw *dålig* < 'unconscious' • Ger *schlecht* 'straight' > 'dumb', also *schlimm* < 'crooked'! • Lith *negeras* 'not good' • Pol *zły* < 'bent' • Rus плохой < 'timid' • Farsi *gast* 'stinky' • Ch *huài* < 'ruin'
dear	OE *déore* 'glorious' > 'esteemed' > 'beloved'
	• Gk φίλος < 'one's own' • Lt *cārus* < 'love' • Rum *drag* < 'precious' • Rus милый < 'pitiful'
evil	OE *yfel* < 'exceeding'
	• Fr *mal* < Lt 'bad, evil', *méchant* 'ill-falling' • Sw *ond* < 'harm' • Rus злой < 'bent' • Ch *xiōng* < 'inauspicious', *è* ‖ 'hate'
fancy	ModE abbreviation of 'fantasy' < Gk φαντασία nomn. of 'make visible'
fine	Fr *fin* 'finished' > 'of high quality'
	• Ch *měihǎo* 'beautiful-good'
GOOD	OE *gód* < 'fitting'
	• Lt *bonus* uncertain • Lith *geras* < 'praise' • OCS *dobrŭ* 'becoming, fitting' • Rus хороший < 'orderly' • Ch *hǎo* poss. < 'nourish'
GREAT	OE *gréat* 'coarse, thick' > 'stout'
nasty	ME 'foul, disgusting' uncertain
nice	Lt *nescius* 'not knowing' > 'foolish' > 'fine' > 'kind'
perfect	Lt *perfectus* 'completed' < 'done through'
terrible	Lt *terribilis* 'frightening'
WELL	OE *wel* ‖ 'will'
+	*foul, naughty, wicked*

Degree

absolute	Lt *absolūtus* 'absolved' < 'loosed away'
	• Ch *juéduì* 'very correct'
(e)special	Lt. *speciālis* 'individual = of a species'
intense	Lt *intensus* 'stretched, taut'
mere	Lt *merus* 'undiluted, pure'
pure	Lt *pūrus* 'clean, pure'
quite	Lt *quiētus* 'quiet' > 'free, clear' > 'clean, complete'

slight   ME 'sleek' > 'thin, weak'

Beauty

beauty   Fr *beauté* < Lt *bellus* < 'good'
• Gk εὐειδής 'well formed' • Breton *kaer* < 'mighty' • Ger *schön* < 'shining' • Dutch *mooi* < 'washed' • OCS *krasĭnŭ* < 'glowing, hot' • Skt *çubha-* 'adorned' • Ch *měi* ‖ 'good'

grace   Lt *grātia* 'pleasingness'
• Ger *Anmut* < 'desire' • Ch *yōuměi* 'superior-beauty'

pretty   OE *prættiʒ* 'tricky' > 'clever' > 'admirable' > 'pleasing'
• Fr *joli* < 'gay' poss. < *Yule* • Sp *bonito* dim. 'good' • Ger *hübsch* < 'courtly' • Ir *deas* 'well arranged' < 'right' • Rus миловидный 'dear-looking'

ugly   Norse *uggligr* 'fearsome'
• Gk δυσειδής 'ill formed' • Lt *turpis* < 'turn (away)' • It *brutto* 'stupid' • Fr *laid* < 'hateful' • Sp *feo* < 'foul' • Breton *divalo* 'unsoft' • Sw *ful* < 'stinking' • Rus дурной 'bad' • Ch *nánkàn* 'hard to look at'

+   *cute, hideous, homely*

Wisdom

fool   Old Fr *fol* < Lt 'bellows' > 'windbag'
• Cz *blazén* < 'err, stumble' • Danish *taabe* < 'fumble' • Sw *tok* < 'crazy' • Ir *baoth* poss. < 'timid'

prudent   Lt *prūdens* 'foresightful, experienced'

silly   ME *sely* 'happy' > 'innocent' > 'pitiable' > 'foolish'

wise   OE *wís* ‖ *witan* 'know'
• Lt *sapiens* 'taste', *prūdens* 'foreseeing' • Breton *fur* < 'cunning' • OCS *mądrŭ* < 'learn' • Ch *shèng* < 'renowned'

Clarity

clear   Lt *clārus* 'bright, clear, manifest'

direct   Lt *dīrectus* 'put straight'

evident   Lt *ēvidens* 'seen out'
• Gk δῆλος 'visible' • Ir *follasach* < 'bright' • Ger *deutlich* 'explained' < 'in the vernacular' • Skt *vyakta-* 'revealed' • Ch *xiǎn* 'bright, clear'

obvious   Lt *obvius* 'in the way' > 'in front of' > 'evident'
• Fr *évident* < 'seen' • Rus открытый 'open' • Ch *míngxiàn* 'bright-appear'

Suitability

exact Lt *exactus* 'driven out' > 'demand'
- Ger *genau* ‖ *enough* • Ch *quèqiè* 'true-agree'

fit ModE uncertain
- Gk εὔθετος 'well placed' • Lt *convenīre* 'come together' • Ger *passen* < 'pass' • Rus итти 'go' • Ch *hé* 'joined, harmonious'

suit Fr *suite* 'following' (> 'pursuing (a case)', 'uniform outfit')

Normality

extreme Lt *extrēmus* 'outermost, most advanced'
- Ger *äußerst* 'out-first' • Ch *jìntóu* 'last-head'

familiar Lt *familiāris* 'of the family'
- Fr *habituel* 'customary' • Ch *shú* 'ripe, ready'

normal Lt *normālis* adjn. of 'carpenter's square' > 'pattern'
- Ch *zhèngcháng* 'always straight'

odd abbr of Norse *odda-maðr* 'angle-man' = 'third man'

queer ModE uncertain

strange Lt *extrāneus* 'external, foreign'
- Ch *qí* ‖ 'irregular', 'put aside'

usual Lt adjn. of *ūsus* 'use'

Hardness

delicate Lt *dēlicātus*, prob. ‖ *dēlicium* 'delightful'

hard OE *heard*, cognate to Gk κρατύς 'strong'
- Gk σκληρός < 'dry' • Lt *dūrus* < 'solid' • Ir *crua* < 'flesh' • OCS *tvrŭdŭ* 'firm'

soft OE *sófte* 'agreeable, calm'
- Lt *mollis* < 'tender, weak' • Sp *blando* < 'smooth' • Ir *bog* < 'pliant' • OCS *mękŭkŭ* < 'knead' • Ch *ruǎn* < 'bend'

Complexity

complex Lt *complexus* 'folded together'
- Ch *fùzá* 'repeat-mix'

plain Lt *plānum* 'flat'
- OE *emnet* < 'level, even' • Ir *má* 'expanse' < 'big'

simple Lt *simplex -plīc-* 'once-folded'

+ *ordinary, popular, regular*

Remember that you can multiply this list by four simply by having a morphological negative *(indirect)* and diminutive *(direct-ish)*.

Words for quality refer to very different things for different referents: consider what *good* means when applied to dogs, paintings, investments, chess moves, mayors, and wines. But I'm not aware of any language that has any trouble with this.

Words for beauty can be culturally complex. Applied to women, I believe English terms are best thought of as having different prototypes:

beautiful	a mature woman: Marilyn Monroe, Angelina Jolie, Halle Berry
pretty	young: Zooey Deschanel, Janelle Monaé, Maggie Cheung
cute	girlish: Audrey Hepburn, Faye Wong

These have fairly close equivalents in French (*belle / jolie / mignonne*) and German (*schön, hübsch, niedlich*). Swedish *snygg* seems to cover both 'beautiful' and 'pretty' (but not 'cute' which is *söt*).

Sometimes terms sound different applied to men or women. Spanish *guapo* is the go-to adjective for handsome males; *guapa* applied to women has more of the connotations of *hot*. *Handsome* applied to women seems to imply 'surprisingly well-preserved'.

Spanish *hermoso* is 'beautiful', but in Peru to call a woman *hermosa* implies that she's fat. Possibly this developed from the sense 'luxuriant, healthy'.

Hebrew cheerfully applies *yāpε/yāpā* 'beautiful', *ḥāmūḏ/ḥămūḏā* 'cute' to either gender.

ally
: Fr *allier* 'make bound'
  - Ch *méngguó* 'oath-country'

army
: Fr *armée* 'armed (force)'
  - Gk στρατός 'spread out' • Lt *exercitus* 'training' • Rum *oaste* < 'enemy host' • Dutch *leger* 'camp' • Ger *heer* < IE 'army, crowd' • OCS *vojĭ* ‖ 'war' • Skt *senā-* 'missile'

arrow
: OE *arwe* 'bow-thing'
  - Gk τόξευμα < 'shoot' • Fr *flèche* < 'feather' • Sw *pil* < 'javelin' • OCS *strela* < 'beam of light' • Cz *šip* 'thorn' • Farsi *tīr* 'sharp'

attack
: It *attaccare* 'attach' > 'commence (battle)'
  - Gk προσβάλλω 'strike against' • Lt *aggredi* 'march toward' • Ir *ionsaigh* 'go after' • Ger *anfallen* 'fall upon' • Ch *gōng* < 'apply oneself' < 'work'

battle
: Fr *bataille* < 'beatings'
  - Gr μάχη 'fight' • Ir *cath* < IE • Sw *slag* < 'blow' • Rus бой 'strike' • Ch *zhàn* poss. < 'tremble'

blade
: OE *blæd* 'leaf'
  - Fr *lame* < 'plate, leaf'

blast
: OE *blæst* 'blow, gust'

bomb
: Sp *bomba* imitative
  - Ch *zhàdàn* 'explode-bullet'

bow
: OE *boʒa* < 'bent'
  - Lt *arcus* ‖ arrow • Latvian *stuops* 'stretched' • Ch *gōng* < 'curved, bent'

camp
: Lt *campus* 'field'

captain
: Fr *capitaine* < 'of the head = principal'
  - [military] Ger *Hauptmann* 'main man' • [nautical] Ch *chuánzhǎng* 'ship-chief'

castle
: Lt *castellum* 'citadel, fort', poss. < 'laid out'
  - Gk τεῖχος 'wall' • Fr *forteresse* 'strongness' • Ir *dún* < 'enclosure' • Ger *Burg* 'fortified place', *Festung* 'firm' • Skt *pūr* 'fortified place', cognate to πόλις • Ch *chéngbǎo* 'wall-fort'

combat
: Fr *combattre* 'fight with'

conquer
: Lt *conquærere* intensive (here a completive) of 'seek'
  - Ger *erobern* 'begin-above' • Ch *zhēng* < 'target' < 'straight'

enemy
: Lt *inimīcus* antonym of 'friendly'
  - Gk ἐχθρός 'outcast' • Ir *namhaid* < 'curse, retribution' • Breton *enebour* < 'against' • Ger *Feind* < 'hate' • OCS *vragŭ* < 'misery' • Avestan *dušmainyu-* 'bad-minded' • Ch *dí* ‖ 'vengeance'

gun ME *gunne,* apparently from a nickname
- Fr *arme* 'weapon' • Ch *qiāng* 'spear' • Ket *bogdóm* 'fire-arrow'

invade Lt *invādere* 'walk into'
- Ger *einfallen* 'fall in' • Ch *qīn* poss. < 'sweep'

military Lt *mīlitaris* 'of soldiers'

raid Scots form of 'road'

revolt Fr *révolter* 'roll back'
- Sp *rebelarse* < 'go to war again' • Ch *gémìng* 'change-life'

ruin Lt *ruīna* 'falling down'
- Qu *pirdichiy* 'make to lose'

scout Old Fr *escoute* 'listener'
- Ger *Pfadfinder* 'path-finder' • Ch *zhēn* < 'test, verify'

shoot OE *scéotan* 'rush, dart, cast'
- Fr *lancer* 'hurl' • Ch *fā* < 'go out, eject'

soldier Old Fr *soudoier,* one paid by the *sou* (Lt *solidus*)
- Gk στρατιώτης < 'army' • Norse *hermadr* 'war-man' • OE *wígend* 'fighter' • Avestan *raθaēštar-* 'chariot-stander' • Ch *bīng* < 'weapon'

spear OE *spere* < 'spar, beam'
- Gk δόρυ 'beam', ἄκων 'spike' • Lt *pīlum* poss. 'pestle' • Ir *sleá* poss. < 'release' • OCS *kopĭje* < 'hoe', *sulica* < 'thrust'

spy Old Fr *espie* probably < Lt 'look at'

squad Fr *escouade* < 'square'
- Ger *Mannshaft* 'man-ness' • Ch *bān* < 'classify' < 'distribute'

sword OE *sweord* poss. < 'pain, wound'
- Gk σπαθί 'blade' • Ir *claíomh* < 'dig, strike' • Avestan *karəta-* 'cutter' • Ch *jiàn* poss. < 'sharp thing'

WAR OE *wyrre* < Germanic 'discord, strife' (> Fr *guerre*)
- Lt *bellum* uncertain, poss. < 'battle' • Ir *cogadh* 'battle with' • Ger *Krieg* < 'defiance' • Lith *karas* 'army' • Rus война < 'pursuit' • Icelandic *ófriðr* 'un-peace' • Ch *zhàn* poss. < 'fear'

weapon OE *wǽpen*
- Gk ὅπλον 'instrument' • Lt *arma* 'upper arms' • Lith *ginklas* < 'defend' • Ch *wŭqì* 'military tool'

+

surrender, retreat, loot, parry, wield

strategy, tactics, logistics, campaign, headquarters

navy, cavalry, infantry, veteran, recruit, fort

bullet, rifle, club, pike, dart

armor, helmet, shield, chainmail, greaves

‣ See the War chapter in the *PCK*, p. 243.

‣ For less blood and guts, see *Conflict*, p. 164.

Military terms are likely to be borrowed from whoever has the best armies. We retain some from ancient times (e.g. *legion, strategy, victory, martial*), but take many terms from the French, once the premier military power of Europe: *army, battalion, campaign, mêlée, sortie, squad, reconnoiter, rapier, parry, surrender, maneuver, combat, battle, fortress, castle, cannon, bullet, camouflage, spy, artillery, cavalry*, as well as the military ranks (below).

As Lakoff points out, war is used as a metaphor for politics, arguments, and even love. For the art-obsessed Xurnese, I created metaphors for war based on painting:

nelima	frame > context, *casus belli*
rímex	sketch > strategy
šonasudo	brushwork > tactics
ravom	canvas > battlefield
šuke	paint > blood

There's a close relationship between war and games— we make games based on war, and obsolete military skills like archery become sports events. The highly evolved and enlightened humans of the far future will probably climb into VR simulators and play at phalanx warfare.

The powers that be, naturally enough, tend to glorify and value war, but there's been no shortage of people who deplore it— many cultures even viewed common soldiers very negatively. It's curious that linguistically, war is almost always taken as a positive— Paul even uses it, bizarrely, as a metaphor for the spiritual life (Ephesians 6). The most frightening sort of destruction, nuclear warfare, becomes a metaphor for using the microwave. Perhaps not even those future pacifists will have a slang expression *That's war* to refer to something terrible.

Military ranks

Here are the basic **British/American** ranks, with their etymologies. This is not enough to write modern military fiction— but I'm not sure why a conlanger would need to translate *senior chief petty officer* rather than creating their own system.

Army		Navy	
General	'general' = 'not limited in scope'	*Admiral*	Arabic 'commander'; cf. *emir*
Brigadier Gen.	Fr 'fighting'	*Commodore*	Dutch 'commander'
Colonel	It 'little column'	*Captain*	
Major	Lt 'greater'	*Commander*	
Captain	Lt 'head'	*Lieutenant*	
Lieutenant	Fr 'place-holder', i.e. deputy	*Ensign*	Fr 'insignia'; i.e. 'standard-bearer'
Sergeant	Fr 'servant'	*Petty officer*	'little officer'
Corporal	It < 'head'		
Private	'private soldier', i.e. 'hired'	*Seaman*	

Marshal (from a Germanic term for 'horse-servant') can be used for a rank above general.

Some ranks are named by two terms. *Lieutenant* can be used for a rank below (a *lieutenant colonel* serves below a colonel) and *major* for a rank above (a *sergeant major* outranks a sergeant). But a *major general* actually falls below a *lieutenant general*.

The great divide in military organization is between the *officers* and the enlisted men. In medieval times the officers were generally nobles; indeed, the feudal system can be seen as a low-overhead way to provide a well trained and equipped cavalry and officer corps. Since the last century, officering has been a profession, taught in military academies.

Another useful distinction is between commanding officers and *staff officers*, who take on logistics, intelligence, planning, personnel, and other functions.

The English names are almost all borrowed from the **French**. The French scale is *général, colonel, commandant, capitaine, lieutenant, major, adjudant, sergent, caporal, soldat.*

There are also special terms for the **units** that officers command:

army	50,000 soldiers	Lt. general or higher
corps	20,000 to 45,000	Lt. general
division	10,000 to 15,000	Major general
brigade	3,000 to 5,000	Colonel
company	60 to 200	Captain
platoon	15 to 50	Lieutenant
squad	10	Sergeant

The ancient **Roman** system, after the reforms of Marius (-2C):

Consul		
Legate	Legion	4800 soldiers
Tribune	(staff officer)	
Centurion	Cohort	480
Centurion	Century	80
Optio	(staff officer)	
Decurion (cav.)	Turma	10 to 30
Decanus (inf.)	Contubernium	10
Legionary		

Under the Republic, *consuls* were the supreme leaders, elected for just a year; during wartime they each commanded half the army. In an emergency a single leader was elected, called a *dictator*. Note how many Roman political terms are still in use, though often with an altered meaning.

An *imperātor* (from *imperāre* 'command') was originally a supreme military commander; it of course became the word for 'emperor'. Legally, the emperor was also a consul (among other offices).

Some of the titles above use the metaphor of THE LEADER IS THE HEAD; for my conlang **Xurnese** I generalized this as THE BODY IS THE ARMY, providing an entire military hierarchy as well as numerous other military terms:

newe	brow > general
juysu	head > commander
teyš	chest > colonel
pučisu	belly > major
reyxu	thigh > lieutenant
xuc	leg > sergeant
neja	foot > infantryman

> *breš*   arm > vanguard
>
> *waysu* nose > scout

The movements of the body are also used for armies: *neymore* 'sleep = camp', *jivi* 'walk = march', etc.

The internal organs are used for nonce meanings, but these have not been lexicalized, except for the general *xímex* 'organs > support staff.'

WATER

bath	OE *bæð*
	• Ch *zào* < 'wash'
clean	OE *clǽne* < 'clear, pure'
	• Lt *mundus* poss. < 'washed' • It *netto* < 'polished' • Fr *propre* 'proper' • Sp *limpio* 'limpid' • Ger *rein* < 'sifted' • Skt *çuddha-* 'purified, cleansed' • Ch *qīng* 'pure, clear'
dry	OE *drýʒe* prob. < 'strong, holding up'
	• Lt *siccus* poss. ‖ *sitis* 'thirst' • Rum *uscat* 'sucked out' • OCS *suchŭ* < IE, cognate to *sere* • Ch *gān* 'dried by heat'
ice	OE *ís*
	• Gk κρύσταλλος < 'frost, crust' • Lt *glacies* < 'icy cold'
pour	ME *pouren* uncertain
	• Fr *verser* < 'turn' • Welsh *tywallt* 'empty' • Sw *hälla* 'lean' • Ger *schütten* 'shake' • OCS *lĭjati* < 'flood, river'
wash	OE *wæscan* ‖ *water*
	• Lt *lavāre* 'bathe' • Lith *mazgoti* 'immerse' • Cz *práti* 'beat' • Rus стирать 'rub'
WATER	OE *wæter*
	• Lt *aqua* < IE 'running water' • Skt *jala-* ‖ 'drip' • Ch *shuǐ* < 'what flows'
wave	OE *wafian* 'move up and down'
	• Gk κῦμα < 'swelling' • Lt *unda* < 'water' • Welsh *gwaneg* < 'course, gait' • Ch *bō* poss. < 'uneven'
wet	OE *wǽt* ‖ *water*
	• Lt *ūmidus* < IE • Fr *mouillé* < 'soften' • Lith *drėgnas* < 'dirty' • OCS *mokrŭ* 'moist' ‖ 'puddle' • Ch *shī* ‖ 'swamp'
+	*steam, liquid, splash, dam, drip, spill, wipe*

Where we have *water*, Japanese has *mizu* 'cold water' and *yu* 'hot water'. This gives a different flavor to the comic *Ranma 1/2*, whose title character turns into a girl when doused with *mizu* and back into a boy when hit with *yu*. In Malay, *ayer* covers both liquid water and solid ice. Yidiɲ has *biriɲ* for salt water, *bana* for fresh.

Indo-European seems to have had two words for water, one animate (**āp-*) and one inanimate (**wed-*).

Lakota distinguishes several types of dryness:

púza	not wet
šéča	withered, applied to something that used to be alive: bones, wood, grass
sáka	dried, hardened: hides, fruits, carcasses

oyáȟe	dried up, applied to things that used to have liquid: empty lakes, a milkless udder
ťhaťhápa	partially or nearly dried (meat, mud, clothes, etc.)

Water can be used informally for any liquid, particularly alcoholic ones. *Vodka* is 'little water'; *whiskey* is Irish *uisge-beatha* 'water of life'; French *eau de vie* is brandy.

Many languages distinguish *washing* the body from washing clothes— e.g. Greek λούω vs. πλύνω. Recall that premodern clothes-washing was a fairly intensive process, thus the words deriving from 'beat'.

We have *flow* for moving water, but many languages just use 'run', e.g. Irish *rith*.

Bodies of water

bank	It *banca* 'bench'
island	OE 'isle land' < *íȝ*
	• OCS *ostrovŭ* 'around-stream' • Skt *dvīpa-* 'two-watered'
lake	Lt *lacus* 'basin, lake, pond'
	• Gk λίμνη < 'depression'
pool	OE *pól*
river	Lt place nomn. of *rīpa* 'bank, shore'
	• Gk ποταμός < 'falling (water)' • Lt *fluvius* < 'flowing' • OE *ēa* 'water' • Skt *nadī-* 'roaring'
sea	OE *sǽ*
	• Gk πέλαγος < 'flat' • Lith *jūra* < 'water' • Skt *sāgara-* 'swallowing (the rivers)' • Ch *hǎi* prob. ‖ 'dark'
spring	OE *spring* 'water spring' > 'source, origin' > '1st season'
stream	OE *stréam* < IE 'flow'
+	*ford, delta, rapids, brook, pond*
	bay, strait, peninsula, coast, beach, cape, archipelago

French distinguishes *fleuve*, a river that ends in the sea, from *rivière*, which flows into another river. In German *Floss* is a river and *Strom* is a subcategory of *Floss* reserved for the largest rivers.

The OED suggests that a *stream* is larger than a *brook*, but I'm not sure if all English speakers would agree. In England a *creek* is an inlet, but in the US it's the same as a brook.

Greek ὠκεανός was conceived of as the sea on the outer edge of the flat earth, encircling all the land; Germanic *sea* retains the larger sense ('the law of the sea', 'at sea') but can also be used for specific large bodies of water (the North Sea, the Caspian Sea). The Low Germans, who had an ocean nearby, called it *die See* (f.); the High Germans, who didn't, used *der See* (m.) for lakes; the standard language retains both terms.

In many areas the *ocean* notionally begins past any coastal islands or reefs; the water in between these and the inner shore is a *sound*— or in Maryland, *the Bay*.

If your conpeople live in the ocean (like the iliu of Almea), imagine the geographical (pelagographical?) terminology they'd create. What are two-dimensional areas to us are just the surface of complex three-dimensional shapes to them.

Ships

boat	OE *bát*, uncertain
	• Gk σκάφη 'tub' • Lt *barca* < Egyptian • Ir *curach* < 'hide (covering)' • Rus лодка dim. 'ship' • Cz *člun* < 'dugout' • Skt *plava-* < 'float' • Ch *chuán* < 'hollow out'
bow	ModE < Low German 'shoulder' ‖ *bough*
fleet	OE *fléot* < Germanic, prob. ‖ 'flow, float'
	• Gk στόλος 'expedition' • Sp *armada* 'armed' • Welsh *llynges* collective of 'ship' • Ch *jiàndui* 'warship-squad'
launch	Fr *lancer* 'pierce' > 'hurl' > 'set in motion'
pilot	Fr *pilote* prob. < Gk πηδώτης 'steersman'
	• Ch *linghángyuán* 'guide-vessel-professional'
row	ME *ráw*
sail	OE *seȝl*
	Verb: • Gk πλέω < IE, cognate to 'flow' • Lt *nāvigāre* < 'ship' • Welsh *morio* < 'sea'• Dutch *varen* 'travel' • Ch *hángxíng* 'boat-go'
	Noun: • Gk ἱστίον < 'mast' • Lt *vēlum* 'cloth' • OCS *jadrilo* < 'ride' • Ch *fān* ‖ 'wind'
ship	OE *scip*, uncertain
	• Gk ναῦς, Lt *nāvis* < IE 'rowboat' • Sp *buque* < 'belly' • Breton *lestr* 'vessel, pot' • OCS *korabljĭ* < 'horned beetle' • Pol *statek* 'property' < 'stand'
+	*galley, raft, caravel*
	deck, stern, mast, anchor, rudder, oar, keel; steer, dock, embark, paddle; navigation

A *ship* is a big *boat*, but in different times or contexts a finer formula may be used. E.g. to the AHD, a *ship* is a vessel large enough for deep-sea navigation. In the sailing era, a *ship* should have a bowsprit and three masts.

A quick review of the major medieval ships:

Sailing ships

cog	smallish, one mast; steep sides with a flat bottom; built with overlapping planks
hulk	similar but larger, good for cargo; also flat-bottomed
caravel	15C — 1 to 3 masts, small, very maneuverable; built with butted planks; mainstay of Portuguese exploration
carrack	larger, with 3 to 4 masts, e.g. Columbus's *Santa María*

Rowed ships

galley	oared, and thus fast and unaffected by lulls in the wind, but not suitable for months-long journeys; little changed from ancient triremes; low on cargo room
longship	the Viking mainstay, cheap to produce; sometimes fitted with one sail

WORK

build　OE **byldan* < 'dwelling'
　　• Lt *ædificāre* 'make building' • Fr *bâtir* < (make with) bark' • Breton *sevel* 'make stand' • OCS *zĭdati* 'form' • Rus строить 'arrange' • Skt *kr̥-* 'make' • Qu *hatarichiy* 'make get up'

able　Lt *habilis* 'holdable'

craft　OE *cræft* 'strength, force'
　　• Gk τέχνη < 'carpenter' < 'cut, hew, make' • Lt *ars* < 'fit together' • Fr *métier* 'ministry' • Ger *Gewerbe* < 'turn, be busy' • Norse *iðn* 'doing' • Ch *yì* < 'accomplished' < 'establish'

fix　Lt *fixus* 'fixed'

maintain　Fr *maintenir* 'hold in the hand'

MAKE　OE *macian*
　　• Gk ποιέω 'construct' • Sw *göra* 'prepare' • Lith *veikti* 'struggle' • OCS *dělati* 'work' • Ch *zuò* < 'get up, start work'

patch　ME *pacche* uncertain
　　• Fr *pièce* 'piece' • Ger *Fleck* 'spot' • Ch *bŭ* 'mend'

produce　Lt *prōdūcere* 'lead forward'
　　• Ger *erzeugen* 'begin-create' • Ch *chăn* 'bear'

provide　Lt *prōvidēre* 'see before'

practical　ModE adjn. of 'practice'

remake　ModE 'make again'

skill　Norse *skil* 'distinction, difference'

supply　Lt *supplēre* 'fill under'
　　• Ch *gōng* 'provide with both hands'

structure　Lt *structūra* nomn. of 'build'

task　Lt *taxa* 'tax' > 'imposed fee' > 'imposed work'

WORK　OE *wyrcan* 'do, perform', cognate to Gk ἔργον
　　• Lt *opus oper-* < 'power, wealth', *labōrem* 'toil, trouble' • Fr *travailler* < 'torture' • Rum *lucra* < 'gain' • Ger *arbeiten*, Rus работать < '(work like an) orphan' • OCS *raditi* 'care for' • Skt *karman-* 'act'

+　*invent, toil, artificial, manufacture, technique, mend, adjust, guild, factory*

English is relatively unusual in distinguishing *do* and *make*— compare French *faire* which covers both. At a first approximation, we *do* <verbs> and we *make* <things>. (At a second approximation, *do* <thing> is generally a quirky idiom: there's nothing common to *do the dishes, do your taxes, do a play, do your hair, we're doing the Islands this year.*)

Dutch has a similar distinction (*doen/maken*), but doesn't always agree on the applications— e.g. homework is *done* in English but *gemaakt* in Dutch.

Not a few of the words for *work* are rather negative— e.g. French *travailler* derives from the *trepālium,* a three-pronged instrument of torture. (The same word gave us *travel,* which doesn't say much for medieval tourism.) Latin *labor* wasn't much more positive— it meant 'labor, toil, hardship'. This may relate to the fact that premodern agricultural societies were all aristocracies, where work was something the dirty commoners did. The aristocrat aspired to not *work* at all, though he might deign to lead armies or governments.

Guilds

In most medieval European cities, craftwork was organized by *guilds*— a self-governing business association. The guilds organized training in the craft (you went from *apprentice* to *journeyman* to *master*), encouraged quality work, participated in civic government, and served as health and life insurance for its members. Less benignly, they kept the trade a monopoly, keeping prices for their work high.

On the other hand, as N.J.G. Pounds points out, in most places trade was controlled by the big merchants, not by craftsmen. The merchants often supplied the raw materials and even the tools. And the guilds had no power to prevent the merchants moving the cloth trade to rural areas— the original *cottage industry.* Rural workers were cheaper and unorganized.

The guilds of **Florence** are a good snapshot of what were the important crafts of the 1300s. There was a strict ordering, the first seven guilds being recognized as the *arti maggiori* (greater guilds)

Arte dei Guidici e Notai	judges, lawyers, notaries
Arte di Calimala	merchants, finishers, and dyers of cloth
Arte della Lana	wool
Arte del Cambio	bankers, money-changers
Arte della Seta	silk weavers and merchants
Arte dei Medici e Speziali	physicians, apothecaries, painters, spice sellers

Arte dei Vaiai e Pellicciai	furriers, skinners
Arte dei Beccai	butchers, livestock dealers, fishmongers
Arte dei Fabbri	blacksmiths
Arte dei Calzolai	shoemakers
Arte dei Maestri di Pietra e Legname	stonemasons and woodcarvers
Arte dei Linaioli e Rigattieri	linen
Arti dei Vinattieri	vintners
Arti degli Albergatori	innkeepers, tavernkeepers
Arti dei Cuoiai e Galigai	tanners, curriers (worked in dressed leather)
Arti dei Oliandoli e Pizzi-cagnoli	olive oil dealers, chandlers, cheesemakers, glass-blowers, soap-boilers
Arti dei Correggiai	saddlers and harness-makers, horse dealers
Arti dei Chiavaiuoli	locksmiths, toolmakers, braziers
Arti dei Corazzai e Spadai	armorers, swordsmiths
Arti dei Legnaioli	carpenters
Arti dei Fornai	bakers, millers

Index